For Kate Laura 1
So she may have

Elizabeth. J. Hazeldine

Published by St Marks Publishing,

Henley-on-Thames

ISBN **978-0-9572636-6-6**

Prelude

It was an exceptionally murky December night, with scarcely any moonlight, what there was of it struggling vainly to be perceptible through the squally hail and rain that fell unrelentingly. A farm trap scrambled at speed along the road, on occasion entangled in sodden overhanging branches. It bumped across potholes, the exhaled breathe of the driver creating crisp patterns, which hung suspended in the air like unwanted visitors before dispersing. The trap pulled up short at the conclusion of its journey, alongside the entrance of Henley Police Station. Its drenched driver leapt from his seat, and rushed headlong through the door. The station superintendent, startled by the strangers' distressed manner, asked his late night visitor what had so alarmed him. The trembling, traumatised figure sank in on itself, and at first failed to utter any response. The superintendent in his impatience to establish the facts spoke sharply. "Speak man." At last, the man took a deep breath, recovered his senses, and exclaimed. "The housekeeper at Lambridge Farm has been murdered tonight."

One

The Froomes Boys

James Froomes, who resided in the hamlet of Assenden, Oxfordshire, had turned thirteen on 29th November 1893, the boy finished with schooling earning his living on the farmland of Lambridge House. It was accepted practice that James would usually sleep the night at afore mentioned property, while its master, Mr Mash, and family were not in residence. The Mash's usually frequented Lambridge House at the weekends, but at the time of the events to follow had not visited the premises for a fortnight. Lambridge House, positioned two miles from Henley-on-Thames, and a full half mile from the main road which led to Oxford, stood on the summit of Assenden Hill, awarding it splendid views of the Thames Valley. A singular building constructed of brick, with an attractive gabled roof, Lambridge House stood just one storey high, boasting two good sized bedrooms, a sitting room, dining room, kitchen, scullery, and conservatory, with two additional double bedrooms in its attic space. The property constituted part of a model farm, a type of small holding much favoured by the professional upper middle class, who found the pursuit of farming a blessed release from the pressures of commerce. The arable land around Lambridge House amounted to just over twenty acres, which incorporated two pasture fields, and an orchard. There was, included in the tenure, a collection of outhouses, a well house, a working dairy, and stabling for two horses. Situated close to a footpath, the main house was enclosed in on three sides by mature woodland, from a distance only its chimney tops discernible above the canopy of many varieties of tree. The open side of the property was separated by the length of two fields (the width of which, just short of quarter of a mile) from a carriage road which carved its way through the countryside, and ran on down towards Henley-on-Thames. Lambridge House could be approached either by using a track which stretched across Henley Cemetery (the tenant of Cemetery Lodge, the burial grounds keeper, Lambridge Farms closest neighbour), or by cutting across a sewage farm. The most arduous route to the house was only manageable on foot, any prospective visitor first having to ascend a steep hill, which lay some two hundred yards beyond the isolated Victorian burial ground.

Line drawing of Lambridge House
The People, Sunday 17th December 1893

After dusk, on the day in question (Friday 8th December 1893), James Froomes, accompanied, as he invariably was, by his eleven year old brother Harry (the lad known more often than not after his schooling to amble along to his brothers place of work), left Lambridge Farm. The two lads, having bid goodnight to the two mature farm labourers who toiled alongside James, returned home to join their family, and partake of the evening meal their mother had dutifully prepared. Duly fed, both boys washed at the sink, and armed with their trusty "Bulls Eye Lantern", James and Harry set out, to travel on foot the one and a half miles they had trudged but a few hours earlier.

The siblings arrived at Lambridge House nearing eight thirty in the evening; the weary children surprised to find the rear door, which led on into the kitchen, locked. The housekeeper, Miss Dungey (the only occupant, there being no additional servants) known to leave the door unsecured in anticipation of the Froomes brothers arrival. The boys, somewhat at a loss, wandered aimlessly around the full expanse of the property's exterior, but this exercise proved fruitless, and so they took it upon themselves to journey from window to window, peering in at each and calling for Miss Dungey. This, as before, did not offer any solution to the children's dilemma, and having made their way again to the backdoor; James clenched his right hand into a tight fist and pounded twice upon the doors glazed upper portion, his efforts delivering no positive outcome. All obvious avenues explored, the Froomes boys took stock of the situation and pondered on where the housekeeper might be. The brothers talked through several scenarios, and the elder of the two surmised that Miss Dungey may have gone to call upon friends, the absent woman known to frequently visit, of an evening, close acquaintances who resided some half a mile away. James and Harry Froomes were aware that the housekeeper of Lambridge seldom remained at her friend's home after nine o'clock, and so determined to await Miss Dungey's return, the brothers no doubt guarded against the harsh wintery conditions by hearty constitutions, sought out shelter. They resolved to sit in the well house, its back wall buffering onto that of the kitchen wall, their youthful optimistic characters leading them to expect the lady to appear at any moment. Time eventually weighed heavy on their confidence, and the boys emerged from their bolthole, and after a last ditch round of kicking at doors and thudding window panes, and hollering at the tops of their voices the name of the woman they so earnestly sought, their cries as if caught by the chill air echoing back at them, the Froomes boys concluded that any further efforts would only lead to the compounding of the feelings of despair that had begun to creep into their immature minds, Miss Dungey could not be roused.

James, increasingly bewildered by the situation, somewhat hesitantly approached the kitchen back door and peered through its upper glazed panel, noting with some difficulty the kitchen clock, just visible in the prancing shadows that invaded the rooms' interior. The darkness that enveloped the kitchen seemed to fight against lights that burnt, James establishing that one illumination was provided by an oil lamp that sat upon the kitchen table, the other pinpoint of light generated from an indistinguishable source, which originated in a passageway that ran off from the interior doorway of the kitchen. The child screwed up his eyes and peered with all the effort he could muster in the direction of the clock, he just able to make out the time as nine fifty. With the realisation that the hour was now late, James and Harrys stoic resolve failed them utterly. Chilled through, puzzled and greatly unsettled, they decided the best course of action was to retrace their earlier journey, and seek out their father.

Two

The Growling of a Cat, When She Has a Mouse

John Froomes had settled down for the evening, no doubt with the hour approaching twenty minutes past ten thinking of his bed. The Froomes's home was located within Lower Assenden, nestled in amongst a row of workmen cottages, and with many of Johns neighbours, for the most part agricultural workers, having retired for the night; the slumbering man was not unduly disturbed. It was therefore a startled individual, who leapt from his chair, when roused from his dozing by the familiar voices of his own children. James and Harry sought the comfort of rapid admittance to the family home, and their father did not disappoint. John Froomes, confounded by his son's tears of distress, and the garbled story they spluttered out between their sobs. Instantly shaken into alertness by what he perceived as the gravity of what his boys had conveyed, Froomes took leave of his wife Emma, who, jolted from her sleep by the hullabaloo, had torn downstairs. Emma, though much agitated by her children's angst, compounded to remain in situ, to mind her other four children, all of whom shaken from their sleep. Thus, once he had tugged on his boots and pulled about him his woollen coat, John Froomes set off, accompanied by his sons; resolved to seek out a Mr George Dawson.
The man Froomes sought lived at Bix Folly, on the very cusp of Lower Assenden, and earned his living in the employment of Mr Henry Joseph Mash. Dawson acted as Lambridges farm bailiff, his role primarily that of Mashs steward, with responsibility for the hiring and supervision of farm labourers. Dawson had been known to spend nights at Lambridge House, but on this particular occasion had opted to sleep at his home. After George Dawson, who was woken from his

light slumber by frantic banging on his door, admitted his unexpected visitors, and listened to a rapid appraisal of the facts known; he wholeheartedly agreed that all was not well, and that the only sensible course of action was to make haste to Lambridge Farm. Harry Froomes whose youthful sensibilities had by now left him feeling vulnerable and emotional, was placed in the care of Dawsons wife Amy, who also had in her charge her infant daughter. Dawson, a powerfully built fellow, sourced a lamp, and armed himself with his bamboo sword stick. This, an ingenious device, appearing to be a cane it incorporated within its shaft a concealed blade, which could be rapidly drawn if a situation necessitated it. Thus the three individuals set off for Lambridge Farm, trepidation causing hearts to flutter and minds to wander, idle thoughts exploring every perceivable scenario.

The journey was taken at a leisurely speed (the walk from Bix Folly to Lambridge Farm, at an average pace, taking eight minutes or so), to allow for the exhausted James, who was traversing the route for the seventh time that day. Upon reaching the property the comrades came upon Jack, Miss Dungeys black Retriever, a gift from her father, whose principal task was that of a guard dog. Jack was known to invariably welcome those he knew with enthusiasm, but as the party approached the creature, who was attached by his collar to a long chain, did not stir, and remained as he had first been observed, laid on his side next to his kennel. The three went closer, and as George Dawson stretched out an arm expecting Jack to respond with his accustomed nuzzling of the farm bailiffs hand, he commented that the dog seemed to be in a state of unnatural stupor. Leaving Jack dozing, the three next encountered Rover, who had the run of the house, he, unusually consigned to the elements, trotting around the yard. A partially deaf Spaniel of some age and quite docile, Rover seemed unaffected by what had blighted the other dog, and greeted the group eagerly.

The adults of the party, resolving to repeat the process carried out earlier by the young brothers, firstly rapped loudly on the pane of the kitchen door, this a fruitless exercise not producing any response from the unaccounted for solitary occupant of Lambridge House. The men were not to be daunted, and accompanied by James strode briskly round to the opposite side of the house, where Dawson, utilising his sword stick, tapped sharply on the window of Miss Dungeys ground floor bedroom, his efforts rewarded with scant success. Thus the three carried on down the length of the house, and in due course came abreast of the sitting room window. Dawson lifted his lamp, and he and John Froomes, in an instant, ascertained that the windows latch was unfastened, and the bottom sash of the bay pushed up. This discovery greatly unsettled James Froomes, who exclaimed that when he and his brother had earlier checked the house, the window had been shut fast. Thus the two men, having first composed the agitated child, took it upon themselves to use the opening as an avenue into the inner confines of the farmhouse. One following another, the two climbed gingerly through the window, James Froomes watching them disappear the two figures swallowed up by the dingy interior of the house. Then comforted by the familiar voice of his father, conveying that all was well, the lad scrambled in after them.

Once within Lambridge House, and having drawn the sword from its narrow hilt, it was observed and commented on by George Dawson, that Miss Dungeys small silver watch, which she was accustomed to keep about her person, was lying upon the seating area of one of the siting room chairs, he having moved closer to the device further observing that it was ticking heartily. The group knew full well that the rest of the house must be scoured, and thus they made their way to the sitting room door, tentatively opened it and continued their journey through the deathly hush of the core of Lambridge House. Their apprehension was tangible, as the investigators inched down the hall corridor, flinging back each door they came upon, finding nothing. Having reached the front door of the property the men momentarily took stock, and the next course of action decided upon, they carried out a rudimentary check of said door, the top bolt found to be fastened, and the key, which lay idol in the keyhole, not turned. The three timidly continued along the passageway, their exploration, leading to the rear of the property, culminating in the kitchen. Using the meagre shimmery light provided by Dawsons' lamp, and the spluttering flames of two household candles, the men had seized upon during their search of Lambridges interior; the three compatriots studied the eerily still kitchen. George Dawsons vision, growing accustomed to the dark, revealing to him Kate Dungeys knitting, which lay abandoned, strewn across the kitchens substantial wooden table, in close proximity to the oil lamp James Froomes had earlier observed, which by now starved of fuel cast but a flicker of light. The three next turned their attentions to the back door, which was found to be bolted at the top, and upon paying particular note as to whether the key in the door was turned they observed the doors brass handles colouring appeared at odds with its construction, on closer inspection it found to be stained with smears of what appeared to be congealed blood. The amateur investigators of this expanding horror now wildly looked about them, and a further splattering of dried blood was duly discovered, when a fragment of broken stick, seemingly discarded on the floor, was the next item to benefit from the aid of the lamp, its bark clumped with bloody clots.

Dawson and Froomes, their responsibilities to the child in their care uppermost, and with fearful realisation that further heinous revelations awaited discovery took drastic action, the men and child hurriedly retracing their steps, and via their previous entrance point hastily quitting the house.

Upon George Dawsons' suggestion the three scoured the well house, where the farm bailiff knew there to be a more substantial lantern. With outbuildings, such as the dairy and stables, being obscured in darkness and the need to reassure themselves that there was no activity in any of said outbuildings the lantern extracted from the well house provided invaluable assistance.

Once back in the raw elements young James Froomes stood cheek by jowl with his father, and in an attempt to bolster his small frame against the biting wintery air shuffled from foot to foot. The lad, as if suddenly compounded to offer assistance, blurting out that he and his brother had heard a peculiar noise earlier. The two adults, straining to hear above the thunderous rain, asked the child where the noise he had just recalled originated. James, who raised an arm and pointed it in the direction of nearby woods, expanding on what he and Harry had heard. 'It sounded something like the growling of a cat, when she has a mouse.' But the noise had been slight and at the time the children had taken like notice of it. John Froomes and George Dawson cut a look to each other, left James, their charge, to his own devices (it to be noted that the child, finding himself in total isolation and much unnerved, did not tarry long before re-joining the men), and with much effort to stay on their feet in the slippery conditions, hurried to the spot indicated by the child. Upon reaching the conclusion of their hasty journey, some forty yards from the main house, the men normally accustomed to an uneventful existence, to come upon a sight of unimaginable horror, the body of Miss Kate Dungey, which provided a terrible spectacle, one of her arms raised, her head unnaturally twisted, and the woman's legs curled, and feet tucked up under her. There were cavernous gashes to the left side of her neck, and Kate Dungeys dress, under garments, and corsetry were torn, which left a section of her back exposed to the stark wintery elements. Dawson and Froomes, pulling their gaze from the body, rapidly absorbed the implications. Making use of the lantern extracted from the well house, the two began to survey the immediate area, quickly coming upon, close to the womans shattered remains, Lambridge Houses kitchen fire poker, and the farms rammer (an implement used to mash potatoes, for animal feed), which Dawson momentarily handled, the surface of which slippery with a combination of icy rain, and what the farm bailiff perceived as blood. Glimpsed through the murkiness, that seemed to claim every furrow, was a stick, almost enveloped by the muddy earth. On closer inspection this stick found to be tacky in texture, the two men gripped by the realisation that this item was also bloody.

Dawson and Froomes straighted up, and manipulated their necks and backs, their muscles strained from the effort of having leaned over at an uncomfortable angle. It was not an easy task to look upon the corpse, and how much the two took in of the housekeepers' ravaged remains they locked within their own thoughts. Kate Dungey had suffered much; her body was bruised and cut, her dress stained heavily with blood, the skirt of which lifted up, so as to reveal her stockinged legs and under linen. The woman lay in a dense thicket by the side of a narrow road, about four yards from the path the Froomes boys had earlier used, the disarranged scene conveying evidence of a fierce struggle, the grass around the body flattered, and the rain drenched ground deeply furrowed. It commented upon by John Froomes that Miss Dungey, being out in such weather, and lying close to the path, must surely have been attempting to reach the sanctuary of the cottage, tenanted by the keeper of Henley Cemetery.

Dawson had seen enough, and promptly decided on his next course of action. The three were in sore need of assistance, Lambridge Farms bailiff rushing to the stable block to retrieve a mode of transport; the farm trap extracted and hastily harnessed to the Mash's pony, Billy. Thus amply prepared for a journey that was in the mind of George Dawson of paramount necessity, he geed up the pony and pulled away, his frame stooped forward in an effort to gird himself against the atrocious weather conditions. John and James Froomes watched Dawson be swallowed up by the blackness, and once all sight and sound of man and beast were lost, the two made haste to the well house to await George Dawsons return.

Henley Cemetery Keepers Lodge, no longer used as such Thought by John Froomes to be the place Miss Kate Laura Dungey had been heading for, in search of sanctuary

Three

The House is Shut Up

George Dawson made an arduously slow start to his journey, as Billy trotted gingerly down the steep incline from Lambridge House. The pony whining in alarm as his hooves, upon coming into contact with hailstones that littered the ground, slipped several times from under him. Once the trap had cleared the steep hill, and was on an even run, Billy seeming to relax, responding more willingly to Dawsons commands.

From the moment he had left Lambridge Farm George Dawson had formed an immediate plan of action, and reaching his desired destination drew Billy to a halt, adjacent to the Red Cross, a hostelry that stood within the boundary of Henley Parish, on the north east side, at the junction of the Fairmile and the road which ran off through Assenden. Dawson, after a day of toil, often partook of a beer in the Red Cross, and was a drinking acquaintance of its landlord, Robert Carpenter Bratchell. Thus Lambridges bailiff, attempting to summon help, pounded heartily on the door of the building, but his efforts were little rewarded, there being no sign of human activity. Dawson was not to be confounded, and hollered up at the windows, but the exhausted and shocked man found little joy.

Opposite the Red Cross, situated at the junction of the Toll Road to Nettlebed, and the road to Assenden, stood the Travellers Rest, like its fellow hostelry shut up for the night. George Dawson, whose nervous energy made it unbearable for him to tarry any longer; not attempting to rouse James Yeatman, the landlord. Returning to the pony and trap, and giving Billy a reassuring pat, Dawson climbed back aboard, and continued along the Fairmile, and on into Henley-on-Thames.

The Red Cross, photographed in 1890

Four

A Dress of Cherry Red

George Dawson, his hefty woollen coat by now drenched through and weighing heavy on his shoulders, made rapid progress, and cleared the Fairmile in good time. Entering the boundary of Henley-on-Thames via Northfield End, he continued on into Bell Street. At the junction, where stood Charles Monks drapers shop, Dawson swung round to his right and headed up Market Place, the end of his journey in sight. On the corner of West Street and Kings Road stood the premises to which George Dawson was headed, Henley Police Station, at the late hour the only building in Market Place where gaslights still burned, their shimmering hue visible through panel glazed windows.

Dawson drew Billy to a halt, hastily tethered the pony, and made for the front entrance of the police station, thrust open the door and careered towards the desk sergeant. The officer on duty, much alarmed by the bedraggled state and erratic manner of the man before him, quickly summoned the stations superintendent, one Francis Keal. George Dawson, by now afflicted by a combination of shock and the effects of his ad hoc journey, made for a sorry figure, and he stuttered and mumbled incoherently when attempting a response to Keals bombardment of questions. The superintendent, no doubt confused by the late night visitors' garblings, grew frustrated and his voice rose in volume as he tried to ascertain the facts pertaining to Dawson having arrived at the station in such a state of heightened agitation. Eventually some headway was achieved and George Dawson, his voice frail and jittery, stammered through his perception of the occurrences that had so distressed him, and necessitated his post-midnight arrival at Henley Police Station.

Henley Police Station in Market Place, not quite as Superintendent Keal would have known it, in the early 20ᵗʰ century the structure extended and modified

Once Dawson had exhausted himself of the details which had bearing on events back at Lambridge, and fully appreciative of the gravity of what he had heard Keal knew his next course of action did not warrant the slightest delay. Thus three men hurriedly emerged from the police station, George Dawson, Superintendent Francis Keal, and one Edward Snelgrove, he holding the rank of constable. They climbed aboard the trap, Dawson and Keal squeezed side by side at the front, poor Snelgrove (his police personnel card detailing him as of medium build, five feet and nine inches in height, with a fair complexion, light coloured hair and blue eyes), somewhat crammed in at the rear of the trap. Billy, straining under the added weight of his additional passengers, pulled away, and made his way out of Henley, and back onto the Fairmile.

The lately acquainted men arrived at Lambridge Farm approaching the hour of a quarter to one in the morning, and once Billy had been relieved of his burden and tack, and settled in the relative warmth of his stable, the two officers of the constabulary, at the behest of Superintendent Francis Keal, were led by George Dawson in the direction of Lambridge House.

Upon reaching the property Keal desired to immediately examine its interior, and thus, accompanied by his constable, he scrambled through the same unsecured window that Dawson and the Froomes had used earlier. It at this juncture observed by the police officers, and duly recorded within the pages of Constable Snelgrove's police issue notebook, that the bay window opened perpendicularly, and according to a snatched conversation with Dawson, which had taken place just before the two men disappeared into the darkness of Lambridge House, the bottom sash had been pushed half way up when the sitting rooms window was initially discovered to be unsecured.

Once safely through the window the two men, aided by their police issue lanterns, set a course for the sitting room door, they emerging, with some caution, into a narrow ominously silent corridor, that led to the front door. Superintendent Francis Keal, crouching forward, paid close attention to this door and satisfied that he had seen all, made a remark that the front door was bolted internally, Constable Snelgrove scribbling all he was made privy to within his notebook. The superintendent, first listening for any sound that might indicate that peril lay beyond the door, and satisfied that it did not, reached up and unbolted it, the two proceeding into a porch way, continuing out onto a lawned area.

The officers, deep in conversation, sought out George Dawson, and once Lambridge Farms bailiff was in his sights; Keal requested that a ladder be sourced as the means of carrying Miss Dungey back to the house. His request met with a nod from Dawson, who (while the police where within the confines of Lambridge House, having sought out the Froomes, both of whom he discovered huddled within the well house) sent John, and his son James in search of the farms ladder.

At the end of a short pathway, which ran off from the front porch, was a small gate, and at the behest of Superintendent Keal, Dawson (carrying the ladder) led the way, the police officer wishing to be guided to the body. The three followed one another through the gate, coming out onto an unmade pathway which ran down into Lambridge Woods. The mastery of the elements was all too evident, the rain pelting down relentlessly, and as such visibility in the area where the woman lay was reduced to a bare minimum. The sight of Kate Dungey was indeed terrible to behold, and once the three had gazed upon her it took several moments for the men to take themselves in hand, even George Dawson, who was looking upon the housekeeper of Lambridge not for the first time, shaken to his very core. Still Francis Keal had a duty to perform, and once preliminary observations had been noted he crouched down, oblivious to the sodden conditions of the ground about him. The Superintendent conscientiously examined every inch of the muddy quagmire, taking particular note of the position of the body. Thus satisfied, as to initial findings, Keal struggled to his feet and resolved that Lambridges housekeeper must be got inside. With hands trembling, as a result of both the cold and jangled nerves, the men lifted Kate Dungeys drenched corpse free of the mud that ensnared her, and laid her lengthwise onto the ladder.

Dawson took hold of one end of the ladder, while no doubt Constable Snelgrove took hold of the other, Francis Keal, as superior officer, taking the responsibility of ensuring that the tragic cargo was securely held within the ladders runs. Progress back up the slippery slope, through the little wooden garden gate, and on into Lambridge House was arduous, those who carried the remains of Miss Dungey taking careful deliberate steps.

Once safely within the confines of the kitchen, and with the various items that were scattered about the table top removed to any surface close to hand, the ladder was laid across the table, and the body lifted clear of it. Superintendent Francis Keal thus took a tentative step towards the corpse, and gazed at the womans upper torso, his eyes travelling up to the lady's head, at which point he visibly flinched at the sight of the young womans badly lacerated face and neck. Keal, recovering his composure, peered closer, he able to ascertain from the angle at which Kate Dungeys head lolled to one side, that the back of her head was severally wounded. Indeed so much of the unfortunate Miss Dungeys blood had been spilt, her dress, which was of indoor attire, was described by the officer, to his two companions, as being stained cherry red.

Superintendent Keal next desired that Lambridge House be searched; at this stage George Dawson, having quit the property, busying himself with an examination of the grounds that surrounded it. There was no indication, at this stage of the investigation, of any involvement of John Froomes and his son, but owing to the childs tender years it was wholly possible that father and son had, as before, retreated to one of the outhouses, in an effort to escape the bitter cold, and unyielding rain of that dank December night.

Keal and Snelgrove moved out into the corridor, kneeled down, and pin pointedly examined the floor, and with the aid of their lanterns they carried out a fingertip search of the hall. The men to rapidly come upon a hairpin, the item under closer scrutiny showing signs that it had been removed with some violence, as attached to it was a clump of hair, torn clear of its roots. The next item recovered was a diminutive brooch of intricate design (such as a lady might wear at her throat), close by it a seemingly discarded lamp, its metal work dented and glass shattered. The latter object led Keal to the belief that some individual had attempted to provide themself with a means of light, this conjecture reinforced by the discovery, a little distance away, of a box of matches. Further along the passageway the men chanced upon a candlestick, which lifted from the floor and examined was found to be streaked with what appeared to be congealed blood, a section of a wooden stake close beside it, the wallpaper splattered with bloody gore. All rooms were next put under scrutiny, and though the search of each was as thorough as conditions allowed no trace or clue, in relation to an intruder, was uncovered by the policemen.

Superintendent Francis Keal and Constable Edward Snelgrove quit Lambridge House via its front door, upon using its handle aware that it was coated in a residue of dried blood, Keal examining the handle meticulously. The two made their way to the rear of the premises and explored the ground in the area of the sitting room, this portion of the garden laid primarily to lawn, a sizable strip of soil directly beneath the sitting room window containing the frosted remnants of an autumn flowerbed. The soil around the wilted flowers was clumpy and heavily waterlogged, the explorers somewhat startled to find imprinted in the cloggy earth an impression of a man's footwear, the boot or shoe appearing to have several nails missing from its sole. At this point George Dawson, who was close at hand, found his assistance required, though this time the task demanded of him was less gruesome. He directed to cover the print, so as to protect its integrity until daylight, when a hoped for upturn in the weather would allow a cast to be taken.

Superintendent Keal was now satisfied as to his initial exploration of Lambridge House and the grounds about it. At this juncture he confident in his rudimentary conclusion regards the timeline of the previous evening's events. Miss Dungey had no doubt been quietly knitting at the kitchen table when her assailant had entered the house. He conjectured that the housekeeper had gone to investigate a noise that said intruder had inadvertently produced, carrying with her the fire poker, which had been initially observed by George Dawson and John Froomes, lying alongside Kate Dungeys body. The unfortunate woman had come across the interloper in the hallway, and at that point in time a terrible struggle had ensued, as indicated by the clues found in the passageway, Miss Dungey seized upon so fiercely that her hair was torn from its roots. It was at this point that she was most probably struck by a heavy implement, thought by Keal to be connected to the fragment of a wooden stake found lying on the hallway floor, the walls around the poor wretch at this stage of her assault sprayed with her blood. Francis Keal further surmised that Kate Dungey, though suffering from the effects of the sustained attack upon her person, had fled Lambridge House via its front door, closely pursued by her assailant. She must have run, still clutching the poker, down the garden path and through the gate, her villainous pursuer at her heels repeatedly striking her, until finally she fell, or collapsed, Miss Dungey then brutally beaten about the body, with a weapon of some description. Keal strongly believed the intruder had returned to Lambridge House, and, possibly hearing the Froomes boys approach, had concealed himself within the shadowy inner confines of the property. The murderous fiend, having bolted both the front and back doors internally, on realising the children had desisted in their efforts to gain entry to the farmhouse and left, taking the opportunity to exact his escape through the sitting room window.

Dawn was fast approaching as the weary group took leave of Lambridge Farm, upon the explicit instructions of Superintendent

Francis Keal, the body of Miss Kate Laura Dungey left where she lay. A Plainclothes Sergeant, one Thomas Allmond, who had not long arrived at the scene, receiving orders from his superior that he was to stay in situ and guard the body. All interior doors were locked, and windows checked to make fully certain they were bolted, Dawson, at the behest of Keal given charge of the house keys. Those vacating Lambridge House thus exited via the front door, with Allmond bolting it behind them. Superintendent Keal and Constable Snelgrove were conveyed back to Henley, thanks to the fortitude of an exhausted George Dawson, and the equally rung out Billy. While the Froomes, without the benefit of pony and trap, made their homeward journey to Assenden on foot.

Sergeant Thomas Allmond

The nights work was not yet at its conclusion, and once the officers were back in Henley-on-Thames, telegrams were rapidly sent (via Henley Post Office) to inform the surrounding towns and villages of the terrible events which had unfolded at Lambridge Farm. The telegrams contents included explicit instructions, from Superintendent Keal, to stop and examine any male, no matter his social position, leaving the area. Indeed on the morning, which followed on the heels of the dreadful events of the previous night, all men who waited to board trains at Henley had their footwear examined by constables, only once eliminated allowed to continue their journey. Also all men, who awaited trains at Twyford and Reading Railway Station, had their boots examined for any similarities to the footprint, which lay concealed under a protective cover, amongst the flower beds, beneath the sitting room window, back at Lambridge House.

Five

The Arrival of the Medical Examiner and the Cruel Nature of the Attack Revealed

New Street, which ran off from the right hand side of Bell Street (its junction dominated by Alfred Austin's provisions shop), consisted of numerous impressive Georgian properties, hostelries and business outlets. The prominent features of the bottom end of the street being the collection of buildings that constituted Brakspears Brewery, and the lapping waters of the River Thames. Doctor George Smith, one such professional who resided in New Street, ran his practice out of number fifty two. On the morning of Saturday 9th December, Superintendent Francis Keal was admitted to the doctors premises by housekeeper Fanny Underwood, she first escorting the unscheduled caller to the drawing room before summoning her master. George Smith, not in attire he deemed suitable to welcome a guest hastily changed, completed his toilette, and set off to greet Francis Keal. As appointed Surgeon for South Oxfordshire Smith was required as part of his remit to examine all those unfortunate enough to meet an unnatural death, and so with the doctors credentials in mind Superintendent Keal stated that he desired that Smith immediately accompany him to Lambridge Farm. Thus on a mercifully dryer morning than the night that had preceded it, Doctor Smith, once he had equipped himself of his medical bag, loaded up with the instruments that would be required, emerged from the surgery door. He took his place in a small trap, alongside Keal, the doctors coachman, Charles Underwood (husband of Fanny), bidding the steed, which he had hastily harnessed, to walk on. And with the horse trotting at an even pace the journey was not to be a tardy one, the trap heading up New Street, at the junction Underwood steering the horse to the right, the vehicle making rapid headway up onto the Fairmile.

Doctor George Smiths Surgery & home in New Street
It being the distinctive three storey flat roofed premises

Upon his arrival at Lambridge House, and after a cordial introduction to those present, Doctor Smith was led into the kitchen, the room dominated by the bedraggled remains of Miss Kate Dungey. The medical man strode up to the sizable table and gazed upon the lifeless woman, his face grave as he glanced back at Superintendent Keal and passed comment as to the dirty and bloodied state of the corpse. It cannot be ascertained if Francis Keal remained to witness any aspects of the examination of the body, but notes taken at the time seem to suggest that only two men were present during the principal stages of the grim procedure required to assert the cause of death. The second man in attendance was one Mr Joshua Watts, how he was conveyed to Lambridge Farm not known; his task that of the doctors clerk during Miss Dungeys post mortem.

At the time of the events at Lambridge it was fundamental in law that every step of a post mortem should be accurately recorded. And in the event of an examination being made by only one medical man, as in the case of Doctor Smith, the medic present was required to speak aloud his findings, notes of such to be made by a colleague. Once the necessary procedures were completed the notes were required to be read over on the spot by the doctor, and following his satisfaction as to the transcript, the document could then be deemed complete, finalised by the signature of both doctor and scribe.

Doctor George Smith positioned his medical bag in a convenient location, and gestured to Watts to indicate that he was ready to commence. Kate Dungey was initially examined in a state of dress; the doctor turning his attentions to the housekeepers head and after a hiatus of some moments taken up by Smith's absorption of the terrible nature of what was before him, he began to convey his findings, Joshua Watts taking down every word the doctor uttered verbatim. Deep wounds were present on the left side of the deceases neck, which, utilising a wooden ruler extracted from his medical bag, Smith measured at three to four inches long, and an inch and a half thick. The wounds were rugged and deep, and upon rolling the body towards him the doctor ascertained that further cuts had torn through the bodice of the young womans dress, sheared muscle, and penetrated as far as the backbone. Doctor Smith, reliant on his familiarity with the nature of injury, surmised that the wounds had been inflicted by an implement not unlike a billhook, a commonly enough found tool in agricultural establishments. Formidable in appearance, a billhook demanded extreme caution during usage, being a sharp curved blade most usually attached to a wooden handle, and used to clear, by means of rough pruning, areas afflicted by stubborn growths of brush. The doctor next turned his attention to the analysis of the numerous cuts which darted through Miss Dungeys hairline, and zigzagged across the crown of her head, each measured in turn. George Smith then examined the ragged sleeves of Miss Dungeys dress, each rolled up to reveal that her arms and wrists were also afflicted with multiple cuts, clearly indicative that the deceased had raised her arms in a desperate attempt to defend herself, as blows were rained down upon her.

The delicate task of disrobing the body was now not to be avoided, a difficult endeavour in relation to the respect for Kate Dungeys modesty, even in death. Utilizing water that had been heated on the stove, the doctor gently washed the corpse clean of the mud and gore which blighted it. Smith thus investigated every aspect of the body, at the conclusion of which twenty four wounds scattered about Miss Dungeys head, neck, arms and hands (the consensus that for the most part said wounds were the result of the wielding of a bladed implement), had been duly noted by Joshua Watts. The final imposition against Kate Dungey, one of a most intimate nature, and once it was carried out Watts to record in his notes that the lady had not been violated. Doctor George Smith stood back from his mute patient, turned to Joshua Watts and requested that his clerk include in his notes that time of death was most likely between five and eight o'clock the previous evening, as the victim may well have clung to life for a time, after the frenzied attack upon her person. Smith redressed Miss Dungey, though since her clothes were torn and blooded remnants of their former selves this task proved not an easy one. The foremost necessity being to retain Kate Dungeys body as closely as possible to the state in which she was first found, for the purpose of a coroner's inquest.

Six

Summon Benjamin Palmer

During his second visit to Lambridge Farm, while Doctor Smith was taken up with the examination of the body of Miss Kate Dungey, Superintendent Francis Keal took the opportunity to explore the crime scene, the process of which greatly assisted by the daylight. The benefit of natural light to enable a significantly more detailed examination of Lambridge House, the gardens, farmland, and wooded area which surrounded it. Keal took it upon himself to pay particular attention to the footprint discovered the previous night. Crouching in the flowerbed, the rainy conditions having abated, he drew back the protective covering, the compression of what appeared to be the sole of a hobnail boot clearly evident. Superintendent Keal had not come unprepared, and, with the use of copious amounts of wax, which had been liquefied at the hearth in Lambridges kitchen, he took a cast, the finished result of which producing an intricately detailed piece of invaluable evidence.

The morning of Saturday 9th December had been an eventful one for those who worked within the local constabulary. Henleys Postmaster, thirty year old Benjamin Palmer, had been summoned from his home "Redlands", located at the bottom end of Fielder Road (in 1895 renamed Hamilton Avenue), some hours before he was accustomed to head out for a days labour, the post offices usual opening time being seven. Once made aware of the urgency of the situation, and after a hasty farewell to his wife Emmeline, Palmer accompanied the constable, who had been charged with fetching him, into town. Henley Post Office, located in Market Place, opened without delay, for the explicit purpose of wiring numerous telegrams, composed by

Superintendent Keal, the contents of which directed to outlying towns and villages, and persons, who were to find themselves sorely affected by the dreadful events at Lambridge.

Henley Post Office in Market Place
The central building, with the letter box in front

The contents of the telegram received at the London home of Mr Henry Joseph Mash sent him in haste to Henley-on-Thames, his unscheduled journey, by means of Great Western, culminating at Henley Railway Station. The time of arrival of the tenant of Lambridge, it being the early hours of the afternoon, had been sent ahead, and a gig was laid on for Mr Mashs convenience. Henry Mash thus conveyed without delay to Lambridge Farm, upon reaching his destination and being escorted into the house, Mash displaying an air of profound emotional exhaustion, his face ashen and gate unsteady, he informing those concerned by his outward appearance that the cause was primarily the abruptness of his summoning to Henley. Mashs wife, Georgiana, who in a show of spousal support had travelled down from London alongside her husband, was profoundly affected by the shocking facts which emulated from the lips of Superintendent Keal, she to retreat to the garden to calm herself. Henry Mash was not as fortunate as his wife, and at the request of Keal, was required to look upon his dead housekeeper. The master of Lambridge House entered its kitchen, in situ Sergeant Allmond (Doctor Smith and Joshua Watts returned to Henley), who nodded an acknowledgement, and at the behest of Superintendent Keal quit the room. The kitchen, which had been in the past the site of much domestic harmony was now a temporary morgue, containing as it did the lifeless form of Miss Kate Dungey. The ordeal of looking upon the corpse caused Henry Mashs complexion to drain, and his legs to buckle, the man clutching at the table, fearful that he might swoon. Mash was clearly in need of some comfort, and was bolstered by the carefully chosen words of Keal, who was not unused to handling those in a state of shock. There was an interlude while the tenant of Lambridge recovered, but the break was but a short one, as Henry Mash was required by Keal to join him in an exploration of the house. This examination was necessary to determine if Mash missed any of his valuables, since there was the possibility of theft as a motive for an intruder to have invaded the farmhouse. Henry Mash, as he strode from room to room, found all as it should be, no household item unaccounted, and Superintendent Francis Keal thus reunited the man with his wife, and determining that there was no further necessity for them to remain, gave them leave to depart. The Mash's relieved to be back in each other's company conversed briefly, acknowledged the kindness shown them by Keal, and swiftly left Lambridge Farm. Their journey to Henley was not a protracted one, and shortly then after their coachman pulled up alongside the Mash's townhouse, thirty seven New Street, which ironically stood almost opposite the surgery of Doctor George Smith.

Miss Kate Dungeys father also was to receive, via the hand of a post boy, a telegram the dreadful contents of which to throw his household into chaos. The Dungeys resided at "Pattenden", located just outside Goudhurst, a small vibrant rural village situated in the county of Kent. It was no short distance to Henley-on-Thames, and as such Walter Dungey, who travelled by rail, did not arrive until the latter hours of Saturday afternoon. Walter was accompanied by two of his daughters, and the Dungey party was met at the station by transport, which conveyed them to Lambridge Farm. Superintendent Francis Keal, fully aware that Miss Dungeys family were en-route, extracted himself from the house and waited anxiously for their arrival, his face set firm. He had a job to do, and do it he must, and as the gig drew up he took charge. The ladies were placed into the care of a constable, and the father of a slain child was escorted, expressions of condolence from those he passed, to the kitchen, where after some moments of heartrending grief Walter Dungey formally identified his daughters' remains.

It was a fact, which caused some alarm to the police officers who patrolled the area, that several dozen curious locals (inaccurately quoted in various tabloids as numbered in the hundreds) visited the murder scene on Sunday 10th December. There some concern that it was most likely that the presence of unchaperoned interlopers might interfere greatly with any evidence that had laid undiscovered, it trodden down beneath sole and heel.

Word was out regarding the outrage, and the local paper, the Henley and South Oxfordshire Standard, quickly issued a transitory report on the murder at Lambridge Farm. "An awful crime, that had not been committed in the town or neighbourhood within the memory of living man, and Friday 8th December 1893, will always be regarded as a black day in the annals of Henley's history."

Seven

The Carpenter and his Boys

Fawley Court, which stands resplendent just beyond the boundary of Henley-on-Thames, was occupied before the conquest of William the Conqueror, under Edward the Confessor. The estate bore witness too much upheaval, during the tumultuous struggle between King and Parliament, its manor house reduced to a dilapidated shell. But from the ashes came forth a phoenix, when in 1684 one William Freeman commissioned the construction of a fine country retreat. The principal house, which benefited from a riverside setting, is much debated as to whether Sir Christopher Wren was directly involved in its design, but, doubts aside, by 1688 a very fine residence was ready for occupation.

Fawley Estate passed through umpteen generations of the Freemans, the house and grounds much adapted according to the architectural and landscaping foibles of the day. And upon the death, in December 1821, of Strickland Freeman, he having no issue, Fawley Court passed to the deceases close relative William Peere Williams, the eldest son of Mary Williams, sister of one John Cooke Freeman. William obliged, upon inheritance, to take the name Freeman, the estate he thus acquired considerable, included within its holdings Henley Park. This estate, situated on a hill at the north side of Henley-on-Thames, lands run down onto the Fairmile, its boundary wall of flint and brick constructed in 1804 under the behest of Strickland Freeman, he fervently wishing to keep out undesirables. William Peere Williams Freeman (honoured by William IV with the title of Admiral of the Fleet), shared his time between Fawley and his other estate, Hoddesdon, in Hertfordshire, and here it was he died on 11th February 1832, duly interred in the family vault at Broxbourne.

The new master of Fawley Court, as with the previous incumbent named William Peere Williams (he also upon inheritance required to incorporate Freeman into his surname), took to his elevation within society with gusto. Favouring Fawley Court as his main residence Freeman had little need of Henley Park, the estate thus for the most part tenanted out. In 1841 John William Newell Birch, aged sixty five and retired (his former job that of Clerk Assistant of Parliament), finding Henley Park to his liking secured a lease for life. The park's main residence (in the Georgian style) had fallen from favour, and having stood empty and neglected was a shadow of the fine dower house it had once been. But John Birch and his wife Diana Elizabeth much cherished the property, and under skilled builders and interior designers the house was given the attention it so craved, adapted to a three storey residence, topped off with an elegant stuccoed frontage. Birch had his country retreat, and although the estates lands had by the 1840s been much reduced, with large swaths held by independent agricultural tenants, John Birch still had the benefit of twenty acres. Within his holdings he desired to keep a small herd of sheep, and once a suitable breed of animal was acquired Birch had need of a shepherd, his estate bailiff employing Moses Froomes.

Moses Froomes, upon commencing employment having turned thirty six, was more fortunate than many others who worked the land, as his position at Henley Park came with the provision of an estate cottage, its upkeep dutifully executed by Moses wife Mary. The Froomes, who had wed at St Mary's in the October of 1827, did not occupy their new home in isolation, they having a five year old son William. A daughter, Jane was born within the Froomes tenancy in 1843; Elizabeth arriving three years after, the last winter of the decade to witness the birth of John.

The Froomes lived an idyllic existence at Henley Park, their lives enhanced by a kindly master, but change was on the horizon. William Peere Williams Freeman had in 1833 suffered a Common Recovery (in very rudimentary terms a legal procedure, quite often as a result of bad debts, used to break entails in wills and settlements, and if a Common Recovery moved successfully through the courts, property and lands could be sold), and compounded to convey some of his holdings to another, to avoid another suing for it, Freeman saw as his best opportunity of extricating himself from mounting financial entanglements, the auctioning off of Fawley Court, and the estates that neighboured it, in entirety. A decision, which at the time seemed the most sensible course Williams Freeman could take, proved anything but straight forward, much argument amongst his extended family, as to his plan, resulting in the fellow getting bogged down in expensive litigation. But financial restraint is a strong motive, and all objections dealt with, in the June of 1853 William Peere Williams Freemans local holdings (including the manors of Fawley Court, Henley Park, and Phyllis Court) went under the hammer, Williams Freeman to relocate to a none too shabby residence, Pylewell House.

The gavel was knocked down for the considerable sum of ninety thousand pounds, to Edward Mackenzie, a Scot who had acquired a fortune in the world of banking, and as a railway entrepreneur. Mackenzie's decision to retire to the country much influenced by the body blow felt at the death of his business partner and brother, civil engineer and railway builder William Mackenzie. Indeed, upon arriving at Fawley Court, Mackenzie was so utterly beguiled by his investment that he was to spend the last twenty seven years of his life upon the estate.

So John William Newell Birch had a new landlord, but life at Henley Park carried on much as it had, the Froomes children benefitting from an education thanks to a school house (consisting of one classroom), situated on the road leading from the hamlet of Assenden, and on into

Henley Park. This place of learning, established in 1849, for the teaching of the poor, funded by none other than Moses Froomes employer, Mr Birch, who also covered the wage of the schools sole teacher, in the 1850s (when the Froomes attended) the schoolmistress Miss Mary Ann Stalwood, this young woman having responsibility for the betterment of twenty children.

John William Newell Birch of Henley Park, Henley-on-Thames in the County of Oxfordshire, and of Wimpole Street, Cavendish Square in the County of Middlesex, died aged eighty seven, on 24th January 1864. He drew his last breath in the presence of his close family, at his beloved Henley Park, much lamented by gentleman and labourer alike, Birch remembered as a godly soul. His widow Diana, having the benefit of a considerable share of her late husband's assets of just over two hundred thousand pounds, continued to reside at Henley Park, until her demise in 1867. So after in excess of a quarter of a century under the tenancy of the Birch's, Henley Park was placed on the lettings market, after a short interlude the house and grounds taken by a Mr Robert Robertson.

Moses and Mary Froomes youngest child, John, flourished, in no small part due to the generosity of his father's initial employer at Henley Park, a well-rounded education enhancing the young lad's opportunities. Not one wishing to work the land John Froomes determined to learn a trade, and thus apprenticed in carpentry, when released of his apprenticeship numerous customer commissions enabling John, aged twenty six, to take a wife. Froomes sweetheart, Emma (one year Johns senior, the daughter of brewers man George Green, who resided on West Hill in Henley-on-Thames), was not adverse to the idea of marriage, and on 5th December 1875, before the Rector of St Marys, she consented to be Froomes wife. Moses Froomes had not lived to see his son wed, he having died in the May, but his widow Mary (by this stage her health delicate) attended her son's wedding, she to pass away near one year after her husband.

John and Emma did not buck the tread of the time, and like countless other couples had a large family, Edith Mary the first to arrive, born the year following her parents' marriage. Florence Emma, Charles Frederick, and James, all born before 1880 was spent. John Froomes, as a jobbing carpenter, found his time taken up with securing the next commission, and with a wife and offspring to support, it was little wonder that the children's baptisms were rather ad hoc. Florence and Charles welcomed into the Christian Fellowship, at Henleys Parish Church, on 30th December 1879, Edith and James baptised on 9th May 1881. The brother to whom James would be most devoted, Harry, was born in 1882, another daughter Ellen arriving two years then after. The birth of George further swelled the familys number, the last of the Froomes offspring, Walter, safely delivered of his mother in 1888, so what abode did John Froomes find able to accommodate his sizable family, why number 128 Lower Assenden.

Life in and around Bix and Assenden was evolving, the early 1880s had seen the closing down of the little school that had served the area well (ironically one of its last school mistresses none other than John Froomes sister, Elizabeth), it thus forward utilised as a tenanted property for the Mackenzie's of Fawley Courts gamekeeper. It had been so ordered, by the regionally appointed "School Board", that the provisions made to meet educational needs within Bix and Assenden were inadequate, and with this in mind, and the school that many, who now found themselves parents, had attended, now closed, said parents turned their attentions to a recently completed school. This establishment, opened in 1878, lay alongside Bix Common, and with the areas children sorely in need of it, the school managed to squeeze in forty pupils. By the time the Froomes offspring commenced their education (the school having in 1881 been enlarged), schoolmistress Kate Frances (her husband, George, one who would sit upon the inquest jury, called to examine the facts pertaining to the demise of Kate Dungey) able to accommodate sixty two children.

At first appearance it seemed that the Froomes household must have been bursting at the seams, but all was not as it appeared. By the latter 1880s the two eldest Froomes girls, Edith and Florence, had gone into service, their employer Mr James Gould (an accountant), he and his wife Elizabeth residing at Howard Road, Croydon in Surrey. Ten had become eight, but there is little doubt that space must have still been at a premium, and it therefore must have surely been a blessed relief that young James and Harry would, due to the forbearance of its master, on countless nights have use of a bedroom at Lambridge House. Thus John Froomes and his two boys would find themselves thrust into events not of their own making, pure happenchance determining the presence of the lads at Lambridge Farm, the night its housekeeper met an untimely end.

Eight

The Bailiff of Lambridge Farm

John Dawson, born 1834 in Steventon in the county of Berkshire, spent his formative years in Milton, Berkshire, and in due course finding himself smitten by local girl, Elizabeth, resolved that she would be his wife. Thus John Dawson, with the blessing of his sweethearts father (agricultural labourer Jacob Howard), in the last quarter of 1859 took twenty two year old Elizabeth as his bride. Since Dawson was not a man having been afforded the opportunities that privilege allowed, he kept his new wife as best he could on the meagre wage he earned as an agricultural labourer. Unable to secure a job that came with a tenancy, or manage the financial burden of rent, the Dawson's took lodgings in Little Lane, Milton, thanks to the kindness afforded them by the properties tenants, Johns brother, Daniel, and his wife Sarah.

The birth in 1860 of Stephen Alfred necessitated the need for John and Elizabeth to secure a more permanent place of abode, and Dawson looked about for a farm labouring job with benefit of a tenancy, and not a fellow to be easily confounded in due course secured a position which came with a cottage, in the quaintly named Old Moon in Milton, to the west and south of the Turnpike Road, which wound its way from Abingdon to Ilsley. Financial constraints never proved a barrier to the begetting of children, the Dawson's blessed with a large brood of offspring they could little afford. George was born in 1863, he joined in rapid succession by Sarah Ann, John Thomas, Henry, Seymore Alfred, and in 1875 Elizabeth. 1877 was marked as a year of heartache; Annie Maria, once delivered of her mother, failing to thrive, the child dying shortly after her hastily arranged baptism of 17th June. 1878 brought about worse misfortune, with the death of the Dawson's first born, Stephen Alfred; John Thomas set to die not long after, Elizabeth's profound grief tempered by the safe delivery, on 25th September of that same year, of a son, duly named Stephen after his recently departed sibling, this child to die in 1895.

John Dawson had not in his formative years had advantage of an apprenticeship, and so it was to the much seasonal work of farm labouring that he extensively relied. By the latter years of the 1870s Dawson toiled at Lower Farm, Milton, misfortune as ever snapping at his heels, the first year of the 1880s marked indelible by the death of Seymore Albert.

George Dawson was more fortunate than those of his siblings who had not survived the perils of childhood afflictions, and by his early teens worked alongside his father, while his mother Elizabeth earned a meagre crust as a carrier. George was literate which gave him an advantage, but agricultural positions had many who sought them, and he was compelled to go where the work was. Thus Dawson took himself off to South Oxfordshire; the bailiff of one Henry Joseph Mash much impressed by the young man's work ethic giving him a job as a stable groom.

Miss Amy Katherine Rathall, not born into money, did as many young women of her status did; she went into service, as parlour maid in the household of William and Grace Robinson, of West Cromwell Road, Kensington London. Time off in such a profession was at a premium, but still Amy had opportunity to visit her family in Lower Assenden, and no doubt while on one such excursion she crossed paths with George Dawson, who although now in his upper twenties was in want of a wife. Amy Rathall had her man, and on 1st June 1892 twenty four year old Amy wed George at St James Church in Bix, their nuptials witnessed by Emily Prince and a Robert Parker, a gentleman who will have cause to be mentioned subsequently. There is within the marriage register an anomaly, Dawson's profession entered as that of a groom, at odds with the census of 5th April 1891, in which he is categorised as holding the position of Lambridges farm bailiff.

So it seems that George Dawson, through the diligent manner in which he executed the tasks required of him, had impressed his employer, and when one particular role had become vacant Dawson had been uppermost in Mr Henry Mashs thoughts. And having first refusal, George Dawson became the envy of many, that being appointed farm bailiff of his masters tenancy, a role that not only offered a wider scope of responsibilities, but also an enhanced salary. George Dawson, with the benefit of his position at Lambridge Farm, and his employers reference, secured a tenancy in one of a terrace of four brick and flint properties known as "Folly Cottages" (in the ownership of William Dalziel Mackenzie of Fawley Court), which stood on the Old Bix Road, in Lower Assenden. And although their home was of a size almost untenable for occupation of any more than two individuals the Dawson's quickly started a family, Elsie Mary baptised at St James's, on 20th August 1893.

And so we have an evolving family unit, but George Dawson's situation as farm bailiff, which appeared on the face of it a fairly innoxious job, would in the lead up to the Christmas of 1893 subject this man of unsophisticated nature, and kindly disposition, to unimaginable adversities. The deplorable murder of the housekeeper of Lambridge Farm sending shock waves through the county, the ripples of gossip rapidly escalating into a torrent, opening up those who had course to be connected with the victim to the stresses of wild speculation, which emulated from the mouths of the ill-informed.

In the days that followed the outrage, those of the press, ferried via the Great Western Railway into Henley-on-Thames, had been directed by their editors to seek out any pertinent facts, the reporters to ferreted out any individual who had crossed paths with Miss Kate Dungey.

And with this uppermost in the mind of one such hack, who on the afternoon of Saturday 9th December having travelled to Lower Assenden and enquired thereabouts, found himself at the door of a neat little residence, in amongst a terrace of properties collectively known as Folly Cottages. The fellow gained entry, and secured from the tenant, George Dawson, he not wise to the duplicities of the press, a protracted statement, as follows.

"I left the farm at about a quarter past five on Friday evening, for my home at Folly Cottages, previous to departing I spoke to Miss Dungey respecting matters connected with the farm business, and she then appeared in her usual spirits. Soon after ten, I was called by Froomes and having heard the boy's story, I went with them to the house. We knocked and kicked loudly at both the back and front doors, and also tapped the windows, but got no answer. I then went round the house and examined the doors and windows; I found that the former was locked, and that the keys were in their bolts on the inside. All the windows were fastened, with the exception of one, a bay window of the sitting room, in the front of the house. This opens perpendicularly and the bottom sash was about half way up, connecting this incident with the fact that the doors were locked from the inside of the house, it became evident to me that something unusual had happened. I climbed in at the window, Froomes and his boy James following, we fastened the window behind us and examined all the rooms, but found nothing disturbed, Miss Dungeys small silver watch was on a chair in the sitting room and was going. We next explored the passage and there found the brooch, hairpins and cudgel, while the walls, floor and door were sprinkled with blood, the knob of the door being simply covered. I opened the door and the three of us proceeded to the spot where a noise had been heard by the Froomes boys, and here we found the body, with head and face smashed, neck and ears gashed, and the upper part of the ladies clothes perfectly saturated with blood."

~ 43 ~

The bailiff of Lambridge Farm had unburdened himself, and his words would in the coming days be rehashed in some form or other, appearing in the columns of various tabloids of differing quality. Some of the articles, accredited to George Dawson, not in any way reflective of what he had actually said to the anonymous reporter, who on the face of it had seemed so obliging.

George Dawson, attired in his Sunday best, sitting for a formal portrait

Nine

Men of the Oxfordshire Constabulary

It is noted that in the year of 1835 Henley-on-Thames had to manage town patrols and outbreaks of criminality with the assistance of just six constables, two of whom appointed annually by the Mayor, or those who sat as Henley Bench Magistrates, and four by the Manor Court, but in the course of the next twenty two years all this was to change. The Oxfordshire Constabulary came into being on 25th March 1857, its headquarters based initially in New Road Oxford, under the watchful eye of its Chief Constable, one Charles Mostyn (on a salary of three hundred pounds, with additional travelling expenses of one hundred pounds) who had responsibility for a force which consisted of seventy two constables (on seventeen shillings a week), six sergeants, seven inspectors, and three superintendents. The Oxfordshire Constabulary was made up of three divisions, 'A' Division, included Headquarters Bullingdon, Henley and Watlington, 'B' Division made up of the areas of Ploughley, North and South Wootten, and 'C' Division, made up of Banbury and Bloxham, Bampton East and West, Chadlington, and Banbury South. There was also provision made for two inspectors at Bicester, Chipping Norton, Neithrop and Woodstock, sergeants working out of Burford, Deddington, Henley-on-Thames, and Thame.

Candidates, who having made the grade, and found themselves a constable within the constabulary, were required to adhere to a strict code of conduct, as laid out by the Chief Constable within his instruction manual, which all those working under Charles Mostyn were made privy to. One subsection of the code specified that all constables, upon completion of their set hours of walking a beat, were duty bound to return to their place of abode to rest, it being paramount that a constable should be found within his quarters until his next hour of patrol, the only exception to this rule being if a superior urgently required a constables services.

Francis Grantham Keal (baptised 6th August 1819, in Wyberton, Lincolnshire) married in 1847 Maria Fisher, she six years his younger. With Keal employed as a labourer the couple took up residence in Cane End, Freiston Boston, Lincolnshire Freeby, and here in 1850 they welcomed the arrival of their first born Elizabeth. The remainder of the decade saw the birth of John Francis, Maria, John (his elder brother known by his middle name) and Richard. In 1864 Thomas was born, by the conclusion of 1865 he joined by his brother, David, the familys principal breadwinner, an agricultural labourer, enjoying the benefit of a tied cottage at Lowe Field, this two up two down property just managing to accommodate the Keals.

Francis, the second born, spent an idyllic childhood tussling with his four younger brothers, his sisters Elizabeth and Maria (while still in their teens to go into service), going against the Victorian dictates to maintain an air of lady like decorum, joining in the fun. Keal proved himself a diligent student, and keen to elevate his status sought a career in the constabulary, subsequently noted in his police application as fully able to read and write skills still not fully assessable to all. As a young man, while still under the roof of his parents (the family by now residing at Flying Horse, in Freiston Boston), and fresh in the world of commerce Francis initial employment had been that of a labourer, he in the late spring of 1872 having wed Miss Mary Allen, finding a tenancy of his own. But all was to change one morning when the post brought news that Keals police application had proved successful, on 17th July 1876 Francis Keal donning his uniform for the first time. Training for his new role was something that presented little problem to the eager young fellow, and Keal successfully passed out, afforded the rank of Second Class

Constable, initially billeted on 29th July at Bampton Police Station, a market town within West Oxfordshire, by the November of 1876 transferred to Watlington in Oxfordshire.

Francis Keal was never one to settle for a lowly rank; he was a man of ambition and thus drew the attention of his betters, who sensing that this young police officer was cut from a different cloth to his colleagues, in the January of 1877 elevated Keal to the rank of Constable First Class. Merit Class followed on 3rd May 1880, and by the next October Francis Keal took up a posting in Bullington; by the census return of 3rd April 1881 residing in Wallingford, directly next door to the Eight Bells Public House, an establishment Keal would often frequent on his days off. But Constable Keal did not tarry long in the rank of constable, on 17th October 1883 made up to Sergeant, promoted to First Class Inspector on 5th January 1885. The rank of Superintendent was the lofty ambition of many who worked their way up through the constabulary, and in the summer of 1885 Francis Keal was elevated to the rank of Second Class Superintendent.

In 1868 two premises that stood at the cusp of West Street, in Henley (one for some considerable time the tenancy of any who took the landlordship of the Kings Arms) were purchased for a most particular purpose. The properties thus extensively adapted to the plans of Oxford based architect William Wilkinson. At the time of his commission in Henley-on-Thames nearing fifty years old, Wilkinson (a confirmed bachelor) had in 1857 superseded Mr T. C. Buckler as appointed architect to the Oxfordshire Police Committee, he already responsible, amongst others, for Watlington and Chipping Norton police stations.

The newly constructed Henley-on-Thames County Police Station stood, as you came up towards the fine Georgian town hall, on the right side of Market Place, and on Saturday 30th June 1888 Francis Keal took up his posting as Superintendent of the Henley Division, accompanied by his wife Mary (two years his junior), and Annie their fourteen year old daughter. The family quickly grew accustomed to their living quarters, situated above Keals place of work, he able to call on a ample supply of police officers, that being one inspector, one sergeant, and if a situation demanded it up to twelve constables. Francis Keal found that his posting was not one where he could rest on his laurels, for a relatively small market town Henley-on-Thames had its fair share of the criminal element, and with numerous hostelries alcohol fuelled disorder proved a seemingly nightly occurrence.

1893 would be marked as a year of mixed fortunes for Superintendent Francis Keal, in the February elevated to the rank of First Class Superintendent, by the December embroiled in a case that would put untold pressure on his resources, and the men under his command.

When first alerted to events at Lambridge Farm Superintendent Keal had been compelled to take a somewhat hazardous high speed journey in George Dawsons pony and trap, accompanied by his duty constable, Snelgrove. Edward John Snelgrove hailed from Heytesbury, Warminster, Wiltshire, his beginnings modest, baptised 23rd May 1871, Edwards father, Thomas Snelgrove, earning his wage as a gardener, while his wife, Rachel (nee Pike), managed the home, the couple, who had wed in 1856, residing at 48 High Street Heytesbury. Edward Snelgrove was not to grow up in isolation, he had a sister, Rosa, six years his elder, and a brother Fred (he born in 1867), who shared the name of an elder sibling, who aged twenty one months had died in 1863.

Edward Snelgrove did not initially show any leanings towards a career in the police, his first foray into employment that of a baker, but better prospects were on the horizon. Snelgrove done with the bakery took up an offer of employment working for the bailiff of Lord William Henry Heytesbury, this gentleman named after Edward's place of birth. But as with those afflicted by the follies of youth money matters proved anything but straightforward, and so Snelgrove resolved that a role within the constabulary would provide him with an enhanced wage, and prospects of betterment. And so it was that on 1st July 1890 Edward John Snelgrove became the proud recipient of a police constables uniform, and a copy of the Police Procedures Manual.

Snelgrove was transferred to Henley-on-Thames in the October of 1890, under the mentoring of Francis Keal, and due in no small part to Keals recommendations was promoted in February 1891 to the rank of Constable Second Class. In the spring of 1893 Snelgrove was again promoted, to Constable First Class, and it was at this rank that he found himself embroiled in a murder.

Richard Allmond (born 1829 in Marsh Baldon, Oxfordshire) had on 3rd December 1849 married Miss Martha Currell, born 1831, Marsh Baldon. Allmonds principal job was that of a wood sawyer, but he pushed up his meagre wage by taking casual work as a carrier. The arrival in 1851 of first born Mary Ann, followed then after by the births of Frederick and Emma, sorely tested Allmonds purse strings, the turn of the 1860s seeing the birth of Ruben, followed then after by Thomas, Charles, Caroline Anna, and Frank (born in 1870), compounding the Allmonds money worries. And so Richard Allmond did as many who had little disposable income did, he took in a lodger, one Amos Cannon (who like his landlord worked as a sawyer), the man squeezed into a vacant corner of the Allmond household.

By the time Thomas Allmond had done with schooling, and commenced his working life, his father was employed as a farm labourer, and as with many a father and son Thomas joined Richard on the land, the work back breaking and poorly paid. But life being fraught with peril, in the January of 1882 Richard Allmond fell ill, an affliction that on the twenty second of that same month claimed his life, his sons left to take up the mantle, as the families breadwinners. Thomas Allmond did his bit and took up employment within the household of Sir John Willoughby (Bart) of Marsh Baldon, but he craved better than his late father, and so it was that on 21st May 1883 he passed out as a constable in Her Majesty's Constabulary. Just two months on from that date Allmond promoted to Constable Second Class, while serving out of Chadlington, a vibrant Oxfordshire village north of Chipping Norton.

In the spring of 1884 Constable Allmond requested of Thomas (an agricultural labourer) and Esther Spicer, of Grove in Berkshire, if he might have their daughters hand in marriage, and with their blessing twenty six year old Emma (previously employed as a housemaid, in Dorchester, Oxfordshire) found herself a coppers wife. The newlyweds financial footing further assured the April following their nuptials, Thomas Allmond elevated to the rank of First Class Constable.

The Allmonds welcomed the birth of their first born Leopold in 1886, following hot on his heels a second son, Percival. By the time a third boy, Frank, arrived in 1889 his father a Constable of the Merit Class. On 9th November 1891 Thomas Allmond, serving at Hook Norton Police Station, achieved the rank of Sergeant, which must have been of some comfort as the year had been marked by the arrival of a fourth son, Horace. Allmonds advancement though the ranks carried on almost unabated (there was one hiccup to be later explored), the spring of 1893 his superior attributes rewarded with promotion to the rank of Inspector Second Class; he duly transferred to Bullingdon, the birth of yet another boy, Tom, necessitating the higher wage.

At the time of the Lambridge affair Thomas Allmond was serving in the South Oxfordshire Region, Hook Norton, with the proviso that he was to make himself available to Superintendent Keal at Henley-on-Thames if events dictated the need. Thomas Allmond was unique amongst those he served with, in so much as he was a Plains Clothes Sergeant, and once summoned to Lambridge Farm, having given assistance to his fellow officers, it was due to this superior rank that Superintendent Francis Keal requested that Allmond maintain a guard of Miss Dungeys body until such time as it was permissible for her to be released to her family for burial. Sergeant Allmonds presence within the confines of Lambridge House was to be rapidly seized upon by the press, who milked it for all it was worth, the newspapers providing its ravenous readership with an image of pathos, as this dutiful officer stood faithful vigil at Lambridge Farm, his charge the mortal remains of a woman cut down by foul deed.

Ten

Oxfordshire's Medical Examiner

Henry Smith (born in Lisonahugo, Lancashire), and his wife Elizabeth (hailed from Penpont Dumfries, fifteen years her husband's junior), by the census of 7th April 1861 resided in Peufillan, Scotland, and enjoyed the elevated status afforded those who had possession of land. 396 acres in all, 180 acres of the sort fit for arable, Henry Smith able to sustain the wages of three men and a boy. There were others who worked for Smith, dairymaid Margret Wilson, who tended to a small herd of cows, Thomas Williamsom, who tended to the ploughing, and Mary Rae, who tended to the house.

Daughters Mary Stewart Janet and the strikingly named Euphemia Logan had been born in the 1850s, their brother Andrew arriving during the last year of the decade. Three further sons were to follow after the census of 1861, George, Henry, and James, the Smith's domestic needs met by solitary servant Mary Rae.

The year 1878 saw Henry Smith turn sixty, and with the burden of advancing age as a bearing on his decision Smith relinquished his lands, upped sticks and relocated across the border into Suffolk. Not a man to act rashly Henry Smith had first secured a position that not only provided a wage but also an apartment, that of estate agent of Levington Hall, a furnished wing of which a useful perk and his familys new home. The Smiths not to relinquish domestic servants cook Elizabeth Moffat producing wholesome meals, while housemaid Elizabeth Dinwiddie kept dust at bay, laid fires, and cleaned the silver plate.

Medicine drew George Smith away from the fold, but the security and close bond of a loving family was never far from his mind, and on 3rd

April 1881, when the census gatherer called, the young man was enjoying a visit with his family. Smith's principal education at Framlingham College had stood him in good stead, but it was as an undergraduate at Edinburgh University (spending some portion of his degree studying in Vienna) where he honed his medical knowledge, graduating with honours in 1885.

It cannot be ascertained with certainty what brought George Smith to Henley-on-Thames (he having for a short time practiced in Acton) in the February of 1888, the young doctor setting up in practice at 52 New Street. Here indeed was a diligent fellow, and he caught the eye of those who held sway in the county. Doctor Smith (also it seems a partner in a practice run out of a portion of Speakers House, Hart Street, alongside Doctor George Alden, and Doctor James Lidderdale) soon adding to his responsibilities that of Medical Officer and Public Vaccinator for the Parish of Greys District, under the direction of the Henley Union.

The Vaccination Extension Act of 1840 had led to new thinking as to the prevention of diseases such as Smallpox that in the past had either proved fatal or left many of those fortunate enough to survive blighted by the affliction of heavy scarring, or due to permanent disability the inability to earn a living. This act provided the very first free of charge medical service, available to all, with no restrictions due to the poverty of any individual wishing to access it, up to that point the wealthy (possessing the funds to privately inoculate their children) having an unfair advantage over the poor and destitute. Mass inoculations were administered under the stringent control of contracts governed by Poor Law Commissioners, the costs of which negotiated by the Board of Guardians of any given parish. On the most part professional men the guardians primary responsibility to appoint medical officers within their derestriction, to administer vaccinations quickly and efficiently. Many found the concept of inoculation of their children alien and frightening, indeed in the 1870s fervent opposition to vaccination become widespread. Though inoculation of minors was not compulsory, with the reluctance of some parents in mind, handbills and notices were displayed in prominent positions at Registration and Union Offices, as a means of encouraging the public to ignore their trepidations and take advantage of the benefits on offer. This new wave of state care, of the most vulnerable in society, was something not seen before on such an impressive scale, and one cannot underestimate the importance of the role of any one particular parishes Board of Guardians.

The Board of Guardians grew out of the Poor Law Amendment Act (passed in Parliament in 1834, under then Prime Minister William Lamb, Second Viscount Melbourne), this organisation orchestrated to replace the heavily flawed Parish Overseers of the Poor, established under the old Poor Law. Under the amended act small parishes were required to combine to form a Poor Law Union. One of the most notable endeavours of this new board the requirement to commission the construction of workhouses for poor relief, funded by a levy paid from the pockets of the property owning classes. Once a Poor Law Union was fully established it could not be dissolved or merged with any neighbouring union, without the explicate consent of the board. Each civil parish was to have at least one Board of Guardians, towns and cities with a larger populace permitted to have two or more, the members elected annually by the owners and tenants of lands liable to pay the Poor Rate. Doctor George Smith, under his new role, commissioned to carry out one of the Henley Board of Guardians paramount responsibility, that being to implement the vaccination of all children within the parish boundaries.

Doctor Smith ran an industrious practice; the availability of a fully competent doctor at the close of the nineteenth century still not as straightforward as one might think. The practices dispenser proved himself a diligent member of staff, he being Nottingham born Arthur Bramman, a man of thirty three at the time of the events at Lambridge

Farm. Bramman had experienced a somewhat different start in life than that enjoyed by his employer, the son of a lace curtain presser, Samuel Bramman (born 1815, Nottingham), his mother, Matilda (the daughter of hairdresser John Hindley, and twenty years her husband's junior), a homemaker. Matilda Bramman therefore took responsibility for the nurturing of her children, who besides Arthur consisted of Ellen Matilda, Frederick William (died but a few months old in the autumn of 1861), Fanny, Frederick James, William Henry, and the youngest Laura, she born in 1873.

Arthur Bramman knew what it was to be poor and strived heartily to advance his prospects from his youthful start as an errand boy. Following the death of his mother in 1876, the Bramman's residing at a modest property on Sherwood Street, West Court, St Mary Nottingham; Arthur commenced work as a light porter, a term used to describe a chemist. His siblings to add to the family coffers from wages earned, Ellen as a glove taylor, Frederick as a coach trimmer, while Samuel, the head of the household, still toiled away at the lace factory.

At the time of the calamitous events at Lambridge, Charles and Fanny Underwood, and three year old son Charles Noel (born 17th December 1890, his middle name reflecting the closest of his arrival to Christmas), lived within their employers residence, between them the Underwood's taking care of Doctor Smiths fundamental domestic needs, acting primarily as coachman and housekeeper. 1893 had seen Charles Johnson Underwood turn thirty one; his previous employment that of coachman to a widow, Mrs Ann Langley, the proprietor of the "Rectory" in Yardley, Hastings, Charles Underwood's town of birth. Underwood's father was one Joseph Underwood (born 1835, Yardley, Hastings), who earned a modest living as a wood labourer, he able to just about support his wife Susannah who matched her husband in both the location and year of her birth. Charles the solitary offspring of the union between Joseph and his spouse, his mother, aged but forty five, to succumb to a sudden malady, she laid to rest on 30th April 1880.

Fanny Underwood was on the other hand a local girl, born 28th July 1862, in Lower Bolney, Oxfordshire, and baptised on 24th August at St Margarets Church in Harpsden. Her father, William Harvey (born 1823 in Fingest) had taken as his bride Elizabeth, eight years his junior, and it was in the brides childhood home of Lewknor, Buckinghamshire, that the newlyweds started their married life. Fanny, unlike her future husband, had not experienced a childhood deprived of siblings, with her father moving where the work was, her elder brother Joseph born 1856 in Sonning. A position as a carter on a farm in Lower Bolney offered stability for William Harvey, and here it was that Richard was born in 1858, followed by Hannah, the aforementioned Fanny, and Elizabeth, the youngest, born 1864.

William Harvey, as did many in his situation, took the decision to leave the Parish of Harpsden, though having employment on the Lower Bolney Farm on the Bolney Estate, he reliant on the monies of lodgers, lads John Parker and George Slade. The Harvey's next found themselves in a small property on Village Road, in Hurley, where the master of the house picked up work as a labourer, thus better able to provide for his household, the birth of Alice in 1869, though a joyful event, to pull at the family purse strings.

What was to draw Doctor George Smith so deeply into the events played out at Lambridge Farm were his duties as Oxfordshire's Medical Examiner, his obligation to the role to override any practice responsibilities Smith may have at any given time. This role required that Doctor Smith attend deaths deemed unnatural or suspicious, he to perform a medical examination of the deceased in his charge, and if required a post mortem, Smith then having the power, if he deemed it necessary, to initiate an inquest.

Doctor George Smith was not alone during the hours he spent examining the corpse of Miss Kate Dungey, forty year old Joshua

Watts, in his capacity as Medical Clerk, attending alongside him. Henley born Joshua Watts had benefited from a fairly comfortable upbringing, his father, Thomas Nathaniel (born 1818 in Bix), a highly sought after tailor, Joshua's grandfather, after whom he was named, having set up the business in the early 1800s. The old gent, into his dotage, had run his business out of premises located at 10-12 Bell Street, but Joshua Watts had died in the March of 1852.

The Watts "Tailor, Clothier and Hatter" business grew beyond all expectations and by the latter 1850s was staffed by six men, and two lads. Home for the young Joshua, which had originally been at a residence on the Fairmile, was now above the shop, his mother Mary (born 1824 in Henley) tending to her children, while her husband tended to his customers. The household was large and lively, and Joshua struggled for attention alongside sisters, Mary, seven years his elder, Fanny and Jessie. There was also within the Watts household younger brothers for Joshua to lark about with, Thomas Nathaniel, named after his father, and Henry, the youngest, he born in 1860.

Thomas Nathaniel Watts, though tailoring was all he had known, in later life took it upon himself to relinquish the business to the next generation. He took himself off to the village of his birth, and finding a property to his liking, and arable land at Bix Hill, Thomas Watts went into farming. Joshua Watts took up the mantle from his father, and he did him proud, and by the time of his marriage, on 10th July 1878 to a local girl (twenty nine year old Jane), Watts was a highly competent tailor. Jane was a young woman any man would be proud to make his wife, she the daughter of one George Wright, a brewers accountant, who resided in New Street. By the time of her marriage, Jane Wrights mother, whom she was named after (Jane Wright in life having been much in demand as a milliner) had been dead for a quarter of a century, and so it was that her stepmother, Margaret fought back tears of pride, as the girl she had raised entered into wedlock. It is of interest to note that amongst her siblings, Jane

Wright counted Arthur as one of whom she was particularly fond, we will have cause to hear of this man again.

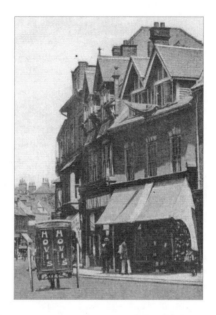

Joshua Watts "Tailors & Outfitters" in Bell Street
Its frontage partly concealed by the Hovis cart

Joshua and Jane Watts were blessed with a large family, typical of the Victorian era; Margaret born the year following their marriage, a son Robert arriving two years after. On 19th January 1883 Thomas Nathienal Watts, who had earned no small crust as a tailor and farmer, died, bequeathing his widow, Mary, and their offspring a share of £4,714 16s 3d. It fitting that when Jane gave birth that same year, the child was named after his late grandfather. There was no let up for the Watt's, Oliver George born in 1885, followed then after by

Harold, Wilfred O'Brien, and last born, Gladys Mary, she in 1889 delivered by a locally based midwife.

Joshua Watts was a man with a strong feeling of civic duty, and the education to back it up; he acting as a Justice of the Peace, reaching the position of Senior JP, in 1865 returned as a Liberal Town Councillor. Watts was Chairman of the Henley Board of Guardians, most notably actively fighting for the rights of a Guardian to gain entry from the Henley Workhouse Master, to better ascertain the welfare of inmates. Through his tireless work Joshua Watts to achieve better accommodation for the parish poor, who found themselves under the care of the Union, he to directly see to it that Henley's almshouses underwent vital improvements, with provision made for the construction of additional almshouses. By the winter of 1893 Joshua Watts had been acknowledged for his efforts with the position of an Alderman of the town. At that juncture Watts to have no inkling that before the year had waned he would find himself mentioned within the columns of the newspapers, on matters far removed from those of his civic duties.

Eleven

Glasshouse Street

During the nineteenth century the name Mash was, in the commercial quarters of the bustling metropolis that was London, the surname of many a provision merchant, their services advertised within the pages of the indispensable Kellys Directory. For the most part the Mash's (it not a wild assumption to presume that these men were related) dealt in the supply of wholesale potatoes for the cities numerous grocery establishments. A James Mash worked out of his premises, 5 Oxford Place, Hackney Road; George Mash earned a substantial living as the proprietor of a potato warehouse at 264 Oxford Street, while George William Mash stored his stock at his facility in Exmouth Street, Clerkenwell. One gentleman, Mr Charles Mash bucked the trend and diversified slightly from his namesakes, he was indeed a purveyor of potatoes, but additionally was a supplier of considerable varieties of fruit, all of which dispatched from his merchant warehouse at 288 Oxford Street. Another of the Mash's, James, did not go down the potato route, but stuck to the dealership of fruit, out of his premises 174 Hoxton Old Town, as did William Mash, who traded from 161 Aldersgate Street. The final Mash in the equation Henry Joseph, this gentleman who had excelled in his chosen profession of wholesale supplier (specialising in tropical fruit, namely bananas) acquiring two properties in Henley-on-Thames, where he in turn consorted with the upper strata of local society.

Henry Joseph Mash came into the world (born Clerkenwell, St James, Middlesex) in the first quarter of 1850, being the eldest son and namesake of Henry Joseph Mash (baptised 11th November 1827), and the grandson of Joseph Mash (born 1787), and Alice nee Gunston, born 1792. Henrys father a fruiterer and green grocer, who supplied to the trade from his retail outlet, 23 Canterbury Road, Brixton; his stock grown primarily at his own farm, the arable lands of which nestled in the heart of Surrey. The lady of the household, Henrys wife Mary Ann (born 3rd August 1828), the daughter of George and Elizabeth Waterford Rose, whose family business was that of a coal and potato dealership located in Great Bath Street, Clerkenwell.

Henry Joseph Mash grew up competing for attention alongside elder sister Mary Ann Rose (born in the September of 1848), and younger sisters, Marianne, Elizabeth, and Alice Emily, she born 19th September 1854. But eventually Henry was granted a playmate of his own gender, Nathaniel George, near six years his brothers younger. But Mary Ann was not done with the begetting of children, Matilda, George William, and the elegantly named William Waterford born in rapid succession, the Mash's by his birth residing above their commercial outlet, the "Potatoe Shop", 39 Paddington Street, St Marylebone, Henry Mash senior a greengrocer of high repute, paying the wages of two assistants. One would think the Mash household was bursting at the seams, but it appears that there was a corner or two vacant, Henry Mash managing to accommodate lodger Henry Cameron (a widower, working as a gasfitter), and no doubt within a corner of the attic domestic servant Sarah Loader. There was no let up for Mary Ann, delivered of three further daughters, Eleanor Bertha, Louisa Emily and Julia Grace Kate, the latter brought safely into the world in the winter of 1867. By now the family resided at 238, Fulham Road, Kensington, the addition of little Minnie Constance to complete the considerable brood, with her arrival on the first day of 1870. Doubtless due to complications after the birth of her last child, on 2nd January 1870, Mary Ann Mash aged but forty two, done with this world.

Henry Mash did not relish the challenge of life as a solitary parent, and resolved to take a second wife, in September 1873 marring Lucy

Austen, born 1834 in Marlow, Buckinghamshire. By the census taking of 3rd April 1881; the Mash's squeezed into their new home, 67 Atlantic Road, funded by the head of the household's fruiterer business, which provided ample employment for three men and three boys.

Now we must look again upon one of the main protagonists of the events which unfolded at Henley-on-Thames in the winter of 1893, Henry Joseph Mash. Before he had turned twenty, Mash had proved himself as accomplished in the provisions market as his father, on 8th March 1869, at Newmarket, Suffolk, he to take a wife. His bride Miss Georgiana Porter, who received into baptism on 26th April 1848 (hailed from Exning, Newmarket in Suffolk), was the daughter of James (a James Porter born 1816 in Exning, by the latter 1830s employed as a bailiff) and Ann Porter. The newlyweds initially occupied a property situated in Walkers Court, in the heart of St James, Westminster, not affected by the constraints of poverty (unlike many who eked out an existence in London) able to afford to keep one servant, young Edmond Cross, aged in his early teens. The start of married life was not a joyous one for Henry and Georgiana, their first child, Rose Harriet, born on 6th June 1870, dying the last day of July, their second child, Henry Joseph, born 28th July 1872, not to live out the month. The weight of grief at the loss of two babies in some way lifted by the arrival in 1874 of Eleanor, and Henry Joseph (the second child to take his father's name), he born 1876. May, a robust little girl, was delivered in 1878, swiftly followed by the birth of Annie, by the early 1880s the Mash's residing at 238 Fulham Road (master of the house, childhood abode) waited on by domestics, sister's Harriett (general servant) and Betsy (nursemaid) Hodson. A larger living apartment all the better, as the birth of two further boys, William James Porter and Martin, added to the family dynamic. Henry Mash of a morning nipping downstairs to see to his shop, fruiterers assistant's widower George Rose, Fanny and Anne Austin, taking instruction from their employer. The last census of the nineteenth century provides a picture of Henry Mashs enhanced fortunes, the time of the census collectors visit on 5th April, Mash relaxing at his weekend retreat, Lambridge Farm, while his wife hobnobbed up in London. This down time permissible due to the considerable profits from Mashs highly lucrative tropical fruit provisions company, run out of Glasshouse Street, Piccadilly. Things were going very well indeed, the Mash family having an enviable choice of houses in which to reside, be it their London house, 12 Redcliffe Gardens (situated in the heart of Kensington, Redcliffe Square built by the Gunter Estates in the 1860s, Redcliffe Gardens running north west, south east through its centre), or their Henley-on-Thames townhouse, 37 New Street. Upon the death on 2nd March 1889, of seventy one year old retired "Coal Merchant and Railway Agent" Robert Dixon, his former home had been disposed of by his widow Caroline, Henry Mash in due course purchasing said property. This New Street premises just what Mash desired, an impressive Georgian construction, entered via a carriage porch way, with considerable grounds to its rear, and at its frontage views down towards the River Thames.

Now I must at this juncture spend some moments to familiarise you the reader with some pertinent facts in regard to Lambridge Farm. A William Hopkins (member of the Bladon family) will of 1881 made provision of two hundred pounds to be used to purchase land. The rental returns of such to be utilised for the benefit of those who had formerly been in service in the vicinity of Bladon, so long as they had been honest and true of character while employed. The charity thus forward became known as the "William Hopkins Charity", affiliated to St Mary Magdalen, Oxford, and Baldon, in due course its trustees acquiring Lambridge Farm. The farm had on 29th September 1866 been let to a Robert Webb (timber merchant), on a rental of twenty eight pounds a year, and as the 1870s drew to a close it seems this gentleman resolved to quit Lambridge. Bickerton Solicitors of Oxford, with approval of the Hopkins Commissioners, in the winter of 1882 to instruct Simmons & Sons of Henley-on-Thames to sell by public auction the valuable freehold estate known as Lambridge Farm. The lots details, appearing in the columns of the Reading Chronicle of 4th March 1882, informing any prospective purchaser that Lambridge Farm was about half a mile from Henley-on-Thames, and consisted of forty two acres of land, with outbuildings and premises there on. So in the rear bar of the Catherine Wheel, Hart Street, on Thursday 6th April 1882, at three o'clock prompt, Lambridge Farm went under the gavel. At this point we have a quandary, who was the individual who successfully outbid all competition, as Mash was tenant only it seems unlikely he purchased the farm. But Victorian terminology can cause confusion, so doubts aside as to ownership by the end of 1882 Henry Joseph Mash had acquired Lambridge Farm, not wasting any time in adapting it to his particular tastes.

In the latter years of the ninetieth century, those in trade who enjoyed the trappings that goodly profits afforded, filtrated into society, and once within this new arena were keen to emulate their betters. Men and woman alike adopted the latest fashions, ate at the right restaurants, attended the theatre, enjoyed social functions, and resided in desirable properties. The upper middle classes to have benefit of an opulent home life, with all of their domestic needs met by servants, the indispensable basics of which to include a housekeeper, cook, and one or more housemaids. Any offspring (if the parents so desired, and if finances allowed) under the care of a nursery maid, and then after a governess, said children able to play within a scenic garden, maintained by a gardener. Henry and Georgiana Mash embraced all the possibilities that money afforded them, and entered with enthusiasm into society, their children having advantage of a private governess, the young woman who had charge over their education being Miss Kate Laura Dungey.

Walter Dungey was born in Cranbrook, Kent on, 11th April 1833, his father; William (born 1793) in possession of sixty acre "Forge Farm", Glassenbury, its arable lands (which stretched out across scenic Glassenbury Hill, able to sustain two labourers. William and his spouse Mary (nee Potten, born 1795) had Presbyterian leanings, and as such Walter was baptised on 28th July 1833 at Cranbrook Independent Chapel on the Hill, which from as early as 1710 had utilised a row of cariers cottages. Young Walter Dungey shared his rural childhood with siblings, Charles, William, Mary, George, Emily, John, Frances, and little James, he born 1838, the children to have benefit of clean air, they not growing up within the industrial heartland.

Walter emulated his father and advanced apace, land management and agriculture his true passion, in due course Walter Dungey to meet at a village dance, or such like, a young lady. And so it was that on 20th July 1858, within the Parish Church of Maidstone, Kent, farmers' daughter Ellen (baptised 13th February 1832) married Master Walter Dungey. The bride daughter of John Corke (born 1797) and Isabella (nee Ashbee, born Stoke, Kent, in the February of 1806), Ellens childhood shared with a substantial number of younger siblings, Julia, Thirza, Jane, Mary, Edwin, James, Charlotte, Samuel, Ebenezer, Isabella and Clara, who had completed the family with her birth in 1849.

Ellen Dungey did not find herself a drudge; Walter a kindly husband, in the early years of their married lives affording to keep house servant Martha Wells, Ellen set to bring eleven into the world. First born Rosa Ellen arrived in 1859, followed swiftly then after by Julia, Ernest Walter (the only son destined to reach his maturity), born in 1862, marked as the year his father achieved sole tenancy of Pattenden Farm (Walter and Ellen having resided there since their marriage), Walter Dungeys partnership with a Mary Upton dissolved with mutual consent on Tuesday 4th March. Kate Laura was born in the November of 1863, she then after to witness the birth of sisters, Alice Jane, Fanny Ada, Helena, and Clara Louise. By the birth in 1873 of Amelia, the elder children of the household under the tutorship of governess Louisa Clifford, housemaid Ann Earon rushed off her feet, and more than earning her salary. All seemed well, but life can deal misfortune to those least deserving of it, and Frank, the Dungeys second son, came into the world in the winter of 1872, only to leave it again aged just thirty months, in the summer of 1875. This greatly lamented little boys sister, Grace Ethel, born in the last quarter of 1876, fared even worse, and failing to thrive died aged just over six months in April 1877.

In the winter of 1875 (as stated on page seven of Friday 15th Januarys edition of the Kent & Sussex Courier) Walter Dungey, from the latter 1850s having been a tenant, had taken possession of the manorial residence and adjoining lands known collectively as "Pattenden Manor" (the borough of Pattenden having been mentioned within deeds drawn up during the time of Edward I, the title Pattenden determining the surname of a long line of those who once possessed the estate), not much distance from Goudhurst. This village (from 1360 onwards, and for many centuries then after, inhabited by Flemish weavers, producing broadcloth), which lies in the Weald of Kent, of a most pleasing aspect, nestled amongst hill and dale, a considerable number of Goudhurst's timber framed buildings ancient in structure. Dominating the highest point of Goudhurst is St Mary's Church, documentation of which stretching back to 1117, when one Ralph de Crevccour presented the church to the Abbey at Leeds. With the petering out of the weaving industry, hop production in and around Goudhurst to increase. During the reign of Queen Victoria, it not uncommon for those local to the region to rub shoulders with Londoners, as many surviving on the poverty line made the journey to

Kent (often on foot), in the hope of securing annual work as hop pickers.

Pattenden Manor, a late medieval half-timbered Wealden type house

Walter Dungeys assets were further swelled upon the death in the May of 1876 of his father, who left an estate of just under three thousand pounds, to be divided amongst his chosen beneficiaries. So it was in this environment that Kate Laura Dungey flourished. The manor house of Pattenden (aspects of which dating to the 1360s) with its intricate oaken panelled rooms, and stained glass windows, never ceasing to fascinate Kate and her siblings, as they played within its centuries old nooks and crannies. A bright vibrant child extracts of Kates diary conveying vivid impressions, she and her siblings, on a heady July afternoon in 1879, gathering wild strawberries out in the fields at Bedgebury. While in the spring of 1880 Kate is hopeful that double daisies and mignonettes will flourish in the portion of the garden she tends, a contented country childhood, unaffected by the restraints of poverty, or the handicap of scant education.

In the winter of 1880 Kate Dungey turned seventeen, and possessed of a keen mind she took work, that of teacher to her younger siblings. No doubt her father Walter (who in many respects did not conform to the scruples of the day) insisting that the role should be a paid one. So while Dungey toiled upon his by now expanded ninety six acre farm (with two men and three young lads in his employee), Ellen saw to matters domestic, while her daughter Kate saw to matters educational.

Kate Laura Dungey had much to offer, and broadening her horizons beyond idyllic Goudhurst; in 1884 she secured employment as governess to the children of one Mr Henry Joseph Mash. Miss Dungey greatly esteemed within her employers household, possessing as she did the essential attributes of any governess worth her salt; impeccable character, musical talents, and diligent teaching of the three Rs. But children have a habit of maturing, and thus eventually Kate was to find herself in need of another position, in 1886 she to secure employment with the agent of the protractedly titled Lord Augustus Charles Lennox Fitzroy, seventh Duke of Grafton. But Miss Dungey had left an impression on the Mash family, and her previous employers enticed Kate away from this new role. And with intricacies, such as hours to be worked, days off, and salary decided upon, Miss Kate Dungey arrived in Henley-on-Thames, to become housekeeper at Lambridge Farm.

The Victorian idea of womanhood was integrated into the psyche of girls from an early age. On the whole these youngsters expected to graduate towards marriage, motherhood and domestic roles involved in homemaking. It was common practice that a woman (once possessed of a husband) would not take work outside the remit of homemaker; her husband to be the sole breadwinner, bound by convention to thus provide financially for his family. Unless blessed with a privileged upbringing, and thus spared the rigors of money worries, single women from their early teens graduated towards teaching (if an acceptable level of education allowed), the textile industry (be it weaver or dressmaker), or domestic service, the majority of these professions offering a merge salary.

The profession of housekeeper, which came under the umbrella of domestic servitude, went some way to being viewed as slightly above average in the eyes of others in service. The role set the housekeeper (who was relied upon to be implicitly honest and hardworking) to act as her mistresses representative within the home, her principal duty to manage the household. Kate Dungey, within her role at Lambridge Farm, would have had several of the housekeepers required duties placed firmly on her plate, not all of which to be described as uneventful. Any housekeeper worth her salt expected to spot the signs of any wrongdoings by other staff within the household, and resolve any ensuing issue, or in the worst case recommend to her employer that the offender be dismissed. A housekeeper would have a solid grounding in the understanding of accounts; and thus keep the books, taking care to accurately register all sums paid for whatever purpose, be it the washer woman or tradesmen's bills. Many housekeepers, if a cook was not employed, expected to attend to matters in the kitchen, buying provisions, and preparing meals for the family. In the absence of a housemaid, such as in Kate Dungeys case, the housekeeper expected to attend to the fires, manage the laundry, and still find the time to tackle a six monthly inventory of everything under her care, with all household losses and breakages, which were recorded as they occurred, transferred into the household books.

Miss Dungey was indispensable; she revelled in her role and with her at the helm of all things domestic Henry Mash could reassure himself that all was well at Lambridge Farm. But this young woman, who after her untimely and violent demise captured the attentions of the press, would be reduced to a collection of generalisations in regard to her gender, one particular journalist categorising her as such. "Miss Dungy was described as of medium height, good looking with a fine figure, and a brunette. If rather reserved she was said to have had a talent for singing, and was an accomplished pianist, not thought at the time of her death to be corresponding or involved with any young gentleman."

Line drawing of Kate Laura Dungey
The People, Sunday 17th December 1893

Part Two

A woman had met her end in a manner most heinous, and the facts which pertained to Miss Kate Dungeys demise were to be determined before a coroner's court.

Twelve

Acacia House, Shirburn Street

Doctor George Smith, in his capacity as appointed Medical Examiner for the County of Oxfordshire, had determined that the extinction of Miss Dungeys life had come about in a manner most unnatural, and as such directed that an inquest be called. The challenges presented by a high profile inquest were ones best met by an individual with the experience and fortitude to carefully and fully examine the facts, and the Deputy Coroner for South Oxfordshire, Augustus Jones, was the fellow deemed best suited for the job.

Augustus Jones was born in Cambridge on 27th August 1834 (baptised 15th November, at St Sepulchre Church), this little boy the last born child of John (born 1796 in Little Port, one of a line of a long established Cambridge family) and Mary Jones, she also of Cambridge descent, born 1801. By the time Augustus made his appearance Mary having begat Elizabeth, twins Mary Ann and John, Amelia, Sarah Ellen Maria, John, Frederick Hart, Adelaide Fellowes and Alfred, he born 1832.

So how did the youngest Jones fare, very well indeed it would seem, excelling in his studies to enter Cambridge University. Law was the degree that Augustus Jones chose to pursue, this young man admitted as a solicitor in the Trinity Term of 1860.

The law could be a hard task master, and when free time permitted Augustus Jones liked nothing better than to travel within the country of his birth. South Oxfordshire, in particular, made a marked impression on the lately qualified solicitor, where county society, enraptured by this vibrant articulate young gentleman, took Augustus under its wing. But however much Jones relished his visits to

Oxfordshire he was regretfully not in the position to take a property there, and thus accepting the financial limitations of a fledgling career he took lodgings (alongside fellow border, estate assistant and auctioneer, Joseph Green) within the household of George (a paper manufacturer) and Martha Durham, at 207 Euston Road, St Pancras.

Whenever he managed to get away Augustus Jones tore down to Oxfordshire, and though he relished spending time in the company of friends, there was one who particularly held his attention, Miss Mary Simmonds (born 1845, in Great Marlow, Buckinghamshire), the only daughter of farmer Mr Joshua Simmons, of Limmer Bucks. Augustus Jones was certain of his esteem for Mary, and thus secured her father's blessing, on 15th October 1863, at Watlington Church, Mary, not yet nineteen, to consent to be his wife.

The newlyweds elected to settle in the village of Watlington, and with Augustus by now on a firmer financial footing took Acacia House on Shirburn Street, both as residence and practice address. Life was splendid, law was most profitable, and before the 1860s were spent the couple enjoyed the domestic assistance of servant, Sarah Hyatt, this young woman proceeded in her duties by Miss Ann Bullock.

For one who had craved a future in the county he so adored, Augustus Jones took little time indeed to involve himself in the affairs of Watlington. Like many of his social strata, a Conservative, Jones keen to assist the party acting as Agent for Watlington Polling District. Never far from the minds of those of influence in the January of 1867 elected Clerk to the Magistrate of Watlington Division, in place of Mr J. H. Maynard, who had recently resigned the appointment.

The family dynamic at Acacia House was not to be changed, the Jones's, for reasons unclear, not to be parents. Thus reliant on their devotion to each other the last decades of the nineteenth century proved a whirlwind for the couple, and what with socializing and entertaining, Mary was grateful for the assistance of two domestic servants, cook, Alice Selwood and housemaid Annie Maunder. Augustus Jones found himself part of a fraternity that looked after their own, and as such was duly appointed as Clerk to Justices, Clerk to the Commissioners of Taxes and District Highway Board, not to mention Secretary to Watlington and Princess Risborough Railways, all of which Jones managed with considerable aptitude.

Shirburn Street in Watlington
Though photographed after the time of Augustus Jones the area little changed

In 1888 the first Chief Constable of Oxfordshire (Charles Mostyn Owen), took the decision, after thirty one years of service, to retire and take advantage of his well-earned pension. And thus having been informed of Owens intention the Police Committee, with input from the Magistrates Board, began the laborious process of selecting his replacement. The Oxford Journal, which hit the newsstands on 23rd

June 1888, reported that. "There have been, as might naturally be expected, a very large number of candidates for the post."

So what did the role of Chief Constable have to offer any prospective candidate? Firstly a remuneration of three hundred and fifty a year, plus a moderate forage allowance. The position, which dictated that any applicant must not be aged over forty five at time of appointment and reside within two miles of the County Police Station in Oxford, involving many diverse roles. One of the fundamental tasks that of the duty to appoint Superintendents and Inspectors of Police.

So after some whittling down, seven found themselves attending individual interviews before the committee. The men, having been verbally examined, sent to a practioner to be medically examined and certified (a most undignified experience), and all being found in good health progressed to the next stage. On Monday 2nd July 1888 the magistrates met, talked, talked some more and took a vote, the top two candidates, Edward Alexander Holmes A' Court (receiving thirty two votes), and Richard Cecil Corbett to secure thirty one. The committee voted a second time, regards the two remaining candidates, Holmes A' Court to secure forty votes, seven more than Corbett, he thus to loud applause duly selected as Chief Constable of Oxfordshire.

Edward Alexander Holmes A' Court was born on 23rd October 1845, in Westover on the Isle of Wight, the fifth son of the Second Baron of Heytesbury, William Henry Ashe A' Court (born 1809, Marylebone), a landed magistrate, and Elizabeth (born 1814 on the Isle of Wight), the daughter of one Sir Leonard Thomas Worsley Holmes.

Edward spent his formative years on the island (his families domestic needs met by butler William Edmonds, and no fewer than twenty one servants), but the family eventually moved to the mainland, residing by the 1861 census at Heytesbury House, in Heytesbury, Wiltshire. Young Edward A' Court enjoying a life of privilege alongside his siblings, the eldest, William Leonard, his birth having swiftly been followed by that of Frederick, Elizabeth, Henry, Emily, and Charles

George. Edward also had a plenitude of younger siblings, Gertrude Anne, Arthur Wyndham, Leonard Worsley, Walter Ashe, and Edith Maria Charlotte, who born on 15th July 1853, died 18th April 1854, the year that followed her demise Margaret born. So here indeed was a horde of children, their educational needs under the direction of Miss Elizabeth Hegarth, their domestic needs met by fifteen household servants.

In the latter part of 1861, Edward Alexander Holmes A' Court (his father having adopted his wife's family name) obtained a military commission within the Kings Shropshire Light Infantry, he to see combat, serving 1879-1880 in the Kurah Division, during the Afghanistan War, his excellent conduct mentioned in dispatches. Edward, as was common for one of privilege, to advance apace through the ranks, culminating with the rank of Lieutenant Colonel.

Military life for a single man could be one of isolation, and Victorian society determined that a man with a wife was one who courted the invitations to dine at fine houses. Thus on 21st December 1880, in St Peters Bournemouth, Adelaide Sophie (born 1852, daughter of landowner Hugh Hamersley of Pyrton Manor in Oxfordshire) consented to be Edwards wife. The couple not to tarry in the area of children, Rupert Edward born 6th February 1882, Adelaide Emily arriving fourteen months later, Ruth Mary, born on 4th June 1885, to be their last child, Adelaide more fortunate than her husband's mother, in relation to childbearing. The family unit, much fond of picnicking within their grounds, able to enjoy panoramic views from their home, The Cottage, positioned as it was at the very pinnacle of Headington Hill, Oxford.

In his fortieth year Holmes A' Court retired from the rigours of army life, spending the next couple of years in somewhat of a quandary as to his future plans, that is until the role of Chief Constable offered him a new vocation.

So Augustus Jones would not orchestrate the inquest into the death of Miss Kate Dungey singlehandedly, the Oxfordshire Constabulary's involvement in the case had quickly drawn some less than favourable comment, and the man at the top (Chief Constable of Oxfordshire, Edward Alexander Holmes A' Court) would travel to Lambridge Farm, his presence to be one that the coroner could not easily ignore.

Thirteen

Twelve Men of the County

Over the weekend that followed on from the fateful night of eighth December, an inquest was called, its remit to examine events at Lambridge Farm, which had culminated in the violent demise of its housekeeper. A jury had to be swiftly assembled, and men of the district found themselves summoned to attend an inquest, to be held on the morning of Monday 11th December 1893. All inquest juries required a chairman, and this role invariably fell to the landed gentry of the district, as such one Richard Ovey summoned to perform his civic duty.

Richard Ovey (son of Richard and Mary Ovey), entered this world in 1789, baptised on 15th December at Saint Paul Covent Garden, Westminster. The man, who experienced the last turbulent decades of the Georgian era, desired a good match (essential for one of superior birth), and Ovey found this in Elizabeth Mary, near thirty two years his junior. The union led to the birth on 26th February 1856 of Richard (his arrival announced in the columns of the London Standard), he born at Park Cottage, Avenue Road, Regents Park, Richards only sibling, Mary, near eighteen months his elder. Richard Oveys childhood was one that others might envy, and in common with all young gentlemen of good breeding he benefitted from a superior education, which culminated in a place at Hertford College, Oxford.

Clara, eldest daughter of John Johnson Broadbent of Horton House (a gentleman of Bradford, Yorkshire, who, fully embracing the industrial revolution had in his employ four hundred, who toiled for their master, spinning worsted wool), was in want of a husband. She found her beau in Richard Ovey, on 19th April 1877, in the Parish of Great Horton, St John, Clara (just short of twenty eight) and Richard to wed. Following family tradition Richard and Clara's first child, a son (born while his parents were up in London, residing at 60 Westbourne Terrace, Paddington, their domestic needs met by ten servants), was bestowed at his baptism, on 15th July 1878, with the name Richard, his middle name being Lockhart. The next two of the Ovey's offspring born in Henley-on-Thames, Esmond baptised at the Parish Church of St Marys (on 25th August 1879); Constance Mary received into the church at her baptism held on 27th October 1880. There was to be one more child born of Richard and Claras union, Darrell, who made his appearance in Bournemouth, this little boy, like those who came before him, baptised in Henley-on-Thames, on 28th February 1882.

The Ovey's had been associated with Henley since the 17th century, a Richard Ovey commissioning in 1812 the construction of a town house, henceforward, due to its location at Northfield End, known as Northfield House. It a masterly three storey structure, boasting an impressive stucco façade, fronted by two curved bays, its doorway sheltered from the elements by a porch edged with finely detailed fluted columns. To the rear Ovey desired, and got, substantial lands, which he had laid to lawn and gardens, and for his horses he had constructed stables and a yard, much of Northfield Houses exterior grounds long since swallowed up by redevelopment.

By the 1841 census Northfield House was devoid of any male Ovey, the premises occupied by Mary Ovey, a widower in her seventy fourth year, her three daughters (all in want of a husband), twins Jane and Mary Ann, and youngest Sarah, residing alongside their mother, with four domestic servants tending to their needs. The old lady died on 12th February 1846, duly laid to rest in the Ovey vault, within St Marys, alongside her husband Richard, he having died in the May of 1834. Her three daughters, as fund holders more than comfortably off living happily in each other's company. Sarah Ovey, aged sixty seven, the first to go, she dying on 4th December 1865, given a send-off befitting her stature, Sarah interred alongside her parents on 12th December. Mary Ann Ovey (just short of eighty) passed away near nine years after her sister, on 19th November 1874, buried six days later. The last of the Misses Ovey (all of whom never to have quit Northfield House), Jane, aged seventy eight, departing this world on 30th March 1878, thus entombed in the Ovey vault on 6th April. The three woman in turn to leave a considerable fortune, Sarah, not much short of one hundred thousand pounds, Mary Ann near fifty thousand pounds, and Jane Ovey in excess of one hundred and ten thousand pounds. The trail left is convoluted, but as far as one can tell Richard was a nephew to the Ovey sisters, and as such he and Clara took charge of Northfield House. Its interior décor, reflecting its Georgian heritage, brought up to the minute, alterations and amendments to better demonstrate the tastes of Victorian high society. Ovey spent with abandon, his finances swelled by inheritance (his father Richard Ovey having died on 24th May 1874, bequeathing an estate just under five hundred thousand pounds), dividends and rents from lands held.

Richard Ovey took to life in Henley-on-Thames with gusto; he sat on the Board of Guardians, attended court, in his capacity as a Justice of the Peace, delighted in country pursuits, and counted many of influence as acquaintances; William Thomas Makins of Rotherfield Court a personal friend.

Oveys interests not confined to Henley, he also in possession of lands at Turville and Shiplake, and wishing to further absorb himself within Oxfordshire, in 1883 he to purchase Badgemore House and its adjoining park, a resplendent estate located on the road to Greys. The former holder of this estate, one Charles Lane, had died on 9th December 1878, and Badgemore House had stood abandoned since, the executors much relieved to commission the transfer of its deeds to a new owner. Richard Ovey launched himself into the enhancement of his latest acquisition, and between 1884 and 1885 he heavily rebuilt the house, the architectural designs of his vision created on the drawing board of John Norton, a renowned designer of country houses, and pupil of architect Benjamin Ferrey. The interior of Badgemore House, that admittedly showed signs of neglect, extensively redecorated; the addition of a Porte Cochere (carriage porch) much enhancing its approach. To take full advantage of the view of the fine garden, Ovey desired that first floor balconies, of the finest stone, be incorporated into the main façade, and by 1886 the house boasted nine bays, a three storey brick façade, three central bays, complete with a pediment, and internally a two storey grand hall with gallery. The finished article was a house of gigantic proportions, staffed by butler William Chapman, footman George Driver, cook Emily Hoare, housemaids, Caroline Tilby, Elizabeth Goddard and Ellen Butler, kitchen maid Ada Smith, scullery maid Lavinia Goffin, and laundry maids, Mildred Russel and Mary Jane Howard. Badgemore to become the principal home of the Oveys, its new master soon held in high esteem by both his tenants and labourers.

Though he had finances to do so, Richard Ovey did not sit on his laurels, and desiring to add to his holdings consulted land agents, the result of which the purchase, in 1892, of the Hernes Estate, in Rotherfield Greys. Ovey was indeed now a country squire, as such establishing in 1892 an annual ploughing match, the event, which proved a great success, taking place on the lands of his neighbouring farmers.

With his time divided between business, family and civic duties, Richard Ovey was never to be one to find boredom a problem, and as one highly regarded within the county, it came as no surprise to Ovey to find himself summoned as Chairman of an inquest jury (the eleven men under his sway to be shortly expanded on), so called to determine on the demise of Miss Kate Laura Dungey.

Henry Lillywhite, who had been widowed the year before the events at Lambridge House (his wife Lucy had died aged fifty six, on 7th January 1892), was born 1830 in Hawkley, Hampshire, on the wrong side of the blanket. Henrys illigimate status duly acknowledged, as he was presented for baptism on 8th August, his mother Elizabeth entered in the register as unmarried. The young man did not suffer unduly from the stigma associated with his birth, in his early twenties Lillywhite employed but a short distance from his mothers, in the household of Henry Warner, a prosperous farmer who resided at Lower Green.

As Henry Lillywhite approached his twenty sixth year, in the first quarter of 1856 he took as his bride Lucy Leming (born 1835 in Oakhanger, her father James having progressed from agricultural labourer to baker), their nuptials held in Peterfield Hampshire. The newlyweds lived off profits from the land, Lillywhite farming three hundred and ten acres at Pokes Lane, Hawkley, his crop fields sustained by the toil of seven men and three boys. Though many village dwellers, in the 1850s, migrated towards the industrial centres of their area, the Lillywhites bucked the trend, and their large contingency of children enjoyed a childhood splashing about in brooks, swinging from branches, and chasing through wild flower meadows. Lucys first born, Henry, arriving in 1856, followed then after by Priscilla, William, Walter, Elizabeth, and in 1864 Emily, the next three Lillywhites all girls; Kate born in 1866, Annie in 1868, and Bertha in 1870. A fourth son, Francis Walwyn, born in 1873, his birth followed by that of Clementina Lucy, and Mabel Gertrude, she born 1876. A mother to twelve, Lucy enjoyed a well-deserved breather (though there could of course be the possibility that she suffered miscarriages) before she was delivered of Louis Patterson in 1881, by the time of his birth the family relocated to Middle Assenden Farm, Oxfordshire.

Henry Lillywhite had all that was necessary to sit on the Kate Dungey inquest jury, he was male (the concept of female jurors still decades in the future), he resided in the district, and had employment, ten others, who also fitted this criteria, summoned to attend alongside Henry Lillywhite.

Enos Clark, who hailed from the same county as Henry Lillywhite, was born 1831 in Farleigh Wallop. His father George (born 1794) earning a meagre wage working the land, while his mother Sarah (nee Silver, born 1804) tended to the needs of her children. George and Sarah had wed on 2nd March 1823, and as was the fate of many women with little to control their fertility, Sarah begat five children besides Enos. John born in 1825, followed then after by sister's Sarah and Mary Ann, the 1830s witnessing the arrival of George and Patience, she baptised 22nd February 1835.

Before Enos Clark had turned twenty his mother Sarah was dead, he and his brother John (who had benefitted from some formal education) joining their father, as agricultural labourers. Mary Ann mindful of the limitations of her gender, and her responsibilities to her widowed father, concentrating her efforts in the running of all matters domestic, within the family home, Farleigh House.

Work on the land had stood Enos Clark in good stead, but like many young men the opportunity of advancement necessitated the quitting of villages and towns known from birth. Clark had in 1852 taken a wife Ann (nee Abdy, born 1832, Weston, Hampshire), and by the latter years of the 1870s the couple had settled in Remenham, Enos Clark having secured employment at Park Place (an estate nestled amongst woodland, in Remenham, held at that time by John Noble), as farm bailiff. This position came with a tied property, known as Farm House, and with no children to fill the place the Clark's were glad of the company of lodger, agricultural labourer Frank Hawkes, and their niece Kate Alice Orchard. This young woman, to whom Enos and Ann were much attached, born 1854 in Basingstoke, daughter of Frederick and Eliza Orchard. Kate, who had formerly been in the service of commercial clerk, Louis Posse of Wellington Terrace, Kensington, London, by the 1890s, could not consider living anywhere but with her aunt, Ann (who cared for the needs of the estates herd of dairy cows), and uncle Enos. An additional lodger, Jane Pettingill (an extremely elderly lady, born 1803) completing the Clarks household dynamic.

Park Place, following the devastating fire of 1871, its frontage and interior much altered by John Noble

George Higgs (born 1799 in Reading, Berkshire) turned a shilling as a white smith, one who worked with tin. He had wed Ann (born 1800 in Bristol, Gloucestershire; daughter of Thomas White) and the couple in due course secured a property at Abbey Wall, St Lawrence. Higgs able to provide more than reasonably for the umpteen offspring he and Ann were to have. The eldest child of the household, George, baptised at Saint Giles on 24th May 1818, he soon joined by a brother, Edwin, who was received into the church on 14th July 1822, this much cherished child soon dead, buried at St Lawrence on 22nd August. Ann, it seemed, had been destined to carry boys; Arthur born in 1823, followed by Job, Alfred, and Elijah, he baptised in the February of 1831. On 18th August 1833, at St Lawrence's, Reading, the Higgs boys, under the watchful eye of their parents, to look on as their brother Frederick was baptised. The brood of boy's swelled in number by the arrival of Edwin (named after his late brother) in 1836, Thomas Octavius in 1838, Theophilus in 1841, and Henry Joseph in 1849. The Higgs for a fleeting time had a daughter, named Ann after her mother, who brought much happiness and profound sorrow to the couple. This little girl had come into the world in the early months of 1845 (at that time her family residing in Newal Court, St Lawrence), only to have left it again before the autumn of 1846.

And so we turn to one of the Higgs boy's, that being Thomas Octavius, the lads initial education courtesy of Blue Coats School, which was run out of premises on the corner of Silver Street and London Street, near St Marys Minster Church in Reading. Once young Thomas was fully conversant with the three Rs he duly dispatched to board at Christ Church School, London. And when schooling was done with, Thomas Higgs, in need of a profession, took up an apprenticeship in Reading, under the mentoring of local printer, Mr Joseph Macaulay. Higgs displayed a natural ability, and when proficient in all matters concerning printing he secured employment (aged seventeen) with Mr Luker, in the back offices of the Faringdon Advertiser.

Thomas Octavius Higgs, with his immediate financial future assured, and in want of a wife, stepped out with Miss Emily Fear. Emily had been born in the St Giles Quarter of Reading in 1833; she and her elder sister, Frances, after the demise of their father William, brought up exclusively by their mother, Jane, the three occupying a modest abode in Spring Gardens. As of many a single girl not blessed with sufficient education, or funds, by the time of the census of 30th March 1851 Emily Fear was in service, her place of work Woodbine Cottages, St Giles, Reading, she house servant to John (a farmer of ten acres), and Elizabeth Norris. But the attentions of Thomas Higgs ended her life of servitude, and in High Wycombe, Buckinghamshire, in the spring of 1859; Miss Emily Fear took her vows.

Thomas Higgs parents had entered the world within months of each other, and thus it was only fitting that they left it within months of each other, the year being 1860. Their son Thomas, now residing in London Street, Faringdon, and funded by the wages earned as a printer compositor, duly, alongside his numerous siblings, benefitting from his parents legacies, thus able to relocate to the more desirable 30 Gravel Walk.

Life in the Victorian era was perilous, and any illness was an event fraught with dangers, Emily fell ill, her protracted condition endured with much fortitude for near four years. But on 16th November 1874, with all her energies spent, Emily Higgs died, leaving her widower childless and bereft. But Thomas Higgs bounced back with aplomb, and with his wife not yet dead a year, on 2nd August 1875, at St Lukes Chelsea, he married Eliza Bridges, who born 1840, hailed from Timsbury, Somerset, where her father James Bridges earned a crust working down the coal mines.

In 1875 Thomas Higgs relocated to Henley-on-Thames, much familiar with the town, his mother Ann (nee White) having taken George Higgs as her husband at the Parish Church of St Marys, on 10th January 1818, the marriage register stating that the nuptials had taken place only once permission of the couples parents had been sought. There was employment awaiting Higgs, as collector of assessed taxes, but printing was in his blood, and Thomas Higgs worked hard and saved even harder. His ambition realised in 1877, when he set up Higgs & Co, a modestly sized printing office located at 4 Bell Street, he just about able to afford the wages of one member of staff. Residential quarters above, to provide a roof over the heads of himself, Eliza, and her widowed mother Mary. The business flourished, and eight years on from its conception Thomas Octavius Higgs commissioned local builder, Richard Wilson, to construct for him a purpose built premises, thus by the end of 1885 Caxton House completed, sitting on the junction of Station Road and Reading Road. Higgs rapidly relocated into his fine new offices, he and Eliza (occupying number one Caxton House) to nip across the road on Sundays, to worship at nearby Trinity Church. Higgs & Co proved itself a valuable addition to the commerce of Henley-on-Thames, and this in turn necessitated the expansion of its printing presses capacity, just in time to win the contract as official printers for the prestigious Henley Royal Regatta.

In the 1880s the town's news was reported upon by two publications; the Henley Advertiser, and the Henley Free Press, the latter of which founded by the Reverend Joseph Jackson Goadby, he a man of Liberal leanings (a tireless worker for local charities) having also established the Foot Path Society. Having proved itself, over seven years in publication, to be a viable newssheet, in 1892 the Henley Free Press passed into new ownership. Thence forward principally a Conservative paper (its primary Director local brewer Archibald Brakspear), it to be renamed as the Henley and South Oxfordshire Standard. The ambition to produce a paper that attracted the gentleman and working man alike succeeded, and circulation increased, in 1892 Higgs & Co securing the much sought after contract to print said paper.

Higgs & Co, Caxton House, Station Road

Thomas and Eliza, alongside with niece Amy Bridges (who resided with her aunt and uncle), socialised widely, and enjoyed the dinner invitations of their neighbours, Thomas Higgs in particular throwing himself fully into community activities. He acted as a correspondent for the Reading Mercury, sat as First Treasurer of the Jubilee Lodge of Druids, and accepted an honorary membership of the Good Samaritan Lodge of Odd Fellows. The latter organisation formed in the seventeenth century to provide aid to those in dire need, its primary principal being to create and run projects which would both enhance and benefit those who sought the Odd Fellows help, as reflected by the society's motto. "Friendship, Love Truth." If Higgs had any time to spare it was taken up by his position as Honorary Secretary of the School of Art, and a voluntary role, that of one of a number of Managers of the towns Saving Bank, conceived to encourage sensible management of the wages of those who worked on the most part for pitiful financial return.

Thomas Octavius Higgs was a resourceful and articulate man, who could rise to a challenge, and finding himself selected to sit upon the jury of such a high profile inquest, he was not the sort of fellow who would mutely observe the proceedings.

Robert Carpenter Bratchell was already a name synonymous with the night of eighth December; he the landlord for eleven years of the Red Cross, the very premises where George Dawson had broken his journey into Henley-on-Thames, in an attempt to summon assistance.

Robert Bratchell was not local by birth; he the son of agricultural labourer, Robert (born 1819 in Etchilhampton, Wiltshire), and Ann (nee Wiltshire), she born 1823 Marylebone, London. Robert was delivered of his mother on 18th May 1849, a welcomed brother to Jacob and John, the Bratchell's, by no means a large family in relation to the times, eking out an existence in Rowde, Wiltshire. Not flush with money, by the taking of the 1851 census they had taken in a lodger, seventy two year old former servant Mary Plank, better to enable them to cover the rent on their meagre property, located on the Piccadilly Bath Road. Ensnared by the confines of poverty there was much to cause the family anguish, the primary of which being the death, in the spring of 1856, of Robert, a man still in his fifties, much worn down in the pursuance of manual work.

Mary Ann Brown was born 1851 in Pensey, Wiltshire, and not yet twenty she had entered into the service of locally based Charles Goode, a farmer of some one thousand three hundred acres, the cultivation of which reliant on thirty one labourers. But like most young women in domestic service Mary's employment ended upon her marriage, her husband, one Robert Bratchell, the nupitals held on 26th January 1874, in Thanet, Kent.

And so we move onward, and by 1876 Bratchell was landlord of the Hinds Head Inn in Lambourn, but his foray into the hostelries trade was not one destined to be a great success. By the taking of the 1881 census Robert Bratchell, though not having quit Lambourn, a coachman, in the service of one George Forbes, Vicar of Eastbury, and incumbent of Vicarage House. Mary Ann grateful for the provision of premises tied to her husbands job, and the company of their lodger Julia Sarah Carr, a certified school mistress, whose contribution to the household budget was much appreciated.

But Bratchell was not done with the pub trade, and with no children reliant on his purse he took a gamble and it paid dividends, he securing the tenancy of the Red Cross, which had run out of a converted former residential property since the reign of George II.

Jessie Webb, at the time of the shocking events at Lambridge Farm having turned thirty, was the son of Silas Webb (born 1821 in Watlington, Oxfordshire), and Caroline (nee Clarke), born 1823, in Clare Pyrton. Jessie whiled away his childhood in the village of Clare Pyrton, which lay not much distance from Watlington in the county of Oxfordshire, the lads formative years spent, as many Victorian childhoods were, playing, squabbling and making up with his numerous siblings. Joseph was the elder of the Webb brood; born 1849, near three years following his parent's marriage, his father employed on the land, tenant of a modest property in Warps Grove, Chalgrove. A daughter, Elizabeth, had been born in 1853, her birth followed by that of Louisa, Frederick, Jessie and youngest Robert, he born 1866. Much can be said of the benefits of country life, but it had its negatives; wages for many were pitifully inadequate, and Silas Webb, an agricultural labourer, reliant on the foibles of the seasons, at times struggled to provide. Some respite provided when one of his daughters, Louisa, while still a child, was taken in as a boarder at the

Domestic Servant Training School, situated within several attached flint and brick cottages on Upper Hill Road, Watlington. But in the latter 1860s Silas Webbs widowed father in law, Joseph Clarke, moved in, further pressurising the familys finances. But with three strapping sons, who resisting all thoughts of marriage still under their parent's roof, the 1880s saw improvements in circumstance, since all three were in employment, Frederick a shepherd, Jessie and Robert, alongside their father, agricultural labourers.

Louisa Jemmett (born 1861, within a small terrace tenement on Greys Hill, Henley, the daughter of a railway porter) caught young Jessie Webb's eye. The young woman a domestic servant who worked at 4 Oxford Villas, the home of widow, Lucy Anne Howard (her husband John had died on 13th August 1878, leaving an estate of some three thousand pounds) and her young son Richard. Having walked out with Jessie (who was at the time employed as a coachman in St Johns, Walworth Newington, London), Louisa nabbed her man, the marriage taking place on 12th May 1888, at Holy Trinity Church, on Greys Hill. Louisa Jemmett, one of four girls and four boys, had spent a considerable portion of her formative years in Cookham, Buckinghamshire, her father a railway guard at Cookham Station. Louisa's father, James, had relinquished his position, and by the turn of the 1880s was once more residing on Greys Hill, his address 1 Prospect Terrace. However James Jemmett had not been destined to proudly escort his daughter up the aisle, as he had been interred in Trinity's churchyard since the September of 1881.

With Jessie Webb a jobbing labourer, finding ad hoc work as a carman (one who drove, or manually pushed a cart, used to transport goods) the newlyweds took a house in Albert Road (Jessie's widowed father, Silas, a lodger at the Old White Horse, Northfield End in Henley, where he would die in the June of 1897), and here in 1890 the Webbs welcomed the birth of Robert Oakley, so named in deference to Louisa's mother Marthanee, nee Oakley, she born 1836 in Kettering, North Hampton.

In a direct reflection of the old adage "it's a small world" by the closing months of 1892 the Webbs quit Henley and secured a tenancy at Folly Cottages, Lower Assendon, their direct neighbour none other than George Dawson.

William Perrin was born 1844 in the vibrant town of Princess Risborough, Buckinghamshire, the son of accomplished tailor John (born 1816 Quainton, Buckinghamshire) and Ann, nee Young, born 1819 Kings Langley, Hertfordshire. William was never short of company, since his siblings were plentiful, Mary, who was five years his senior, Thomas, Henry Stratten, and Emma Sarah, who had been born in 1845. The last born Sarah, who'd arrived in 1848, her mother Ann dead before the year 1849 had drawn to its close.

Life could prove harsh, and John Perrin found himself widowed, with six children to care for, but his tailors, run out of premises situated on Duke Street Princess Risborough, was never short of customers and he more than managed to provide the necessaries. Perrin a skilled draper, reflected in the fact that saw him elevated, by the close of the 1850s, to a shop on the High Street, he thus able to afford himself the title of 'Master Tailor.'

William Perrin grew into a confident young fellow, on 10th May 1864 (at the tender age of just twenty), at Saint Mary Church, Luton, Bedfordshire, taking a wife, his bride Elizabeth Skillman, two years her grooms senior. Elizabeth hailed from Kings Langley, one of five girls and five boys, she born to John Skillman (a tailor, born 1819 in Redbourn, Hertfordshire) and Sarah (nee Pratt), born 1818 in Redbourn. By the census of 1861 the Skillman's squeezed into a house on Albert Road in Luton, master of the house, John, no doubt sewing like mad to keep all the hungry mouths fed.

William (a boot maker) and Elizabeth (a hat and bonnet sewer) started their married life at 71 Hastings Street, Luton, their finances assisted by lodgers Hannah Biggs and Barbara North, she in the same profession as Mrs Perrin. Unlike her mother Elizabeth delivered of only four babies, Elizabeth (her mother's namesake) born in 1865, after a gap of five years she joined by Sarah Ann, known as Annie. Arthur Edward (known as Edward) joined the family in 1874, his brother, William Stanley, born in 1878.

William Perrin's father had instilled ambition in his son, and thus in the latter years of the 1870s Perrin relocated his family to Henley-on-Thames, where he quickly established himself as a boot and shoe maker, and seller of leather, located in the heart of Henleys commercial hub, that being number 26 Market Place.

Market Place, William Perrin's "Boot & Shoe Makers" just visible, being the premises situated just beyond the two canopies. The building still stands, but looks very different, now having a mock Tudor façade

There were many within Henley who sought out Perrin's services, and he took on assistant, youngster, George Emmett, he primarily occupied with running messages, delivery of goods, and when needed assisting in the shop.

Like countless others who earned their living in retail, the Perrin's resided above their business, but within a short time William had the capital required to move his family to 14 Queen Street. A road, made up of a combination of small terrace houses, and Victorian villa properties (principal builders, Robert Owthwaite and Thomas Hamilton), that ran off from approximately half way down Friday Street, its far end culminating at the junction onto Station Road.

John Charles Wheeler was born 1846 in Bradfield, Berkshire, the son of labourer Charles (born 1821 in Bradfield) and Mary (nee Smith), born 1815, hailing from the same town as her husband. We first have clear sight of the Wheeler's, in no small part down to the census of 7th April 1861, at which time the family were residing at Slade Gate, Bradfield. John Charles Wheeler spent his formative years isolated as far as having a brother went, his elder sisters, Mary Ann (born 1843), and Elizabeth (born 1845), a joy and irritation in equal measure. Charlotte was born in 1849, and after her came Hannah, and Caroline, who completed the family dynamic with her birth in 1853. There was scant money to be had; the head of the household employed as a hoop and needle maker, a job which much strained the eyes, the only son of the house, John, aged just thirteen, to share his father's profession.

Within the next decade the Wheeler's had moved onto Buckhold Chapel in Bradfield, Charles working as a woodman, his family settling into a small cottage, situated on Buckhold Row.

John Charles Wheeler, as did many, finished with schooling early in life, and then onwards worked initially in Bradfield, as a carpenter and joiner, the indication being that he had benefitted from the advantage of an apprenticeship. Marriage came relatively late for John, he not taking his vows until Valentine's Day 1874, his wife, one

Caroline Ann (born 1850 in Kingston Bagpuize, Berkshire), daughter of Charles (a stone mason) and Sarah Brown. By 1877 the Wheelers had moved to Henley-on-Thames, John inn keeper from that October of the Kings Arms, 32 Market Place, one of the town centres primary hostelries, with good cellarage, a large garden, and an adjoining cottage (to be later incorporated into Henley Police Station), for use of the landlord. Like many who kept a public house, John Wheeler did not forgo his previous profession, he continuing to work as a jobbing builder and contractor, in the evenings, as landlord of the Kings Arms, privy to bar talk regards the murder not much distance from Henley.

Matthew Stone (born 1812 in Tubney, Berkshire, a landowner and farmer), and his spouse Esther (born 1813 in Lyfold, Berkshire) enjoyed a comfortable lifestyle the envy of many, they having begat numerous offspring. Thomas had been born in 1838, then after, in quick succession, Elizabeth, Matthew Henry, Maria, and Caroline Mary born. George Albert had evened up the boy girl ratio with his birth in 1847, he last of any sons born to Esther. Rosa Ann joined the family in 1849, Eleanor born in 1851, Frances Harriet arriving in 1853. Life for the Stone's, though not at the level of the "Lord of the Manor", was comfortable, and the end of the 1850s saw Matthew Stone retired (his wife a fund holder, one who had investments), the family residing in Newbury Street, Wantage in Berkshire. The elder children of the household by this stage following a profession, Thomas a tea dealer's assistant, Matthew a baker's assistant, Maria a draper's assistant, and Caroline apprenticed out.

At St Saviour Church, Croydon, on 5th January 1870, George Albert Stone (employed as a clerk) took as his bride twenty three year old Harriet, daughter of John Williams from Epsom in Surrey. The newlyweds secured tenancy of a house on Newbury Street, Croydon, and not many months after Stone gained employment, as Steward at Wandsworth Workhouse, a role which involved responsibility of all inmates, and the sorting out of any difficulties or problems that may arise within the inmate's wing. The first born of the Stones, Albert Ernest Brooke, came into the world in 1871, the little boy rapidly joined by brothers, Arthur, and Edward, he born in 1874. Their father earning a none too shabby wage, which had made the taking of a larger house possible, the family residing at 7 St Annes Road, Wandsworth.

What brought George Albert Stone to Market Place in Henley-on-Thames, in the mid-1880s, was his securing of the multi-faceted position of Relieving Vaccination Officer of Henley District, Inspector under Infant Life Protection Act, Registrar of Births, Marriages and Deaths for Henley Sub-District, and Collector for the Guardians, the background to these various roles as follows.

In 1872, in an attempt to protect neglected or deprived children, who fell outside the ambit of the Poor Law, or the judiciary, the Infant Protection Act was implemented. Foster parents (paid a reasonable remittance) whose houses were registered with the local authority, were permitted to take in more than one infant, duly required to maintain said children, and improve their welfare. In 1890 an additional act was implemented to help protect vulnerable new-borns; the babies passed over by their often poverty stricken mothers into the care of women, whose responsibility it was to nurse the child until it turned two. Things did not always run smoothly, as findings by bodies, indicated that some babies, mostly illegitimate, had been placed with "baby farmers", and as such, the Chief Commissioner of Police ordered every department to inspect all registered carers homes, with each police district required to maintain a nurses report.

The business of the Relieving and Vaccination Officer was to sign Birth Certificates, Death Certificates and Marriage Certificates, for the Register Office of Marriages. An officer also required to work alongside the Guardians of the Poor; his duties including receiving applications for relief and examining cases, by visiting applicant's homes, to inquire into health, and ability to work. He, no women to work within the role, had the remit to access the condition of the applicant's family means, reporting his conclusions to the Guardians at their next available meeting; an officer to subsequently revisit (several times) pauper families who had received monetary relief. In the case of sickness or accident the Relieving Officer had a duty to ensure that medical attention was secured, procuring a doctor via the District Medical Officer. It also falling within the officers remits to take on the difficult task to issue orders to immediately admit people in desperate need to the nearest parish workhouse.

The Vaccination Officers duty also required him to hold a record of deaths of infants under twelve months (in a time rife with sudden onset illnesses and disease, there were regrettably many children who did not see out their first year), detailing child's name, date and place of death, father's name and occupation, or mothers name if the child was illegitimate.

So by the early 1890s, with all his responsibilities, George Albert Stone was indeed a busy man, he, his wife and sons, Albert (a brewers clerk), Arthur (a solicitors clerk), and Edward (a bankers clerk), inhabiting the living apartment of 45 Bell Street, a striking flat roofed late Georgian building tucked between a chemists and a corn merchants. As Vaccination Officer Stone would have been familiar to many in the town, and no less so than to Doctor George Smith (the two men involved in the immunisation of children), and as a man of some note within the community, George Stones selection as an inquest juror was of little surprise.

John Eustace was born in the first quarter of 1853, in Henton, in the county of Oxfordshire, his father Frederick (born 21st April 1827, in Henton) a blacksmith, his mother Esther, born the same year and location as her spouse, a homemaker. John to spend his formative years in the company of his three younger sisters Jane, Elizabeth and Hannah, who'd been born in 1862.

Henton, which lay in the Parish of Chinnor, was a scenic hamlet, its workforce consisting of many who were employed in the chair making profession, John Eustace, who did not buck the trend, apprenticed as a chair turner. Having a profession which offered financial security, in the September of 1874 Eustace married his sweetheart, Ellen White, who hailing from Burton in Hampshire, was eleven years his elder. The couple, who took a tenancy in Nettlebed, not much distance from Henley, welcoming the arrival of their firstborn, Florence Jane, in 1875, Cecilia Sarah born in 1878; William John delivered of his mother in 1881.

By the closing years of the 1880s we find the Eustaces relocated to Lower Assenden (ironically the family living directly next door to one John Froomes), where John carried on his trade of chair turning, his eldest, Florence, a dressmakers apprentice, his youngest, William John, a scholar at the village school.

William Francis (born 1815 in Nuffield, Oxfordshire), a man much in demand as a blacksmith (employing five men and one boy within his forge) resided in a property located on Gangsdown Hill, Nettlebed. William's wife, Sarah (also born in Nuffield, a year her husband's younger) had few options when it came to family planning, and as such, as of the fate of many a wife, she gave birth to a great many children. Henry born in 1837, he soon in the company of siblings, John, William, and James, the first girl, Emma, born in 1845, her birth soon followed by that of George Frederick, he delivered of his mother on 23rd January 1847. A second daughter, Sarah, had but a fleeting life; she born 29th October 1848, dying on 5th January 1851. The family's number further swelled by the arrival of Thomas in 1851, Charles in 1852, and following a hiatus of some three years, Charlotte. Three further sons were to be born to Sarah, Edwin in 1857, Joseph in 1859, and Stephen, who came into the world on 22nd November 1862, only to be snatched out of it in the January of 1864.

George Frederick Francis managed to thrive amongst so many, and grew into a strong young man, in the July of 1869 he marrying Kate Stannard, born 1842 in Pakenham, Suffolk. The couple to have three boys (all born in Stoke Row), Frederick John arriving the year following their marriage, Shredic born in 1871, and the year 1872 to witness the birth of Albert Henry. George Francis had learnt at his father's side, and thus run a smithy, out of premises in Bix, Kate, who unlike her mother-in-law not burdened by multiple pregnancies, a school mistress, her family resident at School House, Bix.

By the time of the taking of the 1891 census, the Francis had moved a short distance to Nettlebed, and were living at 23 The Cottage, the eldest boy, Frederick, working alongside his papa, a smiths labourer, while his brother Shredic was employed as a general labourer.

There were to be, as dictated by the rule of law, twelve jurors summoned to sit at the inquest into the demise of Miss Kate Laura Dungey. The last of which, William George Jackson (who seems to have preferred to be known by his middle name) having left no discernible trace, thus to remain an enigma.

Fourteen

A Shocking Spectacle

On the morning of Monday 11th December 1893, the traffic, which travelled through the outer reaches of Henley-on-Thames, and out onto the Fairmile, was unique in living memory, so much so that it included the presence of those called to attend an inquest into a case of wrongful death, the reports of which reverberating countrywide. The various carts and carriages of those connected to the inquest jostled in amongst an influx of individuals, who also made their way to Lambridge Farm (on foot, on horseback, or by carriage or cart), in the hope of securing entry to the inner sanctums, in which the inquest was to be held.

Augustus Jones, Deputy Coroner for South Oxfordshire, was not tardy during his morning routine; he ate heartily, completed his ablutions, dressed and set out from Watlington in good time. The inquest was to be held within the confines of the kitchen of Lambridge House, and as the coroners coachman pulled up adjacent to the farm property, Jones found himself scrutinised by the considerable number of those who had no purpose to be at Lambridge, other than morbid curiosity. Members of the public, thwarted in their endeavours to secure admittance to the farm house, ambled about in its vicinity, and upon the arrival of Augustus Jones the interlopers, on the most part locals, whispered amongst themselves about the possible identity of the well turned out man, who eyed the mob with trepidation, stepped down from his carriage and made haste into Lambridge House.

Once within Augustus Jones was greeted by Chief Constable of Oxfordshire, Edward Alexander Holmes A' Court, resplendent in full dress uniform, which he no doubt felt best reflected the gravity of the situation. Any protracted conversation between these two men, if it occurred at all, not destined to be reported upon through the medium of the press.

Augustus Jones, and those with an interest in the proceedings, made their way to the kitchen, some not familiar with the place, others knowing it intimately. As Deputy Coroner of the district Jones had had much dealings with the tabloids, and regulations dictated his initial task was to provide procedural guidance to the twelve members of the press (the papers they worked for not specified upon), who had been granted leave to report on the inquest.

With all vacant seats taken within the ad hock court, the inquest jury foreman, Richard Ovey (esquire) was sworn in, followed then after by (the running order of this detailed in countless newspapers) Thomas Octavius Higgs, Robert Bratchell, Enos Clark, Henry Lillywhite, George Frederick Francis, William George Jackson, Jessie Webb, John Eustace, George Albert Stone, John Charles Wheeler and William Perrin.

By the time the jurors took their seats, on a dank wintery day, the men had already had dealings with the deceased, as specified within the columns of the Henley Advertiser, of Saturday 16th December 1893. "The room was packed to excess, the jury, witnesses, reporters (12) and a few sightseers, who had managed to elbow themselves in, being cribbed, cabined and confined, in an uncomfortable space, they (the jury) having already visited the copse where Miss Kate Dungeys lifeless body had been happened upon."

The reporter from the Henley and South Oxfordshire Standard, he early on the scene, and having shadowed the twelve jurors, able to specified to his readership that said jury had earlier that morning viewed the young ladies body, which decanted to the sitting room had been laid out on a table, this item of furniture having been lately brought up to Lambridge. The body had not been an easy sight to look upon, those having looked upon it greatly affected, no more so than Robert Carpenter Bratchell and Jessie Webb, who had known Miss Dungey personally, the reporter, supposedly guarded from extremes of sentiment, in his professional capacity, not spared the horrors of what he bore witness to in the sitting room of Lambridge House. Here no doubt was a man greatly stirred, and his notes taken at that time, though brief, in their simplicity of language did not spare the reader. 'Miss Kate Dungeys corpse presented a shocking spectacle.'

Fifteen

She Did Not Mind Being Alone

There was much to get through, the first of which had involved the brief absence of the coroner, Augustus Jones accompanied by his jury assembled in the sitting room, where the body of Miss Kate Laura Dungey was formally identified by her father, for the benefit of procedure. Though this was not the first time Walter Dungey had gazed upon the shattered corpse of his child, his trepidation at the thought of it had not diminished. But the comforting words of Augustus Jones bolstered Walter (though not a parent himself the coroner fully empathic with the man's loss), the acutely distressing process swiftly brought to its conclusion.

Walter Dungey now had the unenviable task, one which would have daunted many, of being the first witness called to give evidence. With the inquest transcripts no longer in existence what follows is compiled from the scrutinizing of umpteen newspaper articules, which detailed the exchanges between coroner, jury and witnesses, verbatim. Augustus Jones, his voice set at an even calming tone, commenced the questioning. 'Please tell the court your name, occupation and place of abode.'

Though provided with a seat, in reflection of the strain the man now in his sixtieth year was under, Kates father chose to stand throughout his evidence. 'Walter Dungey, farmer, residing at Pattenden Manor, Goudhurst near Tunbridge Wells.'

'What age was the deceased?'

'My daughter (Walters voice rose to reiterate this point) had turned thirty in the October.' This is an error on the part of Walter Dungey, his daughter Kate having turned thirty in the November.

The coroner regretful of the insensitivity of his words asked next of his witness. 'When did you last have cause to see your daughter, and at that time what opinion of her did you take away with you?'

'I met up with my child in the October, and she appeared to be in robust health.'

It was evident to those who bore witness to the testimony now taking place, that the coroners primary wish was to set before the jury a picture of the woman, who silenced in death, was laid out in an adjacent room. 'Of your daughter, Miss Dungeys personal attributes, which in your opinion were those most marked in her character?'

'She was a reserved woman with a quiet but neither the less cheerful disposition.'

Now Kate's employer was to be first heard of. 'Did Miss Dungey find her position as housekeeper to Henry Mash to her liking?'

'Yes indeed she very much liked her role as housekeeper to Henry Mash.'

'Did your daughter ever voice any concerns in relation to feelings of isolation while alone at Lambridge House?'

'She did not mind being alone at Lambridge Farm, but we her family never felt settled in our minds about it.'

Though the woman, who lay but a corridors length from the kitchen, had not yet be dead three days, much had been said of her through two distinct mediums, that of the press and that of idle tongues. And Thomas Octavius Higgs had had cause to be privy to tittle tattle, in regards to the deceased, and with leave from the coroner, wished to clarify a matter which had been much speculated upon. Higgs rose and stood forward of his seat (an altogether unnecessary act, as far as court protocol went), and directed a question of some delicacy to Walter Dungey. 'I should like to ask if the deceased was known to walk out with any young man, and was she engaged to anyone?'

'Her family had heard nothing to this fact, and I feel that we would have done, if there was anything of that sort.'

This was the last asked of Walter Dungey, though one bereaved in a manner so heinous, he had with no small effort held his emotions in check. Augustus Jones acknowledged the witnesses stoicism, and excused him from the stand, Dungey to retreat to the area of seating reserved for those who had been summoned to give evidence. If any of Walter Dungeys children were within the kitchen, no reporter in the course of his note taking made reference to it, but I do not doubt that one or more of Kates siblings were present, better to support their father.

Walter Dungey, photographed by his daughter Julia

Sixteen

A Little Matter Regards Ten Shillings

Mr Henry Joseph Mash was next called, and having taken the witness stand gave his principal details as requested. 'I live at 12 Redcliffe Gardens, S. W. and my business interests are that of a self-employed fruiterer, with a company establishment located at 36 Glasshouse Street, Piccadilly.'

Augustus Jones required much of this witness, and thus the exchange between the two was brisk and at intervals brusque. 'Could you clarify for the jury your relationship to the deceased?'

Henry Mash, who seemed somewhat overawed by the gravitas of the occasion, fixed his gaze firmly upon the jury, and with a voice, which at intervals fell away to an almost inaudible whisper, he addressed the court. 'Miss Dungey had been in my familys service for a full seven years, firstly filling the role of nursery governess. When, as the children matured being no longer required, Kate left my employ for two years, but returned when I offered her the role of housekeeper at Lambridge House Farm.'

'Did Miss Dungey have cause to reside alone at Lambridge House?'

'When I and my family were absent from our country retreat (Henry Mash not missing the opportunity to reiterate that he was a gentleman of commerce, not used to such as this), Miss Dungey resided alone, but she was not left isolated during the night time hours, as the two Froomes boys slept in the house.'

'What ages are the two boys you allude to?'

'The eldest boy is aged thirteen, and in my employ, the youngest is still in education.'

The coroner was perplexed as to why the seemingly innocuous house, in which they were all now gathered, had been the seat of such an outrage. 'Sir do you have any reason to feel that there was a possibility of an individual, who privy to the contents of your weekend retreat, and with his sights set on theft, having broken into this farm house, where we are assembled?'

'I have searched, and have not missed anything from the house, my property is modestly furnished and contains no silver plate, it all being electro.'

At this juncture Augustus Jones interrupted his witness. 'It is my belief that the dead womans wages were still present in her handbag, Miss Dungey having been paid seven pounds in the form of a cheque, which she had very recently cashed.'

Mash turned in the direction of the coroner, seemingly momentarily flustered by Augustus Jones interjection, there a distinct interlude before he responded. 'I knew the deceased was likely to have money, as a fortnight ago I gave her a cheque for seven pounds, which was cashed by Miss Dungey in Henley, at Mr Lesters, the Butchers (Alfred Pearse Lesters shop was located at 13 Market Place, directly next door to the Argyll, and though the hostelry still survives, its frontage much altered, Lesters premises has long since been demolished), she had very little money previous to that. She had a cheque after that for two pounds, six shillings and eight pence, to pay the men and boys, and a pound for household expenses.'

Jury Foreman Richard Ovey, mindful of what had been touched upon earlier, required of the witness to comment on the earlier statement made by Walter Dungey. 'Did Kate Dungey feel in anyway apprehensive at the prospect of being alone at Lambridge Farm?'

'My employee was not in any way afraid of being alone in the house, in fact she preferred Lambridge to being in Henley. I suggested that this winter we should go to live in Henley (37 New Street), and my man and his wife (George and Amy Dawson) live here, she said, oh don't do that, I would rather be here.'

Ovey, who seemed somewhat unconvinced by the response, pushed the witness further. 'She never showed any signs of being terrified?'

Henry Mash, with a steely glare fixed upon the jury foreman, and with a firm steady voice answered in a single utterance. 'No!'

The coroner picked up on Mashs abruptness, and as a solicitor much used to dealing with human frailty, determined it best to change tack. 'Could you elaborate on the character of your employee Miss Dungey?

Kate Dungeys employer attempted to respond, but the recalling of his late housekeepers attributes tightened his throat and strangled his speech, and Henry Mash paused, took a generous sip from a glass of water that had been provided for his convenience, and with his voice returned to him answered the coroner. 'Miss Dungey was one of the most pleasant persons that has ever lived, rather reserved, but pure minded, an inoffensive girl, I have lost a most valuable servant, she never complained at all.'

Augustus Jones mindful of his witnesses discomfort, neither the less moved onto a more tenuous subject, that being the possibility of some animosity within the household at Lambridge. 'Is there any substance in relation to a delicate matter that being the inference of some discontent felt by Dawson?'

Mash nodded to convey that he knew what the question alluded to, and replied with no hesitation. 'When I had cause to visit Lambridge in the spring of 1893, my man (George Dawson) had come to me and said that he wished to see me on a matter, on Thursday week.'

'Did you agree to this meeting?'

'I informed my man that I would see him again when I came down in the week.' Urged by the coroner to expand on why his farm bailiff wished to converse with his employer in such an urgent manner, Henry Mash took a moment to mentally prepare his train of thought, and satisfied that he had total recall, elaborated on the events that previous spring. 'I found, upon meeting my man Dawson, that my employee was dissatisfied with his place, he was having a pound a week, but breached the subject on the question of his having to pay rent. I said I would pay his rent, and I have paid it since, it was decided he should not come back into the house.'

This response was somewhat at odds with what was known at the time in relation to George Dawson recently having resided at Lambridge House. Jury Foreman Richard Ovey, like many others of the jury, confused, attempted to deal with any assumptions he or others might have made. 'Was the dissatisfaction on account of Dawson wishing to reside at the farm, or on account of wages?'

'I do not know, he did not give any reason, but of course many could form their own conclusion.'

Ovey pondered momentarily, and then levelled another question towards the witness. 'Where does George Dawson now reside?'

'In the first cottage (that being Folly Cottages, located not much distance from the Golden Ball hostelry, within Lower Assenden,), I can see it from my orchard.'

George Dawson had been drawn to the forefront of his employer's testimony, and the court had not yet finished with the man, as matters moved on to the subject of disquiet between Miss Dungey and Lambridge Farms Bailiff. Richard Ovey, with leave from the coroner, navigated his next question towards an occurrence, which had been much gossiped about. 'Had the deceased ever had reason to complain of anything said to her by George Dawson?'

'There had been some dispute; a little matter regards ten shillings, the fact of which only coming to my attention since the death of my employee. The two had always seemed to agree fairly well, I don't know any reason why there should be any ill feeling between them. Of course, if we and Miss Dungey had not lived here, he would have lived in the house, and had firing and such like.'

As Richard Ovey leaned forward his chair titled slightly, he dominating the witness. 'Do you mean his position was not so good now, was it materially reduced, he would have had use of house firing and light, it would have made a small difference.'

'No!'

Coroner Augustus Jones interjected. 'Has your man Dawson's wages deceased as a result?'

'No they have not.'

The Deputy Coroner had the experience to acknowledge that he had exhausted all avenues with his witness, Jones thus addressed his jury. 'Do you have any further questions for the witness?' Satisfied that the jury was content Augustus Jones thanked the witness, and a relieved, if rather rattled, Henry Joseph Mash was excused.

Seventeen

We Had Parted on Excellent Terms

The Bailiff of Lambridge (George Dawson), testimony followed hot on the heels of the contentious appearance before the coroner of his employer Henry Joseph Mash. This man appeared (according to the transcripts of reporters, who scribbled eagerly in their notebooks) uneasy, and somewhat on the defensive, his mood further unsettled by questions of an uncomfortable nature, levelled at him by Augustus Jones. 'How long have you been in Mr Mashs employ?'
'Eleven years as farm bailiff.' This statement would have Dawson firstly at Lambridge at the tender age of just twenty, and does not correspond with him having first been a stable hand.
The coroner, keen to elaborate on facts that had earlier been explored, progressed onto the nature of his witness's interaction with Miss Kate Dungey. 'It is my belief that there was some verbal dispute, which took place between you and the deceased.'
Dawson intimated, via his body language, that he found this line of questioning exasperating. 'The event the coroner has in mind took place a full three months previously, when Miss Dungey had inquired why the washing had not been taken into Henley, and I had informed the housekeeper that the Froomes boys would collect and take it, when they next passed the backdoor.' It was further left in no doubt that Dawson acutely felt the inference of the question. 'You could scarcely call those words, well we never did wrangle.'
'Are you quite sure of that, and that the two of you parted on good terms that day?' Augustus Jones refers to the day of the murder.
'We had parted on excellent terms.'

Augustus Jones did not leave his witness in any doubt that he wished to press the matter of bad feeling between housekeeper and bailiff, and directed George Dawson to clarify on facts which pertained to an argument between him and Miss Dungey, in relation to her not having wanted him to move into Lambridge House.

'I deny there has been any difference between the two of us over this matter, and I would swear to that!'

It was now plainly evident, to all those assembled within the kitchen of Lambridge House, that the man who acted as its farm bailiff was not to enjoy an easy ride. Jury foreman, Richard Ovey, conversed with his fellow jurors, and the matter of some differences in relation to money (one could infer that certain unnamed individuals, as one might indelicately suggest, had been muck racking) was examined by Ovey. 'It has come into general conversation that you and Miss Dungey had reputedly had words on account of money.'

Dawson, balanced between indignation and downright annoyance, snapped a response. 'We had not argued over money matters!'

'Now be careful, you never had any words about money?'

'No sir!'

'Did you not sometimes buy things for her?'

'Yes, and she paid me back.'

Clearly of the opinion that the line of questioning being pursued was not leading anywhere constructive, and alienating the witness, the coroner relieved Dawson of any further burden regards the subject of money matters, and steered the line of questioning to the events that had bearing on that which had unfolded on eighth December.

But Dawson's rancour had not subsided, and with no prompting from the coroner he clarified in strongest terms a matter he deemed should be heard. 'The shilling Miss Dungey had owed me, the amount had been paid back, and when we parted on that Friday it was as good friends.'

George Dawson had opened the floodgates, and Augustus Jones, somewhat reluctantly visited again upon matters financial. 'Were you privy sir, in regards to Miss Kate Dungeys finances?'
'I had never been privy to or had conversations with her about her personal money matters.'
It was paramount in any coroner's court that all events once touched upon by witness or juror should not escape full scrutiny. And as Walter Dungey had highlighted the secluded, and he felt vulnerable nature of his late daughter's habitation of Lambridge Farm, Jones next chose to explore this avenue. 'Had you ever heard her, Miss Dungey, complain about being alone in this place?'
'Yes, she told me she felt very nervous in the night, this was a fortnight ago. She had been frightened as the dogs had barked fearfully, and she asked if all was right.'
Richard Ovey, a thought pattern developing, interrupted the witness. 'Do you feed the dogs?'
'No the young lady did that.'
'Were the dogs chained up at night?'
'The black retriever was chained up, but the spaniel was loose.'
This brief interlude in relation to the dogs dealt with, Augustus Jones began to explore the events of a day which had seemed like any other. 'On the day of the murder at what time did you quit work for the day?'
'I left the farm about half past four on that Friday afternoon, I had taken my leave of Miss Dungey, finding her sitting in front of the fire in her accustomed chair knitting (Dawsons voice at this stage fell away, his next utterance barely audible), that being the last I saw of her alive.'
'Why had you left so early, on the fateful Friday?'
'Well the horses were fed and we had nothing to do.'
'What was the disposition of Miss Kate Dungey that last afternoon?'
Dawson did not jump in with a reply; he seemed to ponder for a

moment, his pallor noticeable paler from the recollection of the events which had culminated in unprecedented horrors. 'She seemed the same as usual, and made no complaint. I had taken in the eggs collected from the chicken house, and we had conversed briefly.'

'Can you recall for this court what passed between you?'

'Miss Dungey said words to the effect of, you get more eggs now George. I replied yes there are ten, it is better. In all I spent not more than two minutes in the kitchen.'

Juryman Thomas Octavius Higgs, a fellow of sharp wits, glanced in the direction of the coroner, who picked up on the silent prompt, and nodded to indicate that Higgs could interject. 'Having arrived home, during the evening did you have cause to leave your house?'

'I went home and stayed there until twenty minutes to eight.'

'Did anyone call, while you were home?'

Yes Mr Burgis man with groceries, at about seven fifteen.' It is to be noted that the man alluded to was Daniel Burgis, his grocery and provisions outlet located at 35 Market Place, Henley-on-Thames. The late hour of the delivery indicative of the long hours expected of shop lads.

Higgs, the bit between his teeth, continued apace. 'Why did you leave your home?'

'I felt in need of some distraction, and so I went at seven forty to Mr Bratchell.'

Thomas Higgs had no chance to ask more of George Dawson, as Richard Ovey cut in. 'How are you so certain that you left home at seven forty?'

'My wife told me the time and asked when I would be back.'

'When did you return from Mr Bratchells?'

'I returned from the Red Cross at eight forty five.' Just a few hours hence, from the time stated, Dawson would have had cause to return to this public house, his manner at that juncture all together more agitated.

There was now to be an interlude of some moments in which Deputy Coroner, Augustus Jones, having firstly acknowledged Higgs and Oveys contributions, addressed the jury in hushed tones, no word he uttered audible to members of the press. Satisfied on what may have been a point of procedure, and happy to move on, the question next asked by the coroner cut straight to the quick. 'When did you first see the body?'

'It was about eleven.'

'Can you tell the court, as you recall it, what led up to the discovery of the body of Miss Dungey?'

'I had been first called an hour earlier. Froomes had arrived at my home, accompanied by his boys; I was in bed, and was woken quite suddenly by the sound of hammering on my door. I roused from my bed and went to my window and looked out, and initially seeing John Froomes and his lads asked the time, Froomes informed me that it was a quarter past ten. I pulled on my clothes, made my way downstairs, and admitted the Froomes.'

'What did those, who you found within your cottage that fateful night, convey to you in regards to events back at Lambridge Farm?'

It was clearly evident to magistrates, jurors, spectators and reporters alike, that John Froomes had not, on the night of the eighth, had time for pleasantries; Dawson to recall what had passed between them. 'His sons, upon returning to their family home had told their father they could not gain entry to Lambridge House, nor could they make anyone hear, even though there was a light on the kitchen table, as though somebody was home. I felt, sir, and thus agreed that the testimony of the children seemed to suggest that all was not well, and thus it was decided at that point that the two of us, having first settled Harry, the younger boy into the care of Mrs Dawson, would return to Lambridge Farm, accompanied by the elder child.'

'Where did you go first?'

George Dawson, though overawed by his ordeal, was stoical, and thus meticulously articulated all that he had observed the night in question. 'The three of us, having reached the farm, resolved to first investigate the main house, and we made our way to the kitchen door, which we found fastened. The Froomes and I made our way around the house, to the bedroom of Miss Dungey, and I tapped on the young ladies window, with my sword stick. I had taken a bamboo stick with me when I was summoned to the farm on that Friday night, and drew it when I began to examine the exterior of the farm house.'

At this point, at the request of the coroner, there was a hiatus, Dawson's sword stick, lately removed from his home and entered into evidence, brought before the court, this item a long sword cane, the coroner to cautiously draw its blade. 'This is indeed a very dangerous article.'

Thomas Higgs drew in a sharp intake of breath, and with an air of bewilderment in his tone, levelled a question. 'And of this stick you brought along with you that night, was it usual for you to carry such a weapon?'

Dawson did not much like the inference. 'I only brought along the weapon because I thought something was up.'

Thus the sword stick had left its mark (Dawson would later regret its existence), and with the coroners lead George Dawson, by this point seemingly rattled, took up his evidence. 'The three of us called out the womans name several times, but we secured no reply. The hen roost was our next port of call, everything there seeming alright.'

The matter of the dogs, still set firm in the mind of the coroner, and demanding of further clarification, again came to the fore. 'Is the farm dog (the retriever) on the whole kennelled in the yard, and would the dog generally come out to you?'

'Yes he is an outside dog, he did not on this occasion come to greet me, and he seemed sleepy.'

Richard Oveys brow furrowed, he much perplexed by the last comment, compelled to speak. 'Did you take particular note of the dogs altered state?'

'Yes I did sir.'

Augustus Jones thanked Ovey, and continued on in relation to the dog. 'Would the dog rush out at anyone?'

'Any stranger who passed would be greeted by the animal, but any being familiar could pass without event, unless they called out to the dog.'

'Where had you found the Spaniel?'

'The Spaniel was by the door.'

'Would this dog approach a stranger?'

'It is old and deaf and would not take notice of any stranger.'

The matter of dogs again explored, the scene of the outrage came under scrutiny. 'Tell us of your exploration of the farm house.'

'As a group we again turned our attentions to Lambridge House, and tried the kitchen widow, which was secure. We moved on next to the sitting room window.' The window alluded to the one found to have its bottom sash pushed up.

'Mr Dawson, when you had come back to the house would it have been possible that you stepped in one of the flowerbeds?'

'I stood back on the grass in order to look in at the windows.'

Henleys police constabulary, under Chief Constable Captain Holmes A' Court, had put much weight on the evidence, in relation to that window, the flowerbed below it, and the boot imprint pressed firm into the mud, and the Chief Constable thus took up the mantle. 'Did you step on the flowerbeds in order to tap on the windows?'

'Yes sir.'

The coroner glanced across at his interrupter, and requested that the witness expand. 'Did you, Dawson, ascertain at the time if any villain had left any footprints?'

'I did not look about the place for footprints, or for any trace of anyone being about the place.'

'Was it not at this point that the child became agitated?'

'Yes, very much so, upon witnessing the unsecured bay window, James Froomes declared that when he and his brother had earlier investigated the property it had been secure.'

'You thus entered the house via this window?'

'I went through the opened window, carrying a Bull Lantern, with John Froomes and his son following on behind.'

'What route through the house did you take?'

'We went out into the hall and searched the bedrooms, and finding nothing amiss made our way to the kitchen.'

'Was all found to be well?'

'Yes sir, the room seemed as it should be, a lamp was burning, and Miss Dungeys knitting lay on the kitchen table, alongside her handkerchief, the chair in which I had last seen her sitting in, in the same position.'

'What part of Lambridge House did you next explore?'

'I took up a candle from the dresser, but found nothing out of place, and thus we walked along the passage which adjoined the kitchen, and led to the front door.'

'Is it a correct assumption that you subsequently began to feel that something was indeed amiss?'

'Yes, the true horror of the scene was exposed to us, the passageway walls were streaked with what could not be mistaken for anything but splatters of blood.' This comment drew gasps from spectators, who through duplicity had managed to wangle their way into the kitchen. 'Upon reaching the door (Dawson referring to the front door that led out into the porch), after we first ascertained that it was bolted at the top, the key in the lock not turned, we became aware that its brass handle was stained with blood.'

'Did you stay within the premises?'

'No sir, we rapidly made our way to the sitting room and left the way we had entered.'

'Did you explore the outbuildings?'

'As a group we surveyed the stables and outhouses, and found all as it should be. I at this point felt a more substantial light was in order, and went to the well house, where I took possession of a lantern.'

A member of the jury, not named in the press, at this juncture requested that Augustus Jones level a particular question at Dawson. 'Is it a correct assumption that the three of you returned to further investigate the front porch of Lambridge House?'

George Dawson, much perplexed at the line in which his cross examination was headed, clarified this point. 'We came back to the front of the house.'

'It is my belief that an item you thus forward saw has been admitted into evidence.'

'By this do you refer to the short thick piece of blooded stick we found on the front porch mat?'

Augustus Jones did indeed refer to the portion of stick, duly produced for the court. The item held aloft by a clerk, for the benefit of the jury, hence forward taken over to the witness stand so Dawson could look upon it. 'Is the stick you saw that night, the one you see before you now, and are the blood stains on it still?'

'I am sure it is the same piece of stick by the blood stains.'

'Did you handle the stick for any length of time?'

'Yes sir, I did examine the stick with the aid of the lantern, and then I put it back down on the mat.'

At this point there was a brief hiatus, as members of the jury wished to confer with their chairman, Richard Ovey. With leave from the coroner, Ovey leaned in, better to discuss matters with jurors, and satisfied of the direction they wished to take, and with leave from Augustus Jones, Richard Ovey addressed the witness. 'We have heard much of what lay within Lambridge House, and in regard to the horrors thus happened upon, but what occurrence, sir, ultimately led to the discovery of the young womans body?'

George Dawson grimaced, as he fine-tuned his train of thought and with a voice that erupted from his lips in a manner most impassioned, he guided the court through the sequence of events that had led to the realisation that Miss Dungey had met a violent end. 'When I was informed by James Froomes of an alarming noise he and his brother had earlier heard, the two of us (George Dawson and John Froomes) proceeded to the spot the boy indicated as roughly the location the noise had originated from.'

'How did the child direct you to the spot?'

'He pointed to it sir.'

'Who led the party?'

'I did, and in respect of his tender years instructed the Froomes boy to wait behind.' Some versions on this point of evidence, that made their way into the columns of the press, stipulate that James Froomes, nervous of being left in isolation, did not tarry for long, and made his own way down to where his father and Dawson were. 'His father and I were struggling against the darkness of the night, and the heavy rain, so I went ahead with the lantern.'

'What time did you come upon Miss Dungeys body?'

'We found Miss Dungeys body at approaching eleven fifteen.'

'Could you tell the court where the young lady was happened upon, and your initial thoughts when first you observed her?'

Dawson, sore in need of clarity turned to the coroner. 'Do you require distances sir, or how she lay?'

Augustus Jones could well see that the witness was growing weary, and as a gesture of reassurance informed Dawson that he could answer Richard Ovey, as his conscience took him.

'Miss Dungey was a full two yards from the path, and a clear thirty yards from the house. I took note that she was attired in a lightweight dress, considering the inclement weather, and she was lying on her right side.'

Richard Ovey had exhausted his arsenal of questions, and thus gave the floor once more to Deputy Coroner Jones, who, as befitting a gentleman, such as he, thanked Ovey. 'I am grateful indeed for the diligence of my Jury Foreman, and with his leave will expand on matters now in discussion. Did you, Dawson, go directly to the body?'

'Yes I went straight to the body.'

'How exactly was the woman lying?'

'She was lying out straight, and her head seemed to be twisted towards the right, and her arm was up.' Again, as before, there was at this point disquiet within the kitchen, mutterings and audible gasps originating from spectators, possibly (according to a representative of the press) kin of Miss Dungey.

'Which arm was raised?'

'I was too much upset to notice!'

'Where in relation to Miss Dungeys body did you see the rammer?'

Dawson had much to say on this, and did not confine himself to matters relating to said rammer. 'The rammer lay by the womans side, and as I moved to glance more closely at it I was able to see that there was a wound on the back of Miss Dungeys neck.' Richard Ovey cut in, and raised a point of procedure with the coroner, and George Dawson, given due guidance to temper his answers directly to the questions asked, shuffled nervously from foot to foot, his head cast down and shoulders hunched.

'Could you clarify for the Jury Foreman that the rammer had been last used to mash potatoes at five thirty, on the Thursday preceding the murder (one would imagine that the date referred to is Thursday 7th December), and was after left in the pig tub as usual?'

The bailiff of Lambridge straightened up, shoulders back and face set firm. 'Yes sir that is so.'

As of other items displayed during the proceedings, the rammer was now produced, it reported in the press as a formidable looking article. "The farm implement, which required two hands to lift it with anything like ease, was displayed for the benefit of the jury. It measured four feet in length; with the end used to break up the pigs feed massively thick."

'Did you handle the item seen here?'

'Yes sir, I saw the rammer near the body, and when I lifted it from the ground there was blood on it, so I released my grip.'

'There was a poker close to the body (also produced), which came from the house, when had the poker last been seen?'

'Two months ago.' George Dawson not to specify where said poker was usually to be found.

'Did you touch the body when you saw it, to see if there was breath in it?'

The coroners next question caught Dawson off guard, and he breathed in sharply. 'No!'

At this reply, a juror (his identity unspecified), stirred by indignation, and without leave of the coroner, desired to be heard. 'Why not!'

'She did not move, she was dead, she looked dead sir, and we did not stay two minutes.'

Thomas Octavius Higgs gazed at George Dawson quizzically, he like his unnamed colleague upon the jury stirred to speak. 'Having a lantern in your hand, is it a fact you did not see if she had any breath in her body?'

'No I did not!'

'So you did not, by examining the body, satisfy yourself that there was no sign of life.'

George Dawson released a protracted sigh and reiterated. 'I satisfied myself that Miss Dungey was dead, there was no movement. But I was so terrified I did not touch the body, I being under the impression that Miss Dungey had been murdered quickly left the scene!' The bailiff of Lambridge now, to all those who bore witness, seemed shaken to the core by the recollection of what he had been forced to revisit.

The coroner, though he must have surely been aware that his witness nerves were in a fragile state, had a duty to preform, and he did not shy away from it. 'What did you next resolve to do?'

'We immediately returned to the outbuildings, the stables our primary location, to source transport, so I could summon assistance. I drove to Mr Bratchell, he is the publican at the Red Cross, but I could not make him hear, so I carried on into Henley.' To the surprise of many assembled in the kitchen George Dawson thus provided a snippet of information that had not formerly been common knowledge, though many retellings of the night in question had been bandied about. 'I passed on route a policeman (the persificic location of this man not revealed), so I briefly drew up my vehicle. I did not alight from the cart, but never the less informed the officer in clear terms that a young woman has been murdered in the wood. (This policeman, more than likely a constable, identity never established.) My journey ended at Henley Police Station, from which juncture I summoned assistance.'

'I am led to believe that the three of you (the coroner referring to George Dawson, Superintendent Francis Keal, and Constable Edward Snelgrove) searched Lambridge House.'

'Yes sir.'

'Did you notice anything in the passage?'

'Both I and Superintendent Keal saw glass, which originated from a broken Fairy Light Lamp, which had been knocked off its bracket. We also came upon a candlestick stained with a large blood mark. I independent of Keal observed a box of matches.'

'Is it the same kind of matches usually used in the house?'

At this stage, and startling those present, Mr Henry Mash got to his feet and exclaimed. 'When I had searched the premises, I only found one box of matches in the house, and they were of a different brand to those we commonly used!' The inquest jury mumbled in deference to the man's fortitude, in stating unbidden a point of fact he no doubt felt should be heard.

Augustus Jones gathered himself together after the interruption, and taking a moment to examine his notes (Mashs interjection had thrown the coroner of track), requested that George Dawson clarify what else worthy of note he had observed.

'I saw blood on the walls, the match boarding and the floor.'

'And of the body, when you and Superintendent Keal went to where it lay, did you see any difference in its position since you last looked upon it?' The wording chosen by the coroner was regretfully most clinical, and his omission of the deceases name did not go unheeded by those closest to Miss Kate Dungey.

'No sir, I just assisted in carrying the body back to the house.'

Thomas Higgs took leave to speak. 'Can I take the opportunity to cross examine you on your movements; is it correct that once the house was shut up you departed from Lambridge Farm soon after four in the morning?'

'Yes sir, I put up the horse and trap, and went away with the Superintendent.'

Augustus Jones, well aware that his witness was flagging, inwardly acknowledged that any subsequent testimony demanded of Dawson may well be unduly influenced by the bailiff of Lambridges mental exhaustion, and as such, after clarifying that the jury was content, the coroner did not ask anything further of Dawson. The bailiff of Lambridge had thus far found himself subjected to the interrogations of both coroner and jurors, the presenting of evidential objects, some stained with the blood of Miss Dungey, not to mention being privy to the frenetic scribbling's of the press, his every word taken down. Thus it was a relieved George Dawson, who at the direction of Augustus Jones found himself excused.

Eighteen

I Work at the Place, Where this Inquest is Gathered

It was mandatory that Augustus Jones, in his capacity as Deputy Coroner of Oxfordshire, examine, before the inquest into the demise of Miss Kate Laura Dungey, the statements (secured in tied bundles) of all who had been privy to events at Lambridge Farm, and with this in mind Jones requested that his clerk call James Froomes. Augustus Jones took from a bundle the boy's statement, when and by whom it was taken unclear, and pursued it, until such time as James had taken the stand. As a solicitor, Augustus Jones had had cause to deal with minors (regretfully, on the most part as a result of poverty, many a child brought before the bench, charged with some minor misdemeanour), and in deference to the lads tender years he tempered his questions accordingly. 'Please James, could you tell us your age, where you live, and your occupation.'

The child, unlike many of his fellow witnesses, was, within the newspaper columns afforded the privilege of warranting a description of his appearance. "James Froomes is a boy possessing a comely face, his eyes are blue, and his complexion fair, as is his hair." James though finished with schooling and out in the world was never the less daunted by the responsibility of giving testimony, and his voice was initially fragile in tone. 'I am thirteen sir and live in Assenden, I work at the place where this inquest is gathered.'

'Could you tell us where you slept on Thursday 7th December?'

'On Thursday last I had slept at Lambridge House with my brother, in the same bed.'

'Could you tell the jury of your movements the next night, take your time we are in no hurry.'

'I had left for home at about four thirty; I was accustomed to go for my tea at about five o'clock, but left earlier that afternoon. I then come back to Lambridge at about eight thirty to sleep; my brother would always come along with me.'

'How old is your brother?'

'He is eleven years old sir.'

'What happened once you reached Lambridge Farm?'

'We failed to attract the attention of Miss Dungey, and as the house was shut up we retreated to the well house.'

'It is my understanding that the well house adjoins the kitchen, am I correct?'

'Yes sir.'

'Was it unusual to find the house shut up?'

'Oh yes sir, Miss Dungey never had the door locked.'

'Did you try the house again?'

'Yes sir, after we had sat in the well house for a full hour we left it, and with the assistance of a lantern, walked around the exterior of the property in order to see if the housekeeper was present.'

Did you, during your investigation of the houses exterior, notice that the sitting room bay window was open?'

'No, the sitting room window was not open.'

'What did you do from that point?'

'Do you mean what did we see?'

'Yes.'

'Again we had failed to make anyone hear so I peered in through the glass in the kitchen door. There was a lantern on the table, and I was therefore able to make out the time on the kitchen clock.'

'Can you tell the court what time it was?'

James nodded enthusiastically. 'Yes I can sir; it was nearing ten to ten.'

'Was it then that you left the farm?'

James Froomes paused for a moment, took a sip of water, cleared his throat, and continued. 'We set off for home sir, to summon our father.'

'We have heard from the last witness that you then arrived at his home, Folly Cottages, what is your recollection of this?'

'After a few moments we went on to Folly Cottages. Father left my younger brother Harry in the care of Mrs Dawson, and the three of us set out for Lambridge Farm, and just as my brother and I had earlier found, they too realised the doors were indeed locked, and Mr Dawson said something must be up.'

'Did your father and the farm bailiff take you into the house?'

'Yes sir, we climbed in through the sitting room window.'

The coroner, as before, seemed acutely interested in the movements of George Dawson, and as such chose to question his witness on subjects that were no doubt acutely distressing to an immature mind. 'Can you remember that you told the two men about the strange noise you and your brother had heard?'

'Oh yes sir.'

'When did you first inform Dawson of the noise you and your brother had heard in the wood?'

'I did not tell Dawson that we heard a noise in the wood until after he and my father had searched the house.'

The coroner continued, George Dawson now firmly in his sights. 'Did Dawson go straight to the spot, and straight to the body?'

'Yes sir.'

'He did not go to the left, but turned straight to the right?'

'Yes sir.'

'Did he speak?'

'I was standing back, but heard him say, here she is.'

Augustus Jones at this juncture asked his jury if they required clarification on any points, and satisfied that they did not, excused James Froomes.

The lad squeezed himself into a corner of the kitchen, the child under scrutiny of both press and spectator. James had seemed during his testimony acutely nervous, but perked up when he heard his father's name called.

'Can you tell the court your place of abode and occupation?'

'I am a carpenter, and I reside in Lower Assenden.'

As John Froomes testimony corresponded with that of his son's version of events, his evidence was not so thoroughly covered in the newspapers. But the reporters present at the inquest did take note, and include in their respective articules, aspects of the carpenters account.

The coroner, still acutely interested in the movements of Lambridge Farms bailiff on the night of 8th December, did not take long to again touch upon Mr George Dawson. 'How did Dawson react when you first told him that your boy's had been thwarted in their efforts to gain admittance into Lambridge House?'

'Dawson had replied; it seems a funny thing.' Froomes then, as George Dawson had before, described for the benefit of the jury the search of the deserted house.

'Which of you mentioned to the other that there was blood in the house?'

'George Dawson pointed out to me that there were blood splatters in the passage, and dried blood on the brass door handle.'

'Who of you saw the body first?'

'We all saw it at once.' Froomes reply seemingly to suggest that his son James had been in very close proximity of Miss Dungeys corpse.

'What impression of the young womans body did you have?'

'The body was in a very crammed position; the knees seemed to be doubled up, the clothes disarranged.' This testimony caused an individual seated within the kitchen to cry out, the press not to specify if the distressed spectator was a member of the deceases family.

Augustus Jones took a moment to establish if all was well with the individual who had been so sorely affected by the witness's last comment, and satisfied all was well continued. 'Did either of you touch or investigate the body?'

'We could not see any movement; we did not touch or investigate the body, as there was no life remaining.' With this painful recollection conveyed to the coroner, John Froomes prepared himself for the next volley of questions, and appeared surprised and relieved in equal measure when he was excused.

It was duly reported that the youngest Froomes present that day, Harry, was next called to give his account, which on the most part backed up his brother's version of events. Therefore the press took little note of it, and his part in the inquest appeared as a brief footnote within the columns that dealt with his brother and father.

Nineteen

A Brooch and Some Hair Pins

Evidence, which pertained to the analysis of the murder scene, carried out at the behest of Francis Keal, was now to be heard, and thus the superintendent was called. 'Could you inform the court of your rank, and which police station you work out of?'

'Francis Keal, Superintendent of Henley Station.'

'On Friday last, when did Dawson arrive at your station?'

Keal was a thorough man, and all that had seemed relevant that fateful night had been noted within his pocketbook, and with the coroners permission he extracted his regulation pocketbook, thumbed through its pages, and satisfied as to which pages pertained to the matter in hand proceeded. At approximately twelve o'clock I saw Dawson at Henley Police Station, the man informed me that the housekeeper at Lambridge had been murdered, and I asked him for particulars.'

'Did George Dawson seem nervous?'

'Yes sir, I took notice at the time of the fact that Dawson seemed in a very nervous state, visibly trembling, and scarcely able to get the words out of his mouth.'

A juror (unnamed) desired to know if the two men had conversed as they exited the station.

'Is she dead I said, yes quite he replied, there were not two words spoken on the way from the station.'

The coroner momentarily paused to see if the juror had any further need of the witness, and satisfied he did not continued. 'What time did you arrive at the farm?'

'I, my constable (Edward Snelgrove) and Dawson arrived about the hour of twelve forty five.'

'It is correct is it not, that you went straight to the body of Miss Dungey, and did you having gazed upon her feel she was quite dead?'
'That is not quite as it was, I was taken by Dawson to the location of the body after I had firstly briefly examined Lambridge House, and it was obvious to me that Miss Dungey was dead, and had been for some hours.'
'Could you clarify for the jury the positioning of the body?'
At this juncture Superintendent Francis Keal consulted his notes. 'She was lying partly on her right side with her legs drawn up, I found that her under linen was visible, but felt that was accidental.'
'Could you tell us what items you recovered close to the body?'
'I discovered a blooded rammer, partly concealed by the ladies hair (this being the first time the exact position of said rammer had been stipulated), I also took note that a quantity of blood, apparently escaping from a wound on the neck, was still visible on the ground, even though it was raining and hailing in torrents.'   At this recollection, a spectator, their emotions no longer held in check, was heard to be sobbing.
'Is it correct that you organised the removal of the body from the scene?'
'After careful examination of the area where the woman lay, I did have the body removed indoors.' This action of course prevented the examination, by Doctor George Smith, of Miss Dungeys body in situ, but inclement weather, and the forensic practices of the time had much bearing on Superintendent Keals decision.
Much had been said of what the superintendent had ascertained from his exploration of the murder scene, now Augustus Jones wished to explore that which Keal had deemed noteworthy within Lambridge House.   'Could you Superintendent Keal give account of your observations of the interior of Lambridge House?'
Francis Keal, again, heavily reliant of the prompts provided by his small pocketbook, paused and familiarised himself with all he had

scribbled down on the night in question. 'As I, Constable Snelgrove, and Dawson, had travelled through the inner sanctums of the house, I came upon a brooch (subsequent drawings of Miss Dungey, which appeared in several tabloids, would depict this brooch) some hair pins, lamp glass and matches, all of which scattered along the passageway floor. There were blood stains on the wall, as if done by a person's hand. I said to Dawson here's a box of matches are they yours. Dawson replying, that indeed they were and they came out of the candlestick there (this statement contradicts Henry Mashs interjection, during George Dawsons testimony, when he made comment that the box of matches were not of the brand used in the house), so I at that point examined the candlestick, finding it had no matches in it.'

Jury Foreman Richard Ovey, much interested in the superintendent's last comment, desired to hear more on the matter. 'Is it you're thought that some of what you examined was connected with the attack upon the person of Miss Dungey?'

'It is sir, on the Friday I picked up in the lobby, and took note of, a stick, the thick end of it clumped with blood and hair, both of which clearly visible. And on Saturday morning I myself had picked up the poker near where the body had lain, and also recovered the other portion of the stick I have just mentioned. It has now been identified as a small segment of a branch from a cherry tree.' All of the items scattered about Lambridge Farm, that Francis Keal had deemed evidence, had been removed to Henley Police Station, where, once entered by the desk sergeant into the log, they had been locked in the evidence store. Though, as there is no mention of them, it does not seem that the portions of cherry stick were produced during the inquest.

'Could the damage done to the ceiling have been caused by such a stick?'

'Indeed sir, the scratches on the ceiling corresponded with the jagged end of the abandoned portion of stick found in the passageway.'

The coroner, with acknowledgement of Richard Oveys contribution, mindful of the hour and requiring a last answer of his witness took the lead. 'Is it so that you locked the body in?'

'I did sir; at this stage I locked the room in which Miss Dungeys body had been placed, that being the kitchen.'

'I am satisfied, you may step down.' Thus Superintendent Francis Keal retraced his earlier steps, and took a seat within the crammed kitchen. And here the man who had taken the lead on the night the housekeeper of Lambridge Farm had been found brutally murdered, listened keenly to the testimonies of those who followed.

Twenty

Indeed, a Small Knife Could Account for the Injury

The coroner now had cause to make clear to his jury that the next witness, would, on the most part, be cross examined on evidence that pertained to the medical examination of the deceased. Though this portion of evidential material would be of a delicate nature, and could be the cause of some distress to those present, Augustus Jones emphasized the necessity to hear the testimony of Oxfordshire's Medical Examiner.

Doctor George Smith had been sorely affected by what he had seen at Lambridge Farm. He as a medical man, in the course of his duties, had cause to gaze upon deceased individuals who through illness, disease, or accident, had presented a sight that many would find at odds with their sensibilities. But the brutal nature in which Kate Dungey had been dispatched had profoundly affected the doctor, and it was with a heavy heart that Smith, the evening preceding the inquest, had reread the notes so eloquently set down by Joshua Watts.

On the morning of eleventh December Doctor Smith had awoken early, his housekeeper Fanny Underwood, as always one step ahead of her master, having already set in motion all that was necessary to ensure there would be no tardiness. Once Smith had taken a light breakfast, completed his ablutions, and dressed (in a suit he deemed sombre enough for the occasion), he momentarily took himself off to the portion of his residence set aside as a surgery. Within Arthur Bramman greeted the man who he considered not only employer, but also a friend. The two conversed, and with George Smith satisfied that all was well, with provision set in place (both in New Street, and the Hart Street Surgery) for any unforeseen medical emergency, he bade his dispenser goodbye. Charles Underwood, his wife having ensured that he had harnessed up horse and cart in good time, awaited his master without. A goodly number of people, who resided on the opposite side of New Street, to gaze through windowpane and half open doors, to better see one who had cause to be involved with matters at Lambridge Farm.

So with the journey to the farm exacted, and Underwood, either returning to New Street, or joining other coachmen who awaited their charges, we know not which, Doctor Smith took a seat in the kitchen of Lambridge House. He sat patiently, witness to those who went before him, and with his name reverberating, compliments of an usher, Smith now found himself before coroner, jurors, reporters, the deceases loved ones, and spectators.

'For the benefit of the jury can you state your name and occupation?'

'I am George Smith, and I affirm that I am a doctor, practicing out of my surgery in Henley-on-Thames.'

The coroner knew full well that this witness's testimony was liable to be protracted, and before he proceeded Augustus Jones glanced down at the doctor's police affidavit. 'When were you first sought out by Superintenant Keal?'

'My professional services were required on the Saturday morning (ninth December), to examine the body.'

'At what time did you arrive at Lambridge Farm?'

'The Superintenant and I arrived at Lambridge at nine thirty.'

'Could you give to the jury, in as full a detail as you possess, the injuries inflicted upon the person of Miss Dungey?'

George Smith had need of Joshua Watts notes, Augustus Jones requested a brief perusal of said notes, and once satisfied that they had been witnessed by both doctor and scribe, returned them to Smith, and with a flurry of a hand, Jones bid the witness continue. One reporter, moved by the experience of what followed, to later reflect in his editorial that. "The injuries inflicted on the murdered woman, were terrible in character."

Though no definitive record of Doctor Smith's testimony survives, what follows is as full in detail, gathered from subsequent reports that appeared in various newspapers. Those who had attended the inquest, in their capacity as reporters, having noted down the post mortem evidence verbatim.

Before Doctor George Smith is heard one should be familiar with what one can gleam from the procedure the medical man would have followed. The fundamental ethos of a post mortem examination was that one with medical expertise should inspect a body, as soon after death as possible. Before any medical practioner could consider performing a post mortem upon an individual, he had first to ascertain if the person was indeed dead. A doctor practicing in the Victorian era had very rudimentary equipment which could indicate that a person was deceased, and thus on the whole he relied on his senses. Placing his ear close to the body, a doctor could listen out for the beat of a heart, and however shallow detect through sight and sound breathing. Doctors at the time did have the use of listening equipment, but still relied greatly on their medical instincts, and the ability to assess if life was extinct by touch, determining if a body felt warm or cold. The accepted guideline to protect against mistakes in relation to death (and indeed mistakes had been made), no medical man had any justification to commence a post mortem examination of a body until coldness and rigidity have manifested. As to Kate Dungey, even with the wintery conditions in relation to the core temperature of her body, there was no doubt that the young woman had expired.

Established guidelines dictated that an attending medically trained man should carry out a careful examination of the exact location of a body, and the posture of a body, and the area immediately around it. In the case of Miss Dungey, Superintenant Keal had orchestrated the removal of her remains to within the farm house, if she had been left where she had perished, Doctor Smith would have looked about him to see if any visual indications of a struggle were present. It also accepted practice that the medical examiner would search about him for objects that may have been dropped, at, or within proximity of a body. Any medical fellow, worth his salt, was fully abreast with the requirement that any discovery he made was to be immediately recorded in writing. And only when satisfied that his analysis of the scene was exhausted, could the body be removed to a place which was convenient for a fuller examination.

A post mortem, performed on an individual deemed to have met their death in suspicious circumstance, was required to be carried out in natural daylight, as colour changes upon the skin were often hard to distinguish in artificial light. Kate Laura Dungey had lain upon the kitchen table until such time as Doctor George Smith, once the night of the eighth was spent; had been summoned. There was at the time a fundamentally excepted running order of post mortem procedure, and Doctor Smith would have been familiar with it. Firstly the expression and colour of the face was to be noted. If hands were found to be clenched, it should be ascertained if any item was grasped within them, and fingers were not to be neglected, examined for any sign of defensive wounds. A medical examiner was duty bound to make careful note of the condition of the deceases clothes, if they were soiled and disordered this could indicate a struggle, and any blood staining upon clothing was to be catalogued. Once any doctor was satisfied that he had fully explored all visible areas of skin, he could then (as in the case of Kate Dungey) remove the clothing. With clothes clear of the body, tears and cuts sustained to garments could better be compared to the underlying surface of the body, any examiner taking care that marks, such as those that appeared to be bruises, were sponged to make sure they were not in fact dirt. If in doubt, any indication of identification was to be sought, in the form of distinctive moles, scars and the like. The measurement of the length and depth of wounds was paramount, and the examining doctor was permitted to indicate in his notes if in his professional opinion he deemed them self-inflicted. Strangulation was an injury that doctors paid particular note of, and examination of the neck for marks of it was common practice, and sat alongside the search for any signs of gunshot wounds, stabbings, and beatings. A doctor was permitted, within his field of expertise, to include in his notes his assumptions in regards to any kind of weapon that could have produced any wounds he came upon.

One rudimentary post mortem procedure was reserved for women or female children, and it was of a most intimate nature. As in the case of Doctor Smith, when he examined the remains of the housekeeper of Lambridge, it required that an intrusive procedure to verify the existence or absence of the hymen and any signs of violence to that area, be carried out.

It would appear that Kate Dungeys body was not opened up, and if any criminal trial subsequently took place, this lack of an internal examination could be seized upon by counsel for the defence, who could use it as having implications as to cause of death.

With considerable experience as a medical examiner George Smith had taken much care in his investigation into the cause of Miss Dungeys death, and as such he faced the inquest jury with a confident air of professionalism. 'I first saw the deceased about ten o'clock, her face was covered in dirt, and appeared red from the streaks of blood upon it. Immediately over the right eye was a horizontal wound, one and a half inches long, which extended to the bone. Three quarters of an inch above this was a small puncture wound, triangular in shape, which also extended to the bone. One and a half inches above this and towards the right side of the face was a contused and lacerated wound, one and three quarter inches in length and exposing the bone. Two inches above the right eye was another small puncture wound, also triangular in shape. On the upper part of the forehead was another lacerated wound, one and a half inches long extending to the bone, and laying bare a considerable area of it. One and a half inches above this wound, and amongst the hair, was another lacerated wound, two and a half inches long extending to the bone. On the left side of the head, amongst the hair, was another lacerated wound, three inches long. Close to it was another wound one inch in length, and a small wound run parallel with its inner side. Another lacerated wound, about one inch in length, ran along on the left side behind the ear. The left ear was very much lacerated by several small jagged cuts, the largest of which, about one inch in length, was situated behind the ear. At the back of the head was a lacerated wound two inches long, down to the bone, on the right side of the head was a lacerated wound, also two inches long down to the bone. On the lower level was another lacerated wound, one inch in length, on top of the head a lacerated wound also one inch in length, and a punctured wound down to the bone. There were two small parallel superficial incised wounds below the chin, one and three quarter inches in length respectively. On the left side of the neck three incised wounds, three, two and one inches in length, only just through the skin. On the left side of the neck, running horizontally forward was a deep lacerated wound, six inches in length, and one and a half inches deep, severing the muscles down to the backbone. This wound was sufficient to have caused death, the edge was jagged and the sides irregular. Another incised wound ran parallel with this large cut, immediately below it, two and a half inches long, and a quarter inch deep. Both hands and arms were very much bruised, there being several wounds on the arms. The large wound, which began from the back of the neck, must have been done by some cutting instrument, and not by one cut, but a series of cuts. The instrument which would account for most wounds, I think was a stick, which would account for the punterial wounds. The poker might have caused some of the injuries, but no single weapon caused the wounds.'

Doctor Smith stood silent, his stillness mirrored by the hush that had fallen across the occupants of the kitchen at Lambridge House, Mr Richard Ovey to rupture the silence. 'Doctor Smith, how long would it take for a well-nourished body to get cold?'

'It would depend very much upon the weather; the night of the murder had been a very cold and wet one.'

'Would it take three hours?'

'The parts of the body covered would not have been cold in three hours.'

'You say the big wound was done not by one cut but by several, could it have been done by a small knife?'

'Indeed a small knife could account for the injury.'

Thomas Higgs, compelled by a sudden touch of inspiration, sprung suddenly forward of his seat, and levelled a question. 'I would like to ask who prunes the trees here Mr Mash.'

Henry Mash, though caught off guard by the suddenness of his inclusion in Doctor Smiths testimony, answered with forthright clarity. 'Dawson does all that sort of thing.'

'Have you seen him pruning the trees recently?'

'I don't think I have seen him this season.'

Augustus Jones, with leave from Higgs, carried this line of questioning forward. 'I would be much obliged if Lambridges farm bailiff, Mr Dawson, could clarify what type of implement he commonly used to prune his employers trees.'

A slight gasp was audible, as Dawson, squeezed in amongst many others, rose from his seat. 'Sir, I am accustomed to prune the trees with nippers, and not a pruning knife!'

This brief interlude dealt with, and apologies via the coroner for the interruption of George Smiths evidence, Augustus Jones thanked the doctor, and excused him.

Twenty One

The Police are no Wiser Than Before

The Deputy Coroner for South Oxfordshire thus addressed the twelve jurors. 'The police have no further evidence pertaining to the case, that at this stage warrants production within this inquest. If the constabulary are of the opinion that the inquiry should be adjourned, I will adjourn it. But feeling as I do, that you the jury will agree with me, it is scarcely necessary for those assembled to wade through the evidence again. It having been thrashed out and there no doubt that the woman had been murdered, by person or persons unknown.'

Now almost a formality following on from the coroner's direction, the jury were duty bound to consider their verdict. The twelve men thus left the kitchen and retired to another room within Lambridge House, said room unspecified in any newspaper.

Those who remained within the kitchen gossiped in hushed tones, and gazed at the witnesses who were sat amongst them. Their fidgeting's to abruptly cease when the jurors, who had not tallied for any considerable time, were readmitted.

Jury foreman, Richard Ovey, so directed by the coroner, intimated that the verdict was agreed to a man. 'We have come to the conclusion that on the night of eighth December, Miss Kate Laura Dungey was brutally murdered, by some person or persons unknown.'

The verdict was in, the time nearing ten minutes past four, the coroner having been occupied with the inquest for a full four hours.

A newspaper correspondent, who had arrived in Henley-on-Thames on the morning of the inquest, and had made his way to the scene of the so called "Henley Murder" (this terminology already in use in numerous tabloids), turned in his story, his thoughts on the matter subsequently to be rehashed in several regional newspapers. "That so far as the evidence given at the inquest is concerned, the police are no wiser than before, as to the identity of the perpetrator of the crime. The authorities have their suspicions, and it must be said that those suspicions have been greatly strengthened by subsequent events. But up to the present nothing sufficiently tangible has occurred to justify an arrest, although this step may be taken at any moment. Lambridge Farm itself is situated in one of the loneliest places imaginable, and it is difficult to understand how a young woman could consent to live there all alone, except for the protection afforded by two little boys and a couple of dogs."

On Wednesday 13th December 1893, at the behest of Augustus Jones, in his capacity as Deputy Coroner for South Oxfordshire, a death certificate, signed by registrar of the district George Albert Stone (inquest juror) was issued to Miss Dungeys next of kin, the details of the certificate unsentimentally to the point. When and where the individual died stated as 8th December 1893, at Lambridge House, Lambridge Road, Henley-on-Thames, R. B. D. Oxon. Name, surname, sex, age and occupation of the deceased itemised as such, Kate Dungey, female, thirty years, housekeeper. The cause of death to stand out as somewhat ambiguous, wilfully murdered by some person or persons unknown, by a series of cuts and bruises received on the head and neck, supposed to be inflicted by a stick, portion of a poker, and a knife or some other cutting instrument. Now all the formalities of an inquest were tidied away, and with a burial order having been issued by the coroner, the shattered remains of Miss Kate Laura Dungey were handed over into the care of her devastated family.

Twenty Two

The Latest Particulars

A paper, aptly titled the Henley Free Press, came into being in 1883; its conception orchestrated by the charismatic Leicestershire born Reverend Joseph Jackson Goadby, from 1874 Minister of Henleys Congregational Chapel. Mr Charles Henry Smith, a paper bag manufacturer, within the Kellys Henley-on-Thames Directory of 1877 itemised as operating out of premises in Duke Street, alongside him Smiths wife, Sarah, not content to sit idle, a manufacturer of umbrellas. By the commencement of the 1880s the Smith's had relocated to "Bath Place" on the Reading Road, Charles, besides his paper bag production, diversifying into paper manufacture and printing, landing the contract to produce the Henley Free Press. Business was good, and in the December of 1884 Charles Smith took a twenty one year lease on the former "Victoria Oil Mills" in Friday Street, his family tenants of a fine property in Queen Street. One of Smiths two stepsons, Frederick Bendy, took on the role of manager of the company's newly acquired factory, located at 35 Friday Street, and it was here that the Henley Free Press was run off the presses, ready to hit the newsstands on Saturdays. Ernest Edwin Smith, son of Charles, had also been trusted with responsibility for another arm of the business, that of Manager of New Mills, which produced paper, no doubt much of which utilised in the production of the Henley Free Press.

The Reverend Goadby relocated in 1892 to minister in Reading (where he died aged seventy, on 23rd March 1898), his paper taken over upon his departure by the Henley-on-Thames Conservative Newspaper Company Ltd, owned by a number of prominent members of the Conservative Party, amongst them the aforementioned Mr Archibald Brakspear, brewer and councillor. Thus forward, with a much altered political stance, the paper relaunched as the Henley and South Oxfordshire Standard, initially printed by Cambridge born, James Baldwin Bryant (a journalist, editor and reporter), of 31 Market Place, the contract subsequently awarded to Thomas Octavius Higgs, whose printing presses where sorely tested during the fall out from the notorious "Henley Murder."

A reporter (posterity sadly not availing us of his name), affiliated to the Henley and South Oxfordshire Standard, had been dispatched by his editor to Lambridge House, on compilation of the inquest this fellow rushing back to his place of work. His notebook brimmed full with the latest particulars that pertained to the murder of Miss Kate Laura Dungey, and her subsequent inquest, after the reporter had sat in on an ad hoc meeting with his editor, he to transcribe his notes. A special edition of the Henley and South Oxfordshire Standard run off the Caxton Works presses (situated in Station Road), to hit the newsstands at seven o'clock of the day of the inquest. The special edition, which had advertised in anticipation of the inquest verdict, was awaited for in town with, as the standard later boasted within the columns of its regular Friday edition. "With intense interest and great excitement."

A multitude of locals, who wished earnestly to possess a copy of the newssheet, had assembled from early evening, converging at an area of Henleys town centre known as the Cross. The snaking queue commenced from outside 1 Market Place, an impressive structure that stood at the turning of Duke Street into Market Place, occupied by Mr William Thackara's "Hair Artist and Stationery Shop". The column of people, in some sections three persons in width, wound its way down the street, half on and half off the pavement, and stretched all the way to the frontage of Mr Sidney Higgins "Book, Stationery, Musical Sheets and Newsagent shop". Indeed the assembled persons must surely have transgressed onto the road, as Higgins outlet was on the opposite side of the street to that of William Thackara's, situated at the top corner of Hart Street, three doors up from the Catherine Wheel Hotel.

Mr Sidney Higgins Book & Stationery Shop
The rounded building at the top end of Hart Street

The chemist's shop of Albert Richard Awbery was operated out of nine to eleven Market Place, he also just about managing to squeeze onto his shop floor, books and stationery, the offices of local paper, the Henley Advertiser situated on the first floor. In the year pertinent to the Lambridge murder, it is likely that the outlet which distributed copies of the Henley and South Oxfordshire Standard was located in close proximity to the Three Tuns, possibly 11 Market Place; this being unusual in so much as that particular address was the administrative hub of a rival paper. Anomalies aside, those whose task it was to distribute the special edition (with no copies known to have survived its cost unknown) were literally besieged by the considerable crowd who had gathered in anticipation of securing the newssheet, a surge of people bursting through the offices front doors. The snatching hollering melee completely enveloping the front office and passage, the assistance of the police, for crowd control, required on two separate occasions.

The next edition of the Henley and South Oxfordshire Standard, which gave itself a pat on the back, duly reported that. "Never before in Henley has there been such demand for papers, and at seven o'clock there was a rush for the first few copies. By eight o'clock one thousand papers had come off the presses, and such was the clamour for copies, the printers were unable to keep pace, another one thousand were printed on that Monday, many sold late into the evening, the rest snapped up first thing Tuesday." The Henley and South Oxfordshire Standard was not the sole locally based newspaper distributed in the area; there were others available alongside it.

Charles Kinch, whose dispensing chemists, stationers & printers outlet, was tucked in between Gabriel Machin and Alfred Lesters butchers in Market Place, died on 20th September 1859, in his forty third year, but he had one who would carry his commercial interests forward. This person none other than Kinch's widow Emma, who having shared fifteen contented years with her spouse, was determined to preserve his legacy. So with the lion share of Charles's assets of seven thousand pounds, the ownership of her late husbands business, not to mention children Charles James, William Herbert, Edwin, Emma Fanny and six year old Charles, Emma had much that would determine her to succeed. The business carried on much as it had before, with the exception of the addition of a circulating library, run out of the first floor.

In 1867, Emma's eldest, Charles (by now working in the chemists), utilised monies accrued through land ownership, and launched Kinch's Henley Advertiser (the word Kinch's soon dropped from the title), the paper, which hit the newsstands on Saturdays, rapidly growing in popularity. In time Charles Kinch determined to quit the town of his birth, he relocating to 8 West Kensington Terrace, Fulham London, where he established a business not far removed from his previous one, in 1886, Charles Kinch, his wife Matilda, and their children, to emigrate to Tasmania. Emma Kinch, advancing in years, and in possession of lands, tenanted houses, and dividends, also took it upon herself to leave Henley-on-Thames, and settled in Lancashire. But that was not the end of the chemists, or the paper, both taken on in 1877 by a new proprietor, a man we have heard mentioned, Wootton St Lawrence born, Albert Richard Awbery.

The Henley Advertiser, Awbery supported the Conservative cause, consisted of eight pages, and dealt with items of both local and world news, much of which shocking and salacious in detail, its issue of 9th December 1893, carrying within its columns several rather gruesome articles. Amongst them the hanging at Reading Goal of wife murderer, John Carter, and the guillotining in Paris of one Pierre Kuntz, for the robbery and mortal wounding of an elderly spinster, his body taken from his place of execution to the School of Medicine. And with the murder at Lambridge Farm fitting in with the mood of the afore mentioned stories, the Henley Advertiser did not shy away from including it in its pages, though the facts were not covered in as much detail as they appeared in the Henley and South Oxfordshire Standard.

The fate of the Henley Advertiser was that it could not ultimately compete with its rival, and the last issue hit the newsstands on Saturday 11th January 1908, its proprietor, Albert Richard Awbery (his first wife Sarah Emma dead more than twenty eight years), dying aged seventy six, on 14th May 1923, his second wife, Mary Sophia, in due course to receive a share of her husband's legacy of just over two thousand two hundred pounds.

The Henley Times was also in circulation in the town in the 1890s (no copies of which seem to have survived), published and printed out of an office located on the corner of Hart Street. Not much is to be found in relation to this paper, and its existence may indeed have only been short lived, and it is not definitive that the Henley Times carried within its columns articules in regards to the murder at Lambridge Farm, though no doubt it more than likely did.

Twenty Three

What I Do Though Knowest, Not Now
But Thou Shalt Know Hereafter

Messrs Frederick James Davis and William George Leaney operated out of a yard to the rear of Holly House on the Cranbrook Road, Goudhurst. These business partners offered their services as decorators, general plumbers, memorial masons, and undertakers, and it was the latter that saw Frederick Davis set out for Henley-on-Thames, on the morning of Thursday 14th December, his journey to conclude at Lambridge Farm.

As she had been since her untimely demise, the mortal remains of Kate Laura Dungey lay within Lambridge House, where her situation as its housekeeper had in life made it an abode Kate much cherished. Plainclothes Sergeant, Thomas Allmond, since the early hours of Saturday 9th December, at the behest of his superior, Superintendent Keal, posted at the farm, his primary duty to protect the dignity of the deceased, against any attempt upon the part of countless ghoulish individuals, who had trekked out to the farm, to peer in through window pane, glazed door or letter box. Allmond had exacted his responsibilities as expected of one so experienced, he had stood vigilantly at his post, only venturing outside once secure in the knowledge that a constable would remain within.

Undertaker and sergeant met at the doorway of Lambridge House, and conversed in hushed tones, those lurking about curious as to the identity of the sombrely attired gentleman. Satisfied as to the man's credentials Thomas Allmond admitted Frederick Davis, he thus conveyed to where the corpse was laid out, Davis to look upon the dishevelled remains of a woman who he had often had cause to exchange pleasantries with, when Kate Dungey had resided at Pattenden Manor. It is not known, at the conclusion of the inquest, if any of Miss Dungeys family had remained on in Henley, or if Kate's father or sisters had selected a dress, and such like, to replace attire which had been blooded and torn. Miss Dungeys body had been coffined by undertaker John Tomalin, of 48 New Street, and this gentleman, on the morning of the ninth, had arrived at Lambridge House in anticipation of Frederick Davis's arrival.

A hearse had been provided by Tomalin for the convenience of Mr Davis, and this man in awe of the gravitas of his task took charge of Miss Dungey. Who knows if any who knew her in life assembled to witness Kate's last departure, but one would like to think that those of Lower Assenden and Henley-on-Thames who knew her best were present, they to utter prays for their lost friend.

As specified in the press (a substantial number of reporters still milling around the farm) Kate Dungeys coffin left Lambridge House at eight in the evening of the fourteen, and in an effort to avoid prying eyes the hearses coachman travelled via Peppard, and onward to Reading Railway Station, at which point the two undertakers parted company. Frederick Davis, fully aware that hacks may still be lurking, in deference to his charge to keep watchful eyes upon the coffin, while it was placed aboard a train on the South Eastern Line, both man and coffin alighting at Redhill, Surrey. With the assistance of several porters the coffin secured within one of the wagons of a train bound for Tunbridge Wells. The railways served the undertaker well, but once at Tunbridge, Davis was met by his company hearse, the coffin conveyed the final eleven miles by road. The hour was late as the horses drew to a halt alongside the central doorway of Pattenden Manor. Miss Kate Dungey met at the entrance by her parents and siblings, Mr Davis to bow his head in deference as his men dutifully carried the coffin on into the house, where the deceass family would sit in vigil for their slain loved one.

During the morning of Friday 15th December the Reverend Thomas Francis Ken Underwood, a bachelor of forty four, busied himself at the Vicarage. His domestic needs met by his housekeeper Marion Benning, who aware of the gravitas of the day spent that bit extra time seeing that her employer was adequately prepared for the ordeal ahead.

On that same afternoon, at Christ Church Kilndown, in the county of Kent (this striking gothic revival inspired church opened for worship in 1841, its build cost met by an endowment of one William Carr Beresford), the funeral of Miss Kate Laura Dungey was set to take place, the arrangements of which carried out personally by Frederick Davis. The circumstances which surrounded the crime, that had robbed a young woman of life, had, as reported by an employee from the Kent & Sussex Courier, who had been dispatched to Kilndown. "Created a deep impression and great sympathy for the parents of the deceased, who were highly respected in the district in which they had lived for many years. And although the interment of Miss Dungey had not been generally known, a considerable number of friends and neighbours had gathered, both in the church and at the graveside."

The parish hearse (presented in 1877 to the Reverend Henry Harrison, as a supplement to the parish pall, the hearse a gift to the parish, donated in memory of Augustine Beresford Harrison, who had died in 1853, up to that point coffins conveyed to funerals by hand, or if available a farm cart. The hearse, which could either be pulled by horse power, or pushed by man power, painted in sombre black, with a wooden white painted cross at its front, and a cross and crown motif along its side) adorned with floral displays, wound its way through back lanes, it apparent that those closest to the deceased had selected to push the hearse, followed on behind by no less than thirty mourners. The weather that day, described in newspaper reports as favourable, encouraged many to leave house and field, and assemble in the lanes, though even inclement weather would not have dissuaded those who wished to bow their heads in sad reflection as the hearse rattled past. Such was the number of those who wished to pay their respects (Walter Dungey insistent that the cart should be slowed to allow all to see), the mourning party, timed to arrive at the church at two o'clock, did not reach their destination until well after that hour.

The hearse which conveyed Kate Laura Dungeys coffin, kept within Christ Church Kilndown, its black paint work and cross no longer in evidence

The coffin was met at the lynch gate by further mourners, Kates mother, too much unnerved by her terrible and sudden bereavement, unable to attend her daughters funeral. The bearers lifted the coffin and placed it with silent deference upon their shoulders, the full gravity of the service they performed etched on their faces. A striking floral token, atop the coffin, observed and commented upon by a reporter. "With deep sympathy from the assistants of W. C. Burgess

& Sons." This being a grocery and drapers located on the High Street, Goudhurst, at the time under the ownership of Frank Burgess, the business was started by his grandfather William Burgess, who had died in the February of that year. As the party, which was led by the father of the deceased and his children, wound its way up the narrow pathway, the Reverend Underwood, and the church choir, who alongside the considerable number of mourners had assembled at the gate, united their voices in a firm and resolute reading of the opening sentences of the Burial Service. "I am the resurrection and the life saith the Lord." The congregation made measured and solemn progress into the church, some of whom greatly affected by the choir and organist, Mr Ernest Harold Melling, rendition of Mendelsohn's aria, "O rest in the lord." The coffin thus placed adjacent to the altar, the woman within silenced of all retellings of her last ordeal. The coffin, as described by a reporter, representing the Kent & Sussex Courier, who had settled himself into a pew, "was of polished oak, with fittings of brass, the inscription on the plate affecting in its simplicity, "Kate Laura Dungey, Died 8th December 1893, Aged 30 years."

The funeral services solemnity was profound; the choirs unified voices reaching the very eves, as they sung, "Lord thou hath been our refuge from one generation to another." Thomas Underwood, firstly having acknowledged the choir with a nod, stepped purposely up to his pulpit, the previous day having written, rewritten and finalised an especially composed lesson, he to speak his words clearly and impressively. Underwood next turned to his bible, which lay before him on its accustomed lectern, and gazing upon the page it lay open upon, he recited psalm ninety (Pray of Moses the man of god), the rendition of which greatly affecting Kates family, this passage personally selected by the Dungeys. The funeral rites, the necessity of which due to the violence of one as yet unknown, was concluded with the hymn, "When our heads are bowed with woe," the congregation then after filing out in silent procession, to the rendition of Handel's "Dead March", played admirably by organist Mr Mellings.

The mourners made their way to the graveside, where the service was concluded, at this juncture the congregation joined by those villagers, who wishing to pay their respects had waited patiently in the churchyard. The singing of the hymn, "Jesus lives no longer now" concluded the contribution of the mourners, their voices seeming to soar up to the very heavens, on that crisp winter day. Then after Kate Dungeys (noted in the press as greatly lamented by those present) mortal remains confined to the earth, within the churchyard of Christ Church, while Reverend Thomas Underwood recited the Burial Service. Kate Dungey now forever lost to the living, to spend eternity interred alongside the grave of two of her siblings who had died in infancy (Kate during her childhood having had cause to lament their passing), Frank, who had left the world on 11th June 1875, aged thirty months, and little Grace Ethel, who aged but six months had died on 12th April 1877.

Those who had assembled that day sought out friend and colleagues alike, groups huddled together in conversation, the employer of Miss Dungey, Mr Henry Mash, accompanied by his wife and daughters, drawing marked attention. Most noteworthy to those of the press, a magnificent display commissioned by the Mashs, which consisted of an anchor of Arum Lilies, intertwined with other white flowers, the card bearing the inscription. "From one who knew her worth best, and valued it most." Almost eclipsed by this extravagant tribute, a more modest wreath lay alongside the grave (as recorded by the representative of the Kent & Sussex Courier), created at the behest of the dead woman's parents, its card having but two words. "Our Kate."

Grave of Walter & Ellen Dungeys children, who died in infancy

Time, as it always must, moved on, and mourners, villagers, and reporters alike drifted away, some to their homes, some to their work, and some to their editor. The churchyard now deserted, save for one (being the reporter in the employ of the Kent and Sussex Courier), who settled himself at the graveside, pencil and notebook in hand. Confronted by the mass of wreaths (forty in all), each with a card, this anonymous fellow carefully selecting a choice few of the handwritten dedications, to be included in his report of the day's events.

"With deep and loving sympathy from the cousins at Middleton."
"With sincere sympathy from Mrs King, 72 Redcliffe Gardens." It would appear that this lady was one Alice King, who alongside her husband, Livino (his monies made on the stock exchange), resided in close proximity to the Mashs London home.

"With heartfelt sympathy, from Mr & Mrs Eedes, Manor House, Goudhurst." This being George Albert and Annie Eedes, who ran a chemists out of "Manor House", on Goudhurst High Street.

"With Percy and Nelly Tompsett's sincere sympathy." Percy Henry Tompsett ran a grocers and drapers on the High Street in Marden, which lay some five miles from Goudhurst.

"From her sorrowing friends, Mr and Mrs Lindridge, Tunbridge." Edwin and Sarah Lindridge, both of whom born in Goudhurst, had retired in 1888, and were at the time of Kate Dungeys funeral living on their own means in Tunbridge Wells. Edwin had previously run a grocers and drapers out of an outlet on the North Road in Goudhurst, and no doubt had in the course of his business known the deceased.

"With deep sympathy from Mr and Mrs Harry Lindridge, Penshurst." Harry and Fanny Louisa Lindridge, he born in Goudhurst, ran a grocers and drapers, located on The Village Road, in Penshurst.

"With deepest sympathy from Messer's Allwork Bros, & Mrs J. Allwork." John Thomas Allwork, alongside his brothers, William Henry (his twin), and Charles Buss, had assisted their father in the running of a grocery and drapery store on the West Road in Goudhurst. Their father, Thomas Allwork, had died in the May of 1892, having had the shop as far back as the 1840s, and John and Charles had taken up the mantle, while William went onto run a post office and grocery outlet in Kilndown. These three young men, the twins born in 1860, and William born in 1863, contemporaries of Kate Dungey, and thus greatly affected by her untimely demise, their mother Jane Allwork also much saddened.

"With deep sympathy from Rose Villa Cranbrook." This property stood on the North Road, and was occupied by Edwin and Kate Usherwood, Edwin engaged in the profession of wheelwright and smith.

Some of the younger members of the Dungey family, who had been scarcely able to get through the trying ordeal of a public funeral, had been fortified by the support and love showed by others, and the Sussex Agricultural Express, of Saturday 23rd December, reported as much. "Mr Walter Dungey, Mrs Dungey, and all the family are deeply grateful to the many kind friends, who from all parts of the country have sent letters of sympathy, and to those who have forwarded the beautiful wreaths. The funeral, occurring under such exceptionally painful circumstances, one wreath, and not the least prized of these, forwarded by the washer woman at Henley (supposed to be the woman who had charge of the cleaning of the linens and clothes, of both Lambridge House and New Street), made out of her own flowers."

Christ Church in Kilndown
Its churchyard the final resting place of Kate Laura Dungey

Walter Dungey did not let his child lie unmarked for long; and once the settling of the grave allowed, the burial spot was graced with a headstone. This monument (no doubt created at the stonemasons of Davis and Leaney) had along its sides intricately carved scroll effect, and at its top an exquisitely carved spray of country flowers. Which members of the Dungey family carried sway over the wording of the epitaph is not certain, but its sentiments spoke volumes, as to the events which had snatched one much loved from the bosom of her family.

"In loving memory of Kate Laura Dungey, who was cruelly murdered without apparent motive at Henley-on-Thames December 8th 1893, aged 30 years. "Faithful unto death", what I do thou knowest not now but thou shalt know hereafter."

Twenty Four

Penny Dreadful

The "Henley Murder" was an incident of the type that grabbed the headlines, in equal measure both enthralling and affronting Victorian society. A true life "Penny Dreadful" (initially known as "Penny Bloods" these cheap, sensational stories, published weekly, were from the 1860s rebranded "Penny Dreadfuls", and dealt with tales of crime and detection, luridly illustrated), the particulars of the crime to rapidly infiltrate many of the country's newspapers, the editors of which primary source material accessed via the Press Association. The news articules that appeared in countless regional papers, differentiate greatly in their quality, some meticulously thought out editorials, others tawdry in the extreme, and riddled with wild assumptions.

The Shields Daily Gazette, which hit the newsstands on Monday 11th December, initially made one fundamental error, that being the portrayal of Miss Dungey as middle aged. This paper, on the most part, derived its information (as did many other local papers) via a Special Representative of the Central News. This shadowy figure, on the Saturday evening of ninth December, had gained admittance to the home of George Dawson, and finding James and Harry Froomes also present, had seized the opportunity to felicitate in-depth interviews with all three. The representative took note of all said to him, and a reporter of the Shields Daily Gazette, having gleaned this information, on the most part from the source material, could neither the less not help but shy away from the pertinent facts, and include within his article the unsubstantiated.

"All three confirmed the fore going particulars of the case, George Dawson said. I left the farm at a quarter past five on Friday evening for my home, about half a mile from the farm, and previous to departing I spoke with Miss Dungey, who then appeared to be in her usual spirits. Soon after ten I was called by Froomes, and having heard the boy's story I went with them to the house. We found all doors locked with the keys inside, we knocked and knocked loudly, at both the front and back doors, and also tapped the window, but got no answer. All windows were fastened, one exception a bay window of a sitting room."

Superintendent Francis Keal had found himself also in the sights of the Special Representative, and once pinned down at a location not specified, he provided the reporter with tantalising snippets, many of which to find their way into the columns of the Shields Daily Gazette.

"The murder was committed between five and eight, probably about seven, as the body when found was quite cold. Robbery was not a motive, as four or five sovereigns were found in Miss Dungeys handbag. The ladies pockets had been rifled, which suggested the murderer wanted something she possessed, and after struggling to obtain it, killed the lady, and rifled her pockets."

The weekly Lancashire Evening Post, which carried the story on page four of its Monday 11th December edition, headlined its feature with a disturbing, and in relation to the scene of the crime, a wholly inaccurate assumption, as to the grandeur of Mr Henry Joseph Mashs weekend retreat.

"The dreadful murder, with the victim beaten to death in a wood, and a mysteries motive, with Henley residents startled by the story of the crime, at Lambridge House, a fine mansion."

It cannot be substantiated, whether palms were crossed with coinage, but much of the information sourced in Henley-on-Thames, which found its way into the newspapers, was of a sort most dubious. In its edition, of Monday 11th December, the Sheffield Evening Telegraph alluded that a broken hedge stake had been found discarded near the body, and proceeded to give very persificic details of the crime scene, and on-going investigation.

"No razor or other weapon, with which the gashes were made, has yet been found, but it is speculated that police have found evidence of a scuffle outside the front door of Lambridge Farm.

They felt Miss Dungey probably run across the lawn, with a view to going down the hill to the nearest houses for assistance, though no individual interviewed reported having heard anything that stirred up alarm.

People who live nearest to the farmhouse state that they saw nobody of a suspicious character about on Friday, nor did they hear any cries for assistance in the evening, but this would be accounted for by their distance from the farm, about half a mile."

The Derby Daily Telegraph, of Monday 11th December, joined the masses, and also led with the murder of Miss Kate Dungey.

"It seems singular that the murderers were not scared by the barking of the dogs, unless they were familiar with the place, and knew there was no possibility of their being heard, and if they were acquainted with the premises it is hard to account for their presence, for, according to all accounts, there was little in the house that would tempt a burglar.

Miss Dungeys friends repudiate all idea of this being in any way connected with a love affair. They describe the poor girl in very high terms. She was of very superior attainments, and besides being well educated, she had many natural attributes, she was musical and played and sang well. The Mashes were exceedingly fond of the young woman, and regarded her more in the light of a member of the family than a servant."

Reports, sourced from hacks who trawled the vicinity of the murder, certainly seized the imaginations of the wider press, and the Derby Daily Telegraph, of Tuesday 12th December, luridly reported on events that were unfolding in the previously tranquil market town of Henley-on-Thames. Under the headline "The shocking murder of a lady in Henley." The feature got off to a bad start, as the victim was incorrectly aged as twenty five. From that point onward the article deteriorating into concoction.

"At site of the body, here fresh evidence of a struggle was visible, the grass being much trampled down, and up to the present the motive for the crime is enshrouded in mystery. But a close examination proved the poor girl had made a desperate fight for life, for in the cold hand of the corpse was still grasped a poker (the poker was in fact found alongside the body), with which she had attempted to defend herself."

The edition of the London Standard, which was circulated the day following the coroner's inquest, paid particular attention to the events that had played out on Monday 11th December.

"Great interest manifested in the inquiry, and there was a large attendance of the public in the vicinity of the house."

The Yorkshire Evening Post, which hit the newsstands on Wednesday 13th December, surpassed all its rivals, with its usage of exceptionally flowery language.

"It is perhaps unfortunate that Doctor Conan Doyle should have killed off the redoubtable private detective, Sherlock Holmes, at a time when his services might prove of the greatest value. We do not allude to the "Ardlamont Murder" (occurred on 10th August 1893, in Argyll, Scotland. A gentleman's tutor, one Alfred John Monson, who having accompanied his twenty year old pupil Cecil Hambrough on a day of hunting, returned later with the dreadful news that his charge had accidentally shot himself dead. His version of events not believed Monson endured a trial, the verdict unproven, though another suspect, one Edward Scott, who had joined the expedition on that fateful day went on the run) which is now being investigated in Edinburgh, but to the horror which has come to blight the Christmas festivities of the Henley people.

The murder of Miss Dungey at present looks remarkably mysteries, though allegations are made which, if proved, may clear up the matter completely. But it is essentially one of those cases which Sherlock Holmes loved to take up, where the science of deduction may fill the gaps of ordinary circumstantial evidence."

We must not forgo the paper which was printed slap bang in the middle of a town, whose populase craved any information that originated from the scene of the crime. Thus, the Henley and South Oxfordshire Standard reported within its Friday 15th December edition that police enquiries into the outrage at Lambridge were being ably assisted by two detectives, though these gentlemen were not afforded name or characteristics.

"The ponds in the woods and at the farm had been dragged, in an effort to discover any item which may have been used as the weapon, which inflicted the most serious of injuries, during the violent assault on Miss Dungey, but the search proved fruitless."

A further snippet of information to provide the Henley and South Oxfordshire Standards readership with a development its rival papers had as yet not been privy to.

"On the window sill of the porch of Lambridge House, a large flint with sharp and jagged edges, weighing about two pounds has been recovered. George Dawson telling a reporter from the Henley paper that he was certain as he could be that the stone was not there the previous day, the item, the reporter stated, possibly placed there by the culprit, to be used during the invasion of Lambridge House."

The Henley Advertiser included within its edition of Saturday 16th December an anomaly in regards to the access points at Lambridge House, including for the benefit of its readership an expansive description of said house.

"The house, which has by the way the peculiarity of having its front door in the back of the house, the front facing N. N. E. The farm is a small one of about 20 acres, consisting of 2 pasture fields, orchards, outhouses, stables, and the dwelling house. The latter building is of brick with a gabled roof. It is one storey high and contains 4 bedrooms, a sitting room, drawing room, kitchen, scullery, and attic."

Within the same issue the Henley Advertiser to touch upon an occurrence that had not been picked up by the editors of other newspapers.

"A circumstance had been mentioned by Mr Tomlins (no man bearing this name appearing on any census), who on Friday evening (the night of the murder), about ten minutes to nine, saw a man running from the road by the back of the Croft. When the man noticed Mr Tomlins he ceased running and walked quickly past him."

On Saturday 16th December the weekly edition of the Cheltenham Chronicle was snapped up by an eager readership, and following the lead of many others gave an account of the "Henley Murder", its features editor adding his own macabre observation.

"The murderer must have hacked blindly at his victim, as owing to the time of the evening he would be unable to see what he was doing."

On the same day as the previous paper the Blackburn Standard was in circulation, and contained within its pages a very individual take (assisted by unsubstantiated gossip, which generated from Henley-on-Thames) on the crime.

"The murder of Miss Dungey remains a mystery, although police are leaving no stone unturned in their endeavours to trace the perpetrator of the outrage. Opinion locally at one time fixed the crime upon a man who resided in the neighbourhood, and his arrest was considered imminent. As a matter of fact he was put through a searching investigation by local authorities, but was able to account for his movements on the night of the murder in a satisfactory manner.
It has become known that the deceased lady, at a recent date, had a quarrel with one of the labourers engaged upon the farm. It appears that late one night a disturbance was heard proceeding from the hen roost, and Miss Dungey went there to ascertain the cause of the commotion. There it was that she discovered one of the farm hands presumably engaged in the theft of eggs. An altercation was the result of this discovery, and it is said that threats were used by the man. He has now, so it is stated, left the neighbourhood, but efforts are being made to trace him."

The Illustrated Police News, of Saturday 16th December, as befit it reputation, carried on page three several spectacularly grim stories, amongst them the execution at Reading Goal of John Carter, agricultural labourer, for the murder of no less than three wives. One Frederick Foster of Market Street, Paddington, also made headlines, he having rushed into the street proclaiming that he had murdered his wife (she found mortally wounded, dying four days later), upon his arrest exacting a daring escape. The same issue also within its columns on page three, turning its attentions to Kate Laura Dungeys untimely demise.

"Between five and eight o'clock on Friday evening a brutal murder was committed at a lone farmhouse in Lambridge Wood, about a mile and a half from Henley, the victim being Kate Dancy (the typesetter incorrectly spelling the surname), governess and housekeeper for several years past in the family of Mr Mash, a fruiterer, of Fulham Road, London, who resides at the farm part of the year. George Dawson, the farm hand in charge, left Lambridge at five o'clock, when he says all was well. About eight o'clock two boys, who always sleep at the farmhouse, went there as usual, but failed to gain admittance, the house being locked up, although lights were burning in the rooms. The two boys waited until ten o'clock, and then returned to the home of their parents, about half a mile distant.

Their parents informed Dawson (it was John Froomes and his sons who raised the alarm at Bix Folly Cottages), and he went to Lambridge with the boys. (This is again incorrect; Amy Dawson had remained at Bix Folly, taking charge of the youngest boy.) He found the house still locked up, and on making a search in the vicinity he found the body of Miss Dancy in the wood nearby, with her head smashed in, the ears cut, and gashes on the neck. (The pattern of injuries described in gruesome detail not altogether accurate.) She was quite dead, and had evidently been murdered some hours previously.

Word was at once sent to the police. Superintendent Keal was soon on the spot, and with a constable entered the house by a window. It soon became evident that the unfortunate woman was first attacked in the house, for there were signs of a struggle in the passage, blood splashes on the walls, and a brooch and hairpins on the floor. Just outside the door of the passage the police found a portion of a heavy cudgel, about an inch in diameter, and another part of it, as well as an iron poker, were found near the body, where it was evident, by the state of the ground, a second and prolonged struggle had taken place between the victim and her murderer.

The police have not yet obtained any clue likely to lead to the arrest of the murderer. Miss Dancy was about twenty six years of age (yet another editorial slip up, she was in fact thirty), and is described as an accomplished young lady. She was the daughter of a farmer at Tunbridge Wells. (Walter Dungey resided elsewhere.) Robbery appears to have been the motive, although nothing was touched in the house. Deceased's pocket was turned inside out; both doors were locked inside, but the sitting room widow was open.

An inquest was opened at Henley on Monday, on the body of the murdered lady, and a man of the name Rathall was arrested during the day, on suspicion of being concerned in the crime. (This last snippet is not altogether accurate, and although a fellow named Rathall had been identified as a person of interest, he had not been taken into custody.)

Also available at the newsstands, on Saturday 16th December, was regional paper, the St Andrews Citizen, its editor somewhat devoid of sensitivity, in regard to what was a dreadful event.

Interest in the French outrage (on 9th December, within the French Chamber of Deputies, an anarchist, one Auguste Vaillant had thrown from the public gallery a homemade bomb, it injuring several of those seated below) says a London correspondent is divided with the "Henley Murder." Here is what seems to promise a murder which for mystery and its local surroundings may take rank with the romance of crime. The lonely farmhouse at the head of the winding road through the silent wood, the personable character of the woman slain, fair, young, highly educated, the evidence of a struggle, as shown by the poker still held in the dead hand, the body lying in a copse. All this reads like the central incident of a novel fashionable in other days. Nay, Miss Braddon (Elizabeth Braddon, a writer of sensation novels, the most popular of which Lady Audley's Secret) herself could scarcely have conceived a better dressed tragedy.

Miss Kate Laura Dungey was not local to Henley-on-Thames, she hailed from Kent, and as such papers circulated in the vicinity of her family home carried within their columns the most poignant of articles, the Saturday 16th December edition of the Sussex Agricultural Express being of no exemption.

"The tolling of our church bell on Sunday morning was the first public intimation that our villagers received of the sudden death of this amiable member of the well-known and much respected family, so long resident at Pattenden, in this parish. On Monday, a perfect thrill of horror ran through the district when, through the medium of the daily papers, the harrowing details of the barbarous murder of the most inoffensive victim became widely known."

It was brought to the wider public's attention, through the medium of the press, that Mr Henry Joseph Mash had offered, through the police, a reward of one hundred pounds to any person or persons, who could provide such information as would lead to a conviction of the murderer or murderers of Miss Kate Laura Dungey.

"A notice was on Saturday posted at Metropolitan Police Stations stating Mr Mashs offer of one hundred pounds reward to anyone, other than a police constable, giving such information as would lead to the conviction of the perpetrator of the "Henley Murder", any information to be given to the Superintendent of the Oxford Constabulary."

The various tabloids and regional broadsheets (included amongst them, the Cheshire Observer, Birmingham Daily Post, Glasgow Herald, Lloyds Weekly Newspaper, Berkshire Chronicle, Illustrated Police News, and the nationals, such as the Times, which carried the developing story in several of its editions), which run the story of Henleys shocking murder, found that their readership bade for more. And as such subsequent articles swiftly descended to the level of being inherently gruesome.

"A small portion of the stick missing at the time has been discovered by the police, we ascertained two teeth found by side of deceased, belonged to the victim."

The Ashford News took a while to catch up with the masses, but in its edition, circulated on Friday 22nd December, the newspaper's editor followed the now familiar tack of fact intertwined with sentiments of the grimmest sort.

"On Friday night a terrible sad and revolting murder was committed near Henley-on-Thames. The victim being Miss Kate Dungey aged thirty, the third daughter of Mr Walter Dungey, a farmer of Pattenden near Tonbridge Wells, and related to several well-known families in the Weald of Kent. Her head had been crushed by a terrible blow, and her throat gashed several times, one wound being almost from ear to ear."

The Penny Illustrated Paper, Saturday 23rd December 1893
Photographs of Lambridge House and murder scene, taken by a Mr Marshall,
from Henley-on-Thames

The greatly unsettled purchasers of the various tabloids, who spread
alarm amongst its readership (in the latter nineteenth century the fear

of being unsafe within ones home at its height, due in no small part to the newssheets insistence of constantly including within its pages, stories of innocent homeowners coming to harm, at the hands of murderous fiends), no doubt took comfort from the fact that police were working on two theories, as suspicious circumstances had subsequently come to light, that may or may not be connected to the events at Lambridge.

"At just past noon on 8th December, a passenger attracted the attention of Railway officials at Twyford Station, the man jumped on the Henley connection, just as it was in motion, indeed it was remarked upon that he had taken no heed of cautionary cries from station staff. It was ascertained that the same man had turned up at Henley Station the next morning, taking the connecting London train from Twyford." (It was not speculated upon, within the news columns why this individual had not been challenged, so soon after news of the events at Lambridge Farm, and subsequent police appeals, in regard to suspicious individuals, having been widely circulated.)
On the Friday of the murder, the time being in the approximate of 8.50pm, a man had been observed running at considerable pace along the road at the top of Friar Park, towards the road that led to Greys Green. Directly the man perceived that he had drawn attention, he dropped his pace to a walk, quickly cleared the corner, and headed in the direction of Badgemore. On the same evening, shortly after eight, a man employed at Henley's Sewage Works (managing engineer at the time, Mr George Renton) was down a manhole on the road near Lambridge House, when he heard the footsteps of a running individual, and the workman assumed that they must be trying to catch the last post. Eventually, when curiosity got the better of him, the man stuck his head out of the manhole, just at the point when the runner, now identified as a man, came alongside him, the witness noted that the mystery figure neither looked at nor addressed him."

Various papers also carried within their pages theories that had been conveyed to them, via those of the constabulary, though it was not stated if any particular police officer had agreed to an interview.

"The constabulary are working on the premise that Miss Dungey was sitting in the kitchen knitting, when the murderer entered the property, via the sitting room window, the ruffian making his way to the stairs with the intention of robbing the upper parts of the house. The unfortunate lady upon hearing a noise which unsettled her taking up the poker and coming from the kitchen to investigate, meeting the man in the passage opposite the conservatory. It is evident that the villainous individual struck her about the head with a cudgel of some description, at this point a desperate struggle taking place, Miss Dungeys blood spraying the floor and walls, marks on the ceiling made by the wielded weapon, possibly a stick. The woman succeeded in opening the front door, as indicated by the bloody marks on the handle, thus running out into the garden, and on through a little iron gate, the other side of which lay open ground, being the left side of Lambridge House, which over looked the road to Bix. The murderous stranger either managed to overtake Miss Dungey, or being close behind struck her about the head, before the terrified woman got the length of the grounds, a blow felling her, the lady collapsing just short of the top of the road which led to the Fairmile Cemetery."

"Miss Dungey was mortally wounded with use of the "Bill Hook", her shattered body left lying just off the path about fifteen yards from the garden gate. The killer must have then returned to ransack the house, locking the front door behind him, becoming alarmed, possibly by the arrival of the two Froomes brothers, fleeing via the sitting room window, leaving an indentation of his boot in the flowerbed, he then crossed the lawn and slipped out of the gate at the rear of the property."

"Four or five Sovereigns were found in Kate Dungeys handbag, nothing seeming to have been stolen, not even a watch that had been placed by the victim on a sitting room chair. (It not proven that Miss Dungey placed her watch upon said chair.) It was however brought to attention by the investigating officer, that the murdered body of the lady had been scrutinised, Miss Dungeys pockets having been rifled, though no attempt had been made to violate the deceased."

Umpteen reporters ambled through the fields and woods and lanes surrounding Lambridge Farm, and knocked upon the doors of any houses they chanced upon. If their various articules are to be believed, the hacks were welcomed by all they encountered, the locals providing them with valuable tit bits. Those who lived within the vicinity of the farm had not seen any suspicious characters about the area on that Friday, nor that evening did they hear any cries for assistance, but it was pointed out that this could be accounted for by the fact that the neighbouring properties were a full half mile from Lambridge Farm.

Those of Kate Dungeys intimate friends, who spoke with reporters, were as bewildered as any, as to why such a grievous thing had befallen one so unassuming.

"None could suggest any motive that could drive an individual to commit such a heinous crime, and they denied she was mixed up in any love affair. Miss Dungey was well known to many in and around Henley, and those whose paths she crossed spoke well of her. And the crime being the predominant cause of conversation and indignation, it drew people to Lambridge Farm, many voicing their heartfelt sympathies for the family and friends of Miss Dungey."

Into the third week of the inquiry, and with no firm resolution in sight, and the police seemingly chasing their tails, some of the more salacious newspapers carried stories that may or may not have had foundation in fact. One well known gutter rag the Illustrated Police News adding a completely new slant to the dramatic events that had unfolded in the riverside town of Henley-on-Thames.

"It was mentioned during the inquest that a letter was received on Friday 22nd December from the Inspector of the Police at Cranbrook, describing a man who had under gone several terms of imprisonment. Three weeks ago this man was in Cranbrook and asked several people if they knew Kate Dungeys address, as he had heard she was managing a farm and might give him a job. It is believed he eventually succeeded in obtaining the desired information. He however left Cranbrook suddenly, and as the police state he had no money, it is thought that if he did visit Henley he walked the distance from the heart of Kent. The communication concludes by describing the man as a very bad character who would stop at nothing to secure his ends. And advices the Henley police to inquire into his doings, if they find him, for the few days previous, or on the very day of the murder itself. Such a communication as this is not to be lightly passed over, and extensive inquiries are being made. It has been discovered, that a man answering in almost every particular to the description furnished by the Cranbrook police, asked in a small public house in Henley, his way to Lambridge Farm House, on the day previous to the murder."

The edition of the Henley and South Oxfordshire Standard, which came off the presses the second Friday after the murder, carried within its pages particulars of the search for any instrument that may have accounted for the injuries inflicted upon Miss Dungey. The paper informed its readership that George Dawsons house and person had been searched for the knife, thought by Doctor Smith to have been used to inflict the fearful wound on the neck. This piece of information steering away from the doctor's original assumption that a "Bill Hook" (this item not alluded to during the inquest) had caused the wound. The local paper testified within its columns that during the inquest Dawson had stated he had a knife which he had not used for many weeks, as he had not worn the clothes in which he usually left the knife, though during a search a knife was discovered in Dawsons home. Superintendent Francis Keal, assisted by two unidentified detectives and Chief Constable, Captain Holmes A' Court, had, the reader was informed, been pursuing all leads, unfortunately with very little success. Though it was reported that a man had informed the police that he heard screams in the wood between six and half past on the night of the murder, but that information would not prove relevant, as the Froomes boys supposedly heard the dying moans of Miss Dungey, and it is thought unlikely she could have lingered two hours with such terrible wounds.

It is fitting, that as far as the press goes, it should be the paper local to Henley-on-Thames that has the last word.

"One witness has the key to the mystery, the two year old Retriever, sent from Goudhurst by Mr Walter Dungey, the dog, if only he could speak, having no doubt seen the villain."

Front cover of the Illustrated Police News, Saturday 23rd December 1893
Depicting in lurid detail the attack upon Miss Kate Dungey

Twenty Five

Town & Hamlet

Two distinctly different locations had been caught up in the fallout from the "Henley Murder", one consisted of two hamlets, primarily occupied by families who on the most part relied on wages earned through agricultural labour, the other a vibrant market town, which supported the livings of skilled craftsmen, brewers, shop proprietors and the like.

At the time of the events at Lambridge Farm the nearby Parish of Bix was reported as being located some three miles northwest of Henley-on-Thames, off the Old High Road, which ran from Henley to Oxford. This was an ancient settlement, in the time of the Anglo Saxons known as Byxe, possibly the Anglo Saxon term for vow. Those who chose to settle at Byxe saw the hamlet flourish, and by the time William the Conquer and his Norman army swept across much of Britain, the hamlet had evolved into two separate settlements, Bixa Brand and Bixa Gibwin.

Assenden had first appeared in records as far back as 800 AD, known as Assundene, the term derived from the language of the Saxons. Assa the word to describe an Ass, Denu the term for valley or vale, thus Assundene was colloquially known as the "Valley of the Ass", which best reflected its farming community. Over time the term Assundene evolved to Afsington, eventually the hamlet known as Assenden, sometime after the end of the Second World War, henceforward known as Assendon.

The Church of St James (a Norman construction) served the Parishes of Bix and Assenden well, but time took its toll, and found to be deteriorating at an alarming rate the decision was made to close St

James (the remnants of the ancient church can still be seen at Bix), and relocate services (with the blessing of Henley Parks tenant Mr Birch) to Assendens school house. This rural community did not find themselves abandoned, and construction of a replacement place of worship was soon in motion, due to the financial generosity of Lord Parker (sixth Earl of Macclesfield), who resided at Shirburn Castle, Watlington, Oxfordshire. The new Church of St James (in the Gothic Style) opened in the September of 1875, ready to serve the Ecclesiastical Parish of Bix, and the hamlets of Lower and Middle Assenden.

The education of the youngsters of this rural idyll was one that had not been universal, children of the poor on the most part unable to access a classroom. All was to change after the aforementioned "Bix Church of England School" opened in 1860, due to the monetary generosity of Mr John William Newell Birch of Henley Park. This flint and brick building (with its distinctive pointed entrance arch) had but one schoolroom, but neither the less it was to offer an education to many, including John Froomes and his siblings. In the 1880s the school was closed, and thus forward was utilised as a service cottage for Fawley Courts Game Keeper, shortly after the new Board School (situated on Bix Common) taking in its first scholars.

Henley-on-Thames, its boundaries expanding, had by necessity to deal with considerable amounts of human waste, and a sewage farm and refuge tip was opened in 1860, near the hamlets of Bix and Assenden (on land donated by Edward Mackenzie of Fawley Court), in 1887 a sewage works outfall opened within Lambridge Woods. The sewage works (which had a fleeting connection to the murderous events at Lambridge House), which must have been an unwelcome addition to the surrounding countryside, remained active until the mid-1960s, when a new sewage farm opened on the Marlow Road.

As in all things, the landed gentry had great influence, and in the summer of 1894, at a sale that saw the disposal of large swaths of land, the principal purchaser was William Dalziel Mackenzie Esquire of Fawley Court, he to take possession of lands around his estate and on into Assenden, thus in all sense and purposes Lord of the Manor.

Henley-on-Thames, by the latter decades of the nineteenth century, had gone through a process of reassessment, the economic fortunes of this market town, built on by its connection to river trade, which had fortified Henley for well over five hundred years. The arrival of the railways (Great Western Railways branch line, running from Twyford to Henley-on-Thames, opened in June 1857), and building of canals had necessitated the rethinking of Henleys future, and the use of the invaluable Thames as a draw for the wealthy, who were turning to the open waters as a leisure activity and escape from urban life. Kellys Directory of 1891 describing Henley-on-Thames as. "The prettiest summer retreat in the county, surrounded by handsome villas and plantations, a very favourite and fashionable place to resort."

This moderately sized market town in the 1890s (a corn and general market held each Thursday) experienced complicated and far reaching contrasts, with a population just short of five thousand, the wealthy to lead privileged lives in fine town houses, the landed gentry residing at their country estates, which lay both within Henley-on-Thames, and its surrounding villages. Fawley Court the country seat of William Dalziel Mackenzie, Rotherfield Court, nestled high above the town on an area known colloquially as Ancastle, estate of William Thomas Makins, Badgemore House, situated on the road to Rotherfield Greys, residence of Richard Ovey. Park Place, a considerable estate, which lay within the Thames Valleys extensive woodlands, in the Parish of Remenham, home to widow Mrs Lily Noble, John Noble having died in the October of 1890. Within the Parish of Harpsden, the ancient manors, Harpsden Court (tenant Robert Raikes) and Bolney Court, both in the ownership of John Fowden Hodges.

The less affluent of the town's population found themselves crowded into small cottages or terraced houses, such as those on Gravel Hill,

West Street and Friday Street, many of whom failing to maintain the status qua, and with large families to provide for, to turn, in moments of dire need, to Henley's workhouse.

Early photograph of Market Place, depicting Henleys Georgian Town Hall

Life for rich and poor alike was unpredictable in the 1890s, illness took no note of class, and many succumbed to the deadly diseases that were prevalent in the last decades of the nineteenth century. The prevention of the spread of highly contagious diseases aided by the completion, in 1892, of an Isolation Hospital, upon land on the Fairmile donated by William Dalziel Mackenzie, the build costs met by William Henry Smith. This structure, which consisted of four blocks with the capacity to house fourteen patients, duly opened by William Frederick Danvers Smith, his father (posthumously bestowed with the title of Viscount Hambleden), having died in the October of 1891.

There was in the Victorian era a consensus, which gained increasing support that a more substantial education should be provided for less fortunate children. In the latter 1850s a school, funded by public subscription, had opened on Gravel Hill, in 1892 a "British School" constructed on the corner of Reading Road and Norman Avenue (build cost three thousand), able to take one hundred and thirty pupils. The children of the upper middle classes were, on the most part, educated at home, the household staff consisting of the indispensable governess, though private schools had begun to appear within Henley. In 1893 Miss Mina Fahy (who hailed from Galway) ran a school out of Laurel House on Gravel Hill, assisted by teachers Ruth Violet Barwell, and Harriett Ellen Cornick. A Miss E. Harris provided education to young ladies, at 40 New Street, and the Reverend John M. Collard educated young gentlemen at his establishment, Friar Park (the present Friar Park a rebuild), located on the top end of West Street. The Royal Grammar School, under the headmastership of the Reverend P. E. Tuckwell, situated at the former Bell Inn, Northfield End, preparing many of its scholars (all of whom male) for the rigours of university.

Henley-on-Thames, by the closing years of a century dominated by the reign of Queen Victoria, had embraced the modern age, it boasted a waterworks (opened in the June of 1882, by 1893 James Dawes the managing engineer), its water sourced from a well, brought to the surface at the Waterworks Pumping Station located at the bottom end of Deanfield. 1884 had seen the introduction of gas lighting in the town, the Gas Companies works in Greys Lane, in 1893 under the management of Harry Alfred Anderson. And the railways, which would have a significant role in the Lambridge murder, brought goods in, and took goods out of Henley, much of which processed in the elegant Gothic inspired sidings sheds. A Daniel Hayes of Station Road, and Thomas Smith of Thames Side, to provide Carmen to collect and delivery goods

Part Three

There is one who has briefly had mention, who from this point onward much will be heard. A young man of meagre means, who survived hand to mouth, his past connection with Lambridge Farm to have much bearing, in regard to him falling under suspicion of involvement in a murder.

Twenty Six

Questioned on a Lie

In the weeks that had preceded the shocking events that had played out at Lambridge Farm, one Walter John Rathall, his wife, Annie, and their infant daughter, Catherine, had booked in at the Red Lion Beer and Lodging House, that operated out of a premises situated on the steeply inclined West Street, in Henley-on-Thames.

Rathall was familiar with Lambridge House and its master Mr Henry Mash, he in the past having toiled on the small farm holding, that was Lambridge Farm. Indeed the young man had had cause to be within the property itself, and had on several occasions had dealings with its housekeeper, Miss Kate Dungey.

The police were much interested in the movements of Walter Rathall, as both James and Harry Froomes, while in the process of providing statements, had informed Superintendent Francis Keal that they had observed Rathall, lurking in the vicinity of Lambridge Woods, the day before the murder. James Froomes, it would seem, had with the encouragement of his father told a police constable that he had seen a man he did not recognise, stood not much distance from the corner of Lambridge House, this mysterious individual deep in conversation with Walter Rathall. Dusk of that same day (Thursday 7th December), while the boy made his way home to take his evening meal, James again spotted Rathall. And later when James, accompanied by his younger brother Harry, returned to Lambridge Farm to sleep the night at the house, both were much surprised to again see Walter Rathall, who with no reason to be in the vicinity, ambled along in the direction of meadows, which lay just beyond the farms outbuildings.

Though a man never as far as anyone at Henley Police Station could recall to have had a brush with the law, the local constabularies attention was now fixed upon Walter Rathall, a constable (his identity unknown), in the course of inquiries, instructed to ascertain the whereabouts of Rathall. Thus the officer called at the Red Lion (how the police came to hear of where Rathall was lodging unclear), his remit to seek out and question Walter. The establishment's landlady, Emily Ayres, conversed but briefly with the constable, and acknowledged that the man he sought was indeed a guest, but at present Walter Rathall and his family were out.

After the ad hock visit of the constable Emily Ayres was much troubled, and when the Rathalls returned, she sought out Walter, who she found in the guests kitchen. Here was a woman never to be described as a shrinking violet, she cornered Walter Rathall, and demanded to know if he had done the terrible murder. The young man, caught off guard, and much perplexed by his landladys accusation, replied in tones most fervent, that he could never have harmed Miss Dungey. But Mrs Ayres was not to be easily satisfied, and questioned Rathall on a lie he had told about being at work that day (the day of the murder), when it clearly seemed to her he had not. The womans patience with her guest by now much stretched, he seemed to her evasive in the extreme, and the fact that Walter Rathall owed money for board did not help his situation. Emily Ayres was not one daunted by much, and sidling up to Rathall she made him aware that her concerns were as a result of a police visit, her earnest wish being that her guest bring his account up straight. Walter Rathall played down the inference of the constables visit, and informed his landlady that as his sister (we will have cause to hear of her later) had generously agreed to forward him money the next day, his outstanding rent would be paid in full.

If, as he fervently testified to his landlady, he was innocent of any wrong doings, Walter Rathalls next course of action set him in a very bad light indeed. In the late evening, of the day of the constable's visit, Rathall requested that the landlord of the Red Lion, Joseph Ayres, wake him early the next morning, by means of a hearty knock upon his guestroom door. Dutiful in his responsibilities to his boarders, Ayres did as requested, at which time Walter Rathall and his family were found to have absconded from the Red Lion, without providing a forwarding address, and owing the landlord money.

Twenty Seven

Landlord and Lodger

Joseph Ayres (born 1836, in Henley) eked out a living as a general carpenter, on 17th July 1858 having taken as his wife, widower Eliza Trimmer (named after her mother, baptised 3rd February 1830), the daughter of William Clements, a labourer. The couple resided within a tenancy, their abode a modest brick and flint terrace cottage in Adwell Place, which ran off from West Hill. Living in a two up two down space was at a premium, and before long parents, there would have no doubt been times when Joseph and Eliza craved a corner of their home that was free off marauding children. The eldest, Joseph, baptised 10th June 1860, at the Parish Church of St Marys, he by the summer of 1865 joined by sisters, Mary Ann and Sarah Elizabeth. A second son, John, was born in 1868, but he was not to surmount the perils of childhood affrication, laid to rest at Henley Cementry on 1st June 1870. His mother Eliza, heavily pregnant at the time, sorely aggrieved at the death of her little boy, going into labour not many weeks following John's funeral, delivered of a girl, Martha Elizabeth. Lack of income paid no heed to the size of a family in the Victorian age, and though there was no doubting the love felt for their children, many poorer parents found the financial burden of countless offspring insurmountable, the Ayres no exception. Alice was born in 1872, the Ayres brood completed with the arrival of Charles Edward, he baptised 13th August 1876. The familys fortunes rapidly diminished, and even with Joseph now employed as a bricklayer (more often than not involved in many building projects, Henley at the time rapidly expanding in size), the Ayres found themselves not able to meet the rent on their tenancy, and thus they took lodgings at the Red Lion Beerhouse.

The eldest of the children, Joseph, had benefit of a sound education (compliments of the National and Industrial School, Gravel Hill), and by the time he quit school, aged twelve, he was fully literate, and in no small part to the efforts of his father able to turn his hand to bricklaying. Barely out of his teens, Joseph Ayres asked for the hand of Miss Emily Wright, and before the Reverend Greville Phillimore the two took their vows at St Marys on 16th October 1881, their nupitals witnessed by John Norcott and Miss Mary Ayres. Joseph's bride throws up something of a conundrum; she seemingly a young woman, who not to have signed the marriage register was illiterate. Emily Wright specified within said register as being twenty one at the time of her marriage, the absence of both her parent's names leaving little hope of establishing the family line of the new Mrs Ayres.

There was to be little time spent as a couple, the Ayres (residing on West Hill) first child, Joseph, born in 1882, this child bestowed with his father's name enjoying but a fleeting time on earth, he laid to rest (barely fourteen months old) at Henley Cemetery on 27th September 1883. The start to married life had been impacted upon sorrowfully by the death of the Ayres first born, and thus the arrival of John Leonard in the spring of 1884 proved a bitter sweet occurrence. Another son, Edward, was born in 1886, a fourth son, George William baptised on 18th January 1888. Childhood mortality had little regard for social standing, though for those without the funds to afford the fees of a doctor the onset of sudden illness often ended badly. George Ayres succumbed to such a calamity, he dying in the November of 1888, duly buried on the tenth, the year following his death Emily delivered of a fifth son, Charles.

William Poffley, landlord since 1884 of the "Red Lion Beer and Lodging House" (with a side line as a bricklayer), relinquished his tenancy in early February 1892, and thus forward Joseph Ayres, who had during his childhood resided at the hostelry, secured the tenancy. So here were the Ayres, now on a much more stable footing, better to provide for their brood of boys, the birth of Alice Mary (baptised 7th November 1892, at St Marys) to provide her mother with some longed for female company.

This property, which stands on West Street, once the Red Lion Beerhouse

West Hill (by the time of the Lambridge affair known as West Street, though many diehard locals still referred to it as West Hill), at the close of the nineteenth century was considered a somewhat desolate and down at heel area, in no small part due to the fact that admittance to Henley Union Workhouse was via the Porters Lodge, that stood but a stone's throw from the Red Cow (another beer establishment), and the Red Lion. West Street had more than its fair share of overcrowded slum dwellings, many of which, by the last decade of the nineteenth century, in deplorable condition, their brickwork crumbling, roofs unsound and sewerage facilities unfit for purpose. Numerous itinerary workers and those who had not the benefit of a tied house, or monies necessary to rent, turned to lodging houses, the Red Lion never to be short of customers. This hostelry, that could be traced back to the eighteenth century or even earlier, a redbrick building of large proportion, with a frontage of some twenty four and a half feet, its depth near ninety nine feet, paying guests squeezed into every available nook and cranny, better to maximise revenue. The Red Lion best described in a sales notice that appeared in editions of the Reading Mercury & Oxford Gazette that hit the newsstands on 5th May, and the June and October of 1866, the beerhouse under lease to brewers Messer's Byles & Co, their contract not due to expire until Michaelmas 1877. The Red Lion, at the time of this sale, boasted five small bedrooms, a parlour, tap room, kitchen, cellar and backyard, with a side entrance and a well, said to provide good quality water. But as with other properties on West Street the Red Lion seems to have let things slide, and after a narrow escape from closure in 1884, in 1892 there was a directive sent, via the Oxfordshire Bench, that the landlord of the Red Lion Beerhouse was duly ordered to thoroughly clean and whitewash his establishment, this upgrade corresponding with the commencement of Joseph Ayres tenancy.

So from the 1890s the Ayres ran the Red Lion alongside nearby rival hostelries, the Row Barge (on the opposite side of West Street, its landlord Joseph Hardling) and the Red Cow, its landlord Walter Norris, he also running a bakery out of his establishment. The Red Lion was comparatively the same set up as described in 1866, but the interior was somewhat altered, guests having four good sized bedrooms and a miniscule one to choose from, as well as the use of two sitting rooms, an additional sitting room exclusively for the use of the landlord and his family. There was a kitchen, boarders permitted to enter, and a scullery with a copper, washing facilities and two WCs, more than likely located within the yard. And thus in the winter of 1893 a previous guest (wife and baby in tow), having on his initial visit found the lodging house to his liking, took one of the smaller and thus cheaper rooms at the Red Lion, his name Walter John Rathall.

Sophia, daughter of John (born Goring Heath, 1770) and Ann Strong (nee Hains, born Checkendon, 1767), was born in Checkendon on 11th March 1798. On Monday 12th June 1820, at St Marys Church, Henley, Sophia (by now residing in Purley) took a husband, one Stephen Eggleton, but through misfortune of sudden affliction, in the first quarter of 1838 Sophia found herself a widow.

On Monday 22nd October 1838 John Rathall (a widower in his thirty second year), who earned a modest living as an agricultural labourer, married Sophia Eggleton, Johns bride some eight years his senior. The ceremony was brief (witnessed by a Thomas Chalk, and Harriett Giles, she residing on West Hill), and as befitting of those of scant income it was followed by a meagre wedding breakfast.

The match was a contented one and the Rathalls in due course took one of a small terrace of properties, Folly Cottages, Bix Folly, Lower Assenden (later home of none other than George Dawson); John finding employment on the farms thereabouts. But the two were destined to be parted, and after nearly twenty eight years of marriage, in 1866 Sophia died. According to the burial register, Sophia Rathalls (aged seventy at death, though this does not tally up with her supposed year of birth), mortal remains laid to eternal rest at St James Church, on 27th May, thus leaving her widower without a wife for a second time, and with no children from either of his marriages quite alone in the world.

Mary Dyer, born in Lower Assenden on 3rd January 1826, was baptised 12th February at the Wesleyan Church, Reading. Mary was a daughter of Joseph (baptised 22nd June 1788, aged twenty eight days, at St James's Bix, his father, also Joseph, a shoemaker by trade) and Jane Dyer (nee Green, born 1793 in Henley-on-Thames), the two having married at St Marys, on 29th May 1812. Young Mary (her father a shoemaker, her mother a nurse) was never hard pressed for playmates, having numerous brothers and sisters. Joseph born 7th May 1813 (his father at the time an inn keeper), swiftly followed by Emma and William. The first born, Joseph, did not fare well, he dying aged five, just over two months following Williams birth, the little boy buried 28th June 1815. The two surviving siblings, some years Mary's elder, no doubt at times finding the playful attentions of their sister somewhat irksome. The last child born of Jane much more suited in age to Mary; Hannah delivered 13th December 1821, in no small part due to the stalwart efforts of the local midwife. Mary Dyer was grateful that through her formative years her sister Hannah and father were present, but this did not in any way diminish her grief upon their deaths. Hannah to die aged thirteen, in the April of 1835 (buried on the twenty ninth), Joseph passing away in 1853, the Dyers bidding him an emotional farewell at his interment at St James's on 27th February.

Mary Dyer, mindful that she had no father to accompany her up the aisle, took a husband, Assenden based labourer John Herridge. In 1855 Mary to give birth to Joseph Alfred, he baptised on 13th January at St Mary's, Henley. Two daughters to follow, Rosa baptised on 1st November 1857, Emily Jane baptised 5th September 1860. The 1861 census saw the Herridge's living on the cusp of the Fairmile and the hamlet of Assenden, Mary earning what she could through dressmaking (it probable that her husband worked within a flour mill, located at Mill End, Hambleden, his employer widower Mrs Augusta Barnett), the family purse somewhat aided by the wages of relative and lodger, fourteen year old William Dyer. But misfortune again visited upon Mary, she before the year following the census was spent a widow, John Herridge buried at St James's on 3rd September 1862.

How John Rathall and Mary Herridge came upon each other we can only conjecture, but whether it was down to attraction or financial necessity, in the first quarter of 1868 John took Mary as his third wife, he sixty two she forty two. The Rathalls chose to live in Bix, John, who had not experienced parenting, taking on Marys two daughters (Joseph while still in his early teens having taken up a position as a gardener's lad, lodging at the home of Thomas, an agricultural labourer, and Anna Smith, at Wrecclesham Bridge, Farnham Surrey.) Rosa and Emily's life choses much dependent upon their modest financial status, the latter of whom going into service, her master John Davis, landlord of the White Hart, Hart Street, in Henley-on-Thames.

Though Mary Rathall was approaching her mid-forties she was delivered of two further children, Amy Katherine born in the early months of 1868, Walter born 15th April 1870, he baptised 7th August, at St James's. John Rathall, a father of great maturity, being sixty four when Walter arrived, regardless of his age still working the land, while Mary sewed for a living. The family muddled along together, and Rosa, having walked out with one Walter Thomas Frederick Rawlins (son of Edward Joseph Rawlins, Schoolmaster of Henley Lower Grammar, Hart Street), married on 3rd April 1877, at St Matthew, St Pancras Camden, the groom twenty the bride nineteen.

John Rathall was not to outlive a third wife, he dying aged seventy five in 1881, at his home in Lower Assendon, duly buried in the small cemetery at Bix on 11th September. Mary was again widowed, but there was hope on the horizon with the offer of a live in position as housekeeper of Lambridge Farm, at the time held by tenant Henry Joseph Mash, young Walter and Amy permitted to join their mother.

Mary Rathall immersed herself in the various tasks required of her at Lambridge House, but illness, namely problems with her back, was eventually to limit Mary's capacity to meet her obligations to Henry Mash, and with mutual agreement Mary Rathall relinquished her role. But Marys employer was a kindly man, much aware of the limitations of those without profession, or funds, and he saw to it that she was not left destitute, by the closing years of the 1880s Mary Rathall residing at 64 Old Coach Road, Lower Assenden, in the care of her daughter. Emily, like her mother before her having chosen a considerably older partner, there being thirty years between her and her husband, jobbing carpenter Robert Parker.

For Mary Rathall life seemed on a firmer footing, but she was to suffer what is the worst a mother can injure. In early 1889 her daughter Rosa, who resided alongside her husband Walter (working as a commercial traveller) in Sussex, died, the young woman aged but thirty one, on 21st March buried in South Bersted, it of note that Rosa's widower remarried on 14th June 1900, his second wife one Ellen Waters. More misfortune was to follow with the loss of another child, Mary's son Joseph. A married man who provided for his wife Sarah through his earnings as a domestic gardener to one William Snell (a retired barrister, who resided at Belmont House, Bedhampton Hampshire), Joseph Herridge at some juncture decided to move to Southampton to better utilise his gardening skills. And here in his little home on Ranlagh Road in Havant, Joseph died on 13th July 1890, aged thirty five, his young widow inheriting a small legacy of sixty one pounds.

As for Walter Rathall he went into service as a groom at Crookmore House, Fawley, Buckinghamshire (the country retreat of Douglas William Graham), and in the course of his duties met one Annie Long, the households cook and domestic. How Annie came to be working down south is unclear, she born 1867 in Hereford, the daughter of William (born 1840 in Hereford, Herefordshire), and Ann, born 1850 in Little Hereford. Life was not easy for the family, William finding himself often without work, the young Annie and her sister Alice (two years her younger), residing with their parents and grandmother Margaret Long, in one of the Lazarus Hospital Almshouses, located on the Whitecross Road, Herefordshire. These properties, modest in size, originally constructed to provide housing for sick woman, later to be utilised for the maintenance of twelve poor people, one wondering if the managing agents turned a blind eye to the influx of Margaret Long's family. Eventually things took an upward turn, and the Long's found themselves living on Little Berrington Street in Hereford, St Nicholas, William a coach wheeler, fourteen year old Annie in service, two other families, the Nicholas's and the Parchins sharing the premises.

Walter Rathall was to quit service in favour of employment as a labourer, and he and Annie (who up until her marriage remained at Crockmore House) wed at St James's, on 8th October 1891. The ceremony very much an intimate affair (witnessed by Charles Young, a baker and grocery assistant who resided alongside the Old Toll House in Bix, and Mary Spyers, wife of agricultural labourer Thomas, the couple occupying a cottage at Bix Hill), the congregation made up on the most part by direct family and a few close friends.

Walter Rathalls mother (who though infirm had attended her sons wedding) died aged sixty five, the following March, duly buried on the eighteenth in the churchyard of the recently built St James Church. Life had been a challenging journey for Mary Rathall, and with her time on this earth done with she was not to see the arrival in 1893 of her grandchildren, Emily and Roberts first born, Violet Mary, and Walter and Annie's daughter, Catherine Mary, both of whom taking their late grandmothers name. Nor was Mary Rathall to witness the tangle that her son Walter would entwine himself in, following the visit of a certain constable to the Red Lion Beerhouse.

Twenty Eight

They Will Never Find That Out

Early, on the morning of Monday 11th December, Walter Rathall walked but a short distance down from the Red Lion; and once adjacent to a foreboding wrought iron gate he rang the workhouse bell. This resulted in the emergence of the Gate Porter (this role carried out by Mr George Moss), who having ascertained the validity of Rathalls request duly admitted into the workhouse Walters wife and young baby.

Annie Rathall was not unfamiliar with the workhouse system, with a journeyman husband who trod the roads in search of a living, the young woman had before now found herself under the care of a workhouse, though now as a relatively new mother she also had her infant daughter Catherine to consider. Upon admittance it was mandatory that Annie relinquish her clothes, which were itemised and locked away, she then, as many times before, provided with a uniform (handmade by fellow inmates), and when meal times came around a bowl of gruel or broth. But there was no such thing as a free lunch, and as such Annie Rathall was expected to work for her supper, either in the sewing room, laundry, or caring for those unfortunates who arrived unwell, or fell sick within the workhouse.

Henley Union Workhouse had begun life in 1790, a substantial brick construction (that stood tucked back from West Street, just down from the Red Cow Beerhouse), designated as a better alternative to its fore runner, which had operated out of a row of cottages, located in New Street. Administration of a workhouse was placed in the capable hands of a Board of Guardians, individuals (all of whom male) who made up this group carefully selected by local Justices of the Peace.

Guardians on the whole led privileged lives (at the time in question Henleys Guardians, George Edward Brakspear, Frederick Holmes, Alexander Graves, William Dalziel Mackenzie, Sir Francis Stapleton, Colonel William Thomas Makins, Robert Trotter Hermon Hodge, Robert Napier Raikes, Henry Brigham Vanderstegen, said members to hold meetings within the workhouse every alternate Tuesday), and possessed incomes beyond that which those under their care could ever hope to attain.

Annie Rathall bore witness to the evolution of care that had shaped Henleys workhouse, which at a push was able to accommodate up to three hundred and eighty two inmates. The workhouse had benefit of upgraded sanitation, schoolrooms (school mistress, Miss Elizabeth Courtney, had in December 1893 resigned her position), an infirmary, contagious diseases ward, and ten acres of gardened land, the pastoral care of inmates under the dutiful eye of the Reverend William Chapman, who resided at 3 Caxton Terrace, Station Road.

Relieved of the burden of his wife and child, Walter Rathall made haste to Ealing, Middlesex, no doubt his journey a combination of walking, and catching a lift from any passing cart or wagon. His destination a lodging house (where he and his wife had on occasion resided), 42 Bedford Road, occupied by old acquaintances Tom and Maria Brown.

The Browns were surprised indeed by the sudden unexpected appearance of their intermittent tenant, but welcomed him in neither the less, Maria, concerned at Walters bedraggled state, rustling up a plate of cold cuts and bread for her hungry guest. When Rathall had last resided with the Browns he had placed two boxes into their care, and after an interlude filled with pleasantries, Walter Rathall took the conversation around to the subject of his boxes, which duly extracted from where they had been stored were handed over to him.

One of the boxes proved of particular interest to Walter, and he snatched off its lid and pulled from it a pair of trousers. He then fell upon the second box, which he quickly opened and racked through; drawing from the box a buddle of his wife's and babies clothes, informing his friends that he intended to take away with him those garments he felt would raise a bob or two at a ragshop.

It seems that Walter Rathall spent some days grateful of the Brown's hospitality (though he would often be out of the house for hours on end), but after he had breakfasted on the morning of Monday 18th December, Rathall took his leave, to again trudge the roads, on route back to Henley-on-Thames.

So who were the couple who had been such generous hosts to Walter Rathall, well though Tom and Maria Browns family heritage proved somewhat of a tangle, I am as certain as I can be that I have gone someway to unravelling it. Christopher Francis Crook (born Harefield, Middlesex, baptised 20th February 1814, at St Mary the Virgin) took employment as a labourer working within the copper industry, Harefield well known in the nineteenth century for its sheet copper works, much of the metal it produced supplied to the Royal Navy. Crook was married to Elizabeth (nee Farmer), who two years her husband's elder hailed from Savernake, Wiltshire. The marriage was content and productive; during the 1840s four children delivered of Elizabeth, William, the eldest, born 30th November 1840. Frances Emma was born in 1842, Daniel in 1845, the youngest, Maria, baptised 27th June 1847. The Crooks, in need of a more substantial abode, took a property on the High Street, and by the latter 1850s Daniel worked alongside his father.

The youngest of the family, Maria took, on 25th July 1869 James (son of William Sutton) as her husband, and by the following spring, the newlyweds residing in Uxbridge, Frederick William was born. Twenty third March 1873 saw the baptism of the couple's second child, Frances Emma, and all was well, though some time in the 1870s things were to take a dark turn with the death of James.

So what was to become of a widow with two young children, the answer being the help of a family member, Maria Sutton turning up on the 1881 census living alongside her aunt, mutually widowed Maria Franklin, a lady in her sixty second year who earned a pittance in domestic service. Her niece Maria earned a cooks wage (a day servant, who worked under the head cook), the two women, combining their salaries, able to afford the rent on a terraced property, 4 Kerrison Place, Ealing Old Brentford, in Middlesex.

But a life of widowhood was not for Maria, and she in due course walked out with Thomas Brown, so what of Thomas, or Tom as he preferred to be known. He was born 1840 in Dunstall, Burton upon Trent, in Staffordshire, the son of John Brown (born 1789), whose job as a bricklayer provided adequately for the rental of a property on the Main Road. Though it is to be noted that a John Brown (also born 1789), appeared before the County Sessions in Staffordshire on 7th January 1835, on a charge of larceny (theft), and found guilty received seven days in prison. John Brown's spouse, Rebecca (born 1802 in Dunstall), was more fortunate than many others of her gender, she not to endure the perils of multiple childbirth, she, besides Thomas, giving birth to Joseph in 1838, and Fanny, she born in 1843. As of many lads finished with schooling while still tender in years, and requiring of a trade, both Joseph and Thomas learnt at their fathers side, before long competent bricklayers in their own right.

So Maria Sutton extracted a proposal from Tom, and with the nupitals concluded relinquished her former surname, henceforward Mrs Maria Brown, she, Tom, Frederick and Frances securing a rental not a stone's throw from Aunt Maria, 8 Kerrison Place. Many incomes were necessary to keep the household up straight, Tom bricklaying, Maria a laundress, Frederick a general labourer, and Frances working as a domestic cook. Circumstances changed and the tight family unit that was the Brown's vacated their property at Kerrison Place, moving onto 42 Bedford Road, Ealing.

On his long arduous walk back to Henley-on-Thames Walter Rathall was accompanied, the two having come across each other just outside Maidenhead in Berkshire, by a tramp who was, as happenchance would have it, heading for Henleys workhouse. The man (as with many who through misfortune found themselves on the road, not to be afforded a name), who spent much of his life out in the elements away from easy acquiring of a newspaper neither the less well versed in the latest news, and breached the subject of the so called Henley Murder. The conversation between the two became quite intense, the tramp voicing his eagerness that a man should be brought to book for the crime, his walking companion on hearing this declaring quite adamantly. "They will never find that out!"

The men walked down the steep incline that was White Hill, crossed Henley Bridge, and continued on into the town centre, and here they said their goodbyes, and parted company.

Life as a vagrant was one of great challenges, any individual who had fallen into this trap of severe poverty often only one step ahead of total ruin. Admittance into a workhouse provided the necessary to hold body and soul together, but the experience was not one to be relished, the tramp, that fell in with Rathall, having proved that he was not in possession of any money or had about his person any food, permitted admittance to Henley Union Workhouse. The tramp would not have found himself within the standard ward, but instead escorted to the Vagrants Ward (built in 1866), where he had to endure the disinfectant bath, his ablutions overseen by the Gatekeeper, any females in the same predicament bathing's witnessed by the Gatekeepers wife. The tramp, or vagrant (this title often banded about), was thus fed and given a bed for the night, the cost of his meal offset by some form of manual task

Henley Union Workhouse, its white foundation stone bearing the inscription
THIS HOUSE WAS ERECTED A.D. 1790

Before the tramp again took to the open road (limited by legislation to a stay of only one night), his mind much occupied with the man he had met on the road from Maidenhead, the tramp sought out the Workhouse Master, at the time this role filled by fifty two year old Chatham born John Martin. So distracted was the man of the road that Martin, having taken leave of his wife Sarah (Workhouse Matron), spoke at some length with the tramp. The tramp unburdened himself, and the weight of the information now laid squarely on the shoulders of John Martin, who in turn communicated what he had heard to the Chief Medical Officer of Henley Union Workhouse, the protractedly named Doctor Egerton Charles Augustus Baines, a man of forty, who hailed from Eastwell in Leicestershire. Baines did not miss the inference of what he heard, and by use of a lad, who carried out menial tasks at the workhouse, sent word to the local constabulary. Doctor Baines did not share the hardships of his destitute patients; he residing with his wife Rosina and twin daughters, seven year old Clara and Audrey, at a fine townhouse, 78 Bell Street. The family waited on by a housemaid, parlour maid, and cook, the girl's education under the care of governess Caroline King. And one can only imagine that upon his return home that evening, Egerton Baines was full of tales of the startling events that had played out within Henley Workhouse.

Twenty Nine

Lynch Him

Walter Rathall, on Wednesday 20th December, gained admittance, via the Porters Lodge, to Henley Workhouse, and with all regulatory procedures dealt with extracted his wife and child. The three, Walter (little knowing that a certain tramp was to, before long, drop him right in it), mother and child (sorely tested by their ordeal) swiftly leaving the area. The means of their journey, though never to be speculated on, more than likely involved the party travelling on the most part on foot, possibly availing themselves of a passing cart. Rathall, with money enough (much of his wife and babies scant supply of clothes now in the possession of a ragman), during the early morning of Wednesday 3rd January 1894 to take a room at a lodging house in Daventry, North Hampshire.

How much of the furore which had erupted around the location of Walter Rathall the man himself was aware of is pure conjecture, but with appeals in relation to Rathalls whereabouts included within the columns of countless newspapers, Walter Rathall surely must have had inkling that he was a wanted man. The trail was a hot one, and with barely any time to settle in at their digs, and unbeknown to the Rathalls, Daventry's constabulary, with information provided one would think from the landlord of the lodging house, were hot on their heels.

Harry Webster, as Inspector of Daventry Police Station, New Street, acted immediately when via his desk sergeant he heard tell of the strangers who had taken a room. With little regard to protocol he set off in haste, to ascertain the identity of a man and his family, who did not seem to have any perceivable reason to be in Daventry. Webster slipped quietly into the lodging house, so as not to draw attention, and after conferring with the landlord of the establishment determined that his new guests were to be summoned from their room by use of some subterfuge. With their landlord spinning some tale (goodness knows what ruse he and Webster concocted), Walter Rathall, wife and child, thus found themselves in the presence of Inspector Harry Webster, who asked of the man his name, John Brown the name given, causing Webster to raise a wry smile. The tension was almost sentient as Webster paused some moments to scrutinise those stood before him, and with his next move decided the inspector informed the young man that it was his belief that his name was in all probability Walter Rathall, and he was required in Henley to answer criminal allegations. The man stood before Harry Webster would have none of it, and insisting his name was indeed John Brown demanded that the inspector verify the fact with his wife. Having done as requested of the stranger, Walters attempt at deception came abruptly to an end, when Annie bluntly asserted that she was Mrs Rathall.

To immediately apprehend was the only course now open, and Walter Rathall, given no time to evade capture, was seized, handcuffed, and confined, alongside his wife and infant daughter, in a side room. While Inspector Webster sent the lodging house landlord (by this point totally engrossed in the drama) again to the police station, to fetch back a constable.

The journey through Daventry raised eyebrows, those who gazed upon the group ignorant as to the identity of the man handcuffed to a constable. Upon reaching the police station the Rathalls placed under lock and key, Walter and his spouse whispering in anxious tones, their baby oblivious to all. A telegram was hastily composed for the attention of Superintendent Francis Keal, and with a constable sent scurrying off to the post office, those within Daventry Police Station nervously awaited a reply. It was not long after, with an arrest warrant secured, that Superintendent Francis Keal found himself commencing a train journey, its conclusion a railway station situated on the east side of Daventry. Inspector Harry Webster met the train that carried aboard it a fellow officer of the law, and once at the police station, with all legal formalities attended to, the prisoner was passed into the care of Superintendent Keal. Thus Francis Keal, Walter Rathall, Annie and baby Catherine, boarded the next available train, which would in due course see them back in Henley-on-Thames, a town that but a few days since Rathall had fled.

Indiscretion is a powerful force, and word was out, and though it had not been generally known that policeman and prisoner would arrive by train, a large crowd of excited and highly charged locals gathered on the platform at Henley, peering searchingly at any who alighted from the Twyford connection. Something was going to happen, the mob was sure of that, as they found themselves driven back to the entrance of the station, hedged in by a contingency of six policemen, whose (with their truncheons at the ready) role it was to prevent a breach of the peace. And after a journey, which had involved the stares of both startled and intrigued fellow passengers, and the running for connections, the party of four pulled in at Henley's railway terminal at seven thirty in the evening, the cuffed prisoner, under the watchful eye of Superintendent Francis Keal.

The man, who pinpointed as one of interest to the police, and thus the source of much speculation and conjecture, emerged from the railway station, his outward appearance in all sense and purposes somewhat unremarkable. Walter Rathall was a fellow of slender build, his height being not much greater than five feet seven inches. His complexion (no doubt in some part due to the predicament he was in) was pale, and as such his large dark eyes appeared much evident. Rathall boasted a crop of dark brown hair, and if his features had not been obscured by stubble he would have been noted as attractive. This character was in all evidence a man who had not been blessed with an income worthy of note, and his clothes, a jacket of tweed and trousers, which sported a striped design, were much worn, his boots, after Rathalls days trudging the highways, in somewhat of a sorry state.

Henley Railway Station in the 1890s
At its entrance Walter Rathall met by a consignment of police

One enthusiastic Representative of the Press, who mingled amongst the crowd (his article to be rehashed in umpteen papers), turned in a somewhat lurid account of Rathalls reception at Henley. "A report had got abroad that the man was expected, and despite the cold and snow the majority of Henley's inhabitants turned out to meet the train. From Henley Railway Station to the police station is a good half mile walk, and the crowd followed the suspected man, and hooted him to their hearts content, all along the route of the procession. Rathall, who was surrounded by four policemen, seemed to ignore the existence of the populace, and he marched boldly forward, giving little or no trouble. He turned somewhat pale once, when someone shouted out lynch him, and an ugly rush was made towards him, the police were however able to cope with the disturbance."

The prisoner was indeed taken on foot to Henley Police Station, followed closely by the considerable crowd, some of whom had firstly assembled at the railway station, others having joined the melee on route. Once admitted to the station, the rabble milling around its exterior, the group advanced to the charge room, at which stage the prisoner, not having the benefit of gloves, walked under his own steam to the fireplace, and warmed his cuffed hands.

It is evident that several reporters were admitted to the inner sanctums of Henley Police Station, as a reporter, whose feature piece made it into numerous newspapers, conversed with the prisoner. 'I suppose it was very cold travelling?' Rathall, the reporter recalled, to turn in the direction of his questioner and reply cheerfully. 'Oh that it was sir, I am glad it is all over I can tell you.' At which stage a constable stepped forward and removed the prisoners Ratchet Mechanism handcuffs, a fairly new device, which could more easily be snapped onto a suspects wrists. 'Ah, that's better.' Rathall exclaimed, the reporter, who had made conversation, to note that the prisoner rubbed his wrists to take away the smarting from the effects of the cold metal. The constable had not quite finished with Walter Rathall, and at this stage his boots (with their distinctive nailed soles) were removed, upon the orders of Superintendent Keal, thus logged in as evidence.

As it had initially been the intention of the police to obtain a formal remand for Walter Rathall that morning, and up to two thirty in the afternoon of the day of his arrest a County Magistrate having not been obtainable, the late hour dashed all hope of securing a magistrate. The suspect, his wife and infant child (who had made their way separately to the police station, under the protection of a constable), constabulary, and newspaper hacks, all held in an inescapable limbo.

Thirty

Master of Rotherfield

Walter Rathall, suspected of a capital offence, and with the additional burden of a vocally hostile crowd, which had converged outside Henleys police station, spent an uncomfortable two days confined in a cramped cell, the whereabouts of his wife and daughter unknown. The sticking point was the lack of a magistrate to examine the evidence against the prisoner, but after a chaotic flurry of activity the desired outcome was accomplished. Ironically the man in question one William Thomas Makins, who resided but a short jaunt from where Rathall sat dejected, upon a hard unyielding wooden bed.

Though the police station where Walter Rathall was incarcerated is now an eatery, the cells remain in situ, all of which grade two listed

Charles Makins (born 1793, Thorne, Leeds) married on 7th September 1837 (at the Parish Church of St Peter), Frances, she born 1807, the daughter of Leeds based banker Mr Thomas Kirkby.

Makins, a man by the time of his marriage in his forties, desired nothing more than the chance to be a father, and this earnest desire was granted, with the birth on 10th March 1840 of William Thomas. The boys early childhood spent at Kingston Place (a row of elegant three storey terraced townhouses), Leeds, in the company of his younger brother, Henry Francis (baptised 1st September 1841), the second and last child of the Makins union.

William Makins enjoyed the advantages that came with privilege (his father a highly successful proprietor of tenant houses), and in due course he was enrolled at Harrow. Those who secured the best school places invariably attended the top universities, William no exception, going up to Trinity College, Cambridge, to read law. William Makins to graduate at the age of twenty two, shortly then after called to the Bar at the Middle Temple, London, subsequently to practice on the Midland Circuit.

Makins lineage allowed him to move within society, he to hobnob with those considered gentleman. As such William on numerous occasions sat at the table of Mr Lightly Simpson (born 1811, in Tadcaster, Yorkshire, Chairman of the Eastern Railway), who resided at 25 Gower Street, St Giles. The second daughter of the family, Elizabeth (baptised 31st August 1835), to catch Williams eye, and with her father's blessing, on 3rd July 1861, at St Mary Magdalene, St Pancras, the two were wed.

The newlyweds at first took a house at Boyne Hill near Maidenhead (a second residence at Holland Park, Kensington), but relocated to Henley-on-Thames in 1872, upon purchasing Rotherfield Court from a certain Mr Vernon Benbow. This property (which still stands) constructed in the Gothic style, built in 1861 (from the designs of Mr Henry Woodyer of Oxford, a well-known architect of Anglican churches), at the behest of Thomas Baker Morrell, Rector of St Marys. Though Rotherfield Court was a substantial house it was quickly enlarged by the Makins, to better suit the tastes of the day. Thus, once modifications were completed, it boasted a grand hall, library, billiard room, dining room, an oak panelled drawing room, enhanced grounds, and glasshouses.

There was certainly no argument that a sizable home was required, Mary Elizabeth had been born the year following her parent's marriage, William Henry had arrived in 1864, followed in quick succession by Francis Kirby, this little boy, born 28th July 1865, buried at All Souls Kensington on 1st September of that same year. Agatha Caroline was born 1867, then after Basil Thomas, Veronica Luce, and Paul Augustine, he born in 1871, all his siblings (with the exception of Basil, who was born in Maidenhead) delivered at Holland Park. Oscar Matthew was the only offspring of the Makins born at Rotherfield Court, delivered in 1872, his sister, and last born, Audrey Katherine, making her debut in 1875, while her family were residing at their London home, 1 Lowther Gardens, Princes Gate Kensington.

The census of 3rd April 1881 indicated that William and Elizabeth Makins kept abreast of London society, and spent much of the season at their London address, accompanied by their daughters, the sons of the family away at school, boarding at "The Beacon School", Worthey, Nottinghamshire, under the pastoral care of its headmaster, Thomas Lockwood.

At this juncture one must briefly consider the Makins town house, a generously proportioned property, kept upright by an array of domestics. The Makins daughter's educational needs met by governess Ellen Scott, while butler William Pattison, orchestrated the smooth running of the household. Upstairs staff consisted of footman William Newett, housemaids, Elizabeth Viney, Louisa Witt, and Elizabeth Wootton, while ladies maids, Elizabeth Blackburn and

Cecila Pigden, saw to the needs of the ladies of the household. Below stairs, cook, Ellen Cracknell, created fantastical meals, assisted by kitchen maid, Maria Eaton, poor Elizabeth Illesley, bottom of the run, toiling away in her role as scullery maid.

William Makins never having felt the practice of law his lifelong vocation diversified in 1883, he securing the position of Director and Governor of the Gas and Light Company. This company the first gas undertaking in the world, up until the 1880s concerned mainly with the production of gas for lighting, many gentlemen, including Makins, becoming very wealthy on the companies proceeds. Alongside the former, William Makins also selected, due to his father in laws influence, to serve as Director and Deputy Chairman of the Great Eastern Railway.

Like many gentlemen who possessed the financial accruement to do so, Makins interested himself in politics, a man of Conservative persuasion, selected to stand in the Kidderminster seat, for the 1868 Parliament, he losing at that time, in 1874 returned as MP for South Essex. William Makins to hold this seat until the 1885 Redistribution of Seats Act, he then after elected for South East Essex, 1886 to see Makins elected as MP for Walthamstow, a seat he held until 1892.

The Makins did of course have a country seat, and the master of the house took to life within the small community of Henley-on-Thames with gusto. William Makins, clearly a man canny in matters financial (itemised within the 1873 Register of Property as owning properties in Henley to the rental value of £185.10s), investing some of his enviable income in the enhancement of the Parish Church of St Marys, while Elizabeth busied herself with charitably endeavours. This devoted couple deeply affected by the death, on 1st December 1889, of their first born son, twenty four year old William Henry.

So here was William Makins, by now a resident of the area for over twenty years (with such diverse roles as Honorary Colonel of the First Essex Military Volunteers, Justice of the Peace for Oxfordshire and

Essex, and Deputy Lieutenant for Essex, Oxfordshire and the City of London), summoned to attend a Police Court, in the matter of Walter John Rathall. Makins had torn down from his London address, when a telegram requesting his urgent assistance had reached him on the morning of Friday 5th January 1894. Attended by his manservant, and dressed accordingly for the solemnity of court, William Makins thus left Rotherfield Court, and made his way to Henley Police Station on foot, tasked with processing facts to be put to him, and having heard all, duty bound to determine if a remanded prisoner (Walter Rathall) had enough evidence against him to warrant the necessity of his appearance before the Magistrates Bench.

Thirty One

That's Got to be Proved

Justices of the Peace were appointed by the Crown, on the advice of the Chancellor, who in turn made his selection following the recommendation of the Lord Lieutenant of the county in which a JP was to sit. An individual arrested on suspicion of a felony, either under warrant, or by a policeman or private citizen (it permissible at the time for a member of the public to apprehend and hold one suspected of wrong doing), was next brought before one or more local justices, for a preliminary enquiry, to determine whether he (or she) should be admitted to prison or granted bail. The Justice of the Peace in whose presence a prisoner stood required to examine the evidence put forward by accusers, against the accused. Once satisfied that all had been heard the JP duty bound to put the pertinent evidence against the prisoner into writing, and forward it on to the clerk of the magistrate's court, before which the prisoner would next appear.

Thus was the fate of Walter Rathall, who, at three o'clock on the afternoon of Friday 5th January 1894, at a special sitting of the Police Court, was brought before Justice of the Peace and County Magistrate, Colonel William Thomas Makins. Cases connected with Henley-on-Thames, as a rule, were heard from twelve o'clock on alternate Saturdays at "Police Court House", Caversham, Berkshire, but due to the sensationalist nature of the Lambridge House murder it was decided that Rathalls hearing should be held within the confines of Henley Police Station. As far as it went the event to be a private one (not quite) none but police officers, and press representatives admitted.

William Thomas Makins
Always known to be elegantly turned out

Superintenant Francis Keal was the lynchpin of the case, and with his trusted police issue pocketbook clutched in his hand he was sworn in, William Makins to thus examine the facts. 'What of the man arrested into your care?'

'The prisoner in my care is Walter Rathall, who is native to the Henley area, being present in the town on the date of the murder, shortly after leaving the district, his whereabouts being unknown.'

'Where was the prisoner apprehended, and how was his arrest secured?'

'In an attempt to track down Rathall I circulated a description of him in a radius many miles wide. On Wednesday, third January, my endeavours proved fruitful, when I received information, via a telegram, that a prisoner, who was felt to be of immense interest to the Henley constabulary, was being held in custody at Daventry Police Station, Northamptonshire.'

'The prisoner was, I understand, subsequently placed into your care.'

'Yes, only two days previous I travelled by train to the police station where Rathall was held, formally charging the man with the wilful murder of Miss Dungey at Lambridge, on Friday 8th December 1893.'

'How did the prisoner respond to the allegation?'

Superintendent Francis Keal, with permission of the magistrate, flicked through the pages of his pocketbook, and content he had sourced the correct page, read back that which Walter Rathall had uttered in response to the allegation levelled against him. 'He replied, that's got to be proved, I was not out of the lodging house all day, and only went into the town about six o'clock, and returned again before half past seven.'

'How was the prisoner conveyed to Henley?'

'He was conveyed under my charge sir, myself, the prisoner, and his wife and infant child travelling back via the railways.'

William Makins, seated in close proximity to the young man who stood accused on charges, which if proved would forfeit his life, fixed the prisoner with a stare that conveyed scant emotion. 'Have you anything to say regards the charge against you?'

Rathalls voice did not falter. 'No, Sir.'

The Police Court sitting had been a brief one, the prisoner thus remanded until Thursday, returned to the cells within Henley Police Station. The cell (sealed by a heavy wrought iron door), in which Walter Rathall again found himself measuring barely five feet eight inches in width, and nine feet in length, though Rathall did have the use of a small exercise yard, in which to stretch his legs.

How Walter Rathall felt at this juncture only he was privy to, but as he was now on remand facing a capital charge one can hazard a guess. After 1841, with the exception of treason or cognate offences, only murderers were hanged. The Capital Punishment Amendment Act, passed into law in the May of 1868, to legislate that prisoners sentenced to death were executed within the walls of the nearest county prison (prisoners before this date hanged in full public view of the masses), to the location in which they were remanded. The concept of malice aforethought dictated that if an individual did commit an illegal act, and although the sole purpose might not have been to end a life, if life and limb were put in peril by an illegal act, and an individual who committed an illegal act had knowledge or belief that life was more than probably to be sacrificed by an illegal act, it was malice aforethought, and the noose beckoned. Such was the allegation which faced Walter Rathall, and he surely must have pondered his fate, confined as he was within a claustrophobically small cell.

Thirty Two

The Representative of the Press

On Saturday 6th January, a representative from a London newspaper (the newssheet not identified) arrived in Henley-on-Thames, via the Great Western Railway. It is not clear where the man chose to billet himself, but during the subsequent day, and late into the evening, the reporter trawled the streets, commercial outlets and hostelries of the town. He also made use of a hackney cab, venturing out to Bix and Assenden, to seek out those who had cause to be on familiar terms with goings on at Lambridge Farm. It seemed that the representative, dispatched to Henley by his editor, was singularly successful and extracts of his observations found their way into many regional newspapers. What follows, all of which appearing within papers too numerous to mention, serves as a cross section of the innuendo and blatant untruths that had sprung into existence since Miss Dungey had met her end, various tit bits conveyed by those of Henleys populace, who with coinage and note on offer had much to tell the gentleman of the press.

"Walter Rathall was born in Assenden, close to Henley-on-Thames, his father employed on the most part as a labourer, his mother earning a monetary pittance by taking in washing and cleaning. Rathalls father died when the man was still a youth, and soon after the families financial worries were compounded, when his mother became incapacitated (Mary Rathalls ailment a bad back, which forced her to relinquish her job as housekeeper at Lambridge Farm), and thus was unable to do any heavy work. Seeking a position, Walter opted to live apart from his mother, and worked for some time as a gardener, and at

~ 217 ~

that stage bore an excellent character. Mrs Rathall occupied a small cottage on the outskirts of Henley, and was considered by those familiar with her, to be poor. Yet upon her demise a collection of banknotes were revealed (hidden under her bed pillow) as the cottage was cleared. Walter Rathalls share of this unexpected windfall was one hundred pounds (several tabloids stated the amount to be eighty pounds), and this money was said, by those who know him best, to be the ruin of the young fellow, the entire amount spent in less than a fortnight."

"Two years ago Rathall was working on Lambridge Farm and came constantly into connection with Miss Dungey. One day he suddenly left this employment, and the next Mr and Mrs Mash heard of him, Walter had inherited the one hundred pounds, previously alluded to, and was enjoining himself. Naturally one hundred pounds does not last forever, and Rathalls enjoyment came to an abrupt end. He however had to live, and picked up wages doing odd jobs at some of the farmhouses around Henley-on-Thames."

"From information gleaned, Miss Dungey took compassion on the man (now firmly down on his luck) and gave Walter work to do, and even went so far as to offer him a permanent position. He however, churlishly, refused the job, and stated that some friends in London were going to send him another one hundred pounds. On the strength of this statement, he obtained small advances from Miss Dungey, as loans, during the last year. Several times Miss Dungey asked for the return of the money, she had advanced him, but never obtained anything."

"On the morning of her death, Miss Kate Dungey met with Rathall in Assenden, and once again requested payment. And it is stated on good authority (the source of the information not disclosed), that he replied that. "She had better not ask for the money too often, or she might not do so much longer." It is not clarified by those editors, who published within their broadsheets this piece of damming information, whether the press representative was informed by his source where the heated exchange between Walter Rathall and Kate Dungey took place. And why, if this verbal attack launched by Rathall upon the young woman was so menacing in nature, did Walter Rathall allow himself to be overheard.

On the afternoon of the day, in which events which culminated in a dreadful murder were to be played out, the representative of the press emphatically stated that Walter Rathall had been identified in several locations.

"On the afternoon of Friday 8th December, he had been seen by James Froomes in the vicinity of Lambridge House. The child was engaged in his work on the farm, and looking up spied Rathall taking the potatoes that were being got ready for the pigs feed." There was never, during subsequent proceedings, any inference to be made in regard to pinched potatoes.

"Midway between Henley town and Assenden is a sewage works, and the man in charge of them (Mr George Renton) has informed the police that about nine o'clock on the night of the outrage at Lambridge, a man, thought to answer accuses description, passed the works, going in the direction of Henley-on-Thames."

"Approaching ten, on the night of the murder, Rathall went into a public house in Henley (its name not alluded to by the press representative), and called for a drink. He had in his possession money a plenty, and indeed stood "treat" to some of his drinking companions, that he met for the first time in the beerhouse."

"It was understood by the wider press, that Rathalls wife had practically admitted the crime to the police (Annie Rathall did no such thing), and duly stated that it was her husband's intention to give himself up."

The shadowy figure from London did not confine himself to banding about accusations against the character of Walter Rathall; he also steered his attentions in the direction of the victim of the heinous event, which had drawn him to Henley-on-Thames.

"I am not allowed to give names (he never does), but this much I am permitted to say. One police line of enquiry was that Miss Dungeys murder was carried out as a preconceived plot, of a second party, who wished revenge on Mr Mashs housekeeper. It appears that Miss Dungey was enamoured of a married man, their acquaintance had been in existence for a term of about four years. June last, the man and his wife came to reside in Assenden for the summer months, and Miss Dungey was frequently at their home, and the wife's jealousy was aroused. In October the man came down by himself, but was followed by his wife, and a lively little scene took place. It is expected that both husband and wife will give evidence at the trial, which is set to be an event of some drama."

The Special Representative of the Press had done as his profession required of him, and stories in relation to the murder at Lambridge, on the most part sourced after those claiming to have a tail to tell were furnished with money and copious amounts of beer, infiltrated the columns of both the regionals and national newspapers.
Who knows if the representative of the press returned to the small market town of Henley-on-Thames, in the lead up to Walter Rathalls appearance before the Magistrates. But as a considerable number of unfounded insinuations made their way into the broadsheets, during

the days previous to Rathalls appearance, it is probable that the incognito reporter lurked amongst those frequenting beerhouses, listening at tables, better to be privy to scandalous utterances.

Thirty Three

A Cloud of Suspicion

George Dawson had from the very onset of the unprecedented events at Lambridge Farm found himself an unwillingly prominent figure in the twists and turns of the investigation. And as such, it seems, was eventually persuaded that the most sensible solution to the entanglement of lies he found himself caught up in was to give a true account of himself via an interview with the press.

As a local man, Dawson determined that said interview was best conducted by a reporter from the Henley and South Oxfordshire Standard, the meeting of the two men taking place on Thursday 11th January 1894. It was not in due course made clear to the papers readership if any payment had been made, nor was the location of the meeting between the two revealed, though the interview probably took place within George Dawson's cottage. If Amy Katherine was present while Dawson unburdened himself is unclear, but she more than likely took herself off to a neighbours. As a woman under immense strain, with her husband suspected of wrong doings and her brother under arrest, Amy surely was in need of the sympatric ear of a friend, this relatively new mother confounded by anxieties, her spouse, conversing with a reporter, equally in a quandary.

'Now Mr Dawson, for the past month you have been under a cloud of suspicion, and have never had an opportunity of saying anything in your defence. Is there any statement you would care to make through me to the public?'

George Dawson was at first tentative as to his response, much of what he'd said before having been distorted against him. 'I do not know if there is anything to be said to the public. I much think that I will have an opportunity to address the doubts surrounding my character, in relation to the affair at the court. Many papers, both local and national, which have followed the case, have published facts which are wrong, indeed contrary to many articles that stated Miss Dungey managed the farm, I as bailiff ran the farm and paid everyone who worked there.'

'Do you have an alibi for the evening of the murder?'

One of George Dawsons neighbours was Jessie Webb, who resided at 3 Folly Cottages, and earned his living as a carman. Jessie's wife, thirty year old Louisa, who alongside her husband had in the March of 1893 suffered the loss of her only child (three year old Robert Oakley), in the course of her grief often experienced abject despair while her husband was away working. And in an effort to raise her spirits, Louisa, if hearing her neighbours about, took herself into the garden to avail herself of human contact. And, as recalled by Dawson, he and Louisa Webb had come across each other outside the rear of their homes, on the evening of Friday 8th December. 'We chatted in relation to the weather.'

George Dawson, in an effort to reiterate his innocence of any wrong doings in relation to the demise of the housekeeper of Lambridge Farm, stated emphatically as to he having one who could bear testimony to an occurrence which the wider press had much speculated upon. 'I had a witness to the event, in which Miss Dungey returned to Lambridge alone (more of this will be heard later), on the day I had been asked by the lady to pick her up. Mrs Wright, who lives next to 37 New Street, bore witness that I failed to locate the woman, and we two had briefly conversed.' Emily Wright did indeed live next to Mr Henry Mashs town house; the lady alongside her husband George, and children, occupant of an elegant Georgian property.

Now the reporter sensed he had George Dawson's confidence, and he thus began to touch on subjects of a more delicate nature. 'Is it indeed correct that you are no longer in Mr Mashs employ?'

'No I left last Saturday. Since this affair the keys which I have had for eleven years (this point regards the number of years Dawson held the keys to Lambridge open for debate) have been taken from me, and Mr Shepherd has managed the farm and paid me.'

'Did you leave of your own accord?'

'I certainly left of my own accord.'

The reporter, keen not to alienate George Dawson, pondered for some moments on which direction he should take the interview, and with the hot topic in many newspapers the relationship between bailiff and housekeeper, Miss Kate Dungey's name came into the fore, Dawson keen to lay any speculation to rest.

'She was always on friendly terms with myself and my wife. She had on several occasions come to tea at my house, and my wife has been to Lambridge House to tea. She was there about a fortnight before this occurred. My wife met Miss Dungey on Thursday 6th December and had a talk with her.' It is to be noted that the date given is incorrect, whether this is a mistake of the reporter, or Dawson cannot be substantiated.

Questioned next as to Walter Rathalls connection with Lambridge Farm, George Dawson was somewhat damming of his character.

'It is two years last July that Rathall worked on the place, the task of getting in the hay, which he was hired to perform, he lasted only ten days!'

'Was Miss Dungey the cause of Rathall leaving?'

George Dawson, it would seem by his clipped response, was much riled by this insinuation. 'No, Miss Dungey never had anything to do with it; I engaged him and paid him. He left of his own accord. There were two or three days work to do, but he never came back to do it!'

The reporter pressed the subject. 'Do you, Dawson, know why Walter Rathall had left so suddenly?'

'No, he would only work just when he thought he would.' George Dawson at this point in his interview to provide the reporter with a snippet of information that up to that point no other had been privy to. 'Miss Dungey had on Thursday 6th December (the date given, as before incorrect) told me she had seen my brother in law, Rathall, going towards Bix.'

The anonymous reporter, as if saving the best to last, alluded to an incident at the inquest, when Superintendent Francis Keal had stated that on the journey from Henley Police Station to Lambridge House, Dawson never spoke more than about two words.

If George Dawson had cause to again feel irritated it was now, he absolutely refuting the superintendent's remembrance of the night in question. 'That is not true; we were talking a good deal on the way back. He was telling me he was very nervous riding in a two wheel trap after his accident (what accident had befallen Keal unknown), and he said go steady. Keal and I had discussed how dark and cold it was, and the superintendent had commented that I had seemed nervous when I had got to the police station. At which point I had replied, informing Keal in more detail of what had happened, and made the man understand that of course I was upset, any man would be!'

The interview between the two men had now drawn to a natural conclusion, but the reporter still had one more trick up his sleeve. 'Do you feel that Walter Rathall is a guilty man?'

'If he did it, it is to be hoped they will find him out, but I do not think he is guilty.'

Thus the two men parted, one a fully paid up reporter for the local newspaper, the other, a man, who through the happenchance of circumstances he could not have envisaged, without a position.

Part Four

Never in living memory had Henley seen the like, hostelries, hotels and boarding houses bursting at the seams. Guests, consisting of those directly affected by the trial, tabloid reporters, and others, who having nothing better to do, had travelled to Henley-on-Thames, keen to soak up the atmosphere of the ensuing drama.

Thirty Four

A Seat on the Bench

The so called "Henley Murder" had stirred up powerful emotions amongst the local populace, and this did not go unheeded by those with the responsibility to orchestrate a magistrates hearing for the defendant, Walter John Rathall. And here was the rub, where were those qualified to sit in judgement to be found; the answer the Magistrates List, many of those duly selected hailing from Oxfordshire, and its neighbouring county, Berkshire.

Part of an old Suffolk family (settled many generations at Stolangloft Hall), Joseph Wilson (born 1786, Clapham, Surrey) took in 1808 as his wife, Emma. The nupitals held in Adderbury, Oxfordshire, the bride (a vivacious young woman of twenty three), daughter of Christopher D'Oyly Aplin, he not to see his child wed, having died in the July of 1806.

The newlyweds, who took tenancy of a house in Clapham, initial foray into parenthood marred by tragedy; their son Edward, born 10th January 1810, living but a solitary day. Frederick William, born in the November of 1818, to fare better than his sibling, though the child was not to live beyond nine years. Joseph Henry came into the world on 21st September 1821, he duly baptised (aged one month) at Holy Trinity, Clapham. On 22nd February 1826 the Wilsons (who by now resided in Battersea) welcoming into baptism Louisa Emma, she to live but nineteen months, taken by some malady on 8th August 1827. The summer of 1829 offered solace with the arrival of Cornelius William, his younger sibling, and last born, Nathaniel, baptised 5th August 1831. The Wilson boys were not unduly burdened by poverty (their father a fund holder and land proprietor), many children who lived within the Borough of Battersea less fortune than they. London living was all very well, the hub of polite society and such like, but the Wilsons desired a life somewhat less urban, and they thus relocated to Lower Norton, North Oxfordshire.

Young Joseph Henry Wilson (for it is he who would have bearing on events that unfolded at Henley Magistrates Court in the January of 1894) excelled in his studies, and as of many a young man from the right sort of family, he had the pick of the best universities. Wilson selected to stay within the county he had much fondness for, and thus went up to Exeter College Oxford. Law was Joseph Wilson's bent, and managing to fit in some study around the usual flummery of student life, he graduated with a BA in 1843, in 1845 called to the Bar of the Middle Temple.

Joseph Henry Wilson was now a man possessed of a profession, and aged twenty three he found one whose countenance was agreeable to him. And so it was, that on Thursday 17th April 1845, at the Parish Church of St Mary, Battersea, Joseph took as his wife Henrica (born in Clapham, 13th June 1822), the eldest surviving daughter of William (a wealthy merchant) and Elizabeth Haigh. Wilson's bride also one who had enjoyed the benefits of goodly birth, Henrica's childhood spent at Furze Down, a fine town house (which retained seven servants) that sat within sizeable grounds, close to Tooting Common, Streatham, Surrey.

The Wilsons settled in Norwood, Lambeth, and here it was that in 1846 Frances Henrica was born (she to be the couples only issue), the child baptised on 9th April. It seemed that parenthood, and the desire for country living, compelled the Wilsons to look about them for a residence in Oxfordshire, Joseph to consult numerous land agents. In the Parish of Rotherfield Peppard, close to the border of Henley-on-Thames, lay the substantial estate of Gillotts (held by John Fowden Hodges of Bolney Court), its principal premises, Gillotts House (previous tenant John Sedgwick) much to the Wilsons liking. Though it is to be said that Joseph Wilson was not to have benefit of the entire estate, John Hodges keeping hold of much of the farmland and small holdings, the income raised on them in no way meagre.

The Oxford Chronicle & Reading Gazette of Saturday 14th February 1852, informed its readership of an occurrence it deemed worthy of note. "Qualified to act as magistrate for this county, Joseph Henry Wilson of Gillotts near Henley-on-Thames." And now firmly anchored within Oxfordshire, and with his wife and daughter at regular intervals residing with Henrica's father, Joseph Wilson was glad of the company of his brother Cornelius (he later to enter into holy orders), the two, housemaid Elizabeth Harriet Grey, and cook Tabitha Mason, rattling around the considerable estate.

Life in the moderately sized market town that was Henley-on-Thames suited Joseph Wilson well, and he much relishing any spare time afforded him, enjoyed weekend rambles (on horseback or on foot) in and around the surrounding villages. Wilson's civic duty, as a Justice of the Peace, determined that he often found himself creeping into the columns of regional newspapers. But there was an occasion for him to appear within the newssheets, as a plaintiff. As reported in the Saturday 21st November 1857 edition of Jacksons Oxford Journal, at the 19th November sitting of the Petty Sessions of Henley Division, a Samuel Lofting stood accused of wrong doing. It was alleged that within his role as Toll Collector at Hew Gate (the toll positioned on the Reading and Hatfield Turnpike Road), Lofting had taken a greater toll than he was authorised to do so. Said toll demanded for the passage through the turnpike of a dog cart, which should have had the same toll charged as that of a gig or chaise, the aggrieved owner of said cart, Joseph Henry Wilson. The tenant of Gillotts had been much perturbed that one of his employees had had cause to complain to him that he had thought himself charged a toll above what was usually the custom, and Wilson was therefore satisfied, when after due process, Samuel Lofting was fined one shilling, with costs of twelve shillings.

In early June of 1859 the sales columns of Jacksons Oxford Journel carried for the benefit of its readership the following. "Hews & Son have been instructed by Joseph Henry Wilson Esq: who is leaving, to sell by auction on premises at Gillotts, on Wednesday 24th June 1859, about 100 dozen of wine, comprising old Port, Sherry, Claret and Champagne, also lots of household furniture and garden implements, and a very prime in calf Alderney cow. Furniture and garden sale eleven, wine sale two o'clock." So where was it that Joseph Henry Wilson resolved next to reside, a fellow much taken with Devon, he to take possession of "The Elms", Stoke Damerel, Devonport. Although a qualified barrister it is apparent Wilson chose not to practice, he instead satisfied to act as Justice of the Peace for Devon, and unusually considering the considerable distance he would be required to travel, he to also retain his seat upon the Oxfordshire Bench.

Life at "The Elms" was much as it was for those fortunate enough to have the income to employ servants. Meals were the responsibility of cook Francis Wilder, and the ladies of the house, Henrica and Frances, were the responsibility of ladies maid, Mary Ann Jeans. Housemaid, Sarah Sanders, kept on top of the laying of fires, dusting of objet d'art, and such like, while butler William Tatton made certain everything ran like clockwork. Life indeed seemed good for Joseph Wilson, but all was not as it appeared, his wife at intervals noticeable absent, Henrica, suffering from a malady of sorts, residing in Gloucester Square, Southampton, at the home of Elizabeth Mackey, she widow of surgeon, Patrick Mackey. The house in which Henrica Wilson found herself was bustling, Elizabeth Mackey mother to two young ladies, Matilda and Mary, her patient under the care of Elizabeth Crichton Chalmers (wife of William Kelman Chalmers, Army Staff Surgeon), and a highly experienced sick nurse, Martha Young. A general domestic servant, Mary Ann Broadbent, tending to those duties required of her by mistress and patient.

By the latter 1860s Henrica had recovered sufficiently to return to her family, and her husband, mindful that his wife might find a change of scene beneficial, relocated his family to Whitley Hill, St Giles, Reading. Wilson was not a man to sit idle, and he quickly added to his considerable workload, taking on the responsibility of Recorder of Henley, and with an interest in local affairs, a considerable number of voluntary roles, such as Chairman of the Governors Trustee of Church Charities, Joseph Wilson to teach regularly at his parish church Sunday school. Wilson sat on the panel of the Reading School Board, in this capacity he to visit one school each week, until the inclusion of newly opened schools made the logistics of such visits impossible. Joseph Wilson to thus invite children, whose schools fell under his jurisdiction, to his home at Whitley Hill, the considerable cost (often to exceed eighty pounds) of entertainment, laid on for the enjoyment of the children, provided at Wilsons own expense.

Here was a fellow whose Christian faith guided his conscience, and Wilson leant on the support of his faith and his parish rector when his wife relapsed. The family again fractured, Henrica sent to reside at 1 Gloucester Villas, Gloucester Close, Hanwell, Brentford, Middlesex. What ailed the lady is unclear, but General Practioner, Canadian born Robert Burton (a specialist surgeon), orchestrated her care. Indeed Henrica Wilson resided under Burtons roof, she given provision of a companion, Fanny Gulliver, while domestic cook Mary Ware fulfilled the patients dietary requirements.

Joseph Wilson quit Reading in 1882 (presented by those who he had assisted over the years with a commemorative album, that contained within a list of names of its subscribers), he to take up residence at "Caversham Priory", where, as before he threw himself immediately into voluntary works.

Watercolour of Caversham Priory, dated 23rd July 1832

But life has a way of inflicting without warning dire misfortune, and the Wilsons were not to be spared, their only child, Frances (having never married, nor left home) dying on 13th May 1889, aged forty three. Frances left an estate of just short of sixteen thousand pounds, and a mother sorely aggrieved, Henrica during her daughters last week's again falling ill, at last an indication of the malady that afflicted her made clear. On Friday 12th April 1889, just a month before her only child's death, Henrica Wilson was placed into the care of a Mr R. C. Shettle, the lady in a state of acute nervous exhaustion. She admitted to Holloway Sanatorium, located in Virginia Water Surrey, under the doctoring of Shettle, Henrica still registered as a patient in the April of 1892. Holloway Sanatorium had opened in 1885 (funded by the generosity of a Mr Thomas Holloway), and it cared for those afflicted by mental health problems. The ethos of the place that those admitted from wealthy backgrounds paid fees of a higher amount for the best facilities, in order to subsidise the charges of the less well off.

Though not fully recovered from the loss of his only child, and his wife's health still delicate (she often away from her husband), Joseph Wilson resolved to move forward, and thus relocated to "Marchmont" Addington Road, Reading, his domestic needs met by cook, Sarah Harper, and parlour maid, Elizabeth Birl.

Wilson, a man of undoubted fortitude, threw himself fully into his work, he still to sit as County Magistrate for Oxfordshire and Devon, and as Recorder for Henley-on-Thames, he to also take on the role of Chairman of Henley Petty Sessions, regularly sitting upon the Bench.

The autumn of 1893 saw Joseph Henry Wilson turn seventy two, but even at this advanced age he still proved himself a man of agile mind, and thus was deemed the natural chose for the role of Magistrates Chairman, for the appearance of Walter John Rathall before the Bench.

The family that one Robert Trotter Hodge was born into had been connected with Newcastle since the eighteenth century; his cousin, Sir Roland Hodge, having in 1889 purchased the Northhumberland Ship Building Company. Robert made his appearance on 23rd September 1851, the eldest son of attorney at law, George William Hodge (born 1817, Newcastle-upon-Tyne) and Sarah Elizabeth (nee Green), who hailed from Sharron in Yorkshire. Sarah did not find herself often confined; she delivered of just three children, Roberts siblings, Elizabeth Blanche (born 1853), and George William Baldwin, he born 1856.

The boys of the family had benefit of a private education, Robert a boarder at the Vicarage, Broom Haugh, Northumberland, its principal Joseph Jaynes, Vicar of Bywell St Andrew. By his teens Robert Hodge a pupil at Clifton College, Bristol (a keen footballer) then after he to study art at Worcester College, Oxford, graduating in 1873. But this young fellow had a course set out for him, and on Christmas Eve

1873, Robert commenced what was to be a three year Clerkship in Chancery, under the mentoring of his father.

By the winter of 1876 Hodge was released of his apprenticeship, a young man out in society; the better to turn his thoughts to that of the heart. Thus on 16th May 1877 Robert married his sweetheart, twenty one year old Frances Caroline. The bride, who hailed from Middlesex, the only daughter of Edward Hermon, an extremely prosperous Lancashire shipping and cotton merchant (a representative of the East India Company) associated with the firm Horricks Cotton. The newlyweds having no need to secure a tenancy, they to immediately move onto Edward Hermon's humongous rural estate (Wyfold Court), taking occupation of Wyfold Grange, within the Parish of Rotherfield Peppard.

Wyfold Court (built between 1872 and 1878, designed by a pupil of Sir Charles Bary, architect George Somers Clark) was indeed a fine eclectic property, constructed from superior quality scarlet and blue brick, with a yellow stone detail, the front façade having towers with quaint corner turrets, intricately carved gargoyles scattered amongst the brickwork. The windows were traceried, the front of the house installed with mullioned bay windows, and enhanced by crocheted gables, the interior grand hall (its corridor rib vaulted), and staircase, both flooded with light. Wyfold Court not to be admired by all who had cause to comment, described at the time of its completion somewhat irreverently as consisting of French Gothic architecture, with a touch of Scots Baronial.

The early married life of the Hodge's was to be touched by sorrow, Robert and Frances first born, Marguerite, to live but three days, she to die on 9th June 1879. The following spring Robert Hodge to again have reason to lament; his beloved father dying at his home (24 Ellison Place) aged sixty two, on 11th April 1880. Robert one of those to benefit from George Hodge's estate, valued in excess of twenty five thousand pounds.

The Hodge's (their income derived mainly from shares held by Robert) found solace in the arrival in 1880 of a second child, Roland Hermon, not long after he joined by another boy, Robert Edward Udny. But life for this young family was to take yet another dramatic turn; on Friday 6th May 1881 Edward Hermon to fall down stone dead (aged fifty eight) within the corridors of the House of Commons. And thus Robert Hodge found himself master of Wyfold Court, ably assisted by his late father-in-laws domestic staff. Once Edward Hermon's estate cleared through probate the executors to place Wyfold Court in auction, it set to be sold on Tuesday 27th June 1882, in one lot (at Tocken House Yard, London), by land agents Rushworth Abbott & Steven. Whether the auction proved unsuccessful, or the lot was withdrawn due to a change of heart by the beneficiaries of Edward Hermon's estate, Robert Trotter Hodge made Wyfold Court his family's permanent home.

The Hodges now had a huge house to fill, and fill it they did, another son, George Guy, safely delivered in 1884, then after followed by Harry Baldwin, Claude Preston, John Percival, and Leonard St Leger, he born 1893, his father at this juncture paying the wages of no less than seventeen servants.

Robert Trotter Hermon Hodge (taking the name Hermon in deference to his late father-in-law) was now a gentleman of independent means, and thus enjoyed the sport of gentlemen, horseracing; his own bred horses notoriously unsuccessful. But there was a life away from the turf, and Hermon Hodge took on such diverse responsibilities as County Alderman for Oxfordshire, Justice of the Peace, and Conservative MP for Wallingford, his seat abolished following the 1885 Redistribution of Seats Act. 1886 to see Robert Hermon Hodge again sat within the Commons, MP for North East Lancashire; a seat he would hold until 1892, he duly acknowledged with the honour of Deputy Lieutenant of Oxfordshire.

Robert Trotter Hermon Hodge
He sporting a very distinctive moustache

It was Robert Trotter Hermon Hodges position as a County Magistrate (Henley Division) that brought him into the Lambridge affair, duly selected to sit upon the Bench at Henley. Via the Court Clerk, Robert to receive a buddle, held within the pertinent facts regards the upcoming appearance of Walter John Rathall. A gentleman to never underestimate the gravity of the case presented before him, Hermon Hodge to spend hours sat within his study, leafing through witness statements and police depositions. Below stairs, household staff (butler Alfred Warner having under him twelve domestic servants) chatting in excited tones about the murder at Henley, the details of which to enthral those across the full spectrum of society.

Robert Napier Raikes (born 15th October 1813, in Drayton, Norfolk) came from a long line of religious men, he the eldest child of the Reverend Robert Napier Raikes (born 1783), his mother, Caroline (born 1784, Longhope, Gloucestershire), the daughter of the Reverend John Probyn. Roberts paternal grandfather (also Robert) an early advocate of Sunday Schools, his monumental statue still standing resplendent within Victoria Embankment Gardens, London.

Robert Napier Raikes formative years were idyllic, he residing at Drayton Vicarage (his father Vicar of Drayton), in the company of numerous playmates, siblings, Julia Maria, Charles Lewis, Ladbroke Napier, Caroline, Henry, Stanley Napier, and Gertrude, she baptised in the spring of 1829. There were in addition two others who had not matured beyond infancy, Emma, who baptised on 25th October 1816, had succumbed to sudden illness, and Edmund, who having lived but eight days was buried 1st August 1827, within Drayton Churchyard.

In 1828, not yet sixteen, Robert Raikes decided that army life was his bent, he thus to enrol as a cadet at the Addiscombe Military Academy, Surrey, previously known as the East India Company Military Seminary. This attempt at military life destined to end in disgrace, Robert expelled for refusing to give up the names of five fellow cadets, who without permission, in order to enjoy copious amounts of beer and some high jinks had left barracks. Though out on his ear Raikes still fervently desired to serve King and Country, and so it was that in his sixteenth year Robert Raikes gained a commission in the Indian Army, he a Cadet within the Bengal Staff Corps. Before much time elapsed the young fellow dispatched to Portsmouth, and thus forward put aboard a military ship bound for Calcutta, India, Raikes not to return for thirty five years.

1844 saw Robert Napier Raikes made up to Captain, and appreciative that military life could easily be one of isolation, Raikes (recently made up to Major in the Sixty Seventh Bengal Native Infantry), not wishing such for himself wed (on 25th September 1854, in Mussoorie,

Bengal) Harrietta Beckett. Roberts bride, some twenty years his junior (born in Agra, West Bengal), the daughter of Captain William Beckett, he having died aged forty eight, on 15th December 1844.

A commission within the Indian Army was not without its adversities, the Raikes early married life sorely tested during the infamous Indian Mutiny, from May 1857 to June 1858 large sections of the Indian Army to rebel against British authority. At the height of the rebellion Robert Raikes posted as Commander at Mynpoorie; that is until July 1857, when obliged to withdraw due to his men's refusal to stay any longer, Raikes retreated, having secured the Treasury. Robert Raikes wife fared little better, Harrietta to flee Gwalior (destined for Agra) concealed in a bullock wagon, indeed the Indian Mutiny marked the Raikes out for tragedy, daughters Harrietta Justina (born 1st December1856) and Emma Matilda (born 10th September 1858) taken by sudden illness. Harrietta the first to succumb, dying 13th September 1857, duly buried that same day in the cemetery in Agra. Her sibling, Emma, not to survive much beyond her first month, buried alongside her sister on 19th October 1858. Army wives were known for their fortitude, and Harrietta Raikes was no exception, while her husband was posted in Meerut, Bengal, she delivered, on 2nd April 1861, of a son, Robert Haigh Napier, a daughter, Mabel, born in the autumn of 1863.

Major Raikes, a man able to speak many Indian dialects, subsequently entered the Gwalior Cavalry, and having excelled in all he had turned his hand to, Robert resolved, in the autumn of 1864, to return to England. Once back on British soil the Raikes looked about them for a property that fitted their needs, and duly took a tenancy in Cheltenham, where in 1865 Herbert William was born; he joined in 1868 by a sister, Margaret Mary. Robert Napier Raikes subsequently settled on a tenancy in Swanmore, Hampshire, it being better suited to his expanding family, Ethel Florence, Reginald Durie, and last born, Cyril Probyn, glad of the grounds afforded them for play.

The census of 3rd April 1881 saw the Raikes now in occupation of Bennington Lodge, in Bennington, Herefordshire, their lifestyle (funded by Robert's military wage) much enhanced by the abundant array of servants at their disposal. Elizabeth Camp to manage the kitchen and the cooking, and parlour maid, Emily Chappell, to manage the household duties, the children's domestic needs under the remit of nursemaid, Elizabeth Wyman, while governess, Antomien Loewenstein, saw to their lessons. A coachman, James Broadhurst (he residing at Lodge Cottage), much utilised, his wife, Anna, the laundress.

But Robert Raikes (in 1889 made up to a General) fancied life as a country squire, and of independent means (investing in the London property market) by the latter years of the 1880s he secured the tenancy of Harpsden Court. Purchased in 1855 by Henry Hodges (he residing at nearby Bolney Court), Harpsden Court a property of grand proportions, that dominated the village of Harpsden. Accessed via a gravelled carriage road, Harpsden Courts impressive front door led on into a handsome hall, beyond which lay the dining room (with oak floor and panelling), drawing room and breakfast room. The ground floor, dominated by the inner hall, having an oak staircase each side, one of which adorned by the addition of an ornamented balustrade. The courts upper floor having no less than two drawing rooms, one adapted for use as a music room, its ceiling domed. There were eight bedrooms, some of which having addition of dressing rooms and closets, located over the office wing the servant's bedrooms, any domestic staff to have use of a servant's hall, butler's pantry, and housekeeper's hall. Within the grounds several outhouses, such as the coach house and stables, the main house enhanced by attractive park like pasture, and rustic meadow land.

Country living suited Robert Raikes, but he was neither the less a fellow unaccustomed to an idle life, and to curb any boredom Raikes busied himself with local affairs, he to sit as a member of the Henley

Board of Guardians, Justice of the Peace, and as a Magistrate. And it was to be the latter role that brought Robert Napier Raikes into the Lambridge affair (he, by the January of 1894 aged eighty), summoned to sit in judgement at Walter Rathalls trial.

The Brigham's held sway over an ancient manorial estate, Cane End, Caversham, in 1717 the mansion rebuilt in its entirety, set to reflect the fashionable Queen Anne Style. In 1689 a branch of the Vanderstegen family settled permanently in England, they having initially come over in the suite of William of Orange. On 3rd May 1759 one William Vanderstegen took as his bride Elizabeth Brigham, she descendant of Sir Anthony Brigham, and heiress to Cane End. Thus forward the combined dynastic landowning families took guardianship of Cane End, in due course adding to the estates already substantial holdings.

1852 saw the marriage of landowner and magistrate William Henry Vanderstegen (born 1808, at Cane End), his bride Ellen (born 1821), the daughter of Richard Denny of Bergh Apton in Norfolk. The year that followed William and Ellens nuptials to see the birth of Henry Brigham Douglas, his childhood not one of solitude, in 1854 he to be joined by a sister, Grace Ellen. Two became five, with the births of Frederick William, Ernest, and Dorathea, she born 1859. Mindful of his children's education, William Vanderstegen, suitable impressed by the references of Miss Ellen Moore, to take the young lady on as governess.

But the norms of the times dictated that boys of a particular background should be sent away to school. And so it was that the eldest child of the Vanderstegen brood, Henry, found himself bunking down alongside fellow students within the dormitory of a boarding school, located in Kirkley Suffolk. Whether related or not to Henrys mother unclear, the headmistress of this institute of learning, former governess, Miss Charlotte Denny.

Miss Dennys teaching staff did a stalwart job, Henry Vanderstegen to go up to Christ Church, Oxford, he aged nineteen, on 11th October 1872, made Matric. So what did many young men possessed of breeding do with themselves after academia was done with, they enlisted in the army, Vanderstegen proving no exception, he to join the ranks of the Yeomanry Cavalry. Within the announcements section of the Tuesday 28th May 1878 edition of the London Gazette its readership were informed that a certain Henry Brigham Douglas Vanderstegen had been promoted from the Rank of Sub Lieutenant, to that of Lieutenant. That was not all; on Saturday 1st June 1878, at the County Hall in Oxford (in the Quarterly Sessions), the very same fellow before his peers to take an oath, sworn in to serve his county as a magistrate.

On 9th September 1892, William Henry Vanderstegen (Justice of the Peace) died aged eighty four, his estate valued at £1,848 18s 2d, and his widow, Ellen, now mistress of Cane End. Her eldest, a confirmed bachelor and very much incumbent, in the January of 1894 selected to sit upon the Magistrates Bench, at a hearing to be held at Henley Town Hall.

Simonds Brewery was founded 1785 by William Blackall Simonds (his father having been involved in brewing since the 1760s), the man's extended family consisting of farmers, millers, maltsters, lawyers, landowners and bankers. The concept of brewing in Reading was not a new one; with five rival breweries in operation at the time Simonds (his brewery run out of a premises in Broad Street) launched himself upon the industry. This enterprising businessman to rapidly relocate to premises at Seven Bridges, Bridge Street, Reading, locally born architect, John Soane, retained to design for William Simonds a resplendent brew house. By 1805 the company had ownership of ten public houses, in 1813 Simonds to secure the contract to supply beer to the Royal Military College, Sandhurst.

William's son, Blackall, in due course took over the company, he quickly expanding Simonds Breweries holdings of public houses, facilitated in no small way by the 1830 Beer Act, which curtailed the monopoly of long established brewers. In 1834 Blackall Simonds went into partnership with his younger brothers, Henry and George, within ten years Blackall to make the decision to retire. Stepping down in 1845, content to live as a country gent (funded by lucrative investments), Blackalls brothers set to rebrand, the company thence forward known as H & G Simonds.

Henry John Simonds (born 23rd March 1828, baptised 26th September, within the Parish of St Giles, Reading), was the son of the aforementioned Henry Simonds, he married to Mary Ann, the daughter of Mr Hillier Goodman, of Oare House. Young Henry was fortunate indeed, born into a dynasty that had possession of H & G Simonds Ltd, Brewers, Wine, Spirits Merchants and Bottlers, located in Bridge Street, on the west bank of the Kennet. The location of said brewery no happy accident, its position in close proximity to the Thames convenient for river carriage of the breweries output to Simonds stores, Milbank Wharf, London.

Henry John Simonds spent his childhood in the company of older siblings, sisters Mary Louisa and Henrietta, Henrys only brother, Maurice Hiller, some ten years his elder. Initially educated at the Prepatory School (kept by Mrs Bradley), which stood just off Station Road, in Reading, Henry then after attended Eton College, he bestowed with the honour of School Captain. Simonds was a bright lad, and thus went up to Kings College, Cambridge, where in 1851 he graduated with a BA in Law, duly called to the Bar on 26th January 1853. Much of Henry Simonds student days had been spent within the Parish of the Inner Temple, London, and his ambition knew no bounds, he in 1854 to graduate MA in Law. Simonds practiced primarily on the Oxford Circuit, but his time in the law was fleeting, he drawn towards the family business. The position of Manager of the Bridge Street Brewery was determined as the best introduction for Henry, the foundations thus laid for his eventually elevation to business partner.

During his formative years within the company Henry John Simonds chose to reside at Bridge Street, he in 1861 to take the Rectory, Caversham (former seat of his uncle Blackall Simonds, who had relocated to the Isle of Wight), and here it was in 1879 that Henry received news of his father's death. Though much saddened at the loss of a man he held in high esteem, Henry resolved to carry the brewery business forward, by the closing decades of the nineteenth century H & G Simonds expanding beyond all expectations, set to become one of the pivotal breweries in the south of England.

Line drawing of Simonds Brewery
The townhouse, centre front, no doubt the onetime home of Henry Simonds

Life was good indeed for Henry Simonds, hectic and challenging, but never dull, he occupied with his duties as leader of Reading Conservative Party, Justice of the Peace for Oxfordshire, and Lay Rector at Caversham Church.   Politics was many a rich man's passion, Simonds no exception, he elected as a member of the first Oxfordshire County Council, in 1866 returned as Mayor of Reading. In 1868 Henry Simonds an active supporter of the Caversham Bridge Act, to see the dilapidated unsightly bridge that spanned the Thames, replaced with a new structure.   In that same year Henry Simonds to assist in the carrying forward of the Local Board Waterworks Act, which saw waterworks acquired from those water companies who held sway over Reading.   Simonds had much benefitted in his life choices due to a good education, and he wished this for others, his efforts in no small way to lead to the resuscitation of the Reading Grammar School (at one time down to a solitary pupil), simultaneously Henry to act as Corporation Governor of both Reading School, and Kendrick School.

Gentlemen had the time and financial resources required to take part in civic life, as well as the time to take part in leisure pursuits, and Henry Simonds relished his down time, he partaking in country sports, and relaxing in the company of his numerous friends, within the lounge room of the Junior Carlton Club (closely aligned to the Conservative party), a London gentleman's club established in 1866, run out of premises, 30 Pall Mall.

Of course there was a family side to Henry John Simonds, his wife Julia Victoria Pilati (only daughter of Signor Victor Pilati) she born 1836, in Albermaria Street, London, the couple married on 26th April 1859, at Lancaster Gate, Christ Church, Westminster.   Their union producing, in 1860, a daughter, Julia Benina (this child to die in 1869), three further girls to follow, Mary Amelia, Isa Florence, and Mabel Constance, she born 1865.   Henry Caversham (the only son of the Simonds) born in 1868; the family unit completed in 1873 with the birth of Lilian Juliette, the childs mother dead before the summer of 1874 was spent.

Widowhood did not sit well with Henry Simonds (he retiring from politics and the Conservative Party after his wife's demise), and in 1875 he took a second wife, Mary (born 1829, Barnstable, Devon), the daughter of fund holder, George Hartwell Marsack, of Caversham Park. And so we have Henry John Simonds, a gentleman who afforded the wages of eleven domestic servants, his time much taken up by his duties as a County Magistrate, he and those alongside him upon the Henley Bench, ably assisted by Town Clerk, John Frederick Cooper.

John Frederick Cooper was born in Henley-on-Thames on Valentines Day 1855, his father, John (born 1819, Watling Street, London), his mother Ellen, she born 1824 in the county of Middlesex. John, as the Coopers only son thus shared his childhood alongside four sisters; elder sisters Annie Elizabeth and Ellen Lucy, younger sisters, Janet and Marion. The master of the house a man of the law, his solicitors practice very lucrative indeed, he thus able to afford to take his family to reside at a sizable property located at Northfield End. John Cooper considered himself a gentleman, and as such retained domestics, Elizabeth and Sarah Tomalin, Alice Sales and Elizabeth Hatton to appear within the 1861 census, general servants in the employee of Mr John Cooper.

John Cooper (junior) attended Henley Grammar School (which run out of premises that had formerly been utilised as the Bell Tap Inn, its Principal the Reverend Charles Goadby), but a stone's throw from the Coopers residence. John, a dutiful student, to excel in all he put his mind to, set to complete his education at Marlborough College, thus forward articled (a term used to describe one apprenticed to train as a clerk) at Shrewsbury. On 10th July 1879 John Cooper admitted as a solicitor, he to join his father within the company's West Street practice, in due course to take up the role of his father's deputy, in the position of Town Clerk.

They say many a young man is in want of a wife, and John Frederick Cooper proved no exception, he on 14th April 1888 to marry Mabel Bertha (born 1864 in Iver Mae, Uxbridge, Middlesex), she daughter of William (an architect) and Catherine Thompson. The year that followed the nuptials to see the birth of John Alan Rescorla, he soon in the company of a sister, Mabel Norah Periam, the last born, with an equally elaborate name to that of his siblings, Lancelot Head, he delivered at home in 1893.

In 1890 John Frederick Cooper had been returned as Registrar for the County Court, many cases settled by him with no need for a judge. This role was not in isolation, he also Clerk to the Henley Charity Trustees, Clerk to Henley and Caversham Old Age Pension Committee, and Clerk to Commissioners of Taxes for Henley Division. Cooper, a fellow never happier than when in the company of friends, a stalwart member of Henley Habitation of the Primrose League, he at weekends to play in the Henley and Marlow Cricket team. John Cooper also notable one of the earliest members of Henley Golf Club (holding bonds in the organization), it little wonder that he found any time at all to fulfil his role as Henley Town Clerk.

Thirty Five

Prosecution Solicitor for the Treasury

With Walter Rathall remanded, set to appear before the Magistrates Bench, legal dictate determined that a prosecution solicitor be appointed, that duty falling to Sydney Brain, he to act on behalf of the Treasury.

Boot and shoemaker, John Alfred Brain (born 8th December 1827, St Lawrence, Reading) came from a long line of cordwainers, a term commonly used to describe those who made footwear. The Brain's were non-conformists, and thus worshipped at the Independent Chapel, a building that stood tucked amongst retail outlets within one of the commercial hubs of Reading, that being Broad Street. John Brain desired a wife, and found himself much taken with Ann Catherine (born 29th August 1825, in the small hamlet of Bix, Oxfordshire, daughter of Thomas Cottrell proprietor of Redpits Farm), who resided with her aunt Elizabeth Challis (she funded by monies from an annuity), on Castle Street, Reading.

The marriage was a contented and productive one, a son Walter John born in 1854, Katherine was born in 1856, she soon to enjoy the company of a sister, Clara, the siblings residing above their fathers commercial outlet, 108 Broad Street. A second son, Sydney, was born in 1860, John Brain able to both support his growing family, and fund the wages of ten men, two women, and one boy, the lady of the house to have benefit of domestic servant, Elizabeth Hambling, and nursemaid Mary Hutchince.

The latter years of the 1860s saw John Brain (he tenant of 114-115 Broad Street) much in demand, he the employer of twenty men, some of whom benefitted from an apprenticeship. Above the cobblers, within the family apartment, the Brain's were appreciative of the additional space, now parents to six, following the birth of Ernest and Maud Mary, who'd arrived in 1867.

Reading in the 1880s was a town that boasted much industry; many agricultural labourers, tempted by good job prospects and enhanced wages, quitting the countryside. And one essential was footwear, John Brain thus able to reap the benefits, which was just as well as four of his offspring found living at home to their liking. Walter in practice as a solicitor, Clara a private governess, Sydney a solicitors articuled clerk, and Ernest his father's assistant bootmaker. There was another two who resided at the family home, the Brain's nephew, young George Kingham, and domestic servant Mary Luxton, she shoehorned into an attic room.

Line drawing of John Brain's commercial premises in Broad Street
His name visible above the triple glass paned shop front

There is of course one we heard of earlier, that fellow Sydney Brain, a young man of no mean intelligence who excelled in all he turned his hand to. Sydney had from his formative years been much taken with the law, and with schooling done he served his articules at solicitors firm Messrs H & C Collins of Blagrave Street, Reading. Brains mentor one Henry Collins, who in possession of a bustling practice resided at Leopold House in Tilehurst. And so it was that the Reading Mercury, which hit the newsstands on Saturday 20th May 1882, detailed within its columns those candidates who had on 25th and 26th April 1882 sat their final examination, thus duly qualified as solicitors, local young gentleman, Sydney Brain, name prominent.

Brain quit Reading and honed his expertise in practice on the London Circuit, he then after returning to Reading to join his brothers (Walter) solicitors practice (founded 1881), which operated out of 15 Friar Street, Reading. The brothers, much devoted, muddled along together just fine, before long in partnership, the firm going forward known as Brain & Brain.

Sydney Brain on returning from London resided at his parental home, his siblings Clara and Ernest still incumbent. Sydney eventually prised himself away from his childhood abode, and took on "Ashcott" on Alexandra Road (an area that consisted of elaborate detached and semi-detached mid-Victorian properties), his sister Katherine, who shared the property, no doubt taking on household duties, assisted by domestic, Elizabeth Goff.

Brain achieved all goals he had set himself, and as such did not fail to win the hand of the woman he loved; he married in Windsor on 9th April 1891, his bride twenty eight year old Gertrude Mary, daughter of John (a grocer and tea dealer, located on the High Street, Eton, Buckinghamshire) and Elizabeth Atkins. Before a year pasted the Brains were parents, on 22nd January 1892 a son, John Atkins (taking his mother's maiden name) born.

Sydney Brain, prosecution solicitor for the Treasury
Though deteriorated this photograph to still convey the character of the man

Solicitors were relied upon to be at the disposal of the Magistrates Bench, and Sydney Brain was no exception, he appointed as defence solicitor to one Thomas Jennings. Landlord of licenced premises, Jennings was sent before the bench in the December of 1893 to answer an allegation that he had permitted drunkenness within his hostelry. The defendant pleaded not guilty and Brain put forward a stalwart argument, the magistrates not persuaded to impose a fine of ten shillings with costs of eighteen shillings. This type of case was bread and butter to any legal practice, and those who toiled at Brain & Brain were much grateful of them. But within a month of having represented Mr Thomas Jennings, Sydney Brain found himself summoned to appear for the Treasury, on a matter altogether graver. The Treasury Solicitors Act of 1876 established that a selected group of solicitors would act for the affairs of her majesties (Queen Victoria) Treasury, all those appointed reporting directly to the offices of the Attorney General for England and Wales. Those selected to enjoy the benefit of perpetual succession, and the capacity to hold land, government securities, shares in public companies, and real and personal property.

Throughout his formative years Sydney Brain had instilled within him a non-conformists ethos, he in his maturity choosing to attend Trinity Congregational Church, where he acted as Deacon. In the January of 1894 the man had thrust upon him the responsibility to examine the capital case set before Walter John Rathall, and although his Christian faith caused him much inner turmoil as to the possible forfeiting of a man's life, Sydney Brain, with the assistance of his juniors, dutifully prepared the prosecution's case. One can indeed visualize Sydney Brain sat into the small hours pawing over the evidence, closely scrutinising police crime scene notes, post mortem report, and countless witness statements.

Sydney Brain, accompanied by his juniors (who lugged considerable amounts of hand luggage), set off for Henley-on-Thames early on the morning of Friday 12th January 1894. The party, who drew glances from fellow passengers, squeezed into a carriage aboard the Great Western service. The date of this journey much significant, it being that set by William Thomas Makins, for Walter Rathalls first appearance before the Magistrates Bench. Once alighted at Henley the men made their way the short distance to the town hall (whether on foot or by hackney unclear), the prosecution team met by Town Clerk, John Cooper. Refreshment thus offered and gladly accepted, the prosecution team shown into a side room, where Sydney Brain fine-tuned his notes, he in due course formally introduced to the defence solicitor, the two men, not yet rivals in court, cordial, as befit the dictates of their profession.

Walter Rathall was not a man blessed with a steady income; he a journeyman who travelled hither and thither, in an effort to pick up casual work. Here was a fellow who struggled through life, and on umpteen occasions Rathall had found himself on his uppers, forced to enter the workhouse system, or failing that kipping down for the night under the stars, it thus a foregone conclusion that Walter Rathall could not afford a solicitor. It was in the 1890s still rare for a defendant to have the expert assistance of a legal adviser, but in a capital case, which if found guilty a defendant could face the hangman, a defence solicitor was appointed and paid for by the state. Such a solicitor permitted in trial to cross examine any prosecution witness, and question any dubious motive behind any damming testimony. Thus in the January of 1894 Walter John Rathall was formally introduced to his appointed solicitor, whose unenviable task it was to argue for an acquittal, that man Robert Samuel Wood.

Theodora Sarah Sophia (the daughter of Watlington based general practioner John Edward Montgomery Boyton, who practiced out of a surgery on Brook Street), had for some time been courted by a young man, who a student of law had recently qualified as a solicitor. And so it was that in the July of 1889, in the Oxfordshire village she called home, twenty eight year old Theodora took as her husband Robert Wood.

Robert Samuel Wood was born 1861 in Manchester (the son of Richmond Wood), and with a fierce spirit of independence, while still a lad, he took himself off, his destination Bowling Green House, Denbigh, Denbighshire Wales. Thus forward Robert under the care of his maternal grandfather Richard Price, a retired shoemaker in his eighties, who busied himself as Denbigh's Parish Sexton and Green Keeper. The household consisting, in addition to the two afore mentioned, of Prices offspring, Richard, who worked as assistant sexton alongside his father, and Sarah, who acted as housekeeper, a child, Alice Maud Wood (Robert Woods cousin), squeezed into a cramped but cosy bedroom. Though still a minor Robert Wood did not idle by his time, the lad attended to his schooling, he much taken with the law receiving his preparatory training in the field while in his early teens, working as a solicitor's clerk. The law did well for Wood, and with somewhat of a heavy heart, his grandfather having died in 1873, he subsequently left Wales, and required to serve his articules arrived in Watlington.

So where was a newly qualified solicitor to practice, Robert Wood decided upon High Wycombe in Buckinghamshire (arriving in 1890), and declining all offers to join in partnership with well-regarded practices within the town, set up in independent practice, out of premises, 30 High Street. Indeed so enamoured were those of standing in High Wycombe of Robert Wood, the latently qualified solicitor was invited to join the Wycombe Lodge, Wood initiated on Thursday 23rd April 1891 as a Free Mason, his mentor Mr Joseph Bliss. Before long Robert Wood had a much in demand practice, and with the income to do so upgraded his offices to "Saw House", an elegant premises that dominated Easton Street. But this was not the last of it, and not long after Wood relocated to a building on the opposite side of the street, he subsequently opening additional offices in Thame. It would seem that Robert and Theodora Wood lived for some time above the practice, but with ladies often to have sway on such matters the couple took possession of "Bedford House" 159 Queens Road, High Wycombe. It was widely accepted that in order to portray a certain standing in society one should retain a domestic servant, Theodora much gratified of the help of Louisa Vernon, no more so than when in the summer of 1891 she gave birth to Nora Christine Daisy.

Robert Samuel Wood was a recognisable face in the majority of the courts in Oxfordshire and Buckinghamshire, and indeed was no stranger to courts in other parts of the country. One of Woods earliest sensationalist cases to involve the defending of two men charged with the murder of a farmer in Bledlow Ridge (a village some six miles from High Wycombe), an inscription detailing the unfortunate fellows fate upon a stone within the local churchyard. A farmer, one John Kingham of Studmore Farm, had been last seen in Yewsden Wood (which lay between Studmore Farm, and the road which ran from Radnage to West Wycombe), much concern as to his welfare leading to a search, John Kingham found slain. The man's head had been smashed in and his throat slashed, the date of Kingham's violent demise (Thursday 28th September 1893) to pass into infamy. Brothers, twins John and Richard Avery (who resided in Radnage, a quaint village nestled in amongst the Chiltern Hills), were known to poach in the vicinity of Yewsden Wood, and with a reputation as reprobates the two were quickly picked up and charged with murder. The answer to the question of why the constabulary sought them out a simple one, the Avery brother's extended family involved in a protracted feud with the slain farmer.

Three inquests and two trials, the prosecution solicitor of all one Edward Wilkins, failed to convict the Avery's, the outcome of each in no small part down to the diligence of the prisoner's counsel, Robert Wood. The brothers were freed after a protracted last hearing (held in High Wycombe, on Tuesday 24th October 1893), those sat upon the Magistrates Bench, at the late hour of eighteen minutes past seven, dismissing the case through insufficient evidence. John and Richard Avery were, as one can only imagine, much relieved to escape the noose, and thus cast appreciative glances in the direction of their solicitor. It reported in numerous newspapers that Robert Wood spoke only three further words after the Magistrate Chairman ruled in his favour. "Thank you sir." Wood then after escorting the Avery brothers through the centre of High Wycombe (awaiting crowds, as the fancy took them, either cheering or booing), back to his practice office in Easton Street.

Easton Street in High Wycombe
Location of Robert Samuel Wood's solicitors practice

So fresh from his triumph in the Bledlow Ridge affair, and due to continual newspaper coverage not unfamiliar with the dreadful events that had played out at Lambridge Farm, Robert Wood found himself instructed to defend yet another who faced the hangman. Wood had little time for preparation, the judicial system moving swiftly in the 1890s, but what days were allotted him he spent reading, rereading and contemplating legal documents at his disposal. And so Robert Wood made his way to Henley-on-Thames; better to familiarise himself with his client Walter John Rathall, who languished within a cell at Henley Police Station.

Thirty Six

Somewhat Rough and Miserable Appearance

The apprehension of a suspect in regards to the "Henley Murder" did not pass without comment, the Representatives of the Press (either already in situ, or tearing back down to Henley), by facilitation of interview or statement, to turn in articules varying in quality, and truth. These hastily written features arriving, via telegram, upon the desks of countless editors forthwith to appear in numerous regional and national newspapers, many of whom leading with the identical emboldened heading. "Walter Rathall, a labourer, to be brought before the Bench, on Friday 12th January 1894."

By the early morning of the twelfth a crowd, considerable in number, had surrounded Henley Town Hall, many of which having lingered in the vicinity of the buildings portico for many hours, in keen anticipation of the prisoners arrival. Market Place (Henley Town Hall standing resplendent in the upper portion of the square) a hive of discussion and conjecture, those at the front of the melee fortunate souls who found themselves admitted to the public gallery, where Miss Kate Dungeys father and her siblings had been sat since eleven o'clock. The room designated for use as a court quickly packed, those who had been unable to gain admission wandering around aimlessly, in the futile hope that by some miracle they may yet find themselves within the inner sanctum.

Those who had made it into the spectators gallery gazed about the austere courtroom in which they sat, this room not having in living memory borne witness to so many individuals. More than a dozen press reporters were present; an extemporised table placed along the back of the courtroom to facilitate them, some of whom skilled sketch artists, ready with paper and pencil. Newspapers, the length and breadth of the country, set to fill their columns with details of the unprecedented events occurring in Henley, indeed their number so great one can mention but a few (which I will endeavour to do), though it cannot be substantiated which editors sent their own reporters to Henley-on-Thames, and which sourced details of the trial via press representatives.

Lloyds Weekly (circulated via Lloyds Illustrated London Newspaper Group) was founded in 1842 by one Edward Lloyd, he at the time not yet twenty seven. The paper (following on from the considerable success of Lloyds Penny Weekly) promoted Liberal policies, and offered its readership, for the sum of two pence, eight pages crammed with articles, brought to life by the addition of finely detailed illustrations, these produced at the presses by the use of intricately wood cut drawings. By the time of the so called "Henley Murder" Lloyds Weekly's founder Edward Lloyd had been dead in excess of three years, his son Frank, who had inherited control of the paper, having substantially increased circulation, assisted by his editor Thomas Latling, who had worked on the newspaper from its very conception.

The Pall Mall Gazette (its name inspired by a fictional newspaper which appeared in William Thackeray's "The History of Pendennis") was launched on 7th February 1856, by George Murrey Smith (1824-1901), who earned a crust as an India Agent, his paper (which hit the London newsstands Monday through to Saturday, on the cusp of the evening rush hour) one which had definite Conservative leanings. Its first editor, Mr Frederick Greenwood (1830-1909) specifically providing news items for gentlemen, many of the newspapers articles to deal with seminal political and social questions. In 1880 the Pall Mall Gazette came under new ownership and was radically changed in political direction, thus forward to champion the Liberal cause, Frederick Greenwood (who resigned in protest at the papers altered political stance) superseded in 1883 by one William Thomas Stead, he in 1912 to perish aboard the ill-fated Titanic. The revamped Pall Mall Gazette dealt primarily with investigative journalism (at a point in history when the concept was relatively unknown), its primary mission to expose injustice and create causes to fire the passions of its readership. By the time of the events in Henley-on-Thames, the Pall Mall Gazette (under ownership of forty five year old American businessman, William Waldorf Astor, and edited by Henry Cust) had returned to its original Conservative ethos, thus proving itself a firm favourite at the newsstands.

Undoubtedly one newspaper that stood out from the rest was the Illustrated Police News (that included in several of its editions verbatim transcripts regards the enquiries into the murder at Lambridge Farm), which first hit the newsstands of London in 1864, launched by John Ransom of Fleet Street, and owned by Messrs Lee and Bulpin. The tabloid subsequently taken over by George Purkess (a former bankrupt, and onetime publisher of Purkess's Penny Library of Romances), who within the columns of the Illustrated Police News accurately reported true life stories (so he claimed), that dealt on the most part with shocking crimes, fluke accidents and domestic tragedy. As the first (and the longest lasting) Saturday newspaper, its cost a modest penny, the Illustrated Police News was unquestionable a weekly paper that could not in any way escape allegations that it sensationalized the tragic, its coverage of the Whitechapel Ripper Murders a point in fact. The papers readership provided with finely detailed articules (to the point of unsavoury), and if the feature warranted it gruesome illustrations, that is to be remarked upon outraged the more gentile of Victorian society.

Upon the express instructions of Henley Town Sergeant, Mr Edwin Savage (one of his roles that of keeper of the town hall), seats had been reserved within the spectators gallery, for the sole use of well-heeled local businessmen, and councillors. Some of those who achieved what others had so desired, a guaranteed seat, named within the columns of the Henley and South Oxfordshire Standard, which run off the presses the late afternoon of twelfth December. "Present in court, Aldermen Charles Clements, George Fuller, Councillor Charles Michael Roberts, Thomas Riggs, Benjamin Joseph Taylor, Alfred Austin, Reverend J. Taylor, Mr William T. Coates, Mr Paul Makins, Mr Charles Tubb, and Chief Constable of Oxfordshire, Captain Holmes A' Court." At this juncture it pertinent to expand on afore mentioned gentlemen.

Charles Clements was a fellow with a kindly face, he boasting a fine beard, as a former Henley Mayor (served 1885-86, 1892-93) and Alderman of the town, certainly possessing the clout required to ensure him one of the coveted reserved seats, and an unhindered view, better to witness the appearance before the Magistrates of Walter John Rathall. Clements, by the circumstance of coincidence, not that far removed from the prisoner. By the January of 1894 Charles Clements had turned forty eight, native to Henley-on-Thames, the youngest son of one Thomas Clements, a shoemaker, who from 1844 to 1877 had been landlord of the Red Lion, where in the winter of 1893 Rathall, his wife and infant daughter had secured lodgings.

Charles Clements, a builder and contractor who paid the wages of a team of twenty one men and two boys, did not have far to venture on the morning of 12th January, as he resided above his works office, 41 Market Place, a distinctively ornate premises that stood directly next door to Broad Gates Beerhouse, this hostelry under the landlordship of Charles Letchford Shepherd.

Sixty nine year old George Richard Fuller, a gentleman of portly proportions more than a little squeezed in between those sat either side, as an Alderman had much in common with his neighbouring spectator, Charles Clements. A craftsman of no mean ability, Fuller ran his business out of 27-29 Market Place, in the 1869 Post Office Directory he listed as "Cabinet Maker, Upholsterer, House & Estate

Agent", by the census return of April 1871 able to afford the wages of six men and one boy.

By the January of 1894 George Fuller had no hindrance to his attending Henley Magistrates Court, retired the previous year from his profession, his former Market Place premises taken on by John Hatton, who had relocated both his fancy drapery (formerly at 17 Market Place) and his outfitters, which he had previously run out of 69 Bell Street. More than comfortably off George Fuller resided at an architecturally quirky house, in the Arts and Crafts Style, which went by the name of "Rosebery", 4 Queens Villas. This property situated on Queen Street, those leaving it on foot (as I'm sure George Fuller did), after a brief walk up Friday Street, along Duke Street, and on into Market Place, at the very heart of the drama that was unfolding within Henley Town Hall.

George Richard Fuller, looking somewhat sombre
Photographed at the time of his term as Henley Mayor, 1887-88

Yet another councillor, one Charles Michael Roberts, had also managed to wangle one of the coveted seats. A difficult man to pin down, he the proprietor since 1891 of the Catherine Wheel, a hostelry, family and commercial hotel under the ownership of Brakspears Brewery. Roberts beerhouse (a premises ancient in structure, run as a hostelry since the late fifteenth century), which was situated close to the four way junction at the top end of Hart Street (neighboured on either side by John Tranters florists shop, and Edward Melletts veterinary practice), utilised by local auction houses, many of the areas principal estates going under the gavel within the sizable backrooms of the Catherine Wheel.

Wealth certainly afforded special privilege, and Thomas Riggs, a man of commerce and boasting a fine lineage within the town, was never in any doubt that he would find himself settled within the reserved area of the spectators gallery (looked upon in some envy by those mere mortals confined to the overcrowded general spectators gallery), keen as mustard to see all that was to follow.

Thomas Riggs had just turned thirty one; the third generation of a dynasty of maltsters, in his childhood beneficiary of a share of a considerable fortune (in excess of twenty eight thousand pounds), bequeathed by his father George Riggs, who had died 22nd October 1866. Brewing was the Riggs bread and butter, and Thomas Riggs held the maltsters on Hart Street, which his grandfather Thomas Beckett Riggs (died 23rd June 1866) had taken on long lease in 1863. The young gentleman, who now happily conversed with his fellow courtroom spectators, had chosen not to reside within the Georgian house that sat alongside the Hart Street maltsters, occupying instead a none too shabby premises on the Fairmile, Riggs splitting his time between Henley and Twickenham, where he had possession of an additional home.

Benjamin Joseph Taylor, while still a boy, had been placed into the care of his widowed sister, Sarah Jane Grainger. He not an idle lad had realised the necessity to secure an apprenticeship, taken on as a cooper's assistant. No doubt attracted by the Thames Valleys many breweries, who sought out those with the expertise of cooper, in the early 1860s Taylor quit his sister's home in Newbury (75 Northbrook Street), and duly secured employment in Henley-on-Thames, able to pay the rent on a cosy property on the riverside. Skilled men were always in demand, and Benjamin Taylor proved no exception, in due course affording to take possession of 66 Bell Street.

If Taylor, who at the time of Walter Rathalls trial was nearing fifty, was self-employed is not clear, he could have worked for any number of breweries, there being both large and small independent practitioners within Henley's boundaries. But seemingly Benjamin Taylor was his own man, and thus able on 12th January to take a day off to attend the Henley Magistrates Court, the weather on the day bitingly cold, but thankfully for those condemned to remain without, dry.

Alfred Austin, a commercial traveller who specialised in tea and coffee, had ambition to run a grocery shop. In the course of his travels to come to know of a business opportunity in Henley-on-Thames, and thus in the 1880s Austin relocated.

Though there is no particular note of Henley shops closing on the day of Rathalls appearance before the magistrates, one can imagine that not much business was done. Who knows if Alfred Austin shut up his grocers (located at 1 New Street), and if he did not, his staff were left to their own devices, their employer having by early morning nabbed a seat within the spectators gallery.

Like many others settled within the cordoned off area of the gallery that particular morning, Alfred Austin also possessed the gravitas necessary to have been guaranteed admittance, he a councillor. The man sat alongside him was not, his profession neither the less had seen him escorted by a court usher to the reserved area, he a minister. The Reverend John Taylor preached at the Congregational Chapel, which stood on the Reading Road, almost opposite Caxton House. Having taken up his ministry in Henley in 1892 Taylor had rapidly ingratiated himself with those who found life a daily challenge. The poor, both of financial and spiritual worth, found John Taylor a kindly man, and as an active member of the "Brotherhood Movement", in 1893 he had co-founded the Henley Pleasant Sunday Afternoon Brotherhood, its purpose to encourage all walks of life to converge for one purpose, companionship. What decided this congregational minister to attend Walter Rathalls hearing was clearly more than mawkish curiosity; it of no doubt that genuine Christian concern for another was forefront in John Taylors thinking.

1888 had seen the mayoral ship of one William Thomas Coates, this man, noted as possessing a magnanimous disposition (a fervent abstainer from all forms of alcohol, and Liberal in politics), a familiar face around Henley, having run in excess of two decades a drapery business, located at 14 Hart Street.

Advanced age was now upon William Coates, he at the time in question nearing seventy, and recently having taken a back seat his drapery business now in the care of the next generation, son Henry Whittenham Coates. So the bind of work commitments did not burden the old gentleman, and recently relocated to 6 Caxton Terrace, Station Road, and feeling, as many retired did, somewhat at a loose end, in many respects William relished the opportunity to experience a murder trial first hand.

There could be no argument on what got Paul Augustine Makins passed the court ushers, his papa William Thomas Makins, the very magistrate who had remanded Walter Rathall on the charge of wilful murder. Paul Makins, a bachelor of twenty two, down from Trinity College, Cambridge, for the winter break, and with the advantage of his father's direct involvement in the criminal proceedings (and the benefit of a close friendship with Richard Ovey, the Makins frequent visitors to Badgemore House), Paul enjoyed, for his convenience, a position within the spectators gallery which allowed its occupier a superior view of all that was to follow.

The latter years of the 1860s saw one Charles Tubbs arrival in Lower Assenden, where he took on the landlordship of the Golden Ball. But this fellow had other strings to his bow, and by the mid-1880s had acquired Swiss Farm, Old Brick Kiln, located on the Marlow Road, close to the boundary of Henley Park. Having brought the place up to scratch Tubb decided that the primary business of the farm would be that of dairy cattle, and before long much of the milk found in Henley's grocery outlets was sourced from Swiss Farm.

So it was that Charles Tubb took occupation of the very last nugget of space, within the portion of the spectators gallery reserved for those who courted influence, he nodding an acknowledgement to the man seated alongside him. Resplendent in dress uniform that gentleman none other than the Chief Constable of Oxfordshire, Captain Holmes A' Court, who was attending in his capacity as observer for the constabulary.

So with the expansion on the character of the courtroom spectators dealt with, it must be acknowledged that there were others who the reporter for the local paper chose to mark out, that being the Henley Division Bench of Magistrates, and the legal representatives, the latter of whom keenly conversing with their juniors. "Magistrates Chairman, Mr Joseph Henry Wilson is assisted by General Robert Napier Raikes, Henry Brigham Douglas Vanderstegen, Robert Trotter Hermon Hodge and Henry John Simonds. The Magistrates Clerk, John Frederick Cooper, Mr Sydney Brain of Reading, appearing on behalf of the Treasury, for the Prosecution, and Robert S. Wood representing the prisoner."

At eleven fifty precisely Walter Rathall was taken from his cell within Henley Police Station, and walked the short distance across to Henley Town Hall (accompanied by ten police constables and a unnamed detective, this individual, seemingly sent down from London to assist the enquiry, somewhat infuriatingly never given a name), to be met by a now enormous crowd, whose patience was rewarded with a glimpse of the supposed villain.

Photograph of Henleys Georgian town hall
Location of Walter Rathalls appearance before the Magistrates Bench

Some members of the wider press, who had temporally vacated the courtroom, took pencil and notebook from their coat pockets, and dutifully recorded their interpretations on the appearance of Walter Rathall, one hack describing the prisoner rather derogatorily. "He is a tall slender individual, with a somewhat rough and miserable appearance." Walter Rathall (closely supervised by his police guard), pushed through the baying mob, and made his way up into the portico entrance of Henley Town Hall, thus relieved of his handcuffs, brought into the courtroom and placed within the dock. This man, who must have been much daunted by his ordeal, did not sit mutely by, he immediately appearing to follow the preliminary procedures with keen interest, Walter Rathall reported as, "Showing no visible signs of agitation."

The courtroom, that up to that point was alive with voices, fell silent as Court Clerk, John Cooper, stood forward of his seat, and upon direction of the Chief Magistrate read aloud the indictment. 'Walter Rathall you stand charged that on Friday 8th December 1893, at Lambridge House in the Parish of Henley-on-Thames, you did feloniously, wilfully, and with malice aforethought kill and murder one Kate Dungey.'

The trial was now firmly underway and at this juncture Robert Samuel Wood, solicitor for the prisoner, had opportunity to lay the groundwork of his defence argument. He thus leapt to his feet (somewhat theatrically) keen to commence his opening address. 'I draw to the attention of the bench a report which had appeared in the People, on Sunday 7th January, which contained facts pertaining to Walter Rathall's poverty. I characterised this as highly improper as the article had stated that sufficient evidence would be taken to condemn the prisoner, but also imputing allegations against someone else.'

There was from the spectator's gallery a unified gasp as Magistrate Chairman, Joseph Henry Wilson, momentarily halted the solicitor in his tracks. 'I have not seen the paper.'

The defence solicitor was not thrown off his stride by the interruption and continued with a passion often found in those as yet unjaded by the complexities of the legal system. 'The prisoner was not seen in a public house in Henley, nor had he deserted his wife and infant, leaving them in Henley Workhouse. This fact is untrue, he left his family there so that he might go to Richmond in search of work, while there recognised in one of the areas workhouses, but his effort met with no success (the court never to hear again of the supposed trip to Richmond, nor the workhouse witness), and a while later he left the place, returning to Henley-on-Thames.' Satisfied that his opening argument, one filled with heavily laboured pathos in regards to the happenstance of misfortunes that life had thrust upon his client, Wood returned to his chair, and flung himself upon it with aplomb.

Sydney Brain glanced across at the table, behind which sat Robert Wood, and the solicitor for the prosecution half smiled, somewhat insidiously, at the younger man. Here was a fellow of notable legal prowess, and the London Standard, which hit the newsstands on the evening of Friday 12th January, paid particularly close attention to Sydney Brains opening argument. 'I have been instructed by the Solicitor for the Treasury, who have undertaken the prosecution, to support the charge against the prisoner of wilfully murdering Miss Dungey on Friday 8th December. I will show that the prisoner had been seen on the Thursday previous to the murder near the house, and that on that Friday he was absent from the Red Lion, where he was staying, from half four to half past seven, or a quarter to eight, during which time the murder was committed. It will be shown that the prisoner had a cheque on that evening, but that he had not recouped any cheque for wages. On the Monday following the murder, the prisoner went to Ealing, whence he returned to Henley on December sixteenth. He afterwards left with his wife and child, and was subsequently arrested at Daventry.' Sydney Brain had put forward, in some considerable detail, the beginnings of his case against the prisoner, and as he took his seat (somewhat more sedately than his opposition solicitor), many spectators and members of the press fixed their eyes upon Walter Rathall, who stood before them charged with a capital offence, which if proven could ultimately lead to the forfeiting of his life.

Thirty Seven

The Ten Thirty Five From Paddington

The Chairman of the Bench (Joseph Henry Wilson), satisfied as to the fulfilment of each of the solicitor's obligations, in regard to their opening arguments, with a flurry of his hands in the direction of Sydney Brain, indicated that the prosecution could call its first witness.

Henry Joseph Mash (a very heavy set fellow, he in anticipation of his appearance before the magistrates noticeable perspiring) was seated in a corridor in close proximity to the courtroom, lost in thought, abruptly shaken from his mithering upon hearing his name called. The court clerk, who had dragged Henry Mash back to the reality of his situation, John Frederick Cooper, he escorting the witness to the stand; Mash thus required to state his credentials.

'I am Henry Joseph Mash, and I reside at twelve Redcliffe Gardens, and carry on the business of fruiterer at fifty six Glass House Street. I have a town house in New Street, Henley-on-Thames, and am a tenant at Lambridge House.' The Henley and South Oxfordshire Standard for the benefit of its readership (many of whom craved every last detail of the matter) to carry within its next edition a summary of the location of Mashs tenancy, Lambridge House. "It is situated on the edge of Lambridge Wood, and the wood surrounds it on three sides, it is open on the side nearest Assenden, it is separated from the road that leads to the main Oxford Road by two fields, and there are many ways of approaching the house from Henley."

Henry Joseph Mash, described by his friends as a man of generous spirit

As was the custom the prosecution had first crack at the witness, and Sydney Brain, after a hurried conversation with his colleagues, took the floor. 'I acknowledge the difficulty of your situation, and the fortitude of your giving evidence in regards to your employee Miss Dungey. How long had the aforementioned been in your employ?'
Mash took some seconds to respond, he glancing up at the spectators, who to a person seemed to be transfixed on the previously inconspicuous fruit merchant. A moments grace sufficiently steadied Mashs nerves, and he answered Sydney Brain. 'Miss Dungey had been in my service for seven years.'
'Were all seven years spent in the capacity as housekeeper of Lambridge?'

'No sir, she had formally been my children's governess.'

'How many years had Miss Dungey had employment at Lambridge?'

'For close to five years she had been my housekeeper at Lambridge Farm.'

'Did the young lady have servants under her?'

'No, she took on complete management of Lambridge, there being no servants.'

'And what did this role require of Miss Dungey?'

'She managed the running of the house, and cooked for us when we were there.'

'You considered her a good servant?'

There was at this point an audible gasp from the spectator's gallery as the witness faltered, Henry Mashs voice failing him. Sydney Brain indicated, by way of a gentle smile, that the witness was to be allowed time to recover his composure, and in due course Mash found his voice. 'She was more than that, Kate was regarded as one of the family, and when Mrs Mash or any of her daughters were staying at the house she would assist Miss Dungey in the work of the house and dairy.'

Joseph Wilson, whose curiosity was aroused by the last utterances of Henry Mash, interjected. 'When you spent time at Lambridge, how long would your visits usually last?'

The witness pondered for a moment, and then proceeded to give a rather vague example, by way of his reply. 'In December last my daughter had stayed a week with Miss Dungey, but none of the family resided at the property on a permanent bases, Lambridge being mainly used as a summer house for family and friends.'

Sydney Brain, who had stepped behind the table provided for his convenience, better to examine one of the evidence bundles, mindful of Joseph Wilsons sensibilities waited to see if the man had more to say. And content that he did not; Brain emerged from behind the table and again took the floor. 'When had your daughter vacated Lambridge?'

'I took my daughter with me the Friday preceding the eighth of December (Henry Mash to visible pale as he stated this information, no doubt thinking on the fact that his child had been at Lambridge not more than one week before the murder), she having stayed at the house a full week.'

Again the prosecution solicitor to suffer an interruption, as an anonymous magistrate (not named in any subsequent newspaper report) enquired of the witness. 'Which members of the Mash family frequented Lambridge House?'

Henry Mash, to face examination from all quarters, held his nerve, and swung round to face his latest interrogator. 'Different members of the family used to go down, on and off throughout the year.'

'Did Miss Dungey have the company of others while your family were absent?'

'Except when we were there, Kate Dungey was left alone in the house. She did however have two boys, James and Harry Froomes, to sleep in the building at night.' At this juncture Henry Mash, without direction to do so, to insert into his testimony a short impassioned outburst that had cause to send a ripple of inaudible mutterings (compliments of those sat within the spectator's gallery) throughout the courtroom. 'After collecting my child on the first, I here stipulate that I did not see Miss Dungey alive again!'

Solicitor for the prosecution, Sydney Brain, satisfied that there would be no further interruption on the part of the magistrates, addressed his witness. 'Many have pondered, be it press or otherwise, on the out of the way location of Lambridge Farm. How is it that the deceased came to be employed at such an isolated location?'

'Miss Dungey was not unduly concerned about her situation at the farm; she in fact much enjoyed the solitude. Nobody, except family lived in the house for any length of time, though the children often spent their school holidays there, and Miss Dungey had lived in the house under these circumstances all the time.'

'Was the deceased ever to spend time at any other abode?'

'I have another house in Henley (37 New Street), and last winter Miss Dungey lived there for ten weeks, and my man Dawson lived at Lambridge.'

'Could you tell the court the dates Miss Dungey habituated at New Street?'

'I could not say.'

'Why was Lambridge Farm fixed upon as the place of Miss Dungeys employment?'

'It was my familys wish that she should go to Lambridge House, but there was no undue pressure placed upon Miss Dungey, she went to reside at the house of her own free will.'

'How far from Lambridge was the nearest house?'

'It was a lonely place; I cannot say how far the nearest house is.'

At this point the witness was interrupted by Magistrates Chairman, Joseph Wilson, who privy to information he thought would be of assistance, shared it with the court. 'The property is about one and three quarters of a mile from Henley.'

Sydney Brain, though his expression did convey that he was a little irked at yet another interruption, thanked the Magistrate Chairman for this nugget of information. (Though it had little to do with what the prosecution solicitor had asked of his witness.) Again the solicitor made use of his notes, and back on track took up his line of questioning. 'Could you explain for the benefit of the court the arrangement that led to two lads sleeping at Lambridge?'

'I knew two boys named Froomes, James the eldest in my employ, the child and his brother, Harry, coming up to Lambridge House to sleep.'

'And at what time did the boys arrive and vacate Lambridge?'

'I had nothing to do with giving the Froomes boys orders as to sleeping at the farm, and what time they should go to Lambridge. I never interfered in matters of that kind, but left it to Miss Dungey.'

'When did you sir, last sleep at the house?'

Mr Henry Joseph Mash was a man exhausted by the habitual public scrutiny he found himself under (much of which insidious gossip, carried within the columns of the newspapers), and Brains seemingly innocent enquiry caused him much discomfort. 'As a point of fact I did not visit Henley from December first. I was not in Henley the day before the murder, and most certainly had not slept in Henley the night preceding the murder, being at my property twelve Redcliffe Gardens, where I received a telegram on the Saturday of December ninth, being called to Henley after the outrage.'

Sydney Brain had cause for self-chastisement; he inadvertently alienating his witness, and not wishing to hamper his exploration of the facts he quickly changed tack. 'George Dawson was also in your employ, what was his position?'

'George Dawson worked for me as a general all-round farm servant, and did such jobs as milking cows and attending to the horses (the facts Mash alluded to, which pertained to Dawsons job role, to be included within the columns of umpteen regional newspapers), though he resigned the situation last Saturday, having given a week's notice.'

The seemingly innocuous conclusion of Mashs utterance, to cause a flurry of excited chattering amongst members of the spectator's gallery, and the scribbling's of reporters within their notebooks.

'How far did the man live from the site of the murder?'

Henry Mash took time to consider this question before he answered. 'George Dawson and his wife lived some little distance from Lambridge House; his house could be seen from the orchard.'

'How long would it take to walk at a leisurely pace from Dawsons to Lambridge House?'

'I feel that it would be no more than a six minute walk.'

The foundations had been laid, and the solicitor for the prosecution now turned his attention to the prisoner who stood in the dock. 'Could you provide an account of Rathalls character?'

'I have known Walter Rathall some twelve years, Walters mother had minded Lambridge up to about 1889, her son just a lad then.'

'Did the prisoner sleep at the house?'

'Sometimes he slept at the house, from about 1883 to 1889.'

'Did the prisoner work at the farm?'

'During that time he worked on a casual basis for me.'

'Was the prisoner known to the deceased?'

'Rathall was well acquainted with the deceased.'

'Were Rathall and Miss Dungey on good terms?'

'I should think that they were on good terms.'

Sydney Brains nemesis again cut in, Joseph Wilson asking of Henry Mash. 'What terms existed between these two people?'

'They were, as far as I am aware on good terms during the time they were acquainted. Rathall worked on and off at the farm, and would be under Miss Dungeys control. She would pay him his wages.'

'What amount of wages did she pay the prisoner?'

'I cannot remember what the amount was.'

At this juncture a magistrate (their identity unspecified) to level a series of questions. 'What was the reason behind Mary Rathalls ceasing to mind Lambridge?'

'Walters mother was unable to continue as she became incapacitated through ill health (her malady a bad back), and in 1889 both she and her son (this being Walter Rathall) ceased to live at Lambridge House.'

'While employed at Lambridge was Rathall under Miss Dungeys orders, and was it she who always paid him?'

'I am not able to say if Rathall was regularly under instruction of the lady, but Mrs Mash would pay him on occasion, such as when he had 4d a week for bringing up letters from Henley.'

Chairman of the Bench, Joseph Wilson, raised an eyebrow, and rather abruptly interjected. 'Do you know the terms between the two people?'

'I don't know that she had anything to do with him for several years, when she was governess she might have had (Kate Dungey and the children in her charge known to frequent Lambridge House), I should think they were on good terms, they were on good terms in 1889, but since then I don't know.'

Robert Samuel Wood for the defence, who had up to this point sat in abject silence, chose now to cross examine the witness. 'Have you ever seen a stranger visit Miss Dungey?'

'I am not aware of any unknown visitor calling on Miss Dungey.'

'Did the deceased and the prisoner correspond?'

'I do not think there was any correspondence between her and the prisoner.'

'Are you aware of any burdens on Miss Dungey, in relation to emotional turmoil?'

'I do not think she had any emotional troubles.'

Sydney Brain, who had listened closely to Robert Woods line of questions, sure that for the moment the defence solicitor was satisfied, led the witness further down the avenue of questions in relation to the private life of the deceased. 'During her time of employment with your family was Miss Dungey ever engaged?'

'She was not engaged to anyone, nor have I known her ever to be.'

'Did she correspond with any gentleman?'

'She never told me she was corresponding with any young gentleman, and I never have seen any stranger visit Kate.'

'Did the deceased have any mental problems?'

'I do not think she had any mental troubles, Miss Dungey was too happy to be experiencing any personal troubles.'

The prosecution had one fundamental purpose, that to establish that the accused had violently ended the life of Lambridges housekeeper and with this task firmly in mind Sydney Brain moved his witness on to events that followed swiftly on from the fateful night of eighth December. 'Please tell the court when you were first made aware of the terrible event.'

'I first heard of the murder on the Saturday of the ninth, coming immediately down to Henley, then on to Lambridge.'

'What route did your journey to Lambridge take?'

'I came to Henley on December ninth by the ten thirty five from Paddington, and arrived at the house at Lambridge about twelve forty five.'

'Did you travel down in isolation?'

'No sir, I was with Mrs Mash and Miss Julia Dungey (this the first time the source material alludes to Julia Dungey having travelled to Henley alongside the Mashs, this young woman sister to Kate and in the employ of Henry Mash), Mr Shepherd of Broad Gates drove us up.' This would be the aforementioned Charles Shepherd, landlord of Broad Gates Inn, Market Place.

'It is correct is it not that you had cause to search the house.'

'I looked all around, and could not find anything missing.'

'Why did you search Lambridge House?'

'Superintendent Keal had wanted those familiar with the property to check if they could pinpoint any items as missing. We as a party had searched to see if anything had been moved or was missing.'

There had been some conjecture, where it roots lay unknown that one of those who searched Lambridge hid about their person some letters, which they later removed, and Brain now touched upon this matter. 'I have to ask about the matter of some letters that seemingly have been removed from the murder scene, a fact which has caused much speculation.'

Henry Mash was much riled by the inference, and he breathed in sharply, and then after let out a protracted sigh. 'I did not carry anything away; I did not carry away any letters. Miss Julia Dungey took two letters which were unopened on the table; one was partly written by me and finished by Miss Julia Dungey, they were on the kitchen table.'

'Where are the letters now?'

'I do not know where the letters are now, and the father (Walter Dungey) has the satchel (where he supposedly deposited the letters), which was removed from the house, there was nothing else taken away.'

'Where did the deceased keep her money?'

'I do not know where the deceased kept her money.'

What followed, it is lamentable to say, enthralled many sat within the spectator's gallery, while others, Kates family notwithstanding, were greatly distressed. 'You did have to, I understand, look upon the deceased.'

'I saw the body of Miss Dungey, and identified it!'

Sydney Brain stood in silence for some seconds, as if to heighten the tension, and then retreated to his seat, defence Solicitor Robert Wood taking the floor, he to immediately throw a spanner in the works. 'Do you have any suggestion as to why Rathall should commit this murder?'

The witness again put out of sorts, he thus directing a question into the air. 'Am I to answer this question?' Bench Chairman, Joseph Wilson, informing him that he need not.

Sydney Brain, not in his seat for any length of time, leapt to his feet and rounded on the defence solicitor. 'Are we not dealing with facts?'

Undaunted by the utterances of witness, chairman and prosecution, Robert Wood ploughed on. 'Did you visit Henley between the first and eighth of December?'

'No!'

'You swear that you did not set eyes upon Miss Dungey between the first and eighth.'

Henry Mash answered wearily. 'Certainly I did not.'
'Did you sleep at Henley on the night before the murder?'
'Certainly not, I slept in London at my residence twelve Redcliffe Gardens.'
'And of the two letters, which we must revisit the subject of, and the bag (Robert Wood refers to the satchel), where are they now?'
'I have not the faintest idea!'
It was common knowledge that Henry Mash had put up a reward in an effort to bring to justice the person (or persons) responsible for the murder of Miss Dungey, a gesture which had caused some to question relationship between master and servant, Robert Wood keen to explore this matter. 'On the subject of the one hundred pound reward, this surely reflects that you the witness thought a great deal of the deceased.'
I did, she was a very worthy woman, a good servant, faithful servant.'

A somewhat rudimentary line drawing of Miss Kate Laura Dungey
Appeared within the Sunday 17th December 1893 edition of Lloyds Weekly

Robert Wood, surprisingly brief in the course of his cross examination of the witness, uttered not another word; he simply nodded his thanks to Henry Mash, turned his back on the witness stand, and ambled over to his chair.

And thus Joseph Wilson, satisfied that all those concerned had no further need of the witness, excused the master of Lambridge House. But Henry Joseph Mash did not vacate the courtroom, he permitted to take possession of a seat, a reserved area of the gallery at his disposal, and he did just that.

Thirty Eight

Very Much Like Wood, Such as Might Fall From a Tree

Walter Rathalls abiding connection to Lambridge Farm had been introduced into evidence, and Sydney Brain, a highly experienced advocate, was now set to explore the darker elements of the prisoner's character, thus John Cooper called Mrs Emily Ayres.

The landlady of the Red Lion was unfamiliar with the procedures of a courtroom, but, as described by the hacks who reported on the womans time in the witness stand, she neither the less coped with the experience with gusto.

'Can you state your name and occupation for the court?'

'My name is Emily Ayres, and I am married to Joseph Ayres, the two of us run the Red Lion Beerhouse, on West Hill, Henley.' By this time known as West Street, many locals still referred to the area by its former name.

The prosecution solicitor had before him a witness who had much reason to abhor Rathall, and Brain, familiar with the womans police statement, was quietly confident that before him stood one who could prove herself the linchpin of his case against Walter Rathall. 'How long have you known the prisoner?'

'I have known Rathall since the middle months of 1893, when he had cause to stay at my establishment.'

'How long did he stay on that occasion?'

'He stayed but one night.'

'In regard to the prisoner's recent occupation, how long had he been present under your roof?'

'He had been at our lodging house some eight or nine weeks.'

'Was he alone?'

'No, his wife and young child were with him.'

'It is correct, is it not, that the prisoner was at your lodging house on both the seventh and eighth of December?'

'Yes, the accused had been a guest at the Red Lion on both the seventh and eighth of December.'

Key evidence had been introduced; Sydney Brain having set before the court the whereabouts of the prisoner on both the day preceding the murder and the day of the outrage. Rathall's location was irrefutably fixed as to him having been in Henley, and the prisoner was seen to grimace, aware no doubt that more damning testimony was to follow.

Having read and digested witness statements (transcribed at the time of witnesses police interviews, and now at the disposal of both prosecution and defence), Brain, in an effort to cast aspersions on the prisoners lax morals, fixed his next line of questioning upon the delicate subject of money. 'Mrs Ayres, could you specify for the benefit of the court if any money matters had been discussed between you and the prisoner?'

'We had a conversation on December sixth about money; he said he was beating for the shooting at Mr Mackenzie's (that being William Dalziel Mackenzie, who resided at his estate, Fawley Court), I had no previous conversation with him. Though now I think on it he had said before that time that he was picking stones at Mr Oveys Farm.'

Richard Ovey held the estate of Badgemore, his bailiff taking on men as stone pickers, a backbreaking occupation, where those employed to do so removed stones from arable fields, before planting of crops took place.

'Before the times just now alluded to, had you had reason to question the prisoner on the problematic subject of rent?'

Emily Ayres stood transfixed, as if momentarily dumfounded, no doubt poleaxed by the prosecution solicitors overly elaborate turn of phrase. 'I had always had my money before that.'

'Was the prisoner to recant on his promise of payment of rent?'

Mrs Ayres furrowed her brow, an expression of some annoyance clearly discernible. 'Yes, up until that point I had money paid every night for rent, but as Rathall had informed me of his employment with Mackenzie, I had trusted him!'

'Can you tell us of the movements of the prisoner on eighth December?' Sydney Brain had moved onto the night of the murder, and up in the gallery spectators leaned forward, arms rested on the parapet, chins rested on arms, eager to catch every last utterance.

'Rathall went out of the house about nine in the morning, he returned between ten and eleven and it was obvious, in my opinion, that he had not done any work.' The last unbidden snippet determined, by the men of the press, to convey the witnesses scant regard for Walter John Rathall.

'Was he carrying anything?'

Emily Ayres now took the opportunity to further impugn the prisoner. 'Oh yes sir, Rathall had under his arm a straight piece of rough stick, very much like wood, such as might fall from a tree.'

'How long, do you say the stick was?'

'It was a short piece, about three feet that anyone might pick out of the wood and bring home.' This revelation, in regards to said stick (no doubt thought by many present in the spectators gallery to have bearing, in relation to the weapon used against the person of Miss Kate Dungey), drew a unified in taking of breath amongst those who sat transfixed, in awe of every word that erupted from the lips of Emily Ayres. One must at this point explore the matter of the stick, and consider that as an item of some great importance, in relation to the injuries inflicted on the victim, had the stick in question been sought out. And if so, why did it not appear as an item catalogued and placed upon the courtroom evidence table.

Once all had settled down (Joseph Wilson calling for order in court), Brain took up his line of questions. 'Did you speak to the prisoner, when he returned in possession of said stick?'

The landlady of the Red Lion did in deed converse with the prisoner, and recalled (in acute detail) for the benefit of the magistrates, all that had passed between landlady, prisoner, and Mrs Rathall. 'I said you are returned like a bad penny, and he replied.' "Yes Mrs Ayres I am."

'Did you not also converse with Rathalls wife?'

'Yes I informed Mrs Rathall that her husband had returned.'

'Did the prisoner's wife acknowledge you?'

'Yes she did, indeed Rathalls wife could clearly tell that her husband had done no work that day.' At this point the defence to object, the witness informed by the bench that she must stick only to the facts.

'What form did the conversation between you and Mrs Rathall take.'

'She could see concern on my face, and said words in the nature of. "It doesn't matter; the keeper (pheasant keeper at Fawley Estate) is going to let him have a crown on next week's money."

'Is this all the dealings you had with the Rathalls?'

'No, his wife then helped with some scrubbing (Emily Ayres alludes here to Annie Rathall cleaning potatoes, ready for the pot), while the prisoner nursed the baby.'

'How long did the prisoner stay within the lodging house?'

'The prisoner stayed at the Red Lion until half past four.'

'How sure are you of the time?'

'I know that was the time because my sister had just asked the time (this the first, and last, heard of the presence of Emily Ayres sister), and I looked at the clock a few minutes before I saw the prisoner going out of my kitchen door.'

'Did you, Mrs Ayres, have cause to leave the Red Lion, the remainder of that day?'

'I stayed in the house the whole of the remainder of the day.'

'When did you next see the prisoner?'

'I did not see Rathall again until between half past seven and a quarter to eight.'

'Where did you see him?'

Emily Ayres was indeed a witness with an impeccable memory, with recall of the briefest of snatched conversations. 'I was in the kitchen throughout the early evening, and did not at any time see Rathall. But when revisiting the room nearer eight o'clock I met with the prisoner, who was just coming in via the kitchen door.'

'Did you speak to the prisoner at this point?'

'No sir, but his wife duly acknowledged him.'

'Can you recall what Mrs Rathall said to her husband?'

"I can sir; she said words in the nature of. "You are late coming in tonight."

'And what of the prisoners reply?'

'Well he sat himself down and announced to his wife. "I have no money tonight." His wife asking of him how it was he had no money.'

'Did the prisoner reply?'

'I clearly heard him reply.'

'Can you tell the court what the gist of his reply was?'

'I can do better than that; I can recall each and every word (At this point a ripple of laughter reverberating around the court), Rathall told his wife that the keeper could not change a five pound cheque, but that he should have it in the morning. He told his wife he had been to work, but the following morning he told how he had not been to work.'

'Do you know the name of the keeper?'

'No sir, I do not know who the keeper was.'

'You had no rent, you did not object to this?'

The landlady of the Red Lion, clearly a woman mightily miffed with her former guest, not to flinch one bit under the scrutiny of the prosecution, nor the gaze of the prisoner in the dock, his eyes never off Emily Ayres. 'No I said it was alright, as long as I had rent in the morning.'

'Did you see the prisoner again that evening?'

'Rathall, before retiring to his room, at approximately seven forty five, had asked if my husband Joseph could call him up in the morning.'

'Could you lead us now onto the morning of the ninth?'

Emily Ayres took a moment to compose her thoughts, and as before displayed a remarkable remembrance of that day. 'On the morning of the ninth, Rathall came down stairs about a quarter to eight, carrying his baby in his arms, shortly afterwards going out. I did not see the prisoner again until near eleven o'clock that night, the two of us meeting in the kitchen. I asked him if he had been to work or not, he said he had not. I then asked him why he had told me an untruth, he did not answer.'

'Could you tell us of the conversation, in regards to the prisoner's reaction when hearing of the police visit?'

On the ninth of December a policeman had called, during the day, at the Red Lion, and meeting up with Emily Ayres had made enquires as to Rathalls movements. The landlady had then proceeded to question Walter, when the two of them came across each other in the kitchen, and it was this conversation she now recalled. 'I spoke sharply to the prisoner, the nature of the conversation as such, now Rathall I have had a policeman down to see me today, to ask about this murder, I told the policeman I did not think you were out, but I did not have the presence of mind at that moment. I said to him, Rathall did you do the murder, and he replied in a low voice. "No Mrs Ayres, I could not hurt the poor creature." He then changed the subject. "You will be sure to have your money tomorrow, as my sister (Walters sister often called upon to bail out her brother, we will hear more of her) is going to let me have it." They were the last words we exchanged that night, and he was still staying in our house the following day.'

'Did you speak with the prisoner over the remainder of the weekend?'
'I did not have any conversation with him on Sunday and Monday. But on Monday I heard the prisoner say to his wife that he was going to Ealing. He left that morning (11th December, the day of the inquest) about nine, and I did not see him again until the following Thursday.' This fact contrary to the idea that Rathall did a runner and it seems at odds with the assumption that the landlord of the Red Lion (Joseph Ayres) was not privy to Walter Rathalls movements at that time.

'It is correct, is it not, that you saw the prisoner again?'
'Yes I saw Rathall again, when I saw him ringing the workhouse bell, his wife and child were inside the union.' This statement caused a rumble of verbal exchanges within the gallery, the court quickly brought to order by an unspecified magistrate. The witness had been privy to the timeline in which Walter Rathall regained into his care, his wife and child, subsequently the three of them to leave the area, the family in all sense and purposes on the run.

Defence solicitor, Robert Wood, had throughout Emily Ayres testimony made copious amounts of notes, and now with the prosecution done with the witness, Wood shuffled through numerous sheets of paper, and selected one sheet, scanned what he had written upon it, and stepped out from behind his table. 'Why had you allowed Rathall to stay on with rent owned, and he having received no money from his sister?'

'If he had not told me that untruth, I should not have allowed him to stay in the house.'

'How many other guests were in the Red Lion on the day of the murder?'

If Mrs Ayres had use of a guest register it was not mentioned in court, but one would hazard a guess that the item would have been placed into evidence, and the witness would thus have been allowed to make use of it. 'On December eighth there had been two women and six men lodging in the house.'

'Did any of the guests arrive on the eighth?'

'Only one fresh man arrived that day.'

'Did you know the man who came into your house that day?'

'No sir, he was a stranger.' The witness at this point startled by the gasps of the spectators.

'Where were the guests on the day of the murder?'

'I cannot say where they were on the day of the murder, as most of them were out of the house.'

'Did any of your guests leave the lodging house that evening?'

'I did not miss any of my guests between half past four and half past seven, except Rathall, but some of them might have gone out without my knowing.'

At this juncture the matter of the stick was again explored. 'How can you be sure the prisoner was not already in possession of the stick you earlier described, before he left your lodging house, on the morning of the eighth?'

'When the prisoner went out he had nothing in his hand, and he did not offer me any money when he came back.' Again an objection, again the witness warned to answer only that which was asked of her.

'How are you so certain of the prisoner's movements on the day of the murder?'

'I will take my oath sir (Emily Ayres, her hands gripped together, as if in pray, dramatically swinging around to face the magistrates, her action to cause much disquiet in court) that Rathall was not in all that evening, I went by his door, which was open, and I can swear he was not in his bedroom between half past four and half past seven.' At the conclusion of this impassioned statement some applause originating from the gallery, seemingly because Robert Wood could not shake the witnesses evidence.

One of the magistrates (Robert Trotter Hermon Hodge) took leave from the defence to question Emily Ayres. 'Had you noticed anything unusual in the prisoner's manner, when he had come in on Friday night?'

'I had not, though he was very quiet, and did not mix with other lodgers.'

The Chairman of the Bench (Joseph Henry Wilson) carried Hermon Hodges line of questioning forward. 'When Rathall returned to the Red Lion, on the night of the murder, did he attempt at any point to clean himself?'

'There is a tap where the lodgers can wash, but I do not think Rathall went to it.'

'Was the prisoner's behaviour suspicious in any way?'

'There appeared nothing suspicious about him.'

The solicitor for the defence had valiantly attempted to reverse the damage done to his clients character, and thanks in no small part to the intervention of Joseph Wilson, the last words uttered by Emily Ayres had gone someway to clarify that Walter Rathall had not appeared as one who had only hours earlier brutally murdered Miss Kate Laura Dungey.

The prosecution required nothing more of the landlady of the Red Lion, and with the time now nearing two o'clock, the court was adjourned for half an hour, for luncheon.

Thirty Nine

It Might Have Been the Scream of a Boy

The magistrates, in the interlude, provided no doubt with a lunch of some description served in one of the courts side rooms, were not permitted to discuss the case, though personal assumptions must have already been made. As for others in court, one can hazard a guess that the Dungey family, sorely affected by the ordeal of a trial, were also catered for, either at the behest of the Magistrates Bench, or the generosity of some kindly local. Those who had crammed into the spectators gallery, in the pursuit of an eatery within Market Place, would have been fool hardy indeed to risk losing their hard earned seat, and must surely, having thought ahead, brought along with them sustenance, be it a filled roll or pie, washed down with a beverage.

At just past half past two the court reconvened, those present required to stand as the magistrates re-entered the chamber. Joseph Henry Wilson, once seated, to converse with the Court Clerk, John Cooper thus to called the next witness, one Frank Lillywhite.

Prosecution solicitor, Sydney Brain, ably assisted by his juniors, had much he required of this witness, and once familiar with his notes Brain commenced. 'Can you tell the court your full name, your place of abode, and how you are employed?'

'My name is Frank Lillywhite; I live at Middle Assenden, and am a pheasant farmer,'

This young man, who up to now had managed on the most part to keep his name out of the newspapers, was as fate would have it the son of inquest juror Henry Lillywhite. Francis Walwyn Lillywhite (the witnesses full name), aged twenty one at the time of the trial, still resided with his parents, and in the interlude which led up to his appearance before the bench had kept a low profile. Brain knew full well that the witness had not been directly tangled up in the sequence of events that had played out at Lambridge Farm, on the night of the eighth, but Lillywhites indirect involvement could contribute a tantalising piece to the puzzle. 'We commence with the early evening of the night in question, can you convey for the benefit of the court what brought you out of doors?'

'I was required of an evening to feed the pheasants.'

'Can you be certain of the time you were abroad?'

'On that Friday (8th December) I heard the hooter at Mr Frouds go (James Froud & Sons, Timber Merchants, Brush Board & Veneer Cutters, Hive Manufacturers, Importers, Builders, Wheelwrights, Steam Plough Proprietors & Machinists, Steam Saw Mill, was the exceptionally drawn out company name of a considerably large mill operation located in Assenden, which provided employment to men and boys who resided in its vicinity) as I went to the pheasant pen, which would make the time about six fifteen.'

'What would you say is the distance from the bird pens to Lambridge Farm?'

'From the pheasant pen, which is atop the hill, the distance to Lambridge Wood would be half to three quarters of a mile as the crow flies.' The defence solicitor Robert Wood to raise an eyebrow an amused half smile crossing his features.

'Can you tell the court what you heard that evening?'

'The wind was blowing directly from Lambridge Hill toward me, and I heard a human scream.'

'And what of this scream?'

'It was one scream lasting seven or eight seconds, it was rather a hoarse scream. It impressed me at the time, but I thought no more of it until the next morning when I heard of the murder.'

Sydney Brain had heard all he required of Frank Lillywhite, and with a cursory nod in the direction of the defence table, he took his seat.

It was implicit, as far as the defence saw it, that the court was made privy to the location of Frouds Saw Mill, and thus Robert Wood perused the map which had been provided for his convenience. Said saw mill (for the benefit of you the reader) located within Middle Assenden, tucked between Middle Assenden Farm, and an area known as Frouds Plantation, the nearest building of note the Rainbow, a beerhouse. 'Sir the Frouds Mill and Lambridge Farm are some distance apart, and yet you heard both the hooter and the scream, on a night it is known, when the weather was uncommonly bad.'

'I did sir, when the wind is up sounds carry some distance.'

'Sir I wish to know if the time the scream was heard was nearer six thirty.'

'I don't think it could have been six thirty.'

'Could the scream have originated from other than a woman?'

'It might have been the scream of a boy.'

'Could it even have been the screech of a pheasant?'

'It was certainly not the screech of a pheasant.'

Sydney Brain hurriedly vacated his seat, and cut off the defence solicitor. 'What was the direction of the scream?'

Frank Lillywhite, seen to tightly grip the stand, somewhat unnerved by his ordeal took a moment to gather his thoughts. 'The scream came in the exact direction of Lambridge Wood.' Now here it was, a definitive, a scream indelibly connected to the dreadful events at Lambridge Farm, on the storm ridden and bitingly cold night that was Friday 8th December 1893.

Frank Lillywhites contribution to the proceedings was but a fleeting one, but as he stepped down, amid a flurry of hushed whisperings and speculative glances, no one present could have taken lightly the implications of his evidence.

Forty

Did You Find Any Letters on the Body?

The Victorian legal system did not exclude from its procedures the evidence of children, and thus the Froomes brothers nervously waited for their names to be called, James in due course escorted into the courtroom.

Sydney Brain approached the witness stand, and attempting to put the lad at ease tempered his questions accordingly. 'Young man can you address the court as to your name and age?'

'I am James, the son of John Froomes of Assenden, a carpenter, and I am aged thirteen.'

'You have on many occasions, is it not so, slept at Lambridge House?'

'I have sir.'

'How long have you slept at the house in question?'

'I have worked for Mr Mash on and off since I turned eleven, and since then used to go to Lambridge House to sleep, accompanied by my brother.'

'We must now touch on difficult matters, and the court is grateful for your stoicism. What do you recall of your last encounter with Miss Dungey?'

James Froomes was much perplexed at the new line of questioning, and within the witness stand shuffled from foot to foot. The boy's distress did not go unheeded by those sat upon the Magistrate Bench, and Joseph Wilson raised a hand to indicate that the prosecution solicitor should pause, so as to give the child leave to gather his thoughts. The silence in court almost tangible the short interlude fractured by the utterances of James Froomes. 'I last saw Miss Dungey at about three o'clock.'

'Where did you see Miss Dungey?'

'She was standing at the kitchen door sir.'

'On eighth December, the day in question, what time did you leave Lambridge Farm?'

'From half past four to five, I was accustomed to return home for tea.'

'What time did you return to Lambridge Farm?'

'You mean the first journey I made back to the farm, accompanied by my brother?'

'Yes.'

'I returned with my brother, to Lambridge, about half past eight.'

Sydney Brain, whatever his claims to the contrary, had extensive knowledge of the gossip and conjecture that had circulated, in relation to the sleeping arrangements at Lambridge, and thus was not unduly perturbed when his next question produced a ripple of sniggering.

'Who slept in the house?'

'You mean on the night in question sir?'

'No generally.'

'When Mr Mash or his family were not at home, Miss Dungey, my brother and I were the only ones to sleep in the house.'

Walter Rathall had avidly fixed his attention upon every syllable that had emulated from James Froomes, and he now found himself the foremost subject. 'Do you recall seeing the prisoner before the events now played out in this court?'

'Oh yes sir, I had seen the prisoner before, on Thursday seventh December, the day before the murder. I went home for my dinner about one o'clock, and I saw the prisoner and another man, who works for Mr Hayes (the man James saw never afforded a name, though Mr Hayes could have been Daniel Hayes, dairyman and haulier, Hayes running his business out of Caxton Dairy, Caxton Terrace, Station Road, Henley, each Thursday his employees both delivering and collecting commercial and private haulage from Bix and Assenden), Rathall was at the corner of Lambridge Houses garden, and they were standing still.'

'Did you see the prisoner again that day?'

'I did sir, I returned from dinner about a quarter past two, my brother Harry coming back with me, and I again saw the prisoner.'

'Was anyone with the prisoner?'

'No he was alone.'

'How far would you say the prisoner was from Lambridge House?'

'I would say he was about one hundred yards from Lambridge House, on the road leading to the meadows near New Farm.'

Now the night which had culminated in the discovery of the murdered body of Lambridges housekeeper had to be explored, and Sydney Brain knew that such events would be difficult for any man to recall, let alone a lad of just thirteen, he thus softening his voice, in an effort to put his witness at ease. 'Can you relay to the court what occurred when you and your brother returned to Lambridge Farm on the night of the eighth?'

James Froomes took a sharp intake of breath, his eyes cast down, his expression pained. 'On reaching the house sir, we had knocked at the kitchen door but were unable to make anyone hear, Harry then observed that the door was locked, it was generally unlocked.'

'Is it not so that you took refuge in the well house?'

'We were cold and quite wet through, so we retreated to the well house.'

'Where is this well house?'

'It adjoins the kitchen sir.'

'Thank you, how long did you sit in the well house?'

'We sat in the well house a full hour and a half.'

'And when you emerged from the well house what did you next do?'

'Why sir, we walked around the houses exterior calling Miss Dungey by name. We having no joy in this enterprise peering through the kitchen door window.'

At this juncture Bench Magistrate Henry Vanderstegen to interrupt the prosecution Solicitor. 'When you and your brother initially looked around the exterior of the house, looking for an access point, did you have aid of a light?'

'You mean when we first went round the house?'

'Yes.'

'We had no light sir.' This point of fact seems peculiar as the Froomes boys, when making their way to Lambridge House, had with them a Bulls Eye Lantern.

'Did you notice that the window was open?'

'I did not notice if any of the windows were open.'

'Had you been left waiting before, when arriving at the farm house.'

'We had not sir.'

Sydney Brain, content that Vanderstegen was done with his witness, gestured a thanks to the magistrate, and took up where he had left off.

'Looking in at the kitchen door window could you see anything?'

'We could see many things sir.' This innocent response to cause an outbreak of hilarity, quickly suppressed at the behest of a Bench Magistrate.

'I allude in particular to a clock, could you see the clock?'

'We were able to see a clock.'

'Do you recall the time?'

'Yes sir, the time was coming up to ten to ten.'

'What did you do from that point?'

'We were quite anxious, and decided between us that we should go home to father.'

'And you did go home, did you not.'

James Froomes nodded his head fervently. 'I indeed went home with Harry, and told father we could not get in at Lambridge.'

'Your father did indeed go back with you to Lambridge, did he go straight there.'

'No sir, father took up his coat and fetched out George Dawson, the three of us going to Lambridge.'

'Can you recall, for the benefit of the court, how you entered the house?'

'We got into Lambridge House through the dining room window.'

'Now tell us, no need to hurry just take your time and think it through carefully, all you saw inside the property? Sydney Brain had asked much of his witness, and James Froomes took comfort from the words of the Magistrates Chairman who informed the child that he at any time could ask for guidance.

'In the passage we saw a box of matches (at this juncture the matchbox taken from the evidence table, and shown to the court), and some blood on the handle of the front door, which was bolted at the top. We also saw a piece of stick on the mat (said stick produced in evidence), which was lying outside the front door.'

'Now you told others with you, the night in question, that you had earlier heard a strange noise, can you tell the court what you recall of this noise?'

'Oh yes sir, earlier, as my brother and I were coming up to the garden gate I noticed a noise like a cat with a bird.'

'Where would you say this noise originated from?'

'It was not many yards from the garden gate.' It is to be remembered that said gate was at the end of a short path that ran off from the front door of Lambridge House.

'Would you say the noise came from the direction where Miss Dungey was lying?'

James grimaced at this recollection, but a stalwart lad he quickly recovered his composure, and answered the question. 'The noise came from the spot where we all subsequently saw Miss Dungeys body.'

'How did you happen on the body?'

'I had pointed out to Dawson the spot where the noise had originated from.'

Robert Wood, for the defence, leapt up, and gesturing wildly objected as to this point. 'This is a leading question, as it is already had in evidence that Dawson went straight to the spot where the body lay!' Magistrates Chairman, Joseph Wilson, not to allow the defences objection; he satisfied that the question was quite permissible.

Sydney Brain, casting a withering look in the direction of the defence solicitor, to take up his questioning. 'Please continue, go back to when you told the men of the noise, and work forward from that point.'

The child, at this point, seemed to get his recall of events in somewhat of a muddle. 'Dawson had asked me when I had heard the noise, we next going to the hen house, and then to look at the dog, and after I went to show George Dawson where I heard the noise.'

'Did you have a clear view of the route you took?'

'Oh yes sir, Dawson had a lantern and as such led the way.'

'At what point did you see the body?'

'When we got to the spot where my brother and I had heard the strange noise we discovered the body, I running to catch up sir, as I was sore afraid.' It common knowledge that James Froomes, initially left alone, ran to catch up with his father and George Dawson.

'How far from the road would you say Miss Dungey was lying?'

'About a yard or two off the road.'

'Sydney Brain was content; he thus thanked James Froomes and retreated to converse with his juniors.

Robert Samuel Wood had listened, on the most part in quiet reflection of the facts, and with the prosecution done with the witness; he now commenced his cross examination. 'Leading up to the night of the murder, had there been any gap in your night time occupation of Lambridge house?'

'I and my brother had slept at Lambridge every night.'

'You slept there on the night preceding the murder?'

'Indeed, we slept there on the seventh.'

'You touched on the dog, a black retriever, is the creature a house dog?'

'No sir, the dog is a yard dog.'

'Is this dog chained?'

'Yes sir.'

'Is this dog known to bark at strangers?'

'He would bark sir at those he did not know.'

'There is a second older dog at Lambridge is there not, what is the character of this dog; would it say bark at strangers?'

'No sir, the dog did not bark at strangers.'

'Is this dog ever chained up, and if so was it chained up on the night of the murder?'

'The dog was running free on the night of the murder, the dog never being on a chain.'

Robert Wood, during the prosecutions examination of the matter of the noise the children had heard, had scribbled down many notes, and having familiarized himself with what he had written, continued. 'Please tell the court when you first recall hearing the noise that so alarmed you?'

James Froomes, somewhat gruffly cleared his throat. 'It was about half past eight when my brother and I heard it.'

'How long did this strange noise last?'

'About two or three seconds.'

Wood saw a clink in the witnesses armour, and seeming to forego the fact that he was dealing with the unsophisticated mind of a child led James Froomes to comment on matters sourced on the most part from the columns of the newspapers. 'Did you find any letters on the body, and can you add anything to the subject of the deceased receiving and sending letters of a personal nature?'

'We did not search the body, I had never been given letters to Miss Dungey by anyone, but I had posted letters for her.'
What weather conditions were the three of you subjected to as you looked about the murder scene?'
'I stood back sir, and my father and George Dawson examined where Miss Dungey lay. But I can say that it was a dark night, and it was raining very hard.'
'You saw the rammer I believe, can you tell us where was the rammer when found?'
'The rammer was close to the body sir.'
The foreboding rammer, at the behest of Robert Wood, shown to the court, a lady heard to cry out in abject distress. The defence solicitor, thus ending his cross examination somewhat abruptly, with shock tactics, the court duly shocked. 'I have no more questions for the witness.' James Froomes excused from the stand, his place quickly taken by his younger brother Harry.
Eleven year old Harry Froomes warranted little column space within the tabloids, thus mention of his testimony confined to a solitary sentence. 'The boy corroborated his brother's evidence.'

Forty One

Call for an Adjournment

Sydney Brain had honed his expertise over the years he had been in practice, he a wily opponent, and aware that the defence team were hard on his heels he addressed himself to the Chairman of the Bench. 'I have only very recently been instructed by the Solicitor to the Treasury to conduct this prosecution, so I can fully prepare to prosecute and conclude this case, the charge connected with such a cold blooded and dastardly murder, I request the court remand Rathall.'

Joseph Henry Wilson pondered on what had been asked of him, he having seated alongside him four eminent men, who much familiar with the workings of the courts could offer him guidance on the matter now in hand. The magistrates conversed in hushed tones, those in the galleries, who leaned forward of their seats hands firmly gripping the handrail, at a marked disadvantage when it came to earwigging. The spectators to look about them in the hope that by some miracle any of those seated alongside may have gleaned what was being no earnestly discussed by those of the bench. The moments seemed to stretch out, the wait infernal, but at last the hiatus came to a conclusion, when Joseph Wilson addressed Sydney Brain.

'Will you be producing further evidence?'

'I will sir.'

'Does the defence have any objection to an adjournment, with the prisoner being remanded until the following Thursday?'

Robert Wood perceived no necessity to vacate his seat, and gave the briefest shake of his head. But before any other had a chance to interject, said solicitor emerged from behind his desk and took the floor, his facial features set firm. 'I have no objection in principal, but if next week the prosecution does not produce further evidence of a sufficiently tangible character to implicate my client, as up to this present time there being little evidence to justify the charges, I very much doubt whether it would be justifiable to keep Rathall in custody.' This impassioned plea met with a slight ripple of applause, instigated by a few within the spectator's gallery.

Bench Chairman, Wilson, never for one moment appearing anything but solemn, thus took leave to address the prisoner, Walter Rathall, who now visibly affected by the full implications of his predicament trembling just ever so slightly. 'Do you, Rathall, have anything to say in relation to why you should not be again remanded until Thursday next?'

Rathalls response barely audible to those seated any distance from him. 'No sir.'

Legal formalities now attended to, Walter Rathall was removed from the courtroom, into an adjoining side room. One cannot conjecture which individuals were privy to what occurred in that room, but it is known that the prisoner was given instruction to await the arrival of those policemen whose task it was to convey him back to his cell. Some of those of the press had managed to blag their way into the room, and their observations, hastily scribbled down in notebooks, crept into subsequent editions of several newspapers. "Rathall was removed to a side room where he chatted cheerfully with the days witnesses (it peculiar indeed that the prisoner was in the same room as witnesses, let alone able to converse with them), and others who were present, being then taken shortly after, under guard, to Henley Police Station.'

Part Five

Those of Henley, who had as yet not be able, through connection or otherwise, to facilitate themselves of a seat within the Magistrates Court, now saw before them an opportunity to put that admission right.

Forty Two

A Switch is Made

Those magistrates, who had during the previous appearance of Walter John Rathall agreed to an adjournment, prepared themselves for the prisoner's next appearance before them, with one exception, the seat previously occupied by Robert Trotter Hermon Hodge to be taken by one Alexander Forbes. This gentleman, just short of seventy, curiously in regard to conflict of interest, set to find himself seated at the bench alongside none other than Jury Foreman, at the inquest into the demise of Miss Kate Laura Dungey, Richard Ovey esquire.

John Forbes (born 1787, in Cuttlebrae, Banffshire, Scotland) a doctor of some repute, in 1841, due to his diligence in matters medical and personable bedside manner appointed as Court Physician to Prince Albert. Forbes proved himself beyond measure, and thus found favour with Queen Victoria, who after consultation with her beloved husband made John Forbes up to doctor to the Royal Household, a role he would fulfil close to twenty years. Forbes had in 1841, following his appointment, relocated from Chichester, much glad of the support of his wife of twenty one years, Elizabeth (nee Burgh, born 1787 in Caloretta, Scotland), and their sole offspring, seventeen year old Alexander. The Forbes were provided with an elegant residence in Westminster St James, availed for their comfort of servants, by the close of the decade Charles Walters to act as their footman, Elizabeth Holwell as ladies maid, Lucy Burmingham as household cook, and eighteen year old Frances Frogbrook as the housemaid.

Alexander Clark Forbes, with the benefit of superior education, attended school in Winchester, then onward a pupil of a school in

Sunderland, under the tutorship of Doctor Cowan. In 1842 Forbes went up to Cambridge to read law, and admitted to the Inner Temple in 1844, he graduated in 1847. Here was an astute young fellow, and though called to the Bar on 17th November 1848, Alexander Forbes did not relinquish his studies, his efforts to culminate with an MA, awarded in 1851. University done with, Forbes returned to reside with his parents, he in no rush to go into practice. But in 1853 the status quo was however to change, John Forbes was personally knighted by Queen Victoria for his faithful service, and his son, after a decent interlude of courtship, on 30th August secured the hand in marriage of twenty year old Lillias Miller, daughter of James Stewart, of Cairnsmore House, Minnigaff.

The newlyweds before long took "Swanston House" in Whitchurch, Forbes realising that he best start in practice (as a barrister) finding many, no doubt attracted by his family pedigree, who required his services. There to be abundant reasons to earn a crust, not least of which an extremely large brood of children, the first born who bore his father's name, Alexander Stuart, he making his appearance in 1854. Elizabeth Mary was born 1856; her birth followed by that of John de Burgh, and Lillias Elizabeth Marion. Charlotte Millicent, like her siblings born within Swanston House, brought into the world in 1860, but all was not well. John Forbes, who had in the course of his doctoring returned many to robust health, own health to break down. But he found refuge within the household of his son, the elderly gentleman's needs met by privately retained nurse, Sarah Machin. Sir John Forbes (his wife Elizabeth dead some ten years) to die on Wednesday 13th November 1861, this man not destined to vacate this life like so many less fortunate souls, quickly forgotten. John Forbes given an elaborate send-off, and once interred at St Marys, Whitchurch, his son (who would in 1862 co-author a book entitled Memoir of Sir John Forbes) commissioning stonemasons to create a monument most impressive.

Sir John Forbes left a resworn of seven thousand pounds, and his son much grieved, but Mother Nature has a way of readdressing the balance, and in 1862 Lillias gave birth to Eustace Macleod. The household was a large one, and thus Alexander Forbes took on a considerable number of domestic staff. As with all who wished to impart privilege a butler was essential, and Mr William Hammers fulfilled this role, under him footman Joseph Bosier. Nursemaid Mary Knight ran the nursery like clockwork, and Jane Harrington, as cook, produced meals most imaginative, especially when the lady of the house entertained. Of course there were servants who toiled considerably harder than their colleagues, and for less remuneration, such as housemaid Jane Jennings, and at the bottom of the run, laundry maids Sarah Brown and Martha Cross.

It can never be argued that the Victorians had large familys, but the Forbes took this ethos to its extreme. 1864 saw the birth of Alexandra Josephine (in 1865 her father Sheriff of Oxfordshire), she soon in the company of further siblings, Charles Hubert, Ethel Marion, George Chichester, Henry Keith, and Archibald Jones. And with much relief, on behalf of Lillias, Edith Manuela's birth in 1876 saw the family complete the children's educational needs to be met by governess Ellen Richards.

Alexander Forbes, not shackled by financial necessity, forewent the law, he a landowner (tenants rents to bring in more than sufficient income) content to offer his services as Justice of the Peace for Oxfordshire.

Domestic staffs were notoriously difficult to keep hold of, men with ambition seeking out superior positions, women by the norms of the day expected to leave service upon marriage. And many came and went from Swanston House, by the January of 1894 Edward Weston to act as butler. One can imagine that those servants under Weston were much excited at the prospect of their master sitting as a magistrate at Walter Rathalls trial. One able to envisage that below stairs, housemaids, Mary Page, Ellen Yates, and Sophia Wells, chattered excitedly, while scullery maid, Louisa Evans, and page, Samuel Wheatley listened on, Edward Weston not at all impressed by the subject matter.

Forty Three

A Man of Medium Height, and Poorly Dressed

Walter John Rathall spent the days, which followed on from his initial appearance before the Magistrates Bench, again confined to a cell. There was no suggestion made of any ill treatment of the prisoner, and Rathall, not unfamiliar with hardship, ate heartily and relished the opportunities afforded him to stretch his legs in the exercise yard, which thankfully situated to the rear of Henley Police Station enabled the prisoner to avoid any who might have reason, be it reporter or curious local, to endeavour to facilitate a vocal interaction.

Magistrate Chairman, Joseph Wilson, had passed down instruction that the prisoner be again brought before the bench on Thursday 18th January, and so it was that on the morning of the ordained day Walter Rathall was taken from his cell, he as before enveloped by a contingency of police constables. It was a tardy walk to Henley Town Hall, prisoner and police hemmed in by a surging crowd, those constables who led the party forced to elbow aside the rabble, several of whom consisting of members of the press. Those who escorted the prisoner much concerned that order would irreversibly break down, and thus much relieved when they and Walter Rathall surmounted the town hall steps, the prisoner once safely within relieved of his handcuffs and escorted to the dock.

The prosecution were now in full possession of those facts required to argue their case, and Sydney Brain commenced with fiercely worded conjecture, that culminated with him stating emphatically that there was no doubt that the prisoner before the court, with malice aforethought, did wilfully murder, on eighth December 1893, Miss Kate Laura Dungey. Sydney Brains impassioned, and adversely over dramatic legal argument provided much for Joseph Wilson and those alongside him to consider, and after an interlude filled with much conferring between magistrates it was agreed that the prosecution case had merit. The Clerk of the Court, John Cooper, requested of the prisoner that he face the bench, and Rathall did as he was bid, he further charged and remanded to endure a full hearing, which it was determined would take place the following day. Walter Rathall looked up at the gallery, his expression of perplexed puzzlement unmistakable, and those squeezed into the spectator's gallery in turn looked upon the prisoner, as he was taken down from the dock, handcuffed, and escorted under guard back to the confines of his cell.

The hours that remained of Thursday went by in what amounted to an almost unnatural haste, Friday quick on its heels. And in and around Henley Town Hall, on the morning of the nineteenth, the magistrates, the legal teams, the witnesses, the aggrieved family of the deceased, and the morbidly curious, collided

The editor of the Henley and South Oxfordshire Standard had dispatched one of his most experienced reporters, the papers weekly edition set to hit the newsstands on its accustomed Friday, its presses (located at Caxton House) held fast in anticipation of any events of a dramatic nature. Said reporter (not afforded a name) arrived early, but with word out that Walter Rathall would again make the perilous journey from cell to court on foot a mob had converged in Market Place. Thus the reporter found himself at an acute disadvantage, but not one easily daunted he valiantly pushed aside those who encompassed him, better to gain a superior vantage point over any rival. The correspondent of the Henley Standard licked the tip of his pencil, flung open his pocket notebook, and inadvertently jostled by those close about him, valiantly proceeded to make note of all he observed. Once satisfied he had in elegant prose captured a flavour of the chaos that surrounded him, the reporter proceeded on into the town hall, and facilitated a section of a bench which sat alongside a table that had been set aside, at the rear of the courtroom, for the use of representatives of the press. A fraction of the reporter from the Standards meanderings set to appear in print that same day. "There was not such a large crowd outside the town hall as the previous week, but the court was again densely packed, the gallery being crowded."

In anticipation of civil unrest (the crowd that surrounded the town hall also consisting of casual labourers, who swigged from beer bottles, many of whom, felt by those with an interest in the proceedings, idle reprobates) a posse of police had been stationed in Upper Market Place, this act of caution not to be unfounded. As shortly then after Walter Rathall was led cuffed (described in the columns of the newspapers as, "a man of medium height, being poorly dressed") and on foot from the police station to the court, those stood about him, slightly at a loss how best to react to one considered so heinous, booing, hissing and surging toward the prisoner.

In an adjacent room to that of the court a familiar face, that of Bench Chairman Mr Joseph Henry Wilson awaited the prisoner, ably assisted as before by General Robert Napier Raikes, Henry Brigham Douglas Vanderstegen, and Henry John Simonds, with new comers Alexander Clark Forbes and Richard Ovey fully prepped.

While the magistrates awaited the arrival of a man whose future prospects hung perilously in the balance, in the tightly packed courtroom late comers dived, in a fashion most undignified, for any seat found wanting. The town of Henley-on-Thames, like any small Victorian market town, having men of influence within its midst, as such those individuals had achieved what many who flailed about amongst them had not, a reserved seat. The Mayor of Henley, John Weyman, most comfortably sat within the spectator's gallery, Councillors William Simpkins, Alfred Lester and Charles Singer alongside. There were others who had no thought of having to scramble for a seat, Messrs Paulen, Thomas Rose, James Wells, Harry

Simons, Thomas Higgs, and General Robert Parker Radcliffe, men of commerce, or landed gentlemen, in full realisation of the advantages that their status within the community afforded them. They chatted amongst themselves, and turned frequently to look about the court at those less fortunate souls crammed into the less salubrious portions of the gallery, many of whom leant up against any free wall space at the rear of the gallery, the court ushers, arms raised in frustration, failing to gain any semblance of order.

So who were those afore mentioned privileged few; they men who followed a full spectrum of professions. John Weyman was in his middle forties, a councillor part way through his term of office as Henley Mayor. A building contractor and plumber by trade; Weymans father (John Weyman) had at one time been the manager of local builder Robert Owthwaites land portfolio, he buying Owthwaites business interests in 1871.

John Weyman had initially lived in a property on Greys Hill, but in due course had relocated, his business run out of his father's former home, 59 Gravel Hill, Weymans family making use of an upstairs apartment. But with an expanding family, and a growing income, John Weyman had resolved that the premises on Gravel Hill should be solely the family home, while numbers 27-29 Market Place were facilitated for use as the company's commercial outlet. And here it was from where Weyman tore down to Sidney Higgins bookshop and stationers (a sizable outlet that stood at the corner of Bell Street, and curved elegantly round into Hart Street) to peruse the newspaper stand. And having selected a newspaper to his liking, back at his office, John Weyman absorbed all said paper had to say on the matter of the murder perpetrated at Lambridge House, he destined to attend the hearing of one who stood accused of the crime.

Sat in close proximity to John Weyman was Mr William M Simpkins, near eight years older than his courtroom companion. Simpkins had arrived in Henley in the 1870s; and the Mercer & Crocker Directory of 1874 listed him as in partnership with one Benjamin Singleton, the two, drapers, working out of premises in Bell Street, by 1876 the partnership dissolved.

It was not common place at the time for a tradesman to build his own premises, but Simpkins had done just that. Having on Thursday 29th April 1886 secured in an action, held at the Catherine Wheel, a retail outlet, 17 Bell Street, this building formerly a hairdressers, tobacconists and fancy trade shop, in the ownership of umbrella manufacturer, the late John Franklin Avery.

William Simpkins, in 1890 being yet another locally based businessman to reach the heady heights of Henley Mayor, Simpkins Drapery shop, at three storeys dominating Bell Street

By the latter 1880s William Simpkins had commissioned builders to expand and extensively remodel his commercial outlet (thus forward known as 17-21 Bell Street), the result a sizable structure that boasted elaborately carved stonework and plate glass frontage, with spacious window display area, the business within, a drapers, mantle (a type of cloak) and millinery establishment.

One particular fellow seated within the spectator's gallery Mr Alfred Pearce Lester, he up until 1893 having served as a councillor. Lester had those he sat alongside at a clear disadvantage, he for numerous years on familiar terms with Miss Kate Dungey, the deceased a former customer of his butchers, which was situated at 13 Market Place.

Alfred Lester's outlet at 13 Market Place, long since demolished
Being the third building down, positioned next door to the Argyll Beerhouse

It was in Alfred Lester's establishment that the unfortunate Miss Dungey had cashed what was to be the last cheque she was sent by her employer Mr Mash, the monies she received in return to pay the wages of Henry Mash's farm labourers. A particular duty carried out weekly by the housekeeper of Lambridge Farm (not according to George Dawson), the events of eighth December determined that Miss Dungey was never to distribute coinage sourced from the till of Mr Lester, this money found unmolested within Kates purse.

Alfred Lester, once he had been questioned by Superintendent Francis Keal upon the matter of the cashed cheque, and having provided a written statement (his testimony contained within the legal bundles, which were at the disposal of those with an interest), not called to testify by either prosecution or defence. And thus not required within the witness stand Alfred Pearce Lester found himself permitted to observe the trial.

Charles Albert Singer, aged forty eight at the time of Walter Rathalls trial, had in 1868 decanted from Wiltshire, his destination Henley-on-Thames, he to join his brother, John in business. The two had secured tenancy on a premises in Bell Street, and thus they took up the same profession as their father (Charles Singer), that of green grocers. Custom passed all expectations, and by the mid-1870s (as advertised in the Post Office Directory) Charles Singer had gone it alone, his "Henley Grocery and Provisions Store" run out of 14 Duke Street.

Unlike many other local traders Charles Singer had been able to afford to relocate his family from above his work place, and by the 1880s the Singers occupied "Melbourne House", located in Upper Market Place. The town centre of Henley was indeed the hub of all things, but it was also noisy and crowded, and desiring of a quieter life the Singer's took on "Hazeldean", an elegant detached property, which dominated the junction of Reading Road and St Andrews Road.

Charles Singers grocers in 1900, the three storey flat roofed premises, sat alongside the tallest building in Duke Street

Charles Singer busied himself with matters that impacted upon the local populace, and ingratiated within the public psyche, in 1886 he secured a seat on the town council, in 1891 Singer rewarded for his civic mindedness with the honour of mayorship. A man who much considered the welfare of his fellow man, in 1874 Charles Singer had desired to follow the lead set by others, and assist those who through the burden of poverty found themselves with scant education. He took the decision to concentrate his efforts on the illiterate young men of Henley, and looked about him for a venue for his project. A location not easily to be found, but in due course Singer secured rooms within the Society of Friends (Quakers) Meeting House, which it must be said was in a most dilapidated state. Charles Singer found the ethos of the Quakers most appealing, and it was thus no surprise that in 1878 he converted to the faith, thus forward a prominent and active member. It is not difficult to fathom that Charles Singer did not secure his place within Henley's courtroom due to morbid curiosity, but in the capacity of one who had real concerns for Walter Rathalls wellbeing.

Several of the Paulin's strode confidently past the general area of the spectators gallery and sat within the reserved area, most notable amongst them thirty nine year old Alfred Paulin, this gentleman in possession of the three hundred acre Sheephoue Farm (employing twelve men and boys), located in the Parish of Harpsden, he tenant of John Fowden Hodges of Bolney Court Estate.

Rebecca Rose deprived in 1864 by misfortune of illness of her husband Thomas, in 1867 took one Leighton Thomas (a dried fruit salesman) as her second husband. Rebecca had valiantly carried on her first husbands retail business, aptly named "Rose & Co Leather Sellers", but once remarried she chose to take herself off to Lambeth, better to see more of Leighton, who as a seller of produce supplied the fruiterers there abouts. That was not the end of the Rose's enterprise, Rebecca's son, Thomas Rose (born 1849), carrying his late father's business forward (located at 26 Market Place), though he diversified slightly, he a boot maker & leather seller.

Shop trade was all very well but Thomas Rose had other ambitions, and having taken 7 River Terrace (one of a row of three storey Georgian inspired premises, that stood alongside the "Royal Hotel", and boasted spectacular views of the River Thames) he set his plan into action. Rose was clear on what he required of his acquisition, and quickly opened up as a lodging house keeper, a William Perrin (a bootmaker) taking tenancy of his former retail outlet.

River Terrace, the tower of the Royal Hotel clearly visible

It is not too much of a stretch of the imagination to suppose that guest's at River Terrace were enthralled by events that had unfolded in early 1894, and could it have even been possible that Thomas Rose rented out rooms to members of the press, and those just plain curious individuals who had travelled to Henley-on-Thames. Rose had from his retail day's nurtured connections, and as a councillor he had clear advantage over others, and on that crisp January morning Thomas took a well-deserved day off, nipped along River Side and up Hart Street, in due course escorted to the spectator's gallery.

Seventy seven year old James Thomas Wells considered himself a gentleman, and thus breezed into Henley Town Hall and took a seat within the reserved portion of the spectator's gallery, cut off by privilege from the riff raff who milled about in the less salubrious areas of the gallery.

Wells had been in farming, and by the 1870s his arable lands, which fell within the boundary of Middle Assenden, had peaked at some one thousand two hundred acres. There was one key reason for the expansion of his farming interests, and that reason was corn, James Wells at the time having taken on New Mills, and diversified his interests into that of corn miller and paper merchant. Mill Lane (which ran and still runs down to the water's edge of the Thames at Henley, though its upper portion is now known as Peppard Lane), was so called because it culminated near to the location of two water mills, that nestled on either side of the Thames, one Marsh Mills, the other that which James Wells acquired.

James Wells made no meagre fortune from his enterprise, and in 1883 desired to retire, having gradually reduced his farm holdings to four hundred and fifty acres. New Mills was put up for sale with a price of eight thousand pounds, but did not at first find a buyer, but that was not to be the end of its story. New Mills destined to find a new master in the form of stationer Charles Henry Smith, a water mill just perfect for a fellow who wished to expand his paper bag manufacturing enterprise. Meanwhile the mills previous owner relocated to Henley-on-Thames, and able to enjoy the fruits of his labours James Wells took on Alma House, a property which dominated the outer reaches of Bell Street, a stone's throw from Henley Town Hall.

There were some who lingered without or sat within Henley Town Hall; I am sure, who had benefitted from the expertise of the gentleman who sat in close proximity to James Wells. Harry Simons in his so called fancy repository (located for over twenty five years at 33 Market Place) using his enviable skills as an "artist in hair" to transform all those who sought him out. Hairdressers were a breed that in the course of their day were expected to converse with their clients, subject matters on the whole unobtrusive, the murder of Miss Kate Dungey having put pay to that.

Saturday 1st September 1888 had seen the retirement from the army of Colonel Commandant of the Royal Artillery, Robert Parker Radcliffe. This gentleman, now in his seventy fourth year, having for over twenty eight years resided at "Belmore", a more than modest estate within the boundary of Caversham, Oxfordshire.

Belmore House, from a lithograph produced by Clay, Son & Taylor

Robert Radcliffe was an astute man, and even at his advanced age he sat as a County Magistrate, but not selected to take the bench for Walter Rathalls trial, Raikes had to be content to witness the proceedings as a spectator. Robert Raikes knew much of the law and no doubt shared this knowledge with the man sat next to him, one Thomas Octavius Higgs.

It is not to be ignored that amongst the noteworthy peoples crammed into the reserved benches that looked down upon the courtroom, there was a stark admission. As a reflexion of Victorian sensibilities there no ladies present (god forbid they should witness a murder trial), though in the general gallery women jostled for seating, the "lower classes" looked on with incongruity by the well-heeled.

Those closest to Kate Dungey were also seated within the reserved portion of the gallery, the deceases employer, Henry Joseph Mash, and her father, Walter Dungey, in close proximity to each other. The latter aptly supported by several of his children, his wife unable to travel down to attend, due to nervous exhaustion, she in the dutiful care of those dearest to her.

But one individual was glaringly absent from any reports on the trial, Annie Rathall, where had this young woman found refuge. She did not have the benefit of a room at the Red Lion, not owing rent and with its landlady a witness for the prosecution. The police had clearly not held her as an accomplice to her husband's futile attempt to evade apprehension. It has to therefore be conjectured that Annie Rathall was residing in some location unbeknown to those of the press (there was talk that the Society of Friends had offered Annie and her child refuge), her presence at the hearings not deemed necessary, or desirable.

The courtroom was abuzz with conversations, friend talked with friend, and strangers swapped theories with those they found sitting alongside them. But with the appearance of Magistrates Clerk, John Frederick Cooper, followed soon after by Sydney Brain for the prosecution, and Robert Wood for the defence (this gentleman, extremely fond of flowers, seldom known to appear in court without a bloom picked from his garden adorning his lapel), the chattering ceased. All silent to witness the arrival of the accused, Walter Rathall, who had some time previously fought his way through the crowd, and waited apprehensively in an outer room, glad at least to be rid of his handcuff's. The mob that surrounded the town hall had considerably swelled in number since the reporter for the Henley and

South Oxfordshire Standard had made his way indoors to join the ranks of the hacks, and the noise they produced was on occasion audible within the courtroom. To a man (and woman) those in court strained to observe the prisoner, and compelled to make reference to Walter Rathall, a dull drone of combined voices broke the silence, order restored in time for those in court to stand for the entrance of the Magistrates.

Forty Four

A Matter of the Severing of the Jugular Vein

Both locals and transitory persons, who had managed to elbow their way through the melee and nab a seat within the courtroom gallery, were present on the most part in the hope of being privy to any dramatic utterance, what they initially got to hear was a drawn out series of opening arguments. But all was not lost; George Smith subsequently called to submit his evidence, appearing in his capacity as a doctor, he familiar to many within the court, Smiths taking of the witness stand (duly sworn in) met by a flurry of excited whisperings.

Sydney Brain (the days that had followed on from the adjournment taken up by fervent activity on the part of the prosecution team) stepped out from behind a table strewn with documents, straight backed and grim faced, his manner conveying self-assurance. 'How did you come to be at Lambridge House on the morning after the murder?'

'On the Saturday morning of ninth December I went in the company of Superintendent Keal to Lambridge House.'

'What time did you reach the farm?'

'We arrived between the hour of nine forty five and ten.'

There was to be no restraint in the prosecution solicitors line of questions, no thought of effect upon those connected intimately with the deceased, Brain had a job to do, and he was determined to carry it through with gusto. 'Where did you first set eyes upon the deceased?'

'I saw the body of the deceased in a room within Lambridge House.'

'Which room was this Doctor Smith?'

'It was the kitchen, the deceased laid out on the kitchen table.'

'And what observations did you make in relation to the injuries inflicted upon the person of Miss Dungey?'

This is what a vast majority of the spectators had waited for, the ones who had rushed to purchase their favourite tabloid and leaf through pages until they happened on the columns that carried the very latest on the "Henley Murder". Here within the courtroom was to be played out a "Penny Dreadful", the gruesome details to follow to touch directly upon the sensibilities of some of those present in court. The shop assistant who had skipped work, the housemaid who had defied her master to be present, the homemaker who had left her mother in charge of the little ones, the landed gentleman who had persuaded himself that as a man of local standing it was his civic duty to attend, thus witnessed Doctor George Smith set before him the notes so diligently prepared by Joshua Watts. And the spectators leaned forward, those at the front clutching the galleries balustrade (least they should tumble over the edge), some feeling just the slightest tinge of guilt as to their motives; any shame quickly pushed aside, as the doctors moderately pitched Scottish brogue broke the silence.

'As bound by my remit as medical examiner for the county I made as complete an examination of the deceased as possible, with leave from the court I will refer to my notes.'

Necks strained on tense shoulders, as heads turned toward the witness stand, better to observe the Magistrates Chairman, Joseph Wilson, address Doctor Smith. 'So given, pray continue.'

'I found the body cold and stiff, the face covered with dirt and blood, on the forehead, top and back of the head were several lacerated wounds, I counted fifteen of them. In relation to the wounds, the longest three inches, the majority extending to the bone, the left ear very much bruised and lacerated. Below the chin were two superficial incised wounds, one being an inch in length, the other three quarters, running parallel with each other, and only just through the skin. On the left side of the neck, posteriorly, was another incised wound, six inches in length, extending from the back bone to the point just below the left ear, about one and a half inches in depth. It was deepest towards its exterior posterior extremity and tailed toward the front, its edges and sides were irregular, and it severed the muscle of the neck down to the back bone and cut through the external Jugular Vein. Immediately below this wound was another lacerated wound about two and a half inches long and a quarter inch in depth, upon washing the face several bruises and abrasions were seen upon it. Both lips were bruised and the mucous membrane of both appeared very pale, that of the upper lip being lacerated and one tooth appeared to have been knocked out.' At this juncture the clinical manner of the delivery of the deceases injuries proved too much for Kate Dungeys sisters, who visibly in distress rose from their seats within the gallery. Doctor Smith (as reported in the press, a man of undoubted compassion) observed their discomfort, and in deference to the ladies sensibilities broke off momentarily, so as to allow them to hastily exit the court. 'Just below the right knee was a bruise over which the stocking was torn, both arms and hands were very much bruised and there were several scratches and puncture wounds. The knees were dirty, and the underclothing in the neighbourhood of the knees was also dirty. There were no signs of any attempt of violation; there was nothing about the body to indicate that she was other than a virgin. The wounds at the side of the neck were caused by some kind of cutting instrument; the wounds on the head I consider must have been caused by some blunt instrument, that would apply also to the wounds on the arms and hands.'

Sydney Brain, on occasion seen to make notes, chose this moment to interrupt his witness, and clarify for the benefit of the bench, that he wished to produce items into evidence. A court usher, who hovered in the vicinity of the evidence table, firstly held aloft a stick, followed by a poker, and lastly, with considerable effort on his part, Lambridge Farms rammer. 'In your opinion (Brain enquired of his witness), could any of these implements have caused the wounds seen on the deceased?'

'A heavy stick or something of that kind would have caused them, the stick and poker (it was thought that the poker was initially wielded by Miss Dungey, in an attempt to defend herself) might have caused some of the wounds, and there was some hair and blood on the length of the stick. I think the rammer must have caused some of the wounds.'

'Can you see blood on the rammer still?'

Some ladies and notably some men, seeming to winch as the rammer was brought before the witness stand, so to be better securitized by the witness. Doctor Smiths gaze fell upon the rammer, and he spent some moments in examination of it. 'I think there was some dried blood on this when first I was made privy of it but I cannot clearly see it now.'

'There has been much said about the poker, did you examine the poker?'

'Yes.'

'Did you find anything significant on this implement?'

'Yes, I found some hair on it.'

'Was it the colour of that on the head of the woman?'

'Some of it maybe, but it was very difficult to tell.'

'How long in your opinion would anyone with the injuries sustained by the victim have lingered?'

'I cannot say how long a person would live after having suffered wounds like this.'

Joseph Wilson coughed gruffly and raised an arm, his abrupt interruption met by a flurry of garbled voices from the direction of the spectator's gallery, quickly put down by Wilson. The Chairman of the Bench leaned in and conversed with his fellow magistrates, and thus at one with his colleagues, Joseph Wilson asked of the witness. 'I am curious to know if the doctor's last remark would apply to the severing of the Jugular Vein, and in his medical opinion how long Miss Dungey had been dead when first he examined her.'

The doctor averted his eyes from Sydney Brain and fixed them upon those sat upon the bench. 'The body was in a semi-cumbent position (it must be remembered that Superintendent Keal, not Doctor Smith, examined Kate Dungeys body in situ), and under these circumstances the wounds would not prove fatal as soon as if the body were lying down, it is quite possible that a person could live sometime after receiving blows and wounds like this. I cannot say, she might have been dead more than eight or ten hours when I viewed her, but I cannot say with complete certainty how long.'

Robert Wood had heard enough he deemed he must strike now if he was to best serve his client. 'Reiterating on the point in relation to how long an individual would survive with such injuries, can you be fully certain as to the time one so injured would linger?'

Doctor George Smith, now quite disorientated, swung round to face the defence solicitor. 'I could not hazard a guess on the length of time any one person would live after the Jugular Vein was severed, my stated belief is that the deceased could have lived a full two hours.'

The doctor's last comment painful to hear by those closest to the deceased, the Dungeys, under the scrutiny of the men of the press, much distressed.

'Would an attacker who used such violence have escaped unmarked by blood from his victim?'

'I would be unsurprised to see blood on any person finding a body with such injuries; therefore it is in my opinion quite probable that the person who committed the murder would have blood upon his person.'

'Is it likely the victim's blood could possibly have spurted two or three feet?' Audible gasps, which emulated from the spectator's gallery, again resulting in a call for order in court.

'What weight of certainty do you possess, Doctor Smith, that the stick and poker were wielded as murderous weapons?'

Now the defence fell upon a clink in the prosecutions armour, Doctor George Smith's evidence shaky on this point. 'If used by Miss Dungeys assailant I would have expected to see blood on the stick and poker, but the rain, which had been heavy the night of the eighth might well have washed any blood off, though I am as certain as I can be that I still saw specks of blood on both the stick and poker when first I examined them.'

Robert Wood was on a roll. 'What strength would be required to inflict such wounds as seen on the deceased?'

'The wounds were not necessarily done by a powerful person; they might have been done by a woman.' More gasps from the gallery. 'Had there been any medical discovery made during your examination to suggest a personal nature to the murder, or say a motive consistent with an attempted outrage upon the deceased?' Here the defence alluded to rape as a motive.

'I did not make a minute examination, but every appearance was consistent with the deceased being Virgo intact.' Doctor Smith at this juncture, and unbidden, contributed a personal recollection; his voice strangled, an air of acute sorrow in his continence. 'I attended her about twelve months ago, but it was not upon any private matter, hers was a very healthy and well-nourished body.'

The defence was satisfied and Sydney Brain stepped forward, new vigour discernible in his manner. 'Doctor in regard to the relative position of the victim and her assailant, in your opinion would an amount of blood have been deposited on the supposed murderer, and could an attacker himself been blooded by what is felt to be the victims defence weapon (the poker), in other words could some of the blood identified at the scene belong to the villain?'

'I am of the opinion that as it was raining hard all that night the blood might well have been washed off the stick, but I am certain that there

~ 326 ~

was blood on the poker when I first saw it, it being in Superintendent Keals custody, and it may be that this blood emulated from Miss Dungeys attacker.'

Sydney Brain directed that the poker be brought up to the witness. 'Can you see blood on it now?'

'No I cannot.'

'On the subject of the murderous assailant having been a woman, you are of the opinion that it is possible?' If any answer was forthcoming from Doctor Smith on this subject, his response did not make its way into any subsequent newspaper reports.

Sydney Brain was content, and with just the glimmer of a smile he thanked the witness. The Magistrates Chairman sought assurance that the defence did not further wish to cross examine, and quite satisfied that Robert Wood was done with the witness, Joseph Wilson excused Doctor George Smith. The doctor quit the court, but his testimony, some aspects of which intimate in nature in regard to the person of Miss Dungey, left some in court feeling as if they had intruded upon the dignity of the deceased.

Forty Five

A Question of Plans

Sydney Brain, at this point of the trial, had no desire to cross examine the next witness, there was a matter to be ironed out, and the wily solicitor turned the attentions of the magistrates to it. 'If the court allows, can I be given leave to make a statement in relation to an evidential matter?' Magistrates Chairman, Joseph Wilson, now well used to Brains quirky eccentricity's allowing the prosecution solicitor to proceed.

Sydney Brain had the floor, and strutting out from behind his desk he clarified for those present the details of a dilemma he had faced. 'The previous week I had used a plan which had been prepared by Mr Higgs (Thomas Octavius Higgs, who had sat as a juror at Miss Dungeys inquest), which had initially appeared in the Henley and South Oxfordshire Standard. It had been of considerable assistance to me at the time, but I have subsequently commissioned plans which have been dutifully prepared by Mr Chambers. (John Chambers Auctioneer, House and Estate Agent, his commercial premises number 15 Hart Street) One of the newly commissioned plans shows Lambridge House and the surrounding woods, a second plan shows the internal parts of the house, and includes the paths that are adjacent. The interior plan is detailed, so much so, that the spot where the body was found, as shown me by Superintendent Keal, is marked on the plan.' Spectators, and those with a personal and professional interest in the case, had the advantage of seeing before them Mr Chambers plans; you the reader are not to share that privilege, as said plans have seemingly not survived.

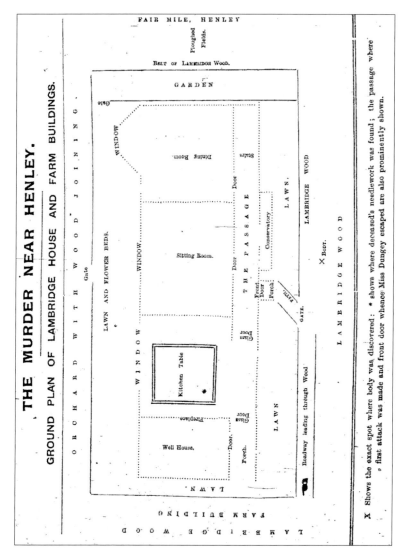

The Plan of Lambridge House and its grounds, that appeared in the Friday 15th December 1893 edition of the Henley and South Oxfordshire Standard

~ 329 ~

Where the plans were positioned, for the perusal of those in court, is impossible to ascertain, though as those of the Magistrates Bench would have need of a clear view of Mr Chamber's handiwork, it is probable that those sat nearest to the bench had a marked advantage over those spectators crammed in at the back of the gallery.

This break in procedure was not to draw to a conclusion just yet, Sydney Brain now to spend some moments exploring facts, as to distances. The particulars the prosecution had prepared for the court were exact, and it is in no doubt that some junior, under the employ of John Chambers, had been dispatched, his remit to trudge from one point of interest to the next, and thus thoroughly check the distances between various sites. The entirety of what this anonymous fellow had discovered had been noted down, and later transcribed for the benefit of Sydney Brain, who now proceeded to convey the findings for the benefit of the court. 'The Froomes cottage is six hundred and twenty yards from Lambridge House going by the cemetery route. (Sydney Brain here referring to the path that ran through Henley Cemetery) From Froomes to Dawsons cottage is six hundred and ten yards, and from the spot where the body was found to Dawsons cottage is six hundred and seventy five yards. The garden gate is sixty feet from where the body (the Froomes boys had passed within twelve feet of Miss Dungeys body) was found, and the copper, where the potato masher was normally found, is three hundred and thirty three feet from where the body was found.'

Those within the court were much subdued, some of those present concentrating on the prosecutions explanation of the plans, others a little bored, eager to return to the more salacious aspects of the evidence. Sydney Brain had had his moment, and thus finished by reiterating to those of the bench the vital nature of the plans, which he had commissioned. 'These plans present a crucial assessment of the facts, in relation to the location of purgative items.' With a flurry of arms, waved in the direction of his plans, and with a self-satisfied expression on his face, Sydney Brain to return to his seat, many in court completely nonplussed.

Court Clerk, John Frederick Cooper, under instruction of the Magistrates Chairman, to summon the next witness. 'I call George Dawson.' Now here was something, the very man whose character had been much maligned, on the most part in print, and by the idle tongues of many a local, much said of the man grossly inaccurate.

One cannot help but notice the Catherine Wheel, alongside it an elegant three storey building (later to be incorporated into the Catherine Wheel), residential premises and surgery of Edward Mellett, Veterinarian. Next to Melletts, an insignificant little building (painted white), being the commercial hub of "John Chambers, Auctioneer, House & Estate Agent, Valuer, Fire, Life & Accident Insurance Agent, and Secretary to the Henley-on-Thames Gas Company"

Forty Six

A Man Most Maligned

George Dawson awaited his summons to appear before the court sat in quiet contemplation, when called by the clerk to the court it said that Dawson looked startled (as noted by a reporter, who had positioned himself not much distance from where prospective witnesses were seated within a corridor), his manner then after said to display an air of heighted agitation.

Sydney Brain had much need of this witness, and once Dawson was sworn, the prosecution solicitor ran through the required judicial formality. 'Can you tell the court your name and place of residence?'

'My name is George Dawson and I reside at Bix Folly.'

'What was the nature of your employment at the time of the murder?'

'I acted as foreman for Mr Mash.'

'How long had you been fulfilling this role?'

'These past ten years.'

'Now we must turn to matters pertinent to the murder (Dawson seen to avail himself of a swig of water), how far would you say your cottage is from Lambridge House?'

'I live about half a mile from Lambridge House.'

'Were you well acquainted with the deceased?'

'I knew Kate Dungey very well.'

'Do you know the accused?'

'I should think I know Rathall, he is my wife's brother.' George Dawson here alludes to Amy Katherine Dawson, her patience, in relation to the exploits of her brother, on many occasion sorely tested.

Amy Katherine Dawson, long suffering sister of Walter Rathall

'Is it not correct that the prisoner had lived at Lambridge House?'

'Yes sir, he formally lived at Lambridge House.'

'When did the prisoner reside at Lambridge House?'

'That would be when his mother was in charge of the house.'

'Can you recall when the prisoner last lived at Lambridge House?'

'It is between seven to nine years ago that he last lived at Lambridge House.'

'And from that point on, where did Rathall reside?'

'Walter went where the work was, but after his marriage he relocated to Assenden.' The prosecution never made privy to Rathalls location within the village.

'Has he had cause to work at Lambridge recently?'

'He has worked for Mr Mash, but the last occasion was two years last July.'

'When Mr Mash took on the prisoner what task was required of him?' George Dawson's brow furrowed, and he clenched the stand as if to steady himself, his mood pensive. He knew Walter Rathall well, and in the past, as well as this particular moment, he'd had reason to despair of his wife's brother. 'It was I who engaged and paid him, he was helping to get in the hay, but the prisoner left before the job was finished. He was paid his money but did not come back.'

'Can you recall how many times you have seen the prisoner since his departure from the job he undertook at your bequest?'

'Since that time I have seen him two or three times.'

'Were any of the times you saw the prisoner close in date to the night of the murder at Lambridge.'

'About seven weeks before the murder he came to my house to ask if we would pay two night's lodgings for him, he said he was staying at the Red Lion Beerhouse. On Thursday seventh December I saw the prisoner about a quarter to one; he was standing at the stile in the Old Bix Road.' The road alluded to by Dawson, which culminated at Saint James's Church, ran through Lower Assenden, past Bix Folly Cottages, it commencing at the turning off from the main road.

'Did you converse?'

'I said hello Walter, no work, and Rathall replied. "No I finished up yonder yesterday."'

'What did you take this to mean?'

'I took him to be referring to Mr Ovey. (Richard Ovey of Badgemore House, inquest juror and trial magistrate) I said it was a nice day, but he made no reply, that was all that passed between us.'

'Did you see Rathall again that day?'

'I did not see him again during the day, but on getting home that evening I looked out of my widow and I saw Walter going along the pathway to Lambridge House.'

Line drawing of George Dawson
Appeared in the Sunday 17th December 1893 edition of "The People"

Sydney Brain now took momentary leave of his witness, and George Dawson glad of it took a sharp intake of breath. His voice had faltered during the bombardment of questions he had been required to answer, and tightly gripping a water jug, with hands that were visibly trembling, Dawson poured a long draft of water and drank heartily. Brain (having pursued his notes, and conversed with his juniors) settled as to the direction his next wave of questions would take. 'If it pleases the bench, on the Thursday afternoon before the murder, I have two witnesses who will speak as to the fact that Miss Dungey was in Henley arranging with a dressmaker, about a dress.'

Joseph Wilson asked of the prosecution solicitor, his manner terse. 'Will the testimony you propose necessitate Dawson having to step down.'

'It will sir, but I will recall him once you have heard the evidence of those connected with the matter of the dress, as their evidence will have bearing on Dawsons.'

Wilson much perturbed and having consulted his fellow magistrates, to give his answer. 'I know of the testimony you allude to, and the bench does not consider this evidence you propose to produce of sufficient enough bearing on the case.'

Sydney Brain had been thwarted (and it was never to be revealed what the matter of the dress fitting had in common with events that had culminated with the murder of the housekeeper of Lambridge), but he was much used to this, and stepping somewhat nearer the witness stand, than he had had cause to stand before, Brain turned his attentions to the night of the murder, and thus George Dawsons ordeal continued anew.

'On Friday eighth December, the day of the murder, at what time did you last see the deceased alive?'

'On that day I last saw Miss Dungey alive about four thirty, she was sitting in her accustomed chair by the kitchen fire, knitting.'

'How long did you stay in the kitchen with the deceased?'

'I was there but two minutes.'

'Where did you go from the point you took leave of Miss Dungey?'

'I went round the orchard.' Said orchard located to the rear of Lambridge House.

'What time did you leave Lambridge House?'

'It was a quarter to five when I left the building.'

'Did you leave alone?'

'No sir, the two boys Froomes went with me, we all walked straight down to the stile in the Old Bix Road together.'

'And when the boy's left you where did you go?'

'I went home, had my tea, and then I went to feed my pigs.'

'Did you meet or converse with anyone at that point?'

'Yes, coming back from the pig house I spoke to my neighbour Mrs Webb, she remarked to me that the dogs at Lambridge House were barking very much.'

'Did you hear the dogs barking from the direction of Lambridge Farm?'

'I heard the retriever barking.'

'Can you recall what time this was?'

'I would say it was about six forty five.'

'You are sure it was the yard dog at Lambridge.'

'Oh yes I am quite sure, the dogs bark is very familiar to me.'

'Did you remain at your cottage the whole evening of the night of the murder?'

'After I had seen to the pigs I went out to get some wood and coal, at twenty to eight I went to Mr Bratchell at the Red Cross, Assenden, (Robert Bratchell, juror at Kate Dungeys inquest, and though he provided a statement regards Dawsons arrival at the Red Cross on the night of the eighth, he was not called to give evidence), and I left there at a quarter to nine.'

'Did you go straight home?'

'I did sir; I had some supper and went to bed about quarter to ten.'

The prosecution solicitor was taking George Dawson little by little towards the inevitable, the events that necessitated his presence before a court. 'Can we move forward to the point at which John Froomes and his sons arrived at your home?'

George Dawson, concentration etched upon his features and confident of the facts replying without hesitation. 'I was asleep when I was called up, but my wife was not, I went to the window and I saw John Froomes and his sons James and Harry.'

'Why did you go to Lambridge House?'

'In consequence of what they told me, I got up and went to Lambridge House with them.'

'Now Mr Dawson can you now take us through what occurred once you arrived at Lambridge Farm?'

'I can sir. I went to the kitchen door first and it was locked, a light (the lamp that the Froomes boys had earlier seen) was on in the kitchen. We went to the front door but found it fastened; we then went to the back of the house to the deceases window. I tapped the window several times with a stick (Dawsons infamous swordstick) and called out Miss Dungeys name several times, having no joy from this we then went to the hen roost.'

'Were you ever alone as you examined the exterior of the house?'

'No, the Froomes were with me.'

'We know of the farm dogs, what did you gather of their state?'

'We went to the dog, a black Retriever, and this dog seemed to be drowsy.'

'Was this the first time you noticed anything untoward about the dog?'

'Yes sir, it had been alright when I went to tea.'

'Did this dog have free run of the place?'

'No, he is kept chained up.'

'How long has this Retriever been at the farm?'

'Mr Dungey gave it to Mr Mash two or three years ago.'

Dawsons comment to stir one of those present within the gallery to call out, none other than his former employer Henry Mash. 'It is three years sir!'

The Magistrate Chairman saw no need to chastise Henry Mash, and Sydney Brain quickly recovered his composure. 'Where was the dog?'

'It was lying in the kennel.'

'This is, is it not the very animal you say you heard barking earlier.'

'Yes, I had heard him barking about a quarter to seven, when I went to feed the pigs.'

'Was there another dog at the farm?'

'There was another dog, a Spaniel, which ran loose.'

'Would this creature bark at strangers?'

'Oh no sir, it's old and very deaf, and made a fuss of anybody, even a stranger.'

'It is correct, is it not, that you searched about for this creature?'

'We did sir, and we found it lying on the exterior kitchen door mat, the cat lying with it.' This is the first and last heard of the cat.

Even Brain, keen to glean every last bit of information, knew he had quite exhausted the matter of the dogs, and thus he again turned his attention to Lambridge House. 'As we have heard from others, it was decided to try the widows at the farmhouse, can you convey for those present what occurred at this juncture?'

'We had made up our minds to try the kitchen windows, the first window was shut fast, and then we tried the middle window, which was likewise. We went to the bay window of the drawing room and found the sash pushed right up, the Venetian Blind was also up. Froomes wanted to get more help (this the first time that this point of fact had been heard), but I entered the house, I had a swordstick with me, which I drew.'

'Can I clarify for the bench one point of fact, Dawson were you in possession of a means of lighting your way?'

'We had a Bulls Eye Lantern with us.' Run on oil, this type of lantern, once lit, focused light to some extent in one direction, not unlike the modern flashlight.

'I see, pray continue.'

'The boy fell into the room (this statement caused some amusement, and there was laughter in court, which was quickly suppressed, at the behest of an unnamed magistrate), and we quickly left the drawing room (in the Henley Standards plan seemingly labelled as the sitting room), its door being shut. I went to the kitchen and from the dresser took a candle which I lit. We thus went to Miss Dungeys bedroom, and we searched under the bed and found everything as it should be. (What George Dawson was expecting to find under the bed not made clear.) We searched all the bedrooms, and after came down stairs (Miss Dungeys bedroom is not shown on the plan, but it was on the ground floor, some further bedrooms appearing to have been in the attic of the farmhouse), where we found blood on the inside door knob of the front door, there also some splashes of blood against the front door.'

'Were the bloodstains still wet?'

'I rubbed them with my fingernails, and they were quite dry.'

'Pray continue.'

'We next went to the kitchen; its door leading to the porch locked from the inside. In the kitchen we found knitting and a book (these items, seemingly abandoned by Kate Dungey, if examined, not to be included in evidence), and the lamp was burning. The chair Miss Dungey had been sitting in was in the same place.'

'Did you have cause to notice anything different from when you were last in the kitchen?'

'The only thing I saw different was that Miss Dungey had had her tea. The tea things had been put on one side of the table, and I saw two teacups and only one saucer (in the coming weeks, within the press and through the medium of tittle tattle, these two teacups would be the cause of much debate, in relation to an assignation on the part of Kate Dungey), a packet of salts was on the table, it had been upset.'

'Once you had satisfied yourselves that you had checked the kitchen where in the house did you next explore?'

'We went back along the corridor to the front door, which was bolted at the top, I unbolted the door and we all went outside. On the outside mat I found a small piece of stick, which I examined and then put down again, I then went to the well house and got a Hurricane Lamp.

(Run on kerosene or oil, and suspended from a metal handle, this type of lamp had the benefit of not being easily extinguished by inclement weather.) The Froomes boy told me about something, and we all went to the front gate. It was a dark night and raining, and I carried the lantern, I was going straight across to the ash pit, but the boy said. "Not there, further down." I went towards the path leading to the cemetery and found the body.' George Dawson's voice faltered, his train of thought interrupted by a combination of gasps and murmurings, curtsy of those seated within the spectators gallery, up to that point they having been transfixed by the witnesses exact recollection of all he had experienced the night of the eighth.

**Line drawing of Lambridge Woods, where Kate Dungeys body was discovered
Appeared in Lloyds Weekly, Sunday 17th December 1893**

'How would you describe the positioning of the deceases body?'
Dawson sighed, the remembrance of this matter seeming to cause him much anguish. 'The body was nearly straight out, the legs doubled up a bit. She was lying back with her head on one side towards the right and away from the road. One arm was up, and I noticed a mark on the side of the neck, and some blood.'
'Did you examine the deceased?'
'We went within about a yard; but I did not touch the body.'
'How long did you linger?'
'We stayed approximately two or three minutes.'
'There was a poker lying beside the body (said poker produced for the benefit of the court), where was it normally found?'
'It was generally kept on the rack over the stove.'
'Did you see the masher?'
'We all saw the masher (the masher being the rammer), it was about two feet from the body.'
'What service did the masher perform, and where was it accustomed to store it?'
'It was kept by the copper, and used to mash potatoes for the pigs.'
'Would the prisoner have had dealings with the masher?'
'The prisoner used to feed the pigs when he was engaged there as a boy.' Upon this utterance the defence solicitor, Robert Wood, sprung from his seat and requested leave from the bench to consult with his client, and with permission thus granted he talked at some length with Walter Rathall. Although the two men kept their voices low spectators were seen to lean forward of their seats, straining to catch but the slightest word.
This little interlude dealt with, Sydney Brain, taking a moment to straighten out his jacket, continued. 'Can you tell the court what course of action you then determined to take?'
'I put the pony in the trap and drove to Henley Police Station.'

'It is a point of fact, is it not, that the police travelled back with you to Lambridge Farm.'

'They did sir; I drove the superintendent and a constable to Lambridge House.'

'Who took the police to the body?'

'I took them to the body.'

'Had the position of the body altered since last you looked upon it?'

'It was lying in the same position.'

'Did you carry the body to within the confines of Lambridge House?'

'I helped take the body in, I asked the superintendent to let me have a sack, so that I should not get covered in blood.' George Dawsons testimony interrupted, he startled by a womans cry, thought by those of the press to originate from one of the Miss Dungeys, who having left during the evidence of Doctor George Smith had again taken their place within the gallery.

Sydney Brain, also much perturbed by the distressed womans outburst, took some moments to gather his thoughts, before continuing. 'We must now turn to matters that pertain to Lambridge House, the superintendent, assisted by you and a constable, examined the house did he not, what can you recall of this?'

'Inside the house we saw a broken nightlight, in the passage we also saw a matchbox (said matchbox produced for the benefit of the court), I noticed blood on the match boarding and the floor.'

'There are some flowerbeds at the back of the house, where the foot print was happened upon, when last were the flowerbeds tended to?'

'I last dug them over in the autumn and planted them out.'

'Have you had cause to notice any footprints in the beds before the night of the murder?'

'I was working in the garden on eighth December, and was in and out about forty times. I did not observe any footprints in that part of the garden that day.'

'When did you first come upon the footprints?'

'On Saturday morning (ninth December) I saw two foot prints, one by the drawing room window, the one nearest the drawing room window I covered up.' This is the first clear indication that George Dawson was present at Lambridge House on the Saturday.

'Had you not seen the footprints before then?'

'Yes sir, I saw footprints the previous night, but it was raining awful hard, and so I quickly covered them as best I could. Superintendent Keal said to me. "Get there as early as you can in the morning (Saturday ninth December), and cover up any suspicious footprints."

'What time did you cover the footprints?'

'Are you referring to the night of the murder?'

'I am.'

'I covered them up about seven forty five.' The time given is incorrect; it unlikely that Dawson would have slipped up, it therefore a mistake on behalf of a reporter.

'Did you notice the direction any of the footprints were facing?'

'That I did sir, one of the footprints was near the bay window, going from the window to the white gate.' Here George Dawson is referring to the gate that led out into the orchard, any using this route to eventually find themselves within a wooded area.

Sydney Brain retreated to where his notes lay, flicked through them, and satisfied that he had exhausted all avenues of inquiry addressed the magistrates. 'If it pleases the bench, I have no further questions of this witness.'

Joseph Wilson acknowledged the defence solicitor in terms most cordial, and aware of the time, and experiencing pangs of hunger, he adjourned court for lunch.

An usher escorted the witness to an adjoining room, if George Dawson thus provided with refreshment the reporters who observed him not to deem this fact in the public interest. The magistrates most certainly took of a hearty meal, laid on within the council chamber. Those who chose to forgo their seats in the spectator's gallery spilt out into Market Place, the frontage of the town hall crowded in on all sides by a gathering of locals, whose number had been swelling throughout the morning. Shops nearest Upper Market Place were abnormally quiet, shop lads creeping to the entrances to better witness the commotion. It would be of no surprise that some chose to shut up completely, and one wonders if William Hamilton's cash drapery, and Stephen Hales bakery remained closed, their proprietors and staff hung precariously out of top floor windows, better to witness the ensuing drama.

Of course, as in all things, there is always a winner, and on the day of the trial the winners were the local hostelries. Henry Russell, landlord of the Victoria, barely able to keep up with the demand for beer, Mrs Mary Ann Vokins, at the Greyhound, kitchens abuzz, as barmaids hurtled back and forth, laden up with plates of sandwiches, pies and the such like. Those courtroom spectators who had dared risk a visit to a beerhouse guzzled down their drinks, and consumed their lunches with undignified haste, their bench seats within the gallery (many of which reserved by the placement upon them of some personal belonging) awaiting their return. And in all this confusion the local bobbies patrolled, their remit to quickly contain any trouble and look out for dippers, the presence of so many offering a good opportunity to pilfer a wallet or a purse.

As the appointed hour to return to the courtroom grew near, those with an interest in the proceedings took their seats, while those there purely to observe piled into the gallery, it being noted that the courtroom was considerably more densely packed than it had been before lunch. The magistrates to duly enter, chairs scrapped back as those in court stood, with varies legal matters ironed out between solicitors, and those on the bench, George Dawson was again called to the witness stand.

Robert Samuel Wood, for the defence, shuffled through some papers which lay before him on a large solid wood table, he perusing one particular sheet, his features contorted in concentration, and decided upon the course his questions would take, Wood approached the witness. 'Now Mr Dawson you told the court that your wife is the prisoner's sister, how long have you been married?'

'I was married twelve months ago last June.'

'Is it not so that you did at one time live at Lambridge House, and remained there for some considerable time?'

'Yes sir, I lived in the house for about nine years with Mr Mash.'

George Dawson would in point of fact also have resided at Lambridge House alongside Mary Rathall, onetime housekeeper, and Walter's mother.

'After you quit the farm who then lived at Lambridge House?'

'When I left Lambridge House only Miss Dungey lived there.'

'Did Miss Dungey have responsibility for any servants within the house?'

'There were no servants.'

'Since you vacated Lambridge House, have you had cause to live within the property at any time?'

'Last winter (this would have been roughly the February of 1892) I slept in the house, about four months before I was married.'

'After you quit the house who usually slept at Lambridge?'

'I knew Miss Dungey and Mr Mash, and any of his friends who had cause to visit, used to sleep in the house.'

'Why was it so that you no longer slept at Lambridge House?'

'After I was married it was arranged that I should live away from the house, and the boys Froomes should sleep there.'

'Have you slept at the house since your marriage?'

'I did sir, my wife and I slept at Lambridge House last winter.'

Dawson is referring to the winter of 1892/93.

'Was Miss Dungey present?'

'No sir, Miss Dungey slept at New Street in Henley.'

'Last winter, while you were at Lambridge, did Mr Mash spend any nights at the house?'

George Dawson let out a protracted sigh, no doubt exhausted by the continual questioning as to the sleeping arrangements at Lambridge.

'During that time Mr Mash did not come there to sleep.'

'Did Mr Mash sleep at the house when only the housekeeper Miss Dungey was present?'

'No sir, Mr Mash only came to sleep there unaccompanied while Miss Dungey was away for her holidays.'

'How do you know this to be true?'

'I used to drive Mr Mash there, and I have had supper there and have been as late as one o'clock.'

'Did Mr Mash stay at New Street while Miss Dungey was in occupation at Lambridge?'

'While Miss Dungey resided at Lambridge I have driven Mr Mash on several occasions to the house in New Street, and I have on two or three occasions collected Mr Mash from New Street on a Monday morning, and driven him to the station.'

'Did Mr Mash visit Lambridge House during these visits to New Street, while the housekeeper Miss Dungey was present?' Robert Wood was certainly keen to put Mr Mash and Miss Dungey within each other's company.

'I have had cause to drive him up to the house and remained there until Mr Mash desired to be taken back into Henley.'

'And during these visits were the Froomes boys present.'

'When I have been kept waiting until late the boys have not been there.' George Dawson, at this point in the proceedings, suddenly startled, his gaze falling upon (as did the rest of the courts) Henry Joseph Mash, who having vacated the spectators gallery now took a seat by the side of Sydney Brain.

Robert Wood glanced across at Henry Mash, but undaunted continued. 'When would you say was the last time that Mr Mash spent time alone with Miss Dungey at Lambridge?' Now here it was, the defence solicitor touching on rumours that were circulating, in regard to an improper relationship between master and servant.

'On a night in November I drove Mr Mash from Lambridge (he having been alone in the house with Miss Dungey), picked up Mrs Mash from Satwell (a small hamlet located close to Highmoor Cross), and then drove to the station.'

Robert Wood had the bit firmly between his teeth, he hoping his next move would shatter the prosecutions confidence. 'Did Miss Dungey ever tell you about a scene at the house?'

'No more than she had words last summer.'

'Could you elaborate for the court?'

Dawson, seen to glance at his former employer, looked pensive, and it was some seconds before he answered. 'One day last summer I found Miss Dungey crying, she said there had been a rare scene and asked me if I heard it.'

Robert Wood interrupted his witness, no doubt to an effort to heighten the tension. 'And what was this scene?'

'She said Mrs Mash was going to hit her with an umbrella stick but Mr Mash stood between and deflected the blow.' An umbrella stick was a term used to describe an umbrellas handle which was made to unscrew, so to make the packing in a trunk of a full sized umbrella easier. An umbrella stick could be an item of extravagance, finely carved, or enamelled, and if the owner had the financial means elaborately jewelled.

At this stage in the proceedings the Magistrates Chairman, Joseph Wilson, cut in. 'I fail to see how this affects the prisoner (Walter Rathall himself looking somewhat nonplussed), it is really nothing to do with the case can you prove it is?'

Joseph Wilson's reaction was somewhat unexpected, as the defence had cause to believe that the incident with the umbrella stick was pertinent, and Robert Wood's response, reproduced verbatim in countless newspapers, left those in court in no doubt that he felt he was duty bound to explore all avenues. 'All I can prove is my client is not guilty, this is a hypothetical case, things have been imputed to my client, a poor man, and much with only a case of suspicion, and I have a right to state that things might also be imputed to other persons.' Robert Wood's heartfelt declaration met with loud and prolonged applause.

Joseph Wilson did not leave the matter there, and discussing hurriedly with his colleagues he turned his attention to the prosecution solicitor. 'Are you Mr Brain of the opinion that this evidence is relevant?'

Sydney Brain, put on the spot, was neither the less quick to answer. 'With the courts leave I am not prepared to say if this was a relevant question or not, I represent the Treasury and not any particular individual.'

More drama to ensue, Henry Joseph Mash, who had remained seated alongside the prosecution solicitor, rising to his feet and addressing the bench. (Spectators craning forward, better to catch every last word) 'One word please!'

Robert Wood swung round to face Mash, and with just the slightest indication of amusement in his voice addressed the bench. 'I have no doubt that if Mr Mash wishes to be called the bench would hear him, as he wishes to make a statement.'

Sydney Brain, irked by the defence solicitor's sarcasm, saw a window of opportunity. 'Mr Mash was not cross examined on this point, he surely thinks it would only be justice to him that he could be recalled and heard upon it.'

Joseph Wilson, eager to restore just a modicum of order to the proceedings, curtly ended the matter. 'The bench cannot hear him.'

Those in court were aghast, mumblings, and cries of "Hear the man", and general unruliness, quickly put down by stern words from the bench.

George Dawson, throughout all that had unfolded in the last few minutes, showed scant emotion, he too had been dragged through the mire, both at the hands of the press and the court, and thus knew fully well that legal procedure had little regard of the damage inflicted on a man's character.

Robert Wood had by now completely lost his train of thought, and with the magistrates leave he returned to his table, to familiarize himself with the direction he had been heading, before the incident of the infamous umbrella stick had thrown all into chaos. He read his notes, slurped some water, and clearing his throat stepped forward. 'We must now explore another matter which is in itself unexplained, can you tell the court of the incident in which Miss Dungey visited New Street on Thursday thirtieth November.'

'I know sir to what you are referring, on the Thursday before the murder I drove Miss Dungey to the New Street house, she told me to call for her at four thirty. I called for her but she was not there.'

'Had Miss Dungey, before this date, ever behaved in such a way?'

'Oh no sir, at other times I have fetched her, and she has not disappointed me before.'

'Did you attempt to seek out Miss Dungey?'

'I made my way to Lambridge the long way round, but could not see her in the town as I drove back.' No doubt Dawson would have driven to the end of New Street travelled along Riverside and turned up into Friday Street. Next he would have gone along Duke Street, into Bell Street, and on into Northfield End, before leaving Henley via the Fairmile.

'Where did you next see Miss Dungey?'

'I found her in the house (Lambridge House), the woman having returned under her own steam.'

'How had Miss Dungey made her way back to Lambridge?'

'She told me she had walked home, and that she had left word with Mrs Wright (this being Mrs Emily Wright, who resided at 35 New

Street, next door to the Mash residence) that she was going to do so.' This evidential statement does not tally with George Dawson having inquired of Mrs Wright, in relation to the whereabouts of Kate Dungey, the two puzzled as to her absence.

'Moving on to the night of the murder, the rammer (this menacing looking item again produced in court) was kept in the copper was it not, would this copper be easily seen from the path up to the house.'

'Anyone could see the rammer from the path and lift it out.'

'The footprints you saw, how many was it in all?'

'I saw two foot prints in the flower bed.'

'And what led you to the body?'

'When I went to see the body it was by direction of the boy.'

'When you left Lambridge Farm the night of the murder who had possession of the keys?'

'Do you refer to the final time I quit the farm on that night?'

'Indeed I do Mr Dawson.'

'Superintendent Keal took possession of the key to the room where the body was (that being the kitchen), I took possession of the keys to the house, as well as keys to internal rooms.'

'How many days did you keep hold of these keys?'

'I had the keys for a week.' One suspects that others, such as Henry Mash, had keys to Lambridge House, as there were logistics to consider, such as access for those of the constabulary, undertakers, and those related to the deceased.

Magistrate Chairman, Joseph Wilson, now cut in, and in a manner that displayed irritability addressed the witness. 'You say the keys were left with you for a week?'

'Yes sir.'

'It passes any comprehension that the superintendent could have allowed you to have anything to do with the house on the night of the murder, let alone leave you in possession of the house keys for a week, and how is it that he did not leave a constable in charge of the house.' His outburst answered by loud applause, which Wilson (mightily annoyed) immediately supressed. There was of course one who remained within Lambridge House, Sergeant Thomas Allmond, ably, it would seem, assisted by various constables. Allmond instructed to guard the deceased, though he not to be left in charge of the keys to the property.

The defence solicitor, much used to interruptions during the course of his job, continued to cross examine. 'The afternoon of Saturday ninth did you search the upper rooms of Lambridge Farm?'

'No sir, the only two who searched the rooms upstairs were Mr Mash and Julia Dungey.'

'So you know nothing of what they discovered during their search?'

'No sir, I was not made privy to anything of that sort.'

So there the defence solicitor left it, Robert Samuel Wood having crossed exanimated the witness on matters which he strongly felt had not been satisfactorily explored, small points, that neither the less combined as a whole created elements of doubt as to the prosecution's case. His client, Walter John Rathall, had paid acute attention to all that had occurred in court, the prisoner noted as particularly fixed upon the testimony of his brother-in-law, George Dawson (he given leave to step down from the witness stand), who, if only inadvertently, had thrown the floundering man within the dock a life line.

Forty Seven

I Did Not See Him at All

Sydney Brain had prepared his prosecution case with the upmost diligence (he well aware that if his legal arguments resulted in a guilty verdict, and thus forward a further trial before a jury, Walter Rathall could ultimately forfeit his life), and as such had sought out all those whose dealings with the accused proved pertinent. Thus John Cooper called Mr Thomas Good.

'Can you state for the court your name and occupation.'

'I am Thomas Good, head keeper to Mr Mackenzie of Fawley.'

'You had cause to employ the prisoner did you not?'

'I did sir, about twelve months ago I engaged Rathall as a beater.' The work Thomas Good alluded to not to offer Walter Rathall continual employment, the social calendar of the gentry dictating demand.

'On the day of the murder did the accused ask you for wages?'

'On eighth December I did not owe him anything for beating, and he did not come to me and ask me for any money.'

'You did not see the prisoner on that day?'

'I did not see him at all.' This was all that was required of Thomas Good (he a man not having left any discernible mark, in census or otherwise), his brief appearance within the witness box (the defence choosing not to cross examine) proving, as Sydney Brain reiterated to those sat upon the bench, Walter John Rathall both a liar, and a fellow desperate for money.

Forty Eight

To Guard the Deceased Alone

Next called to take the stand was Sergeant Thomas Allmond (he described within his police record card, as of proportionate figure, some five foot ten and a half inches tall, with a sallow complexion, hazel eyes and dark brown hair), this fellow somewhat of a celebrity, due to his having stood, as the press liken it, "in dutiful vigil over the body of Kate Dungey."

Sydney Brain sensed his witness, though much used to the courtroom, was nervous, and thus tempered his voice accordingly. 'Can you state your name and occupation?'

'Thomas Allmond, sergeant in the police.'

'You were, I understand, commissioned by Superintendent Keal to estimate the timings of a journey made on foot, from the Red Lion to the site of the murder, can you tell the court the results of this exercise?'

'On Tuesday last (the date referred to 9th January) I walked from the Red Lion lodging house along the Badgemore Road to Lambridge House, it took me twenty seven minutes.' The sergeant would have travelled up to the top of West Street, turned left onto Gravel Hill, and carried on up to the turning into Badgemore Road. Thomas Allmond would have passed two properties, "The Croft" and "The Lodge", thus forward crossing fields and arable land, he to enter Lambridge Woods. After making his way through the woods, via an ad hock path, Allmond would have arrived at Lambridge Farm.

'Which route did you take upon your return journey?'

'I returned by road through the wood, leaving the sewage farm to the right.' Thomas Allmond would have started his return journey from outside the front porch of Lambridge House, thus going through the gate, he to follow the path down into Lambridge Woods. As the sergeant made his way through the wood, on his right hand side he would have walked close by the tanks of Henley Corporation Sewage Works, and an area known as Fairies Hole. Allmond from that point to cross numerous fields, he emerging on the road that ran alongside the considerable estate that was Friars Park (weekend retreat of Frank Crisp), the sergeant thus continuing down into West Street.

'How long did it take to return to West Street, and the Red Lion lodging house?'

'It took me twenty six minutes.' It important to note that the pace at which Sergeant Thomas Allmond walked was never touched upon by prosecution or defence.

Brain had much to ask of this witness, and thus moved onto a matter that had been alluded to in various tabloids. 'It is also known that you in the course of the inquiry came upon an item of some interest.'

'I did sir, on Wednesday thirteenth December I was at Lambridge House, and I found a stake (this somewhat alarming item, which lay upon the evidence table, held aloft) against the hay rick.

'And is it not so that the stick (the stick in question also held aloft) recovered at the murder scene was found to fit the stake exactly.'

'It was sir.'

'How had this stick been separated from the stake?'

'It was partly cut and partly broken.' This utterance of Sergeant Allmond resulted in an excited cacophony of voices, Magistrate Joseph Wilson calling for calm.

'On Saturday ninth December you were placed in charge of the house, can you tell the court what time you took on this responsibility?'

'From ten o'clock, on the day after the murder, I was in charge of the house.' It is to be remembered that Thomas Allmond had spent the previous night at Lambridge House.

'Did you leave the house at any time?'

'I slept in the house until the body was removed.'

'Were you left to guard the deceased alone?'

'No, there was another constable with me.' This part of Allmonds evidence throws up somewhat of a conundrum, George Dawson had earlier stated that the keys to Lambridge House were intrusted to him, and therefore one would suppose that he would have to be on hand to unlock doors. Whether he and Allmond crossed paths during the time leading up to Kate Dungeys removal for burial is unclear.

The prosecution had no further need of Sergeant Thomas Allmond, and thus Sydney Brain intimated to the defence that they could, if they so wished, cross examine the witness. Robert Wood had listened and taken down innumerable notes, but he did not cross examine, and only one sentence escaped his lips. 'Having heard this witness, not a word of evidence has been produced against my client.'

Forty Nine

Two Pairs of Trousers

Maria Brown, who had travelled from Ealing accompanied by her husband and son, the cost of their train fare met by the Treasury, was next summoned by the prosecution, to give account of her dealings with the prisoner.

'Can you state your name and place of residence?'

'I am the wife of Tom Brown, and live at 42 Bedford Road, Ealing.' The answer she gave causing some derision in court, Maria at a loss as to what those within the spectator's gallery found so amusing.

'Do you recognise the prisoner?'

'I know Rathall and his wife; they lodged in the same house as I did.'

'Where was this house?'

'Number 6 Bayham Road, Ealing.' A road primarily made up of late Victorian terraced houses.

'When did the Rathalls leave this address?'

'They left in July last.'

'When the prisoner left he gave into your care items, what were these items?'

'The prisoner left two boxes in my charge.' The boxes in question do not seem to have been displayed upon the evidence table.

'When did you next see the prisoner?'

'I did not see Walter Rathall again until the late evening of eleventh December.'

'What time was it would you say, on the night of the eleventh, that you saw the prisoner?'

'It would have been about eight thirty in the evening.'

'Was he alone?'

'No sir, a man named Woods was with him.' The witness is referring to Robert Woods.

'Was there a purpose to the prisoners visit?'

Maria Brown did not answer, she instead to look directly at the prisoner, she having to be prompted by Sydney Brain. 'I am sorry sir, can you assist me do you refer to the boxes that Rathall had left in my care?'

'That is the matter that I wish to explore.'

'He asked me if I had his boxes and I said, yes, he said "I want them", he said "I don't want them particularly tonight, but I want a pair of trousers out of them."'

'Did the prisoner take from one of the boxes a pair of trousers?'

'He did sir; he took the trousers out and put them under his arm.'

'Have you seen these trousers since?'

'I have sir they are the ones he is wearing now.'

Sydney Brain stepped nearer to the prisoner, and waved his arms dramatically in the direction of Walter Rathalls trousers, the solicitors somewhat dramatic gesturing's causing some within the spectator's gallery to laugh. 'After the prisoner recovered the trousers what next did he do?'

'He said good night.'

'Was anything more noteworthy said by the prisoner?'

Maria Brown dropped her gaze, a scowl distorting her features, it obvious that Brain had caused her offence. 'Rathall said he would call for the boxes in the morning, and went away.'

'Did the prisoner return as he had said he would?'

'The next morning, Tuesday twelfth December, Rathall came to the house.'

'Can you tell the court what the prisoner did while under your roof?'

'He first had some breakfast, and then he packed some things out of one box into another.'

'Why did he do this?'

'He meant to take one box away, the other he left with me, at my suggestion he changed his coat.'

'Did the prisoner tell you what he meant to do with the box he left with?'

'He did not.'

'Did the prisoner have cause to visit your home again?'

'He did sir, after that he came for some more things, some of which he put in his pocket, and some he put in a brown paper parcel.'

'He took this parcel with him when he left?'

'Rathall went out with the parcel, and said he was going to pawn the baby's clothes, as well as some of his wife's clothes.'

'The items he wished to pawn in the parcel he carried off with him.'

'Yes that is so.'

'Do you know why the prisoner wanted to pawn these items?'

'Oh yes I do sir, he told me it was because he wanted to get back to Henley-on-Thames.'

'And when did the prisoner quit your home?'

'He left my house on the Wednesday.' This would have been Wednesday 13th December 1893.

'Have you seen the prisoner since that day?'

'Only now sir, stood before me.'

Sydney Brain had used Maria Browns recollections in regard to the boxes to great advantage, he wishing to cast a shadow of suspicion over the accused, in relation to his sudden appearance at the Brown's door. The insistence on Rathalls part of accessing his boxes in search of a pair of trousers, remembering that as a poor man he would not be flush with clothing, begging the question of what became of the ones he left Henley wearing.

Maria Brown (her husband Tom not called to give evidence) had played her part, and thus excused she stepped down from the witness box, necks craning, as those seated within the gallery looked upon the woman who had been summoned from London. Much had been said of the reward of one hundred pounds (offered by Henry Mash) having been the primary reason behind the Brown's volunteering of information to the constabulary, and Maria left the courtroom glad that the defence had not seized upon this fact.

Fifty

It is a Cruel Job About the Henley Affair

The prosecution had not yet done with the party from London, and with great excitement the spectators (who were by this stage crammed into every orifice of the gallery) stood forward of their bench seat, better to see one Frederick William Sutton enter the court. Sydney Brain, having acknowledged his witness with a formal nod, tempered his voice to allow for Suttons nerves, the man within the witness stand trembling. 'Can you tell the court your name and occupation?'

'I am the son of the last witness (Maria Browns son from her first marriage), and I work as a plumbers labourer.'

'Do you recognise the prisoner?'

Frederick Sutton, he having no inclination to direct his gaze toward Walter Rathall, to answer this question in the affirmative. 'I know the prisoner; he lodged in the same house as me.'

'It is right, is it not, that when the prisoner left 42 Bedford Road after his initial visit, you accompanied him?'

'I did sir.'

'And what pray did you experience, while in the company of the prisoner?'

Sutton staled, he perplexed by Sydney Brains turn of phrase, and it was only after clarification from the bench that he replied. 'On twelfth December I went up to the station with him (unfortunately it not made clear in subsequent newspaper reports where this station was), I went with him to sell a teapot, some spoons and knives.' The last portion of Frederick Suttons testimony alludes to a visit to a pawnshop, we never to know its exact location, the owner of the business, as far as one can tell, if he provided a statement, not called to give evidence.

'From this point where did you and the prisoner next go?'

'We then went to Mr Carpenters Rag Shop; Rathall went in taking a bundle of rags with him?' During the Victorian era the very poor would often resort to selling their worn clothes at a rag shop. An owner of said establishment would purchase for a pittance items brought into him; and having sorted through would prepare items for reuse, which he in turn sold on.

'Can you tell the court what was in this bundle of rags?'

'I know there was a coat in it because I saw it.'

'Can you tell the court what else was in the bundle?'

'I cannot sir, but I can tell you that subsequently as we walked down the road Rathall borrowed a Star (a London weekly newspaper) and read it, and he said. "It is a cruel job about the Henley affair.' There audible gasps and tittering's at the witness's last comment, Sydney Brain looking much amused, he struck by the irony of Walter Rathalls quip.

If Frederick Sutton was cross examined by the defence it did not warrant a mention within the newspapers, and his ordeal before the magistrates was mercifully, as far as he was concerned, over very swiftly.

Fifty One

Have They Any Clue to the Henley Murder?

Yet another had been provided with the expenses necessary to finance his journey down from London, now called to appear as a witness for the prosecution. 'Can you tell the court your name and occupation?'
'My name is Robert Woods; I am a gardener from Ealing.'
'How do you know the prisoner?'
'My wife's brother married the prisoner's sister, and at one time the prisoner lodged in my house with his wife.'
'While the prisoner was up in London did you have cause to see him?'
I did, on Monday night (eleventh December), about six o'clock, the prisoner came to my house, I asked him what he was doing up here and he said he had come up for some boxes he had left at Mrs Browns. I said have you walked up today, and he said, "yes, I started between eight and nine this morning."
'Did you and the prisoner discuss the murder at Lambridge?'
'He had tea with us, and my wife said. "Have they any clue to the Henley murder?"
'And how did Rathall react?'
'He said. "They had not at nine o'clock this morning." I told him that the murder had been well documented in our Sunday paper.'
'Did the prisoner respond to this comment?'
'He said it was not in his paper on Sunday. I still had hold of the Sunday paper and told him he could read it.'
'What paper was this?'

'It was Lloyds Paper.' The murder at Lambridge House had been covered in some detail, within the Sunday 10th December edition of the Lloyds Weekly Newspaper.

'Did the prisoner read about the Henley case?'

'He looked at it, but he did not read it. But he did say what a cruel bit it was, as she had thirty eight knocks on her head.' This comment, if indeed Walter Rathall made it, is unusual in so much as it had not any foundation in fact, the tally of injuries he quoted seemingly plucked from his imagination.

Sydney Brain now wished to explore what followed on from the interlude, in which the three had partaken of tea and cake. 'It is in record that when the prisoner left your house you went with him, can you tell the court what occurred as the two of you made your way to Mrs Browns?'

'I told him I would walk with him to Ealing Dean, and on the way we saw a newspaper placard which stated. "A man arrested at Henley today." I brought the paper (the name of this particular paper not referred to in court), and we read that a man had been arrested at Henley named Rathall. (This newspaper, though it had come up trumps regards the suspects identity, far off the mark regards an arrest.) He said. "That is not Rathall, it is Rattall; he has been a solider and lives in Henley." At this juncture the witness put off his stride, laughter, which emulated from the spectators gallery, causing a hiatus in proceedings.

Once those amused by what had gone before had managed to suppress their mirth, Sydney Brain, his facial expression grave, to reflect that chortling during a murder trial was most unsavoury, continued. 'We have heard from an earlier witness that you accompanied the prisoner all the way to Mrs Brown's, is that so?'

'I went with him to Mrs Brown's.' It is a point of fact, not clarified in court, that Robert Woods did not witness Walter Rathalls exploration of the boxes.

'Did he leave Mrs Brown's in possession of anything?'

'Yes he came out with a pair of trousers on his arm.'

'And what did he do next?'

'Why sir, he went into the passage and changed his trousers, he put on a pair of cloth ones, he said he had another pair underneath (this the first mention of two pairs of trousers, and there is no evidence to suggest that once arrested the constabulary seized from the lodging house in Daventry all of Rathalls belongings, though one would think they did. And we are not privy to whether the trousers the prisoner wore on the day of the murder were recovered, and examined for blood stains), but he was afraid to take them off as he should catch cold.'

'So the prisoner took off one pair of trousers, leaving one pair upon his person, and then put on the pair he had collected from the Brown's.'

'That sir is the long and short of it.'

'What became of the trousers he took off?'

'He took the trousers that he had taken off away with him.'

Sydney Brain had done his worst, but Robert Wood, for the defence, also required much of the witness. 'It is true, is it not, that you informed the police of your day spent with the prisoner, that being Monday eleventh December?'

'Yes, I gave information to the police.' If the Police Station at which Robert Woods gave his information was mentioned in court, its location was not to appear in any subsequent newspapers.

'During your journey to attend this hearing it was brought to my attention that you were heard to say that you very much hoped you would receive some portion of the reward. Is that the reason for the version of events you have given this court?'

'I said at Twyford (the station at which those travelling to Henley-on-Thames would alight, to await a connection) I hoped to get half the reward.' Again those in court, some spectators heard to hiss loudly, not made privy as to the mystery individual who gave information to the defence, as to Robert Woods hopes regards a share of the reward. But it had been commonly banded about that the fellow was none other than Twyford Stationmaster, George Kenerrick North.

Sydney Brain was much annoyed by Robert Wood's inference, and following on from a dramatic leap from his seat, the prosecution solicitor addressed the bench. 'Do I have the magistrate's permission to re-examine this witness?'

'You do?'

'I thank the bench. Now Mr Woods, did you contact the constabulary before or after the offer of a reward?'

'I gave information to the police before a reward was offered.' Disaster had been averted, and with the defence stumped, Robert Woods, who ironically (and somewhat confusingly) name was almost identical to the defence solicitors, excused.

So who was this Roberts Woods, to answer this question we must retreat back to the 1820s. A George Woods of Greys in Oxfordshire, did, on 29th December 1848, in his twenty second year, marry Ann Crutchfield (two years his junior), the young lady hailing from Woodcote, Oxfordshire. The newlyweds, though not destitute, were neither wealthy, and thus only found themselves in possession of the funds necessary to afford the rent on a small premises in Greys Green, George picking up work as a labourer.

As with many of meagre means the Woods were delivered of more offspring than they could afford first born John, starting them off with his birth in 1852. Mary was born in 1855; she then after followed by George, Rosa Ann, Henry, Robert, Anne, and thankfully proving the last, Walter, who was born in 1876. So how on earth did George Woods provide for eight hungry mouths, as like many who had not had benefit of a protracted education, he to find manual work as a "sawyer" of wood (one who saws up wood), his family residing in Shepherd Greens Cottage.

The sixth born, Robert, spent his formative years in Greys Green, and much smitten by a certain Sarah Ann Dawson (George Dawsons sister), and with her much taken with him, the two walked out. They were wed in early 1891; the groom having good prospects, that being a police constable, rather ironic in light of what Robert was to become entangled up in, just under three years later. The Woods were not destined to reside in the country; by the census of 1891 they living at Burton Crescent, St Pancras London. So it was at this address, on the evening of 11th December 1893, that Walter Rathall came calling, his decision no doubt in some part determined by the fact that Robert Woods had quit the force (why he gave up that particular career path unknown), he earning a lesser wage picking up gardening jobs.

Fifty Two

He Replied, John Brown

Those of the local populous who flocked outside Henley Town Hall (their number having grown beyond any hope of control by the glaringly insufficient contingency of police constables) had to content themselves with hearing second hand all that which was occurring within. Snippets of information gleaned from courtroom spectators, who on occasion (having left instruction to those sat either side, not to under any circumstance relinquish their vacated seat) momentarily left the confines of the gallery, to stretch their legs, and take advantage of the fresh air, the atmosphere within the court by now quite stifling. Others, to wander aimlessly in amongst the crowds, picked out phrases from the overheard conversations of reporters, who dashed across to the post office (in an effort to beat a rival), desperate to forward (via telegraph) hastily composed articules.

Within the court Sydney Brain, having taken a pause so as to swig a glass of water, while he'd simultaneously studied his notes, was now satisfied that he had re-familiarized himself with the next witness's statement, and thus he nodded to the magistrates, he ready to proceed.

John Cooper did as he had done before, summoned the next witness. 'The court calls Harry Webster.'

So who was Harry Webster? He was a man of thirty three, born in Brafield, Northamptonshire (baptised 9th November 1860), to local man one James Webster (born 1824), an agricultural labourer. The Webster's, who inhabited a largish farmhouse at Brafield-on-the-Green, Hardingstone, their income largely sourced via a trade familiar to the area, that of lace making, Harrys mother, Sarah (nee Smith, born 1827, in Hardington, Northamptonshire) highly proficient in the craft. Harry Webster was one of many, his elder siblings, Charles, born 1848, Alfred, Eliza, George Thomas, and Ada Maria, she born in 1857. His younger siblings, Martha, born in 1862, and Frederick John, he baptised on 7th August 1864. As with many families reliant on industry, several of the Webster children once finished with schooling, mirroring their parent's professions, Charles, Alfred and Harry working the land, while their sisters, Eliza, Ada and Martha, under their mother's tutorship, produced fine lace, primarily for the beautification of ladies garments.

Sophia Ayris (born Maidford, Northampton) had taken employment as a shop assistant, at a large scale hosiery outlet (11-13 Drapery, under the ownership of John Blacknell), in Northamptonshire, and in the course of her day she had cause to converse with a fine young man, Constable Harry Webster. After the two had walked out together they determined to marry, and on 4th September 1882, in the Parish Church of Blakesley, their nupitals took place, the groom twenty one, his bride five years his elder.

Harry Webster had first served as a police constable in Tidmarsh, he on 19th January 1880 recruited into the Thrapston Division. May 1882 had seen Webster transferred to Rothwell, Harrys wage more than sufficient to provide for his new wife and son, Montague, he born 18th July 1883. Harry Webster, much favoured by his superiors, was swiftly promoted, in the June of 1888 elevated to sergeant, and transferred to Kettering; the Webster's allocated an apartment above the police station, on the London Road. First November 1892 saw Harry Webster promoted to the rank of Inspector of Police, thus forward transferred to Daventry Police Station (the Webster's taking occupation of the flat above), where in January 1894 intelligence (courtesy of a boarding house proprietor) reached the front desk of the police station at 43 New Street. This information, once conveyed to Inspector Harry Webster, to see the man scurrying off to a lodging house, in the hope of apprehending a fellow wanted on suspicion of murder.

The appearance of witnesses, who had travelled from outside the local area, caused the most excitement within the spectator's gallery, and Harry Webster proved no exception. Sydney Brain having to wait some moments for order in court to be restored, once satisfied that he faced no further risk of interruption, he to take the floor. 'Can you state for the court your name and occupation.'

'Harry Webster, Inspector of Police at Daventry.'

'You were on third January called to a lodging house; did you there see the prisoner?'

'On Wednesday third January I went to a common lodging house in Daventry, where I saw the prisoner, his wife and child.'

'Can you now tell the court what occurred once you had hold of your man?'

'I asked the prisoner to accompany me to another room, I told the prisoner that I was a police officer, and I asked him his name, he replied John Brown (some of the spectators heard to laugh), I said you answer the description of a man wanted at Henley for the murder of a young lady on the eighth of last month. It is not a matter to be played with, you had better give me your proper name, he replied it is Brown; if you don't believe me ask her.'

'By the phrase her, was the prisoner referring to his wife?'

'Yes he was.'

'Can you tell the court what passed between you and the prisoner's wife?'

'I said to the woman are you his wife, she said "yes." I said what is your name and she replied "Rathall, I won't tell a lie."'

'From that point what actions did you then resolve to take?'

'I read the wanted description to him and he said. "Yes I am the man, but you've got to prove it. I can prove I was not away from the lodging house more than half an hour on the night of the murder, and arrived home at seven thirty as near as I can say." I then took the prisoner into my custody, and afterwards handed him over to Superintenant Keal.'

That was all that the prosecution required of the witness, Walter Rathall had attempted through duplicity to evade capture, and Robert Wood, for the defence, had to implement damage limitation.

'Why did the name the prisoner gave you raise concerns?'

'John Brown is ten a penny as a name we meet with.' Within the spectator's gallery many heard to snigger.

'When you took the prisoner into custody were you in full uniform.'

'No, I was in plain clothes.' It was now apparent that when Inspector Harry Webster had been informed of the suspicions of the landlord of the lodging house he had been off duty.

'Did you caution the prisoner?'

'I did not formally caution him.'

Robert Wood pausing for effect, so those upon the bench might fully absorb the implications of Inspector Harry Webster's last utterance. And once satisfied that the desired effect had been achieved, the defence solicitor casually addressed the witness. 'I have no further questions, you may step down.'

Fifty Three

No Knife, But a Small Pocket Knife

Superintendent Francis Keal was next called, and thanks in no small part to the revelation that was photography, and the stalwart efforts of those employed to maintain the personnel records of those employed within the Oxfordshire Constabulary, an enduring image of Keal survives. He a man of some five feet eight and a half inches tall with a proportionate figure, his complexion fresh, eyes grey, and hair brown.

Sydney Brain had by this stage cross examined many witnesses, but this particular mans (Keals investigative procedures much criticised by those of the press) testimony had to be extracted with the upmost care. 'Please state for the court your name and occupation.'

'Francis Keal, Superintendent of Police, at Henley-on-Thames.'

'Can I take you back to the night of the eighth, can you tell this court of the arrival at Henley Station of George Dawson?'

'On December eighth, about midnight, I received word that Dawson was in the station, and that all was not well at Lambridge, I thus went back with him.'

'Once at Lambridge Farm, who took you to where the deceased lay?'

'Dawson took me to where the body was lying.'

'What were the weather conditions on that night?'

'It was a pitch dark night, and was raining and hailing in torrents.'

'You closely observed the body did you not, how was the deceased lying?'

'The left leg was drawn up, and the legs were turned towards Assenden. Her head was on one side, the rammer was partly under her hair, and when I moved the body blood came from the neck.' The superintendent to break off, a woman heard to cry out; she thought by those within the spectator's gallery, who turned to gaze at her, to be closely connected to Kate Dungey, this young womans sobs causing much disquiet in court.

Sydney Brain did not have a heart of stone, he much perplexed by the distress of another, and thus he waited for the sobs to subside before he continued. 'Were there items close to the body?'

'I found a poker and a stick (both of which produced in court) against the body.'

'You also, I believe, recovered a short piece of stick (produced in court), where did you discover it?'

'I found it inside the door.' The witness is referring to the front door of Lambridge House.

At this juncture, a magistrate (not identified in any subsequent newspaper reports) interrupted. 'Did you converse with Froomes?' This being John Froomes, father of James and Harry.

'I did sir.'

'Did he seem agitated?'

'No.'

Clearly the magistrate had some conundrum he wished to resolve, but he did not volunteer any more on the matter, and thus Sydney Brain was not to be silenced for long. 'Can we now move forward to the time in which you inspected the house, the passageway found to have items scattered about, can you tell the court what they were?'

'In the passageway I found a brooch and a hairpin (both of which identified as having belonged to Miss Dungey), a nightlight, and a discarded box of matches.'

'Did you see any blood?'

'There were smears of blood about.'

'Who locked in the body?'

'I locked up the body, and left the place.'

Line drawing of Lambridge House, which depicts the front door, thought to have been Kate Dungeys escape route, also shown the path she ran down, some moments later Kate felled by a series of heavy blows, she mortally wounded and left to die. Appeared in Lloyds Weekly, Sunday 17th December 1893

'You returned on the morning of the ninth, who accompanied you?'
'I returned in the morning with the doctor.'
'We know of Doctor Smith's role on that day, but what did you resolve to do?'
'With the benefit of daylight I made an examination of the house.'
'We have heard much of the footprints, what of these footprints?'
'On the flower bed, at the back of the house, I saw a footprint, the toe pointing from the house. I had a cast taken of the footprint, it having been covered up in the meanwhile.'
'Did the cast match that of the prisoner's boots?'
'When the prisoner arrived at the station on January third, I received the prisoner into custody in answer to the charge and he said. "It has

got to be proved, I was not out of the lodging house all day, until I went into town about six o'clock, and returned about seven thirty." I first noted down all the prisoner had uttered, and thus forward examined his boots (Rathalls boots stood upon the evidence table, a court usher holding them up for the benefit of the magistrates), on the right boot the rows of nails are distinct; there are four rows, which are shown on the cast. The measurement of the boot also compares with the cast.' The superintendent's recollection was damming, and Walter Rathall slumped forward, while those within the spectator's gallery collectively gasped. Sydney Brain had done his worst, and as he took his seat he allowed himself a self-satisfied smile.

Robert Wood was out of his seat in a flash, and not a fellow easily daunted, and with the magistrates leave, he took hold of one of the offending boots. Wood minutely examined the boot, and after some moments of spellbinding silence he addressed Superintendent Francis Keal. 'It is indeed a boot that has definite characteristics; did you compare the cast against any other boot?'

'I looked at Froomes and Dawsons boots.'

'Would you say your cast (the cast produced in court) compares completely with the prisoners boot?'

'The measurements of the sole and heal of the boot compare with the prisoners boot, as do the nails.'

Robert Wood stepped toward the witness stand, the cast clutched in one hand, and its corresponding boot in the other. 'You see that distinctive mark on the toe of this boot; can you show me that on the cast?'

'No, because it is the end of the cast, and a flower interposed between the sole and the earth.'

'No, you mean because it is not there.'

Sydney Brain, his voice raised in agitation, cut across the defence's argument. 'The witness can only show the resemblance which existed, and not those which were non-existent. Some marks did not appear on the cast, as the latter was imperfect, owing to the flower and other circumstances.'

Wood chose not to pick up the prosecutions argument, the man to simply return boot and cast to the evidence table, and continued upon another subject. 'When you apprehended the prisoner were his clothes blooded, and did he possess any weapon that may have fixed him to the murder scene?'

'I found no blood on the prisoners clothes, and no knife but a small pocket knife.'

'It is of note, is it not, that the prisoners clothes were unsullied by blood stains.'

'The prisoner had ample opportunity to dispose of his clothes.'

'Before his arrest had the prisoner been questioned by any other officer?'

'Rathall was not approached by any constable or questioned before his arrest by Mr Simmonds (who this Simmonds is, unclear), though an officer did make enquires at the prisoners lodging house, but the prisoner was not in.'

It is a strange point of fact, that, although Superintendent Francis Keal was the lynchpin of the investigation into the heinous events at Lambridge Farm, he spent a relatively brief time being cross examined by Walter Rathalls defence solicitor. But the matter of the boots was not yet finished with, Robert Wood had another who could muddy the waters, and thus the next witness was called.

Fifty Four

A Pair of Boots

'Can you tell the court your name and place of work?'
'Thomas Blake, Fawley Court Farm cowman, in the employ of Mr Mackenzie.'
'The prisoner is known to you?'
'He is, we having met when Walter Rathall was hired to work for the Mackenzie's.'
'What was the job that the prisoner was taken on to do?'
'He was taken on as a beater at the Fawley Court estate shoot.'
'While working alongside the prisoner you found the prisoner in need of a pair of boots.'
'I did sir, his boots were awfully worn, and I had given Walter a pair of boots in October.' The witness is referring to October 1893.
'At the time of the murder, was the accused still in employment at the estate?'
'He was sir?'
'And would he have been in receipt of wages?'
'He would sir.'
There it was, the witnesses account given, not taking much time at all, and with no rebuttal from the prosecution, Thomas Blake stood down.

Fifty Five

To Put the Prisoner in his Coffin

Within the corridor, the bench reserved for those who had been summoned to testify, was deserted, all the witnesses having been heard. Magistrates Chairman, Joseph Henry Wilson, conferred with his colleagues, and satisfied that there were no further legal avenues to be explored (not until the Criminal Evidence Act of 1898 it permissible, after the close of the prosecution's case, for the accused to be called by the defence, to give account of themselves) he gave the defence leave to sum up.

This was no time for nerves, and Robert Samuel Wood (who under the directives of the Criminal Procedures Act of 1865, had been permitted to cross examine witnesses who had previously submitted a written statement) stepped out onto the floor. He looked first at the prisoner, then up at those sat within the gallery, and then he attended to his buttonhole (the flower within it a little jaded), and finally, with his next course of action decided upon, Robert Wood addressed those upon the bench. 'I am a vigorous and able defence, a cruel and blood thirsty murder had been committed, but because a young man happened to be poor and was unfortunately thrown upon the world, that was no reason to say he was the most likely person to have committed it. I submit that it would be the bounded duty of the magistrates, after they have reviewed the evidence today, that twelve reasonable men would not on the evidence adduced by the prosecution send the life out of the young man. What evidence has the prosecution adduced against my client, absolutely none, there had been suggestions outside the court and inside that the young man had been driven away because he had quarrelled with Miss Dungey. But there is not a tittle of evidence to show the prisoner had any reason for revenge, as motive to commit such a brutal murder, Miss Dungey and himself on very good terms. On the day of the murder my client was seen on the pathway which led up to Lambridge, he had a perfect right to be on the pathway. As to the night of the murder, in reviewing the evidence it was pointed out by a medical man that it would be impossible for the deceased to have lived two hours after the Jugular Vein had been severed, and the same doctor stated that the murder must have been committed by a person standing close to the deceased to have severed the Jugular vein, and that blood might have spurted three feet, and yet no trace of blood was found on the prisoner. There nothing strange about the prisoner, he did not even wash himself when he came home. Mrs Ayres evidence is not to be believed, as she told the police that the prisoner was out of her house all evening. It is a mere matter of suggestion, in the same way that the prosecution endeavoured to put the prisoner in his coffin, that another man was very often alone with Miss Dungey, and is not the imputation just as strong against him, as strong against my client. (It seems likely that Robert Wood was casting aspirations in the direction of Henry Joseph Mash.) As to the boot (Robert Wood requesting that said boot be shown to the court), it might correspond in width, but it did not in length, and did not in heel, and was a common farm boot, and indeed the boots have been worn a month since the murder. The Ealing witnesses had indeed come forward, for the sake of the reward, but they had proved nothing. The prisoner had indeed changed his clothes, but had not tried to conceal the old ones. I conjecture the murderer had got in by the kitchen door, locked it after him, then bolted the front, and Miss Dungey had gone out of the house by the bay window (some within the spectators gallery to shake their heads in disbelief, not convinced that this scenario might have played out), as it is highly improbable that the murderer should have returned to lock up the house. (This statement of Robert Woods not to explain the blood stains found on the front door handle, Miss Dungey thought to have fled Lambridge House by this route.) There was no motive why the prisoner should have committed the murder, and the murder does not seem to have been committed for robbery, but to get possession of some papers or other things the deceased had. Indeed we have heard that letters and a bag had been seized and not handed into the police, or produced in court. (This utterance, directed toward Henry Mash, to suggest that the letters removed by Kate Dungey's sister, Julia, and carried off by the deceases father, Walter Dungey, contained correspondence between housekeeper and employer of an improper nature.) A weaker lamer or harder case had never been brought against a man because they had found he was somewhere for an hour.' Robert Wood was done, with a last flurry of his hands, in the direction of his hapless client, he to step back behind his desk, Walter Rahall by the conclusion of his solicitors address moved to tears.

Suddenly there were murmurings from the bench, all eyes upon the magistrates, who rose as one, spectators, witnesses, and those connected with the deceased standing as they left. The court was aghast, what was happening, reporters licking the tips of their pencils, ready to dash down any pertinent fact. The spectator's gallery seemed to groan under the weight, as many abandoned their seats to hang precariously over the front balustrade, courtroom ushers attempting, with little success, to bring order. The Dungey's and the Mash's, who had endured a day that no one would envy, glanced across at each other, and all awaited the return of the magistrates.

After four minutes of deliberation the magistrates shuffled back into the courtroom, and once reseated, Chairman, Joseph Wilson (order having been restored), addressed the court. 'The Bench do not find there is sufficient evidence to support the charge, and therefore the prisoner is dismissed with no stain on his character.'

Walter Rathall, who collapsed in tears, given a loud cheer from the gallery; he having endured a six and a half hour hearing, the time now approaching six twenty five. Robert Wood rushed toward his client, and gave him a reassuring pat on the back, the prisoner now free to go. Upon leaving Henley Town Hall, Rathall (now left to his own devices) presented with a collection of money (word of the prisoners acquittal had quickly reached those assembled in Market Place), donated by the many who had not made it into the courtroom. A crowd of excited (and in some cases inebriated) people surged towards Walter Rathall, cheering loudly, the young man overcome with emotion, and a little unsettled by his celebrity, thanking all who congratulated him.

Walter Rathall was a free man; he had endured a trial that had been weighed heavily against him, the legislation of which dictated by statuary law. A pre-trial bench was required to be made up of magistrates, sourced more often than not from the counties more eminent male citizens, their duty, before any full trial could commence, to hear the case for the prosecution. If the evidence put across by the prosecution indicated there was a case to answer the magistrates would endorse the indictment, and a full trial would be sanctioned. If, after hearing the defence argument, they felt the case against a defendant had not been adequately made, the Chairman of the Magistrate had the power to release the prisoner. However a defendant would not formally be acquitted in law, and could therefore be subsequently rearrested, if more evidence against him (or her) came to light.

So Walter Rathall, though he had been released "without a stain on his character", did have the weight of possible re-arrest hanging over him. Though to his advantage the public had swung over to Walters side, a man (who a few days previous found himself being escorted under police guard from Henley Railway Station, while a mob cried out for a lynching) now in possession of a pocket full of money, while strangers rushed over to congratulate him. The scene that played out in Upper Market Place, reporters tearing off to the telegraph office, the Henley and South Oxfordshire Standards reporter making rapid progress back to his office to turn in his story, surging crowds of locals straining to catch sight of Rathall, and police running hither and thither, in an effort to bring some semblance of order, in acute contrast to what occurred within the courtroom.

Back in court some others were not so exuberant; Henry Joseph Mash slumped back in his seat, slighted by the attacks upon his character, while his wife Georgiana offered spousal support. Walter Dungey sat dejected, while his sorrowful daughters sobbed; their heads leant against their brothers (Ernest) chest. And as for George Dawson, who had found himself on many occasions used as a scapegoat, he took one last look about the court and quietly slipped out of the town hall, and pushed his way through the crowd. And one hopes that this much maligned man made his way to the nearest hostelry, as he was surely deserving of an alcoholic beverage.

The adage that life goes on was never truer in the case of the "Henley Murder". The representatives of the press stepped aboard trains and headed back to their news desks, at the ready to pounce on the next high profile story, that would send people scurrying off to purchase a newspaper, better to read the very latest.

And those who lived and worked in Henley-on-Thames settled back into life as they had known it, before the unprecedented events of the last two months.

But for one family there was much bad feeling, the columns of the newspapers, and idle gossip, had caused considerable damage to reputations, and one amongst the family had much to say on the matter. Mrs Georgiana Mash had an axe to grind, and grind it she did, speaking exclusively to a newspaper reporter.

Fifty Six

The Rich, the Privileged, the Prosperous, Need no Guardian or Advocate

During his cross examination by the defence George Dawson had alluded to there having been ill feeling between Miss Dungey and Mrs Mash. Dawson under oath, maintaining that on one occasion he had a brief but telling conversation with a tearful Kate Dungey, the housekeeper of Lambridge much distressed by an attempt by her mistress to strike her with an umbrella stick. This peculiar event (which had been touched on in the columns of countless newspapers many of whom as the "Gutter Press" drawn to the more salacious aspects of the murder inquiry) to draw the attention of a particular tabloid. And so it was that a representative of The Sun Newspaper, under the behest of his editor, in an effort to secure a statement from one who had been much aggrieved, called at the Mash's London residence. He thus managing, whether paying his quarry or not (I would imagine that Georgiana Mash would have found the idea of a paid interview somewhat vulgar) to secure an interview with the mistress of Redcliffe Gardens.

The two, once formalities were dealt with, settled in the front room, and as an exemplary host Georgiana providing her guest with lashings of tea and sandwiches, the reporter, though grateful of his hosts generosity eager to begin. 'Mrs Mash, could you provide in the fullest terms the reader with a history of Miss Dungeys service in the family.'

'Miss Dungey became governess in our London house about nine years ago, and remained in our London house in charge of our children for two years.'

'Why did this arrangement cease?'

'As the children matured, I felt there was no further need to retain a governess and Kate Dungey left our service.'

'Did the young woman quickly secure new employment?'

'Miss Dungey had been an excellent servant, and aided by excellent references quickly secured a position with the Duke of Grafton's Agent, and remained with him a full two years. Though I must make it clear that Miss Dungey did not become a stranger, she visited us at our London home on numerous occasions. I should tell you that Miss Dungeys sister was then, and still is, in our service here.' Georgiana Mash refers to Julia Dungey, who was employed in her husband's commercial outlet.

The unidentified representative of The Sun, in sore need of a unique angle, to better avail himself of his editor, to lead his interviewee gently towards more current matters. 'When did Miss Dungey return to your household?'

'About five years ago Miss Dungey returned to us as housekeeper at Lambridge, she spent sometime of every winter with us in London.' Georgiana Mash at this juncture to drop into the conversation a somewhat startling snippet of information; in an attempt, no doubt, to reiterate to the reporter her fondest for Miss Dungey. 'Last winter she lived here for nearly three months, as she had to undergo the painful operation of having seventeen teeth drawn.' This statement, in itself, is somewhat ambiguous, and any reader of the subsequent article would have been sore pressed to know if the matter of the teeth in fact alluded to Mrs Mash, not Miss Dungey. It could be that the reporter misinterpreted Georgiana's revelation, as there was no mention of such an alarming amount of missing teeth, during Doctor George Smith's post mortem examination of Kate Dungey.

This misplaced anecdote did not seem to throw the reporter off course; he required knowledge of the salacious, and thus he next touched upon the by now infamous "umbrella stick incident". 'Was it

Mr Mashs mother or yourself (he knew full well it was Georgiana) who is spoken of in the umbrella incident?'

'I suppose it must be me (Georgiana knew full well the incident alluded to her), but I state strongly that the statement was not a correct one, and should not be relied upon. It was made by Dawson on the strength of what the man believed Miss Dungey said to him. (Georgiana Mash to seize upon the opportunity to cast aspersions on the man, who as she saw it, had during the fallout from events at Lambridge Farm, via newspaper interviews, and court testimony, damaged her reputation.) 'With what I knew of Miss Dungeys attitude towards George Dawson, I am sure that Kate had no confidence with him. Indeed I feel most heartily that Dawsons grievance would be that he felt that Miss Dungey was too reserved for him.'

'Was Miss Dungey a reserved character?'

'She was a woman who would sit for an hour in a room with a person and never speak.'

The reporter had a job to do; his editor demanding of him that the very core of the shocking events at Lambridge were delved into. 'May I ask where you were on the night of the murder?'

Georgiana answered with definitive clarity. 'Certainly, the murder had taken place on the Friday of London Cattle Show Week (in 1893 this agricultural show commencing on Monday 4th December, and although the weather was at times bitterly cold, with occasional squally hail and snow showers, on one particular day twenty eight thousand passed through the turnstiles), and I was at home, as I had been all week entertaining friends including Kates father Walter, who was up at the show and stayed as a house guest.'

'And where was Mr Mash?'

'My husband was also in London, he had been to meet his brother-in-law Mr Boyce that night, the gentleman having travelled from

Rutland. Indeed Mr Mash, Mr Boyce and our daughters, arrived all together from Glasshouse Street at about nine that evening.'

The interviewer, with tone of voice best suited to the solemnity of the subject to be touched on, now moving inevitably to the crime. 'How did you come to hear of the outrage at Henley?'

'We heard of the murder through a telegram the next morning, calling us to Henley, but we did not hear a fuller account of the events until we reached Twyford Station and conversed with the Station Master.' Georgiana is referring to George Kenerrick North.

'When had you last visited Lambridge House?'

'It was a full nine weeks earlier, when I and my husband had attended a card party in the neighbourhood. A group of us subsequently deciding to take an excursion over to Satwell near Lambridge House, being up all night, I had not been near the place since.'

'Do you know anything of Miss Dungey having a lover?'

This question, coming out of nowhere, riled Georgiana; she shifted her posture, fixed the reporter with an icy glare, and stated emphatically. 'No, but Kate had been invited to London as it was London Cattle Show Week, but for some reason unknown she refused to come (the irony being that had Kate Dungey not declined the offer, and stayed in London the full week, she would have been out of Lambridge House on eighth December), although her father was present.'

The reporter from The Sun, having benefit of expertise in such matters, knew that his subject was wearying of his barrage of questions, and mindful of Georgiana Mashs sensibilities drew the interview towards its conclusion. 'Have you had cause ever to have words, or quarrel with Miss Dungey?'

'Never anything more than naturally occurs once in a while with an employee'. Georgiana to cast her eyes down, her voice trembling as she touched upon a matter which had much perturbed her. 'I have been greatly distressed by the case, and feel most strongly that if my husband had been represented by counsel at the trial the evidence might have been refuted.'

With these last heartfelt utterances the interview was at its conclusion, and the two parted, the reporter eager to turn in his story, and Mrs Mash, in an effort to find some diversion, eager to busy herself with household affairs.

But this was not the last time the Mash's would find their way into the columns of a newspaper, events unfolding in Henley-on-Thames to see a reporter from the Henley and South Oxfordshire Standard, make his way to Lambridge Farm.

Fifty Seven

Without Reserve to the Highest Bidder

On the afternoon of Tuesday 23rd January 1894, the tenant of Lambridge Farm, Mr Henry Joseph Mash (desiring to forego his tenancy), placed in auction a substantial portion of the properties contents, offered in one hundred and ninety seven lots. Simmons and Sons had been retained to dispose of that which the Mash's desired sold, and aware of the delicacy of the circumstances that surrounded the matter, sent one most experienced in navigating his way through difficulties, William Anker Simmons. The day which had preceded the auction to see the erection of a marquee in a meadow situated not much distance from the side of Lambridge House, to better accommodate any prospective attendees.

As reported in the following Friday's edition of the Henley and South Oxfordshire Standard, the day of the auction was frenetic indeed. Some one thousand five hundred, many of whom having travelled considerable distances, attempting to cram into the marquee, many forced to spill out onto the meadow. It has to be acknowledged that a considerable number of those present were clearly not after a lot, morbid curiosity making them eager to inspect Lambridge House; under the subterfuge of wishing to scrutinize an item they wished to bid on. Better to view the grisly remnants of the crime, it much reported that blood stains were still visible in the passageway, and that there were marks on the ceiling apparently made by one of the murder weapons, it of little wonder that those of an inquisitive, and in many respects indelicate nature, wandered within Lambridge House. The scrutiny's of the curious were not confined to the house, several people to slip through the little gate in search of the spot where Kate

Laura Dungey had lain in her final anguished moments, before the mortal wounds inflicted upon her, took her from this world. The allotted time of the sale arrived, and thanks in no small part to the reporter from the Henley Standard, a verbatim account of the words uttered by William Anker Simmons, as he stepped upon the podium gavel in hand, survive. 'I have sold under many different circumstances but never before under such painful circumstances, as those which brought me here this day. It is not necessary for me to allude to the cause, because you are all well acquainted with it, and everyone deeply regrets the cause of this sale being held. But there it is, and all present can quite understand Mr Mash leaving the farm. His instructions are to sell everything without reserve to the highest bidder.'

So there it was, William Simmons had summed it up admirably, and so began the auctioning of all the Mash's had grown familiar with, during their tenancy of Lambridge Farm. All the lots, the days previous to the auction, had been numbered, and though some of the smaller items were in due course held aloft by employees of Simmons, larger items had been left in situ, the initial lots being the household furniture. "Good prices on the whole being realised." The contents of bedroom number four creating the greatest amount of interest (both from bidders, and the ghoulish), this having been the room of the young woman who had met her untimely end not far from the comfort and security of her sleeping apartment. Miss Kate Laura Dungeys brass and iron French bedstead, described as in the region of four feet six inches in width, knocked down to Mr Stevens (there was living in Lower Assenden at the time one Alfred Stevens, employed as an agricultural labourer) for fifteen shillings, he also purchasing the deceases spring mattress for sixteen shillings. The lot that followed (also having been utilized by the housekeeper of Lambridge), a wool bolster (long thick pillow, that was placed under pillows for support) and pillow, purchased by Mr West, for one pound.

And so it went on, the Mash's (notable by their absence from the proceedings) possessions passing into the ownership of another. The lot which had the dubious pleasure of attracting the most attention (drawing gasps from the crowd), a piece of linoleum (not long since purchased by Henry Mash), and eight yards of Brussels carpet, both of which previously laid in the hall at Lambridge House, having suffered greatly on the night of the murder. The concept of the police retaining material evidence still relatively unknown, and so it was that these items came up for sale. It specified upon by the reporter from the Henley Standard, that both floorings were much marked. "It will be remembered that the first struggle took place in the hall, and the carpet and linoleum, which offered in one lot, were stained with spots of blood. Mr Simmons, the auctioneer, in offering the lot remarking "that if the murder was ever brought home, as he hoped to god it would be that carpet would be worth a lot of money." With this somewhat unfortunate turn of phrase, on behalf of William Anker Simmons, it little wonder that no one seemed anxious to bid, eventually a starting bid being made for two shillings. And then, after others joined the race to secure the lot, a bid of eleven shillings to see it knocked down to a Mr W. Hawkins.

Next to go under the hammer were the garden implements, followed by the farms livestock, five cows, three calves, poultry and some pigs. Special attention placed upon the sale of a chestnut nag gelding "Punch", and a grey pony "Billy" (this particular creature the pony that had been hastily harnessed to the farm trap by George Dawson, on the night of the murder, the two then at a canter travelling down into Henley), as well as a Brougham, Wagonette, pony carriage, pony trap, tradesman cart, Phaeton, and harnesses, all of which achieving good prices. The number of horse drawn vehicles, none of which cheaply obtained, included within the auction lots; a clear indication of the lifestyle the Mash's enjoyed. A Brougham, drawn by one horse, a vehicle for everyday use its carriage closed in, but the driver's seat exposed to the elements. The Wagonette a light weight open topped carriage, commonly utilised for day excursions, with two lengthwise seats that faced each other, the driver sat upon a crosswise seat. The Phaeton, a vehicle much favoured by Henry Mash, an open carriage drawn by two horses, being very lightly sprung it not a carriage suited for long journeys, but having extremely large wheels the Phaeton was fast.

The day, which had been unprecedented in the memory of many of those present, went without a hitch, and William Simmons disposed of all the lots, and thus secured a tidy commission. This was the severing of the Mash families relationship with Lambridge Farm, the secluded retreat which over many years had provided a place of sanctuary from the hustle and bustle of London living. There would be a last visit, Henry and Georgiana Mash anxious to check that no personal item (upon their instructions excluded from the auction, to be subsequently forwarded on to the Mash's London home, Redcliffe Gardens) had been inadvertently left behind. We have no knowledge if the two reflected upon the events that had culminated with the auction, or took a moment to think on their murdered housekeeper, but one would think they did, their last act to hand over the keys to the land agent.

The edition of the Oxford Journal that hit the newsstands on Saturday 14th April 1894, to give details in relation to the sizable reward Mr Henry Joseph Mash had offered the previous December. "Mr Mash, who formally lived at Lambridge House, has increased the reward of one hundred pounds, formally offered by him, to two hundred pounds."

Fifty Eight

Auctioneer, House and Land Agent

The fall of the gavel, which saw the last of the lots at Lambridge Farm sold, did not signify the conclusion of William Anker Simmons commission. There was much to be done, and those who worked under Simmons took possession of many cheques, and no small amount of coinage, from those who had secured a lot. Smaller items sold, were taken on the spot, loaded onto cart and carriage, some who lived close to Lambridge choosing to carry their purchase. Larger items, such as household furniture, farm machinery, and livestock, conveyed to their purchasers abodes, by means of Simmons and Sons own vehicles, each of which adorned with the companies emblem. The remainder of that day and into the next Simmons and Sons accountant to process a multitude of payments, juniors to convey said takings to the bank. All this activity closely monitored by William Simmons, who aware of the delicacy of the matter was not tardy, and before the day that followed the auction was done a cheque (minus commission) thus forwarded onto Redcliffe Gardens.

So what of William Anker Simmons, he thirty six at the time of the horrific events at Lambridge House, born in Farnborough, Warwickshire, the eldest child of Charles Simmons (born 1826, Rotherfield Peppard, Oxfordshire) a land agent and malster. Williams middle name that of his mother's (Ann Emma, born 1832 in Bampton Oxfordshire) maiden name.

William Simmons had certainly had benefit of a good start in life, his father in possession of Manor House in Farnborough, his son not short of playmates, the brother, who would prove to be William's closest confidante, Charles Franklin, born in 1858. John Deane was born in

1860, his younger siblings, Amy Elizabeth Dinah, Edward Henry, and Robert Odiedo, he born 1866. There was one besides who had not fared so well, Joseph Henry, not to live beyond his infancy, buried aged but a few months, on 11th June 1861.

Before William Anker Simmons had turned twelve his father had resolved to relocate his brood to Henley-on-Thames, and once possessed of a tenancy at Northfield End, Charles set up as an estate agent, he and his family occupying an apartment above. And so why Henley, the answer being that the area was much familiar to Charles Simmons, he not the first of his family to operate out of premises within the town. The Simmons's had benefitted commercially in Henley-on-Thames since the early 1800s, a William Simmons (a land agent and estate agent), from the early 1850s, having occupied a commercial premises in New Street, by 1864 he relocated to Hart Street, by the end of the decade affording to reside in a fine house in Bell Street. In the early 1870s the gentleman, just now alluded to, to rename his company, hence forward known as "William & Sons Estate Agent & Valuers & Auctioneers", the decision made to run the firm out of 46 Bell Street.

And so we return to young William Simmons, he advantaged by a superior education (complements of Henley Grammar School), aged seventeen taking up rowing, in 1878 amongst the crew that won the Town Cup at Henley Regatta. But the year that had brought Simmons sporting success also brought sorrow, his mother Ann dying aged forty six, she, after a fittingly solemn funeral service (held on 18th July at the Parish Church of St Marys), interred at Henley Cemetery.

Widowhood did not sit well with Charles Simmons, and with not a year passed since his wife's demise, and not yet out of mourning attire, he took a second wife, his bride, Sarah (born 1842, in Middlesex), the daughter of one Richard Child, a proprietor of houses, who resided at Leicester House, Northfield End. And so it was that William (still firmly encamped within the family home, Crandem

Gate, on Bell Street) acquired half-brothers and a half-sister, Joseph Bruce, Hilda Mary, and Charles Eley, he baptised at St Marys, on 22nd February 1886.

William Anker Simmons was a gentleman, and like many of his stature he enjoyed sporting activities, his enthusiasm for rowing not to go unrecognised, rewarded for his prowess in the sport with the first Captainship of United Rowing Club. But Simmons rowing career was to end quite abruptly, the cause of his reluctant withdrawal from the sport a fall from a tall bicycle (no doubt a Penny Farthing), William sustaining breaks to both wrists. Undaunted by this turn of bad luck the young fellow looking about for a sporting pursuit better suited to his reduced capacity, in due course taking up swimming, and rather ironically cycling.

Of course it was not all idol folly; William Simmons earned a living, he finished with education having joined his father's firm. All was just perfect, living at home (waited on by a cook, housemaid, and under housemaid), William trotting down to St Marys Church on Sundays, possessed of a voice most superior, singing in the choir.

The woman who finally persuaded William Simmons to fly the nest was one Edith Nora (born 1856 in Newington, the daughter of Edward Smith Beddome, an underwriter), after a decent interlude of courtship, the two married on 2nd June 1883, in St Johns Wood, the groom a chartered surveyor.

The newlyweds took Wilminster Cottage (a property affiliated to Wilminster Park, Remenham), and their first child, Philip Golding, was born at home in 1884 (baptised at St Mary's on 31st July), he later joined by sisters, Irene Nora, and Marjorie Yvonne (their father primarily a land agent and valuer), both girls baptised at St Nicholas, Remenham.

William Anker Simmons was not a man to sit on his laurels, and interested in social welfare and politics, in 1885 he secured a seat on Henley Town Council (which he never lost), Simmons also able to fit into his exhaustive schedule memberships of the Charity Trustee Governing Body of Royal Grammar School, Conservative Party volunteering, and membership of the Primrose League, the latter founded in 1883 by Randolph Churchill, to better promote the ethos of Conservatism.

William Anker Simmons, looking most distinguished

It is little wonder if Simmons was ever at home, he so often required to attend this or that meeting, or fulfil a voluntary obligation. Never one, if he could help it, to miss a meeting of the Masons (their Lodge on the Reading Road), Simmons also availed himself of the time to attend to his duties as a Warden at Remenham Church. An active supporter and long term member of the Ancient Order of Druids (founded in London in 1781, its key mantra to promote justice, benevolence and friendship), William Simmons in regular attendance of its meetings, held within the Lodge Room, Argyll Hotel, Market Place. The Royal Antedilovian Order of Buffialues, a society founded in 1822 (existing long before the welfare state, primarily to action its members to carry out acts of philanthropy), to also have benefit of Simmons input, as did the Henley Water Works Company, he their Secretary.

So here was William Anker Simmons, no stranger to his community, and a gentleman with a scrupulous reputation. And it was therefore little wonder that when the Mash's had need of someone of the upmost discretion, to deal with the delicate matter of the disposal of the contents of Lambridge Farm, they had turned to Simmons & Sons, Auctioneers House & Land Agents, who at that stage operated out of 18 Hart Street.

Part Six

This too shall pass.

Fifty Nine

Pattenden Farm

For Walter Dungey the adage life goes on was never truer, though the shadow of grief was on occasion to cast darkness upon him, and at times the burden of the loss of one of his offspring, in such a manner as befell Kate, weighed heavy. Walter's wife, Ellen, did not fare as well as her spouse, the mother, who had found it untenable to attend her childs funeral (let alone the trial of the young man accused of Kates murder), not to live ten years on from the fateful night that was Friday 8th December 1893. Ellen Dungey, whose health had been delicate for some months (her affliction Brights Disease, historical classification of kidney disease), found herself upon doctor's orders confined to bed. On Thursday 12th February 1903, in her seventy first year, having suffered for five days from the extremely unpleasant affliction Erysipelas (infection of the upper dermis, known as Red Skin), Ellen died. There to follow somewhat of a drama, the duly issued death certificate incorrectly stating the date of Ellen's demise as 12th January, the deceases family much perplexed at this glaring error. And so it was that on 30th March, Registrar, Mr J. Dunant, in the presence of Miss Rosa Dungey, amended said certificate.

The Saturday 21st February edition of the Sussex Agricultural Express carried within its columns an emotive tribute to Mrs Ellen Dungey, those inhabitants of Goudhurst, who took said paper, to agree fully with the sentiment. "The deceased lady well known in the parish for geniality of disposition and kindness of heart, one old parishioner said of her. Ah, we've lost the best woman in the parish."

On the mid-afternoon of Monday 16th February Ellen Dungey departed Pattenden for the last time, her family in solemn procession behind the coffin. At the lynch gate of Christchurch, Kilndown, the Reverend Thomas Francis Ken Underwood (he who had led Kate Dungeys funeral service) met the mourning party, the coffin lifted upon the shoulders of those in the employ of funeral directors Messrs Davis & Leaney, Ellen in due course buried alongside the graves of those of her three children who had predeceased her.

The year following his wife's demise Walter Dungey found himself within the newspapers for an altogether different reason than that of the December of 1893. The Friday 20th May edition of the Kent & Sussex Courier to include within its columns those who had been called to appear before the bench, a Mr Walter Dungey summoned for causing four pigs to be moved along the highway at Brenchley without possession of a Movement Licence. It was also reported that on Monday 9th May, the defendant had pleaded guilty, Sergeant Frederick J. Packman (the fellow who had intercepted Walter Dungey and his infamous pigs) providing evidence to the Magistrates Bench. The plaintiff finding himself at the conclusion of deliberations offered the option of a fine of five pounds and nine shillings costs, or seven days in prison, Walter opting for the fine.

By the taking of the 1911 census Walter Dungey had turned seventy seven, he residing as ever at Pattenden, the man, though now great of age, content to work his farm, in his employ estate farm labourers Charles Wheeler and Edward Pooley, the latter of whom residing at "Little Pattenden". Dungey did not manage his domestic burdens alone, his daughters Rosa Ellen and Julia (both unmarried) assisting with the indoor duties (recorded in the census as housekeepers); their father paying both a goodly wage. On the day the census enumerator came calling two grandsons, four year old Leslie William, and three year old Percy Walter, in the care of their grandfather.

The winter of early 1917 was a harsh one, and Walter Dungey fell ill, his daughter Julia, much alarmed summoning Doctor D'Andy Harvey, who was concerned to find his patient afflicted by a particularly virulent bout of bronchitis. Walter was now eighty three, and no amount of medical care prevailed, he to die on Sunday 1st April 1917, at Pattenden, surrounded by those who cherished him.

On Saturday 7th April, a funeral, that numerous locals attended, was held at the Parish Church of Kilndown, amongst the throng of mourners a reporter representing the Kent & Sussex Courier, he scribbling fervently within his notebook, to turn in the following. "The funeral of this old and much respected inhabitant took place on Saturday afternoon at Kilndown, the vicars of Goudhurst and Kilndown officiating. The hymn "On the resurrection morning" was sung after the burial lesson, the late Mr Dungey an ardent lover of oratorio music, he occupying the position of leading amateur tenor vocalists in the district, and as one of the most good natured of men, there was a beautiful collection of floral tributes."

In life Walter Dungey had been a pragmatic man, and in death this trait was in evidence, his will (drawn up on Sunday 2nd May 1909, the calligraphy of which most elegant in style) duly carried through by trustees, Walters son Ernest Walter Dungey and a Mr Ernest Albert Honess (both farmers), they orchestrating the division of the deceases earthly assets (calculated at £3,120 1s 3d) equally between Walters offspring. Any leasehold properties held at the time of Dungeys death, able, if so wished by mutual agreement, to remain unsold, and let out. Indicative of a time when the eldest child (particularly male issue) carried a father's legacy forward, Walter Dungey to specify that his son Ernest could, within three months of his father's death, offer to purchase any of Walter Dungeys freehold properties.

Walter Dungy lies with his wife, he and Ellens headstone intricately decorated with a carved sprig of hop leaves and cobs, its epitaph most poignant. "In ever loving memory of Ellen, wife of Walter Dungey of Pattenden Goudhurst, born Feb 13th 1832, died Feb 12th 1903. There shall be no more death, neither sorrow, or crying, neither shall there be any more pain. Also of the above named Walter Dungey, born April 11th 1833, died April 1st 1917.

Ellen & Walter Dungeys final resting place, their headstone having fallen

Kate Laura Dungey had not grown up in isolation, she enjoying the companionship of a large brood of siblings, the lives of which altered inextricably by their sisters murder.

Rosa Ellen never married and lived out her days in the district where she was born, first with her father Walter, and after his demise, with the blessing of her brother Ernest, on the farming estate she had known since childhood. Rosa Dungey died at "Little Pattenden", Pattenden Lane, on the Goudhurst to Bedgebury Road, on Thursday 19th July 1934, her will proved by her nephew Leslie William Ernest Dungey (solicitor), the deceases resworn just over one thousand pounds. Rosa Dungeys funeral service (arranged by Messrs Penn & Son), led by the Reverend H. G. South, took place on the Monday that followed her demise, she in due course buried at the New Cemetery, Goudhurst. The interment, besides the deceases family, attended by many of Goudhurst who had been on cordial terms with Miss Dungey, the old lady a familiar sight within the village.

Goudhurst at the tail end of the 19th century
To this day much as it was during the time of the Dungeys

Julia Dungey, in stark contrast to Rosa, did experience life outside the close bonds of her family, in the latter years of the 1870s employed as a governess. The couple who retained Miss Dungey, Charles (a tea dealer) and Mary Search, Julia in residence at the Search's town house, 14 Argyle Street, Bathwick, Bath, she in sole charge of the education of Lillie, Bertie and Marie.

When Julia Dungey had found herself no longer required as a governess, she secured a position as a fruiters assistant (alongside a

Miss Helen Clarke), working out of premises on Green Street, St Martin-in-the-Fields, London, the neighbouring commercial outlet a Billiard Ball making factory no less. And so it was that Julia Dungey, in the days that directly followed on from her sisters murder, had found herself mentioned within the columns of the tabloids, duly noted as in the employ of Mr Henry Joseph Mash.

If it is indicative of the traumatic sequence of events that surrounded the death of Kate Dungey, Julia found solace at home, having quit London returning to Pattenden, she set to reside at the property during the lifetime of her parents.

Julia Dungey never, through choice or otherwise, entered into marriage, and so she died (on Monday 1st October 1951) with neither husband nor issue (ingeniously described as a spinster) at her Goudhurst home "Limney", Julia's accumulated chattels worth a paltry £276 5s 2d.

When done with schooling Ernest Walter Dungey worked the arable lands of Pattenden alongside his father. Indeed it seemed that Ernest, like several of his sisters, would forgo marriage, but on Wednesday 15th June 1904, Edith (seventeen years younger than her groom, the only daughter of William Burfield, butcher and shopkeeper on the High Street, Goudhurst) managed to nail her man. Such an event warranted particular mention in the local paper, a society reporter despatched to Goudhurst Parish Church, he milling amongst guests and well-wishers, to take particular note of Edith Burfields frock. "The bride, a resident solo pianist, wore a cream Merveilleux Silk dress trimmed with crepe de chine, orange blossoms and lace, with embroidered veil, the carriages for the wedding supplied by Messrs E. Davis & Sons."

So Ernest Dungey, the wrong side of forty and newly married, took Forge Farm, Glassenbury, his wife delivered of three boys, the eldest Leslie William Ernest (later set to qualify as a solicitor, practicing out of premises in East Grinstead) born in 1906, Percy Walter making his appearance the following year (this child to die Tuesday 15th March 1921, aged thirteen), Alan Cecil born in 1912.

Upon his father's demise Ernest Dungey resolved to return to Pattenden, and as such quit Forge Farm. The Friday 12th October 1917 edition of the Sussex Agricultural Express to carry within its upcoming auctions segment, information placed in the newspaper at the behest of Messrs Winch & Sons, regards the disposal on 23rd October of farming items and furniture, presently at Forge Farm. Pattenden Farm was dear to the Dungeys, no less so than to Ernest, and he and his wife and boys soon felt right at home, Rosa very much part of the equation. Husband and wife rapidly integrated into the community, Ernest Dungey (a local employer), in the company of his wife, performing in singing concerts throughout the district.

Edith Dungey, a sweet kindly lady, in later life was not to enjoy robust health, and for several years various afflictions had left her incapacitated (the death of Percy to further impact upon Edith's wellbeing), she in need of frequent medical interventions. Ill health it was that led to Edith's demise, on Saturday 29th May 1943, after near forty years together, she parted from Ernest. Edith Dungey, on the Wednesday that followed her death, buried at the New Cementry, Goudhurst, her widower and surviving sons to be bequeathed a share of some one thousand eight hundred pounds.

Though considerably older than his spouse, the blight of illness had dictated that Ernest had outlived Edith, he dying at Pattenden on Friday 16th January 1948, his estate, a sizable £24,426 1s 10d (duty paid £1,304), reflective of the success Ernest Dungey had made of his farming concerns.

Alice Dungey, in contrast to her elder sisters, did have a significant other, Sidney (born 1863, the son of Ebenezer Russell, Miller Master at The Mill, Cranbrook), and in the late spring of 1898 they were wed. The couple settling in at their marital home, "Windmill Cottage", close to the Union Mill (with its strikingly picturesque windmill),

Cranbrook. Sidney Russell was an educated fellow, and with the funds necessary to pursue self-employment he forewent his initial profession of engineer apprentice at "The Hill Union Mills", and followed his dream, that of journalism. Russell initially working for an auction house, having responsibly no doubt for the completion of sales catalogues and the such like, in no time he to resign, able to earn a sizable salary solely as a journalist.

The Russell's were not to have children, and after their relocation to "Arnewood" (a building on the High Street, Cranbrook, dating from the seventeenth century, with a nineteenth century façade), they took in a lodger, Arthur Colbran Couchman, a married man of middle years, who earned his rent as a clerk at Cranbrook Post Office.

Sidney Russell did not enjoy longevity; he, suffering ill health in his middle years, dying on Monday 19th June 1922, his widow to benefit from an estate of £685 12s 10d.

Alice had no offspring to support her, and as old age bit at her heels she took as her residence "Taywell" in Goudhurst, her widowhood to stretch out some thirty six years. Alice Russell to die at home, on Monday 21st July 1958, her surviving siblings at her bedside, she in due course buried within Goudhurst Cementry.

Fanny Ada Dungey had had benefit of her sister Kate's tutorship, and like her sister Fanny found the position of a governess to her liking. But Fanny Dungey did not commission an agency to place her with a family, she preferring to teach at a small independent school (Mill Hill College, under the ownership of one Marianne Russell), Fanny having no concerns regards lodgings, she residing at the home of her employers parents (in Edenbridge, Kent), Henry and Elizabeth Russell.

Marriage for a young lady invariable meant the end of ones career, and so it was for Fanny Ada Dungey, George Usher Brenchley (born 1869 in Pimlico) the young gentleman who stole Fanny away from her pupils. 1893 proved a catastrophic year for the sweethearts,

Georges father (George Usher Brenchley, a watchmaker working out of Haxted Cottage, Edenbridge) to die unexpectedly, on Thursday 2nd November, less than six weeks later Fannys sister brutally murdered. The drama that ensued, following the events at Lambridge Farm, delaying the couple's nuptials, but on Wednesday 8th August 1894, at the C of E Church, in the village where Fanny Dungey had grown up, the marriage ceremony took place.

The Brenchley's relocated to Wellington, Surrey, and here it was in 1896 a daughter, Margery, was born, George Walter born the year after that. The young family moved onto Reigate, and resident in a smart townhouse ("Edenhurst", Betchworth) they welcomed in the last year of the nineteenth century, daughter Evelyn; a final child, Hilda, born in 1902.

In due course the Brenchley's resolved to move back to Kent, and once content of their chose of abode settled at "Sunnycote" (a double fronted house on the High Street, Marden), George commuting to London, in his capacity as Senior Assistant within the London County Council Municipal Service.

Though the Dungeys were a close knit family, Alice, in support of her husband's ambitions took the brave step of selecting to emigrate to Australia, Evelyn and Hilda to accompany them, the travellers to join up with Margery and George, who had quit England some years previous.

The Brenchley's were never to return to England, and they ended their days in Brisbane, Queensland, on Thursday 8th March 1951 George dying, his widow, Fanny Ada, reunited with her spouse upon her demise on Saturday 15th December 1956.

In St Martins in the Fields, West Minster, on Sunday 7th July 1895, Amelia Dungey wed twenty nine year old Arthur Ernest Wood (son of Charlotte West Wood, Kingstone landowner and farmer of 580 acres, her husband John having died on 20th January 1870), at the time of her marriage Amelia resident at a London property in the ownership of the Mash family.

The newlyweds hankered after a house in Kent and successful in this endeavour settled down at "Sheffield House", which stood on the High Street, Cranbrook. Arthur, a ironmonger much in demand, having the funds necessary to provide for a family, which was a good thing as he was to be in due course father to three boys, Donald born 1896, Walter Gordon (another child to be named after his grandfather) born 1900, and Arthur Finn born in 1907.

The so called "Great War" saw many men join up, and Arthur Wood proved no exception, though not far off fifty he enlisting in the Royal Sussex Regiment (billeted in Brighton), a member of the territorial force. The war did not leave to much of an indelible mark on the Wood's, but sudden malady did, the youngest of the household Arthur Finn, aged but seventeen, expiring in 1924, on 14th November the lad buried at Kings Down near Eynesford.

Arthur Ernest Wood died on Tuesday 11th August 1953 (aged eighty seven), at his home "Maplescombe Farm", Farningham, his effects valued at £1,476 12s 11d. Arthurs widow carried on as best as she could, but Amelia sorely missed the man with whom she had shared her life near sixty years, and upon her demise, on Friday 9th March 1956, at Joyce Green Hospital, Dartford, Kent (executor of Amelia's will, Leslie William Ernest Dungey solicitor, deceases effects £1,619 0s 11d), it is earnestly hoped that Amelia Wood was reunited with Arthur.

Clara Louise Dungey shows up in the census of 1891, a guest at "Great Cheveney Farm" (its main house late 16th century and timber framed), Goudhurst Road, Marden. Cheveney was farmed by one Thomas Honess (550 acres of arable land, under 20 labourers and 8 boys), the young lady under his roof courting his son, twenty nine year old Ernest Albert Honess. A marriage was the outcome, Albert, with the death on 1st January 1897 of his father, to take on "Great Cheveney Farm", in partnership with his brother Percy.

Ernest Honess had reason to wish for financial stability, by 1896 a parent, his first born child, a girl, at the bequest of Clara, and in recognition of her late sister Kate, named Katherine Grace. Nora Clara was born in 1898; she joined by brother's Walter Thomas, and Ernest John, Albert Beeman delivered of his mother in 1909. Cheveneys arable lands bringing in a goodly income; the lady of the house able to avail herself of a domestic servant, Doris Mabel Foulsham.

Ernest and Clara (in childhood, home tutored) held education for girls in high esteem, and thus their daughters, Katherine and Nora, were enrolled at Claremont House School, Cranbrook, under the mentoring eye of its headmistress, Katherine Huntley.

Ernest Albert Honess (member of Marden Council from its inception in 1894 until his retirement in 1936) died on Tuesday 25th January 1938, one week short of his seventy sixth birthday. On 29th January, at two o'clock prompt, the family, former employees, and friends of the deceased to shuffle solemnly into St Michael & All Saints Church, Marden, at the behest of his widow, Ernest's life reflected upon joyously, Clara's late husband in contented partnership with his brother Percy in excess of forty five years, at High Tilt Farm, Cranbrook and Great Cheveney. Clara Louise Honess never quit Cheveney, and here it was that on Tuesday 22nd January 1963, in her ninety first year, she passed away.

It is often said that some good comes from misfortune, and a child of Walter and Ellen Dungey, as yet unmentioned, goes someway to proving the point. Henry Joseph Mash (eldest son of Henry Joseph Mash senior) was a young gentleman of seventeen when his family became embroiled in the so called "Henley Murder", and it is not too much of a stretch to imagine that Henrys parent's tried to protect him and his siblings from the gossip and conjecture flying around in the tabloids, though Henrys mother did of course cross paths with a reporter.

After Henry and Georgiana Mash quit Lambridge House, their eldest in time was to reside at his parent's former Henley town house, 37 New Street. And with the Dungeys seemingly inextricably bound up with Kate's former employer, on Tuesday 14th August 1900, Henry Joseph Mash junior found himself availed of a guestroom in Goudhurst, set the next day to wed Miss Helena Dungey.

Henry & Helena's wedding portrait, standing in the back row Henry Joseph Mash, alongside him his wife Georgiana, and Walter Dungey, seated in front of her husband is Ellen Dungey, the two bridesmaid's identities unknown

The newlyweds took as their residence 2-4 Garrick Street, Covent Garden, and here it was that in 1903 a son, Henry Joseph, was born, he in 1915 joined by sibling Ernest Martin.

The master of the house followed the family trade, Henry a fruiterer working out of commercial premises below his family's apartment, his wife the company bookkeeper. It indeed a family affair, Henrys brother Martin (set to quit his job upon his marriage in 1910 to Miss Lillian Richmond, Martin to then after set up as a fruiterer and florist, at 9 Museum Chambers, London) a fruiterers assistant, alongside his cousin, Minnie Constance Mash. Minnie upon her marriage to Frank Thomas Steene (an oil and colourman, one involved in the supply of victuals) to relocate to 40 King Street, Maidenhead. The end of the first decade of the twentieth century had seen the death of both Queen Victoria and her son, by the census of 1911 King George the fifth upon the throne, and the fruiterers on Garrick Street turning a tidy profit, Sheffle Barnes, Henry Mashs principal sales woman.

In what was to be the last year of the war in Europe, Henry Mash (occupying business premises 36-40 Glasshouse Street, Westminster), in recognition of his commercial prowess, on 25th July applied to be formally admitted to the Freedom of the City of London, on Friday 27th September 1918 he duly admitted.

For a woman who had grown up in the "Garden of England" marriage to Henry Mash had brought the opportunity to travel, and with bananas the fruit on which fortunes had been built, Helena and her husband made frequent journeys to Kingston, Jamaica, and Barbados, to observe first-hand the produce on which they heavily relied. Indeed sea travel remained a passion of the Mash's throughout their married life, the two in 1948 on board the Queen Mary, on route to New York.

What lasting tinge of sadness was left in the psyche of Helena, regards her sisters murder, she locked within, the lady never to speak of it, her grandchildren not to fully know of the events of December

1893 until both their grandparents had died. Helena Mashs twilight years were spent at "Westhorpe House", Little Marlow, in Buckinghamshire, she aged eighty seven (on Sunday 16th June 1957) to die, a patient at Heatherwood Hospital, Ascot, Sunning Hill, in Buckinghamshire. Henry Joseph Mash remained on at Westhorpe, and here he died aged ninety two, on Monday 30th September 1968, his estate valued in excess of thirty eight thousand pounds.

Chapter Sixty

Winter Hill Farm

The auction of relatively the entire contents of Lambridge Farm signified the end of the Henry Mashs residence within Henley-on-Thames, though he did retain, besides his former New Street address, a commercial premises, 23-25 Duke Street. It common practice, amongst those possessed of the funds necessary, to purchase investment properties, and thus receive a goodly income from the rental return. On Thursday 30th November 1893, at an auction held at the Catherine Wheel, auctioneer John Chambers sold the afore mentioned property, and as such Henry Mash (who rather ironically, under the conditions of sale, had to pay the vendors solicitor in person, he none other than Sydney Brain) had gained commercial tenants, number 23 let to James Scott (butcher), number 25 let to Charles and Frederick Johnson, photographers, gilders, and picture frame makers. Of course Mash did not forgo his tenancy of 37 New Street without having first secured a property to his liking, he and his family in due course to occupy Winter Hill Farm (previously tenanted by a Richard Gibbs), Cookham Dean, Berkshire.

Henry Joseph Mash had built up a profitable market garden business, and thus he commuted up to Glasshouse Street (making use of Great Marlow Railway Station, the train which served the line quirkily known as the "Marlow Donkey") on a regular basis, better to keep his finger on the pulse. Though it is too be said that Mash gradually acquired arable land, much of which not much distance from Winter Hill Farm, the gentleman desiring to farm, as he had at Lambridge.

On Tuesday 18th May 1897 Henry Mashs father (Henry senior residing at 26 Canterbury Road, Brixton) died aged sixty nine, after a fittingly lavish funeral interred at Norwood Cemetery, Norwood Road, Lambeth. Probate was proved in London on Saturday 5th June, Henry Mashs assets of £2,542 8s. 9d duly divided by the executors of his will. Death and mourning held a somewhat morbid fascination in the Victorian psyche, and Georgiana Mash, not long after her father-in-law's passing had reason again to ensure that her black taffeta dress, black braided cape, and jet jewellery were up to the mark, the Mash's on Monday 26th July to bid a tearful farewell to Henrys stepmother Lucy, dead (aged sixty four) not two months following her husband's demise.

Life, as it invariably does, carried on, and in due course Henry Mash, in the company of family and friends, saw in the twentieth century. The household of Winter Hill Farm by now somewhat reduced, with only one of the Mash's children, unmarried daughter Annie, still in residence. Of course Henry Mash retained servants, housemaid Mary Clayton, and cook, Jane Lovell, the gardens without, though slumbering through the winter of 1899/1900, set to explode into colour once spring was done with, gardener David Tompkins (a widower) truly green fingered.

On Sunday 11th April 1911 the census enumerator called at Winter Hill Farm, and made welcome by its occupants the fellow scribbled away in his regulation booklet. Annie (her father's assistant) still in situ, Henry Mash (now working primarily at home, as a market gardener) at this point in time retaining domestic servants, siblings Daisy Louise Pheby and Clara May Pheby (daughters of Frederick Pheby, a paper mill labourer, and Lizzie a laundress), the latter at twenty, some nine years her sister junior. There another Pheby in the equation, the women's brother William Frederick (residing at Lea Cottage, Winter Hill), his employer Mr Mash, affording to own a car, in need of a chauffeur. And what of Georgiana Mash, she had no less than three indoor servants to organize, Mrs Sarah Pheby (wife of William), as her mistress required, toiling alongside her sisters-in-law.

During the war the country had much need of farmers, and Henry Mash utilised as much of his arable lands as crop rotation would allow, cultivating both fruit and vegetables. Just six months after the armistice, Mash in the course of a day that had seemed like any other, to suffer a cerebral haemorrhage, the stricken man to fall into a coma. Doctor E. Downs, his patient unresponsive to all stimuli, spent much time at Winter Hill Farm, and here on Sunday 11th May 1919, with his son William James (of Torringham Farm, Chesham, Bucks) at his bedside, Henry (aged sixty nine) died. Henry Joseph Mash, by the end of his life a fellow of an increasingly corpulent physique, buried within the graveyard of the Baptist Church, Church Road, Cookham Dean.

Probate of Henry Mashs estate was granted in London on Tuesday 23rd September 1919 (legal notice regards claims on the deceases estate having appeared in the Wednesday 21st May edition of The Times, at the behest of Churchill Smallman & Co, of 1 Broad Street Place, EC2, solicitors to the executors), to his sons, Henry Joseph Mash (a fruit grower), William James Porter Mash (a farmer), and Martin Mash (a fruit grower), their fathers resworn £24,465 0s 7d.

Henry Mash had been a sociable fellow, he sitting at the tables of his friends, taking of rich food and fine wines, but there had been a price to pay, and in the knowledge that his health was not as it had been, on Friday 8th November 1918 Mash had drawn up what was to be the last draft of his will. This will, in Henrys own hand (his writing sprawling, and a challenge to decipher), most persificic in detail, duly followed to the letter by the deceases executors. Mash upon his demise, wishing as soon as legal remit allowed his widow and daughter, Annie, to be in receipt of one hundred pounds each. As expected Georgiana bequeathed Winter Hill Farm, and its entire household chattels (furniture, plate, glass, linen, clothes, and pictures), though her husband specified that a few select items were to be passed onto named individuals.

Henry Mashs daughter, Eleanor (married to Walter Frost, he a fruit broker who worked out of Covent Garden), found herself the owner of her father's freehold property, Radnor House (formerly known as 37 New street) let out, under the provision of the Poor Law, to Henley Union Cottage Homes, a Mr N. F. Cave its Superintendent, his duty to care for the fifteen children who resided at Radnor. Eleanor to also inherit the freehold commercial outlets 23-25 Duke Street, at the time of her father's demise, number 23 let to Wilkins & Sons, house furnishers, and number 25 let to butcher Herbert Saunders.

23-25 Duke Street, at the time it was under the ownership of Henry Mash
Being the double fronted commercial premises, topped off with four chimneys

Another daughter (Mrs May Puddephatt) bequeathed her father's Fulham commercial outlets, as well as her childhood family home, leasehold premises 12 Redcliffe Gardens, the very house where nearly twenty six years earlier, on the morning of Saturday 9th December 1893, her parents had received notification of the murder of Miss Kate Dungey. May had in the past caused her father much distress, she married on 18th September 1900, at the Parish Church, Cookham Dean, to one William Mash Fuelling (a fruiterer), by the summer of 1904 May expelled from her marital home in Radcliff Square, her husband on 25th June filing for divorce. Yet another scandal had entwined itself around Henry Mash, his daughter the guilty party, May an adulterous, her lover Mr James Neilson. The whole sorry mess resolved by the courts; Neilson ordered to pay the cuckold husband damages to the sum of three hundred pounds. May Fuelling did not easily dip her toe again in the water, but some ten years after her divorce she remarried, her husband Mr William Puddephatt (yet another fruiterer), nearly thirty two years his wife's senior (he to live to ninety seven), the couple, who lived on the Fulham Road (never to beget children) very content.

Property had always been the way to go, and Henry Mash had in the latter years of his life brought "Holly Croft" located in Cookham Dean, and the one acre that surrounded it. He having also taken possession of Little Marlow Post Office, and in what was to prove his last year, a freehold cottage in Little Marlow, which stood on the corner of the village on Church Road, close to the Kings Head Public House. And so it was that his daughter, Annie, found herself the owner of all but one of the aforementioned premises, as well as the furniture and fittings held therein.

Henry Joseph Mash did not forget a sibling, to whom he had been most devoted, Minnie Constance, his little sister, she left forty acres in Maidenhead, and the Post Office (let to a Mr Hestor) previously alluded to.

The Mash's had seen the coming and goings of numerous servants, and Henry Mash duly showed his grateful appreciation of the service given to his family by several of his most loyal retainers. William Pheby, who his master described as a faithful servant, bequeathed a cottage, barn (let to Walter Frost), and tiled shed known as "Lea Cottage", all of which situated in Cookham Dean. Though there was a sting in the tail, the deceased stipulating that his sons could, if they so wished, have the option to purchase the properties, upon paying over the sum of three hundred pounds to William Pheby. Daisy Pheby, also described in flowing terms, gained the freehold of "Diamond Lodge" in Bourne End, the interest in a policy (number 62079), held in Prudential Assurance, and a picture entitled "Pilgrims", which had hung for many years in the breakfast room of Winter Hill Farm. Daisy had shown great kindness to her master during his frequent illnesses, and Henry Mash earnestly requested from beyond the grave that his family should be certain to show her the greatest respect. Those employed in the shop in Glasshouse Street not forgotten, William Ryder and Edward Leith, in receipt of the sum of fifty pounds each.

Henry Mashs sons to wait for the conclusion of their fathers will, to discover what assets were to be theirs, it worth the wait, Henry, William, and Martin to jointly receive a freehold house (known as "Richard Leigh House"), and four grand villas at Orchard Leigh Corner in Chesham. And as was accustomed, the males of the family duly bequeathed all financial residues, monies in the bank, rents, and life policies.

So the drawing up of Henry Joseph Mashs will (witnessed by Lilian Sarah Ann Pheby, though if she read through the document before lending it her signature, how she managed to decipher her masters handwriting beyond me) had settled his mind that all would be well after his death. But the deceased did die with one matter unresolved, Henry, who had offered a one hundred pound reward (in the April of

1894 increased to two hundred pounds) to whoever brought the murderer of his housekeeper, Miss Kate Laura Dungey, to book, never to see the money claimed.

Georgiana Mashs health had in recent years broken down, she since 1917 much blighted by osteoarthritis, and with her mobility sore affected the lady was tied to her home. Loss of movement carried with it series implications, and Georgiana (aged seventy three) suffered what proved to be a fatal cerebral thrombosis. The lady languishing for two months, and in the company of her son-in-law, Walter Leaver Frost (of Ridgemount, Cookham Dean), on Monday 4th July 1921 she died, Mrs Mashs attending physician (Doctor R. Shephard), content to forego a post mortem, releasing the body for burial.

Georgiana Mashs will, she not in possession of the plenitude of properties and moneys (her effects, £1,256 19s) that her late husband had owned, the more touching for what was bequeathed. Her niece, Ada Mary Royce, receiving two hundred pounds, her late husband's cousin, Frances Mash, left fifty pounds. The mistress of Winter Hill Farm not to forget those in service to her, coachman George Tuck (only on the previso that he was still in her employ) set to receive twenty five pounds.

Her children had brought Georgiana much comfort in widowhood, and Annie (never having left home, her mother's primary carer) found herself left all the furniture held within Winter Hill, and her mother's sapphire necklace and mourning earrings. Annie's sister, Eleanor, receiving her mother's gold curb bracelet, wedding ring, and large signet ring. May bequeathed an opal and diamond ring, pearl and sapphire ring, sealskin jacket, mourning brooch (a jewel that routinely contained a portrait of a deceased loved one), and upon her mother's implicate instructions one gold thimble. Another gold thimble left to Georgiana's niece, Ada Mary Royce, she also to receive a watch and chain, opal and ruby brooch, and small signet ring; the deceases four daughters bequeathed the residue of their mother's estate in equal share. Henry Mash left the illuminated address given to his late father, upon the occasion of the celebration of his parents golden wedding, William and Martin bequeathed one of their mothers opal and diamond earrings, they directed to remount them into scarf pins.

What Georgiana Mash felt regards her sons marriage to her former housekeepers sister, Helena Dungey, can never fully be substantiated, and Helena did indeed benefit from her mother-in-law's will. Though it is to be said that she received a somewhat less salubrious piece of jewellery than her sisters-in-law, that being a plain gold brooch.

So once Georgiana Mashs assets were distributed as she had so wished, she was released of all worldly connection, and the facts that pertained to the incident of the umbrella stick, that Georgiana never quite fully explained, were forever lost in death.

Final resting place of Henry Joseph and Georgiana Mash
As the epitaph states Georgiana "rejoined" her husband in 1921

And as for Annie Mash, she ended her days at "Orchardleigh Cottage" Cookham Dean, where she died on the first day of 1938; her estate (proved by Annie's brother, Martin Mash) valued in excess of five thousand pounds.

Sixty One

At Lambridge No More

Many, who through happenchance had found themselves embroiled in the events at Lambridge Farm, had no option but to return to the lives they had known previously, John Froomes no exception. With carpentry much in demand in the prosperous households thereabouts, Froomes picked up numerous commissions, better to support his wife and children. Indeed John (taking into consideration the immortal souls of his as yet unchristened offspring), on 26th November 1894 just about finding the time necessary to attend the baptisms at St Marys, Henley, of Ellen, George, Walter and Harry.

The dawn of the twentieth century saw John Froomes near neighbour, Robert Carpenter Bratchell, still landlord of the Red Cross, the two no doubt to often reflect upon the events of the winter of 1893. Of a summer evening, upon leaving his local, would John Froomes have gazed upward, he able to just about distinguish amongst the treeline the chimney stacks of Lambridge House, long devoid of inhabitants. The Froomes (who still counted amongst their neighbours chair turner John Eustace), having under their roof considerably less children. But James and Harry had not yet flown the nest, the first a domestic gardener, the second a railway porter, neither had George, a telegraph lad, nor Ellen and Walter, both of whom not in employment.

By 1905 John and Emma Froomes resided at Lower Assenden Post Office (an 18th century build), one of a pair of brick and flint cottages, the properties water once sourced from a common well. Ellen was still in situ, and James, who also resided at home, picked up gardening jobs, the Froomes neighbour, Mr John Grove of Wistaria Cottage, a close friend.

With the closing of the Red Cross, less than four years after the dreadful events at Lambridge House, John Froomes, like many other locals, chose to drink at the newly built Travellers Rest, its landlord Robert Carpenter Bratchell a familiar face. After Bratchells untimely demise in 1903 (more will be said of this), and his widows departure in 1905, new landlord William Grove a man John Froomes much enjoyed the company of.

Even with advancements in matters medical, illness was still perilous, Emma Froomes not to experience much of the twentieth century, she dying aged sixty one in the September of 1907, her children and sorrowful husband laying her to rest at Henley Cementry on third October.

Besides the two, James and Harry Froomes, whose names had crept into the pages of the tabloids, there were many other offspring born of John and Emma's union, these children having in the December of 1893 looked on as their siblings, searched out by representatives of the press, were interviewed. The Froomes eldest, Edith, resisted marriage until she turned thirty, on Saturday 17th March 1900, at Holy Trinity, Haverstock Hill, Camden; she marrying stables job master Frederick George Proctor, the newlyweds set to reside at Eton Livery Stables, Eton Avenue, Hamstead, Middlesex. Their union to produce a son, Frederick John, he born 1900; the little lad by age two without a father, Frederick dying in his thirty second year on 5th October 1902, his widow beneficiary of assets valued in excess of one thousand pounds.

Florence Emma Froomes went into service at 36 Highbury Park, Islington, the London home of William Huntsman, this gentleman, as the contractor for the supply of trams goods to the government and public corporations, able to afford a domestics wage. Florence was a young woman with ambition, and she later took lodgings at the home of Walter Perryman (110 Savernake Road, Saint Pancras), she a post office clerk. Florence Froomes never wed, and in later life returned to live at Fircot (her childhood home, so named after the closure of the post office), and on Friday 8th February 1963, at the Battle Hospital in Reading, she died aged eighty five. At ten thirty, on the sixteenth, in the village where Florence had spent much of her life, her siblings, friends, and fellow villagers gathering to bid one, who had been a stalwart of Lower Assenden, farewell.

Charles Frederick Froomes set himself up as a domestic gardener, after his marriage on Monday 16th April 1906 to Ethel Emma Snell, choosing to reside at 1 Club House Cottages (a row of three smallish properties located alongside Paul Makins Chilterns End Estate), Greys Road in Henley-on-Thames. The war to see Charles, nearing thirty seven, on 10th December 1915 register to serve, allocated into the Labour Corps, whose role it was to build and maintain roads, rails, and bridges, so that vital equipment could reach allied troops.

In later life Charles Froomes required the care of a nurse (his wife had died in 1949), he often confined to his house much relishing the visits of his long term friend, partially sighted Mr Gurdon. Having resided at Langthorne, Wootten Manor, Greys Road, some twenty five years, and aged eighty four, Charles Froomes died. His last hours had been spent at 21 Hawthorn Drive, Willow Bank, Denhan Buckinghamshire, Charles at the time holidaying there with relatives, the old chap dying suddenly on Monday 8th July 1963. Ironically the day that followed his death, Charles's son Frederick, who had been admitted to the Royal Berkshire Hospital, Reading, losing his battle for life. At eleven in the morning, on the Saturday that followed the deaths of father and son, mourners gathered at St James's Church, Assenden, after an emotionally charged service Charles and Frederick laid to rest.

Ellen (known affectingly as Nellie) never left the Old Post Office, the 1951 Phone Directory itemising her as Post Mistress. Ellen Froomes did not find a husband nor have a family, and with those she loved at her bedside she died aged seventy five, on Monday 2nd March 1959.

Ellens demise, though sudden, following on from a protracted illness, she a patient at Townlands Hospital in Henley, Florence orchestrating the division of her sister's assets of two hundred and seventy seven pounds.

George Froomes continued on for some time as a telegraph boy, he later to follow the same career path as two of his brothers. In October 1901 George went to work for the Great Western Railways, out of Maidenhead Station, employed as a lamp boy (the role of which to light the oil lamps in signal boxes) on 1d a week, he seemingly not much liking the job resigning in the August of 1903. Leaving home and taking lodgings at 1 Grange Road, Henley (the family home of domestic gardener William Day), by 1909 George Froomes took a similar job as another of his brothers (that being James), working as a domestic gardener, but the shadow of war was on the horizon. George Froomes enlisted in London on Saturday 29th September 1915, as a Private in the Royal Army Medical Corps, on 22nd November 1915 the young man, who had only known life within a small community, shipped to France. And there it was, on Saturday 18th November 1916, aged thirty, Georges life was snuffed out, as he conveyed the wounded to a dressing station, an exploding shell killing him outright. Private George Froomes, never again to play cricket on the village green, mortal remains to be interred within Euston Road Cemetery, Colincamps. John Froomes (he sent from France his sons personal effects, as well as £4 17s 10d, retrieved from within Georges kitbag) left reeling by his loss, neither the less mindful of etiquette, he within the pages of the Henley and Oxfordshire Standard acknowledging the kindness of others. "Mr Froomes and family, wish to return thanks to all kind friends for their kind sympathy shown them in their sad and sudden bereavement."

On 22nd October 1906 Walter John Froomes took work as a platform cleaner within the Old Oak Common Division at Slough Station, for the Great Western Railways, transferred in the December of 1909 to

Aylesbury, Walter to quit before he'd worked a full day at his newly allocated station. Walter Froomes (with war raging in France, serving in the Army Service Corps) married at Willesden, St Mary, on Saturday 11th November 1916, his bride twenty two year old Florence Mary Bence. After the cessation of hostilities Walter Froomes to return to his home (71a Denzie Road, Willesden), he by the latter 1920s relocated to 149 Church Lane, Barnet Hendon. The last we hear of Walter John Froomes, the registration of his death, that being in the summer of 1975, he aged eighty, resident in Hillingdon, Greater London.

John Froomes, in his dotage in the care of his children, died near forty years after he and George Dawson had looked upon the murdered body of Miss Kate Laura Dungey. On Saturday 14th May 1932 (aged eighty three), much worn down by the effects of fatty degeneration of the heart, and dropsy (diagnosed by a certain Doctor George Smith), John Froomes to expire, duly buried on the nineteenth alongside his dear Emma.

James Froomes, who as a lad of thirteen had found himself mixed up in matters detrimental to the delicate psyche of a child, to again, some twenty three years after the murder at Lambridge, experience the effects of the inhumanity of man. The event that led James into peril, war, on Thursday 16th November 1916, aged thirty six, he relinquishing his profession of gardener, volunteered into his majesty's service. The Royal Navy was where James found himself; recruit number K37791, on Ship Vivid II, it never to leave the shores of England the name in fact that given to the Royal Naval Barracks, Devonport. Froomes was more fortunate than many; and after being demobbed on Saturday 12th April 1919 he came home, returning to live at the address he was never again to relinquish, the Post Office Lower Assenden, as before taking up employment as a gardener. Some might describe James Froomes later life as uneventful, but it was the life he chose, and as a man who felt secure within the close community of Lower Assenden, James (who was never to marry) was content to earn his keep maintaining the gardens of those who lived thereabouts, a familiar face known and respected by his fellow villagers.

Advancing years can prove harsh, and James Froomes was to suffer considerably from coronary arteriosclerosis (hardening of the walls of the arteries), Doctor Landsdell attending him on numerous occasions. But it was a coronary thrombosis that proved James Froomes undoing, on Monday 19th November 1956 he dying within the bedroom he had occupied near fifty years. Probate duly granted granted to the deceases sister Florence Emma (she witness to the death), her brothers effects valued at just over two hundred and twenty pounds. The Post Office at Lower Assenden closed in the latter 1950s (possibly immediately after the demise of James), set to remain as the home of the Froomes, thus forward (as earlier stated), known as "Fircot". Immediately following the loss of this village facility a new post office opened in Middle Assenden, it now also no more.

Harry Froomes took an altogether different path to that of his sibling James, by the age of sixteen working at Henley-on-Thames Railway Station. Registered in the May of 1899 as in the employ of Great Western Railways, Harry a uniformed lad porter, taken on to carry baggage and assist passengers. The December of 1900 saw Froomes (having not yet left home) elevated to the position of station porter (no more mention of the word lad), he not destined to remain working out of Henley Railway Station for much longer. In the September of 1901 Harry Froomes to take on the role of a Shunter (a task which involved sorting items of rolling stock into complete trains) at Acton Railway Station, London. But this young man craved new challenges, and better wages, and in October 1902 Froomes was appointed as a Brakesman (a job with some hazards involved, Harry required to manually apply the brakes of a train, and if necessary the brakes of individual carriages), in Southall, West London. On Friday 11th December 1903 a very proud Harry Froomes admitted into the Amalgamated Society of Railway Servants General Register of Members. In early 1905 Harry to secure a position somewhat less taxing, that of Goods Guard (one who took care of passengers goods, and ensured goods reached their destination safely), working out of Slough Station, Berkshire, in the April of 1907 he transferred to Neath, Wales. June 1910 saw Harry Froomes back down south, based at Reading Railway Station, a Goods Guard, his digs within a terraced property on De Montfort Road, Reading.

Harry Froomes (not having had want of a wife) in later life suffered from cerebral thrombosis and hypertension, and with his health failing was admitted into Townlands Hospital, where consultant, Doctor Staines-Read, diagnosed a heart murmur. Harry was not to be discharged, and on Monday 25th June 1962, aged sixty nine, his sister Edith Ruddock (of 2 Lower Assenden) at his hospital bedside, he died.

The December of 1893 had seen two young lads embroiled in murder, the eldest James having gazed upon the body of a woman who had shown he and his brother Harry much kindness. Miss Kate Dungeys mutilated and blooded corpse laying close to a path the brothers had often trod. Tenderness of age had not spared the boys, they stood within a witness box, required to give evidence in a capital offence trial. The two had always remained much devoted to each other, and James and Harry lie united in death, buried at Henley Cemetery, the path that ran through its centre, out through a gate, into Lambridge Woods, and onward to Lambridge House, no longer in existence.

For George Dawson, he deprived of the keys of Lambridge Farm, at the behest of his employer Henry Mash, and much affronted by this resigning his position as bailiff; life was eventually to be set on a more even keel, his wife, Amy Katherine, delivered of a son in 1897, Reginald George baptised 25th July, at St James's. Dawson had since the January of 1894 flitted from job to job, but in due course he had secured the tenancy of a cottage at Windmill Hill, Nettlebed (so named because of a centuries old tradition of a windmill in its vicinity, the last one in existence accidently burnt down in 1912), within its boundary many brick kilns. Whether George Dawson turned his hand to brick making is nigh on impossible to establish, but with Windmill Hill heavily populated by self-employed men who produced bricks, Dawson could well have dabbled, any small outfit that manufactured bricks not sophisticated, those in Windmill Hill making use of Clamp Kilns. The aforementioned the most rudimentary of construction, this type of kiln on the whole consisting of a pile of green bricks interspaced with combustible material, any bricks produced sold to builders located in close proximity.

Louis John was born on 8th August 1899, his father mindful that he had a growing family to support seeking out those who had need of staff. George Dawson thus securing employment as a poultry man, his family squeezed into a small tied cottage in Bradfield, Berkshire. Dawson would never again find himself bailiff, but he was glad of the work, his master William Chillingworth, proprietor of Barn Elms Farm. There was much that was advantageous to life on the farm; neighbouring cottages lived in by personable folk, shepherd Philip Partridge, and general agricultural labourer Albert Ludlow. But George Dawson, never again, it seemed, to experience the stability of his long term position as bailiff of Lambridge, quit his job. He next taken on as a cowman, his family relocating into yet another tied property, located not much distance from the dairy of the sizable estate (Greenlands, Hambledon) of one William Frederick Danvers Smith, he involved in the management of family business, W. H. Smith.

Though not to be described as moneyed, the Dawson's to have a pleasant enough living, their residence on Dairy Lane neighboured by those they considered friends, carpenter John Silvester, electrical engineer Henry Rose, and residing above Greenlands "Laundry House", estate washer woman, Miss Rachel Davis.

Greenlands Manor House, an impressively overblown structure
George Dawson employed as Greenlands estate cowman

On the morning of Wednesday 23rd January 1907 Amy Dawson rose slightly later than usual, she feeling somewhat under the weather. By mid-afternoon feeling no better, having tended to her children, Amy retired to her bedroom. George Dawson returned home from work early that day, and much concerned when finding his wife lying in bed complaining of a terrible pain in her abdomen, he quickly sent out for a doctor. Doctor Egerton Charles Augustus Baines duly arrived (ironically the very same man who thirteen years early had conversed with Henleys Workhouse Master John Martin, regards the suspicions of the tramp who had fallen in with Walter Rathall, on the road down into Henley), upon examining the stricken woman immediately diagnosing appendicitis. Doctor Baines, possessing surgical skills, resolved to operate, and with his patient thus under anaesthetic, and medical instruments sterilised, and hands scrubbed clean at the Dawson's sink, Baines commenced surgery. All seemed well, but suddenly and without warning Amy Dawsons heart gave out (it possible that the use of chloroform as an anaesthetic caused disaster, this liquid known to bring on respiratory and cardiac arrhythmias), her husband George looking on as his wife expired. Downstairs Amy's children had sat anxiously waiting for news of their mother, and upon seeing their ashen faced father, and Doctor Egerton Baines, descend the stairs in silence, the little ones realized their mother was gone, the children's distraught wailings sorely affecting the two men. The day of Amy's demise was a bad one all-round, it the same day her half-sister Emily was set to bury her husband, Robert Parker. Who knows if the Dawson's had been set to attend the funeral, but one can imagine that if they had been, the mourning party would have been shocked indeed, upon hearing of events back at Greenlands. With no blame attributed to Doctor Egerton Baines, Amy Dawsons death certificate to be issued on 25th January, by registrar George Albert Stone, the mother of three; just thirty eight, interred three days after her death.

Amy Katherine Dawson had in 1899 drawn up her will, witnessed on 6th July by one William Pether (a joiner) of Assenden, and Walter Lovegrove (a carpenter) of Marsh Cottage, Henley. She so instructing that all debts and funeral expenses be paid as soon as conveniently possible after her decease, and then after all her real and personal estate (of every description) to be passed into the possession of her husband George Dawson, for his separate use, after probate the sum in question just short of eighty pounds.

1901 saw the end of the momentous reign of Queen Victoria, and with many looking to a new era; George Dawson resolved to do likewise. As a man still in his forties the thought of life alone was not one he much relished, and it seems George found the companionship he craved in the form of a second wife, the nuptials held in early 1908. The lady Dawson wed, Emma (born Hurst 1872, daughter of Charles King, a groom), a dairy woman on the farm at Greenlands. The new mistress of the house taking into her care Georges two boys, their sister Elsie away in service, she a housemaid at St Marks Rectory, Englefield, Berkshire, in the employ of the Reverend Granville Gore Skipwith.

On 11th November 1913, the eldest son within the Dawson household, sixteen year old Reginald (having quit both his dairy assistant job, and the country of his birth) arrived in Sydney, Australia, aboard the "Irishman", Reginald barely out of his boyhood to quickly find domestic gardening work. The outbreak of war saw the young man return to the country of his birth, on 13th October 1915 docking at Plymouth, aboard the "Omrah", under the Orient Steam Navigation Company Ltd. Reginald Dawson wished to do his bit for the war effort (having failed to gain entry into the Australian army), and thus returning to his family home at Hambleden, he enlisted on 4th November 1915, aged nineteen and six months, his regiment the Oxford and Bucks.

But Australia was not far from Reginald's thoughts, and with the war over he duly returned, the enterprising young man quickly securing work as herd milkman, at a farm situated close to Melbourne, he later to gain employment on a farm in Northern Victoria. In 1930 Reginald Dawson married Doris Mary Fox; like his father before him taking work as a poultry farmer, at Winters Flat, Castlemaine. During the 1930s George Dawson to lose his other son to Australia (though not permanently), Louis, with the assistance of his brother, finding work as a labourer on Netherby Farm, in the state of Victoria.

Later in life Reginald Dawson took up as a storekeeper, his shop located on the Sandhurst Road, and after a long and fulfilled life he died aged eighty, in Bendigo, Victoria, the year 1977. It curious to note that Reginald never, if indeed he knew much of it himself, conveyed to his nearest and dearest the facts which pertained to his late father having been mixed up in a murder. George and Amy's youngest, Louis, who also to live into the 1970s, he dying aged seventy five, in the spring of 1975, his death registered in Slough, Buckinghamshire.

So what of George and Emma Dawson, the Kellys Directory answers this conundrum, the master of the house in the 1920s landlord of The Pheasant, Lent Rise Road, this hostelry, which was first licensed in 1870, now sadly gone the way of many a public house.

In his twilight years George Dawson found contentment living at "The Bungalow", Lent Green, Buckinghamshire, just a short jaunt from his old stomping ground The Pheasant, the old chap earning a small crust as a cowman. George Dawson died, aged eighty three, in the arms of his son Leonard (residing with his father), on the morning of Monday 9th September 1946, his demise as a result of Pernicious Anaemia, the condition brought about by stomach cancer. After a funeral attended by those of Lent Green, who much lamented one considered a good sort, George Dawson buried within the churchyard of St Peters (located in the centre of Burnham), his grave no longer discernible, its headstone removed, and another burial placed on top.

George Dawson's widow, Emma (her late husband not as practical as his first wife, having left no will), to come into a modest inheritance. And living to witness the accession of Queen Elizabeth II, Emma died in the winter of 1952, her demise duly registered in Maidenhead, Berkshire.

George and Emma Dawson in later life
George, as during the trial of Walter Rathall, much fond of his headwear

Sixty Two

A Gratuity of Fifty Five Pounds

Superintendent Francis Keal had thought he had his man, but after the abrupt conclusion of the trial of Walter Rathall, he and those who served under him did attempt to bring to book a culprit, Keal valiant in his efforts to find the person (or persons) responsible for the savage murder of Miss Kate Dungey. But whether subsequent inquiries were tempered by a general feeling that the constabulary had seen the guilty man slip through their fingers, no one else was to be questioned, or indeed held on suspicion of murder. It may well being a reflection of criticism from those in authority over officers who worked out of Henley Police Station; that shortly after the trial debacle Superintendent Keals team was broken up.

In the February of 1894 Francis Keal transferred to Banbury Oxfordshire, on 26th October 1897 he placed in charge of officers who worked out of Chadlington Police Station, some three miles south of Chipping Norton. What was to be Francis Keals final posting, that of Superintendent of Chipping Norton Police Station (on the London Road), he availed of an apartment above the station.

The so called "Henley Murder" was to be Francis Keals last high profile investigation, though he had cause to issue further arrest warrants, some of which to directly affect those in whose town Keal served. On 31st August 1900 Superintendent Keal to take into custody a man he knew well, cabinet maker and upholsterer, John Morgan (his commercial outlet located at 16 New Street), a fellow who preferred to be known by his alias, Harry Wilson.

On Thursday 6th July 1893 Morgan had married, at Chipping Norton's Parish Church of Saint Mary, Sarah Ann Laura Bryan, he to prove himself a good husband, and provider to their three children. There was however one underlying problem, that being John Morgan's other wife. On Thursday 6th January 1876 the nuptials of John Morgan and his initial bride, Gertrude Maggie, having taken place within the Parish Church of Trebethin, Monmouthshire, Wales, the guests to thus partake of the wedding breakfast. What in time blighted the union (which produced six off spring) was clear, Morgan liked a drink, and in 1887 he requested a separation, headed for the nearest dock and took passage, bound for America. One year later, having recently returned to live with his wife and children, John Morgan to again up sticks, his deserted wife, Gertrude, left to her own devices.

Duly held on remand at Chipping Norton Police Station, and with no defence against the allegation, John Morgan was brought before the magistrates on bigamy charges, Superintendent Keal required to give evidence. Those upon the bench listening intently as the defendant argued his case, John Morgan to state that he thought his first wife long since dead, Gertrude anything but, she, having travelled down from Gloucester, sitting across from her ne'er-do-well spouse. Morgan's version of events did not rub, and not able to raise the one hundred pounds bail, he was further remanded to be sent to trial at Oxford. As an aside it apparent that Sarah Ann was a forgiving sort (local gossip alluding to the fact that she knew full well her husband had another wife), she and Harry Wilson (John Morgan) to face down the scandal, and remain on in Chipping Norton.

The dawn of the twentieth century hailed much, the end of the rigidity of the Victorian age, the coronation of Edward VII, and new social, inventory, and scientific innovations. But this new era did not bode well for Francis Keal; he on Friday 26th July 1907 losing his wife Mary, she dying aged fifty five within the flat above Chipping Norton Police Station, her estate a meagre £235 0s 2d. Widowhood was not for Keal, he lost without his wife, to remarry rather hastily, in the last quarter of 1907. The new Mrs Keal one Elizabeth Lewis (forty three at the time of her marriage), a spinster who had previously been in service, one time parlour maid, in the household of James Honour, a farmer who resided at Hill Lodge, Norton Road, Chipping Norton. But this new life embarked upon by Superintendent Keal not to be one blessed with years of contentment, the man was ill.

Superintendent Francis Keal (sitting second row centre) resplendent amongst his constables, and proud looking dog, outside Chipping Norton Police Station Photographed 1907 by Mr Percy Simms

If drink was a factor in Keals malady cannot be substantiated, but with his liver irreversibly damaged by cirrhosis, Francis retreated to his living quarters, he a shadow of himself, struck down by a particularly virulent bout of influenza. Keals new bride coped as best she could, but her husband worsened by the day, and Elizabeth was grateful of the assistance of her husband's niece, who hearing of her uncle's ill health had travelled from Bath. Elizabeth Keal did not spare her purse when it came to paying a doctors fee, but the patients underlying health problem prevailed, and Francis Keals heart gave out (dying aged just fifty six, Francis niece at his bedside), on Wednesday 29th April 1908 Elizabeth to don widows weeds.

John Francis (throughout his life known by his middle name) Keal had served the constabulary well, and in recognition of this service a gratuity of fifty five pounds was awarded to his widow, Elizabeth Keal, after a decent interlude, required to quit her late husbands tied apartment. Francis Keal bequeathing (his will drawn up on 10th December 1907) his gold pocket watch and chain (an item he wore throughout his career) to his eldest grandson, his furniture and household effects left to his widow, for, as he stipulated, her own absolute use and benefit. Keals assets, valued in excess of four hundred pounds (after the settling of any outstanding debts and funerary expenses), placed into the hands of the trustees of his will, for the benefit of Elizabeth Keal.

Less than six months on from Walter Rathalls appearance before the bench, Constable Edward John Snelgrove (on Monday 9th July 1894), took up a posting at Wootton South Police Station. The grass was not allowed to grow under the young officer's feet, he on 21st April 1895 relocated to Ploughley, Oxfordshire, in the October Snelgrove promoted to the rank of Constable Merit Class. On the fifteenth of June 1896, Edward Snelgrove due to be transferred back to his old stomping ground, Henley-on-Thames, this transfer cancelled (if the debacle of the Lambridge affair was a factor unclear), Snelgrove, given scant opportunity to feel settled anywhere, on 25th October 1899 posted to Wootton South Police Station.

Constable Edward Snelgrove did eventually make it back to Henley-on-Thames, his first day, serving under Superintendent Thomas

Jennings, Monday 3rd September 1900. Indeed Henley Police Station had need of many men (Snelgrove working alongside two sergeants, and fifteen constables), much of their time taken up with the various flare ups in Henleys considerable number of drinking establishments. Exactly a year after his arrival back in Henley, Snelgrove was again on the transfer list, his next posting Watlington. It can be argued that life within the constabulary had much to recommend it, but it lacked stability in regard to putting down roots, Edward Snelgrove reliant on lodgings, at the close of the nineteenth century the constable boarding in a premises on Station Road, Goring, his landlord, Mr William Dover, a coal merchants manager,.

On 28th October 1901 poor old Snelgrove was off again, posted at Bullington, and having in the August of 1903 achieved the rank of Sergeant, found himself back again in Henley-on-Thames (as before under the command of Superintendent Thomas Jennings), near ten years after the murder that had in some way impacted upon his career. Snelgrove was ambitious, and those in authority over him did not fail to notice, and in acknowledgement of his dedication to the constabulary, he found himself elevated to the rank of Second Class Inspector (promoted 6th December 1910), posted on 24th July 1911 to Wootten South.   Further advancement on the cards, Snelgrove promoted to the rank of First Class Inspector, he set to work out of Woodstock Police Station.

Edith Emmeline Wood (born 1872 in Chipping Norton) spent an idyllic childhood in Somerset, Thomas, her father, having secured the tenancy of the Three Mariners on the High Street, Taunton St Mary, the coffers assisted by Woods brewing of his own beer. Publican's were always on the lookout for a more profitable beerhouse, and Thomas Wood found one such business, he to secure the tenancy of the Vine Terrace, located in North Town, Taunton Street, not much distance from the Three Mariners. This not to be the last premises the Wood's would reside in, they by the tail end of the old century resident at 13 Paul Street, Taunton, Thomas Wood now exclusively a brewer. The area in which the Woods children grew up boasted a long history of the production of fine linen, and with schooling finished with young Edith, alongside her sister Elizabeth (Thirza, their mother, having given birth to twelve), found work as a buttonholer, within a linen factory.

In-between being transferred all over Oxfordshire, Edward Snelgrove had managed to fit in a personal life, and in the late autumn of 1901 he married the aforementioned Edith Emmeline Wood. In 1904 the couple to welcome the arrival of their first born, Winifred Rosa, while her father was posted at Henley Police Station, the little girl, on 5th February 1905, baptised at St Marys, a son, Frederick Thomas born in 1908, while his father fulfilled a short posting to Bradfield Police Station, Buckinghamshire.

On 21st April 1919 Inspector Snelgrove took up a posting in Witney, Oxfordshire, this proving to be his swansong, with his removal from the force (Edwards last day, Sunday 22nd August 1920) Snelgrove having retirement forced upon him, a superannuation of £233 6s 8d, paid annually, going someway to soften the blow.

Edward John Snelgrove chose in later life to reside at "Southlands", The Roman Way, Glastonbury, and in his eighty fourth year (admitted to Wells Infirmary), on Saturday 19th November 1955, he died, Edwards death certificate to state that nothing more than old age his undoing.

Edith (bequeathed a legacy of just under fifteen hundred pounds) not to linger long after her husband's demise, she dying on Monday 17th September 1956, at Mount Avalon Nursing Home, Glastonbury.

Plain Clothes Sergeant, Thomas Allmond, dispatched on eighth December 1893 to assist Superintendent Francis Keal at Lambridge Farm, was a man who had very much blotted his copy book. On 9th November 1891 Allmond reprimanded for drinking in a public house while on duty (thus neglecting a conference point), after a hearing demoted to Sergeant First Class, not until 27th February 1893 to regain his former rank.

By the early1900s Thomas Allmond serving out of Kirtlington Station, Oxfordshire, his son Leopold working for the Great Western, out of Bordesley Railway Station. The first day of April, 1902, to see Sergeant Allmond take up a posting in Bullingdon; he in the April of 1904 transferred to Bampton West Station.

With his past misdemeanour now firmly behind him, on 11th April 1904, Thomas Allmond promoted to Second Class Inspector, by the close of the September of 1905 elevated to the rank of First Class Inspector. Allmond, like Snelgrove, moved from pillar to post, on Saturday 26th March 1910 to commence a posting in Ploughley, having been promoted to the rank of Second Class Superintendent earlier that same month. Subsequently Inspector Allmond to take charge of the Bicester Division (a position he held in excess of six years), the rank of First Class Superintendent awarded in the November of 1910. By the taking of the 1911 census, Thomas Allmond stationed at Bicester, Market End, Oxfordshire (two sons in situ, Tom a harness maker, Reginald having no occupation), ably assisted by two constables, Francis Eugene Cash, and Arthur Henry Wilkins, both of whom living under the same roof as their superior.

It fortunate indeed that Thomas Allmond had advanced apace, his increased salary going someway to maintain his family, sons Tom Alan (born 1893), and Reginald (born 1896), adding considerably to their fathers financial burden. The outbreak of hostilities in 1914 to see Thomas and Edith's sons, Tom (a saddler), and Horace (both of whom living alongside their parents, above Bicester Police Station) recruited into the Army Service Corps, Horace shipped out to France.

The years raced by apace, and on Sunday 22nd February 1920, having served near thirty eight years within the Oxfordshire Constabulary, Thomas Allmond retired, he duly granted a superannuation of £306 13s 4d, paid yearly.

In 1923 the Allmonds came to live at 76 Albert Street, Aylesbury, Thomas to quickly make new acquaintances, particularly amongst bowls devotees. Being a sport at which he excelled Allmond a devoted member of Aylesbury Bowls Club, he not letting barely a day pass, be it winter or summer that he visited the club, often to be spotted down on his knees, garden tool in hand, removing offending weeds from the green. But in the spring of 1927 Thomas Allmond was to fine his energies sapped, upon the insistence of family and friends he to consult a doctor.

Tests (too numerous to mention) were carried out, but with Thomas Allmonds voice failing him the specialists concentrated their efforts in the region of his throat, the diagnosis devastating, carcinoma of the larynx, an operation the patients best option. And thus it was that Allmond found himself admitted to the Royal Northern Hospital, Holloway Road, London, the midmorning of Monday 18th May 1927 he to go under the knife. Later within the ward Thomas's wife, then after reluctant to leave her husband's bedside, to witness, two days after his operation, her husband succumb to post-operative bronchial pneumonia. Though barely out of recovery, a Doctor Heath (attending medical practioner) to rule a post mortem upon Allmonds remains unnecessary, he content to sign the death certificate.

Thomas Allmonds funeral service (taken by the Reverend Morton, Vicar of Holy Trinity Church, Walton) held at Aylesbury Cemetery, on the afternoon of Wednesday 25th May. The Bucks Constabulary represented by Superintendent A. C. White, Allmonds family (sons Tom and Reginald living in Canada, and Percival living in America, unable to attend) greatly moved by the considerable turn out of those who wished to pay their respects to one they considered a friend.

Emma Allmond (bequeathed the relatively modest sum of £322) never vacated her home on Albert Street; she to die there on Thursday 5th March 1931, her son's to have benefit of their mothers legacy of just over two hundred and fifty pounds.

One wonders if the Chief Constable of Oxfordshire, Edward Alexander Holmes A' Court, was dragged over the coals, due to the unsuccessful outcome of the investigation that followed on from the shocking events of eighth December 1893. He having attended both the inquest and the trial, and with the Lambridge case no doubt the biggest event in his career, and no one ever brought to book, the Chief Constable surely carried the stigma of failure with him. Holmes A' Court to quit his home "The Firs" in 1910, relocating to "The White House" in Iffley, Oxfordshire, taking into his care his widowed sister Gertrude Ann, parlour maid Elsie Smith, and cook Elizabeth Mary Spackman, keeping the household running along just fine.

In the last year of the war, with the country reeling from the continual bloodshed and loss of young lives at the front, Edward Holmes A' Court took the decision to retire as Chief Constable, his army and police pension, not to mention the monies gained due to his privileged background, more than enough to offer financial security. Edward and Adelaide had in the past enjoyed visiting their in-laws, both in Pyrton and the Isle of Wight, and it was the latter location that the couple decided to retire to. "Rosery" a fine premises in Fresh Water Bay, to become the final home of this much devoted couple. Holmes A' Court had for some years been plagued by gall stones and mitral incompetence (disorder of the hearts mitral valve), and in the spring of 1923 his health began to fail him utterly. On Saturday 23rd June 1923 Edward's life to reach its conclusion, he aged seventy seven, his children about him, though his demise shortly after the visit of a medical practiner (Doctor A. H. Hopkins) a post mortem deemed unnecessary, the body thus released for burial.

The funeral of Edward Alexander Holmes A' Court to take place at the Parish Church of All Saints, Freshwater, on Wednesday 27th June, it a quiet affair, apart from the deceases relatives only a few select locals attending, one of which no less that Lord Hallam Tennyson (son of Alfred, Lord Tennyson), of "Farringford House". The service, officiated by the Isle of Wight's Archdeacon, Dr Lewen Greenwood Tugwell (his duties on the day shared by All Saints Rector Reverend G. C. White), reflecting on a life well lived, those closest to the deceased inconsolable. At the graveside buglers of the Second Battalion K.S.L.I. (posted at Tidmarsh) to sound the Last Post, Edwards widow, children, and mourners alike, moved to tears by the emotive rendition of a melody so poignant.

The Honourable Adelaide Sophia (who received a substantial portion of her husband's resworn of £1,285 5s 11d), carried on at "Rosery", until such time as age and infirmity dictated that she needed the support of others. A pragmatic woman, Adelaide moved back to the mainland, to reside at a substantial detached house, "The Lodge" (assisted by a daily), which lay just outside the village of Cressage in Shropshire. Adelaide Holmes A' Court dying, aged ninety two, on Sunday 6th May 1945, at the North Oxford Nursing Home. She not to join her husband in death, Adelaide having desired to be buried in the village of her childhood, duly laid to rest within the churchyard of St Marys, Pyrton, in Oxfordshire.

Sixty Three

To Witness a Hundred Years

Remenham, nestled on an incline of the chalk hills which surrounded Henley-on-Thames, and lying on a bend of the River Thames, afforded its residents splendid views of the surrounding countryside, the church of St Nicholas, and adjoining Rectory, at the very heart of the village. On 20th January 1872, in her thirty eighth year, and married less than six years, Eleanor Madelene Skottowe died at Remenham Rectory. The Reverend Charles Mills Skottowe (born 1820, Portsea, Hampshire), Eleanor's widower, with two young daughters to consider, appreciative of the assistance of housemaid Esther White, cook Elizabeth Pheby, and most vitally, nursemaid Charlotte White, he thus able to offer a nurturing hand to his girls, as well as fulfil the many diverse duties required of one of the cloth.

But misfortune was to again visit at the Rectory, with the death in the March of 1875 of Charles's eldest child, Madeline Amy Katherine, who left this world aged but seven, she laid to rest on 10th March within the churchyard of her father's parish. Four was now two, but the fates had not finished with the Skottowe's, and on 13th May 1878, Laura Emily Anne (baptised 21st July 1869, at St Nicholas's) found herself alone in the world, upon the death of her father, he three days after his demise interred alongside his predeceased wife and daughter. The Reverend Charles Skottowe to leave a resworn just short of four thousand pounds; and his orphaned eight year old daughter in the care of her late mothers sister.

Amy Henrietta had been born on 21st August 1836, in Pusey, Berkshire, the daughter of the Rector of Pusey (William Evans), and the sister of Eleanor Madelene. Amy grew into an independently minded young woman, and whether through desire or circumstance she, against the excepted norms of the time, did not rush into marriage. Charles Hammerton (a highly productive brewer) was left widowed upon the death in 1878 of Rosa Ann, his wife of twenty six years. Though he enjoyed the loving support of his offspring, widowhood did not sit well with Charles, and as such on 9th October 1883 he took as his second wife, forty seven year old Amy Henrietta Evans, their nuptials held at St Nicholas, Wimbledon.

Charles Hammerton's business interests were on the whole based in London, and as such he spent much time in the city, residing at his premises in Stockwell Green, kept company by his daughters Rosa and Marianne. Amy Hammerton, a lady now having a considerable allowance at her disposal, not keen on city life to take residence of an impressive three storey town house in Henley-on-Thames. Much saddened at the loss of both her sister and cherished brother-in-law, Amy did not hesitate when her niece had need of a home, and it was within her aunts New Street premises that Laura flourished, the bereft child to benefit from the unconditional love shown by her aunt.

Destiny is a word much banded about, Laura Skottowe, who had grown into a bright young woman possessed of a good education, drawn toward a young Scot, Doctor George Smith, who in the latter 1880s had set up in practice directly next door to Laura's aunts home. The relationship between the two advanced apace (George Smith to often sit at his neighbours table), and at St Marys, on Thursday 30th August 1894, George and Laura were wed. Their marriage ceremony (witnessed by Aunt Amy, and Georges father and brother, both Henrys) conducted by one Charles Wyrnne, Rector of Gantby, Lincoln.

On 5th January 1896 the Smiths first child, Eleanor May, was received into baptism, a second daughter, Dorothea Elizabeth, born the following year. Bucking the trend of many of his patients, George

Smith not to be father to a multitude of offspring, Henry George (baptised 5th February 1899), set to be the last born of Laura.

Doctor Smith's career was one of no meagre triumphs, and as appointed Surgeon for South Oxfordshire (a role that enabled Smith to accrue a sizeable income) his family enjoyed a privileged life style. Within two years of the dreadful events at Lambridge Farm, Doctor George Smith in practice with Doctors William Hugh Macpherson (resided in Harpsden Village), and James Lidderdale, he tenant at the former home of Richard Ovey, Northfield House. By the end of the century George Smith to quit his New Street address, and relocate to the former home of Doctor Alden, being Longlands, Hart Street (an elegant three storey building of some age, which boasted a Georgian façade); the Smith's waited on by housemaid, Lily Purcell, and domestic cook, Minnie Louisa Purcell. Young Henry Smith, under the mentoring of schoolmaster Thomas Erskine Wilson, a pupil at Hilltide School, Bradfield, near Reading.

Longlands, standing resplendent alongside the Parish Church of St Marys

Laura Smith was diligent in her responsibilities to her aunt, who had cared for her when as a child she had been in need of stability, and shortly after George had taken Longlands, Amy Hammerton moved in, she, somewhat frail, under the care of nurse domestic, Mabel Annie Betts. Charles Hammerton still pursued his business interests in London, and how much he actually saw of his wife is debateable, the two to be parted for ever, upon Charles death on 29th October 1903 (he interred at Norwood Cemetery, Lambeth), his widow to benefit from her late husband's estate, valued in excess of eighty six thousand pounds.

The Smiths were tireless in their voluntary works, Laura a Sunday School Teacher, and District Visitor on behalf of the Children's Welfare Council, she just about able to find the time required to assist her husband in his bustling children's clinic. Outside surgery hours George Smith to enjoy moments of leisure, which he filled with the perusal of a good book, botany, and walking, he often to be seen admiring Henleys medieval buildings, the study of ancient structures a particular passion. A portion of one such medieval building, positioned adjacent to Bridge House (it stood on the corner of Hart Street and Thames Side), the Surgery of Doctor Smith.

Amy Henrietta Hammerton died aged seventy five, on 24th July 1912 (leaving a legacy of £4,356 4s 10d), in the care of those who loved her most. She buried on the twenty seventh (close to her long lamented sister), within the secluded picturesque little cemetery of St Nicholas Church, the gravestones epitaph indicative of how her earthly efforts were perceived by those who had cherished Amy Hammerton. "The soul's of the righteous are in the hand of god."

Laura Emily Smith was to die in her sixtieth year, on Thursday 10th April 1930, her funeral service (orchestrated by George Thomas Savage Undertakers, Bell Street) taking place on the afternoon of 12th April. Said service (attended by family, friends, and representatives of the numerous societies Laura had supported in life), held at St

Nicholas Church, officiated by the Reverend Stephen Charles Rees-Jones, he ably assisted by Allen Edward Dams, Rector of St Marys. Laura Smith duly interred at the east end of the churchyard, laid to rest in a grave decorated with Daffodils and Wild Moss, her final resting place adjoining that of her daughter Eleanor Mary Gibson (who had died aged twenty three), wife of civil engineer Harold Kenneth Gibson. In the February of 1919 Eleanor, having been brought back from her home, 7 Vine Street, Hillingdon, West Uxbridge, to spend her last days at Longlands, she dying there on the twenty second. As the mourners made their way from the churchyard (which now had added to its number a woman who had met much adversity with fortitude), as a mark of respect for Laura Smiths passing and her aggrieved husbands role as Rectors Warden, the bells of Remenham Church, having been muffled, were rung. Indeed throughout that evening the bells tolled continually, a solemn tribute to Laura Smith.

Doctor George Smith was a faithful servant to his patients, and into his seventies he could be found tending to the sick and infirm within his Hart Street surgery, from 1920 he to act as Medical Officer for the Henley Poor Law Institute. Many a child, upon spotting the doctor in the streets of Henley, to run alongside beside him, George Smith, often seen with his hands clasped behind his back, concealing within his clenched fists sweets, duly claimed by his young followers.

Doctor George Smith retired in 1937 (the Hart Street partnership at that time made up of Doctor Thomas Staines-Read, who resided at Bird Place Remenham, and Doctor Walter James Susman, who resided at "Hawthorne" on the Reading Road), he thus to quit Longlands in 1938, the property to then forward be occupied by Mr R. W. Cotton. The war put pay to retirement, and with many a practioner serving abroad, and the Hart Street Surgery sorely pressed by the needs of its patients, George Smith (now nearing eighty) again had need of his medical bag, he to take a small apartment above the surgery. With peace came change, and with hostilities at an end, accompanied by his unmarried daughter, Dorothea Elizabeth, George Smith took up residence at "The Oaks", in Warborough, Oxfordshire. After some fourteen years of domestic harmony, Dorothea to die at the relatively young age of fifty five, she interred on 29th July 1952 within the churchyard where her sister and mother lay buried.

Smith, now in his ninety's, was a practical fellow, and aware that he needed the security of family around him, he decanted from "The Oaks" and took up residence at a small private nursing home in Little Polberro, St Agnes, Cornwall, in close proximity to his son Henry, himself enjoying retirement (formerly a farmer) at "The Sheiling", Mount Hawke, near Truro.

Doctor George Smith, who had been born at the height of Queen Victoria's reign, had found himself early in his long career as a medical practitioner embroiled in a murder case, the implications of which to question the notion of extreme poverty as provocation to commit murder. It had been a fundamental lynchpin of the case, that the doctors medical examination of the body of Kate Laura Dungey (the violence of the attack upon her person clearly evident), had left no doubt that the perpetrator of such a frenzied assault could not have escaped unblooded. The fact that Walter Rathall had been seen at the Red Lion by its landlady Mrs Emily Ayres, on the evening of 8th December, his attire unblemished by blood and gore, tantamount to his acquittal.

George Smith, who witnessed the reign of six monarchs (one of whom abdicating), to die at the dawn of what was to be the Swinging Sixties. He to leave the world aged one hundred (Smiths landmark birthday 9th March), on Friday 14th April 1961, many of Henleys populace saddened to hear of the demise of Doctor Smith. The

Henley Standard, of Friday 21st April, marking his passing, Smith referred to, as. "The best liked man in Henley."

A small gathering came together at St Nicholas Church, on Sunday 16th April, they to attend the private funeral of Doctor George Smith (his body having been brought down from Cornwall via the railways), he duly interred with his beloved Laura, in the old churchyard at Remenham. Simultaneously to the funeral those wishing to mark the doctors passing shoehorned into St Marys Church, Henley, the service thus held a dignified memorial to a man who during his long career in medicine had always acted with the utmost care and compassion. Rousing hymns (accompanied by church organist Mr Edward R. Allwright) were sung, psalms 23 and 130 recited, the Reverend J. Bone (standing in for the Rector, who was in a nursing home), paying emotive tribute to Doctor George Smith.

Grave of George and Laura Smith, Churchyard of St Nicholas, Remenham

Doctor Smith who had written what was to be the last draft of his will the year his daughter (Dorothea) had died, never one to forget a kindness. And in recognition of the friendship shown to Dorothea, her father bequeathed the amount of one hundred pounds each to a Mrs Marjorie Ogilvy, and Miss Maude Montford, a favourite nephew of Georges, Ralph James Dalziel Smith, left three hundred Pounds. All monies (held in trust), plate, plated articles, linen, china, glass, books, pictures, furniture, jewellery, wine, liquor and consumable stores, coming down to George Smiths son, Henry George Skottowe Smith, he to, also take possession of "The Oaks".

By the close of the nineteenth century, Doctor Smith having taken Longlands, Arthur John Bramman, in need of lodgings, took a room at 9 Kings Road. Though the boarding house, a terraced property with provision of an outside privy, was not substantial, even with its limitations Arthur to share his lodgings with another, Albert Bristowe Francis, he employed as a stock clerk. Indeed two others also resided at number nine, its housekeeper Sarah Taylor; she assisted by her young niece, Annie Smith. Arthur Bramman, now working within the surgery in Hart Street (alongside medical assistant Edgar Masters), advanced a pace, with his employers encouragement, and having availed himself of books on medicine, he was duly elevated to the position of Doctor Smiths Surgeon Assistant.

By the close of the first decade of the new century, Arthur Bramman, having worked under Doctor Smith nigh on twenty years, quit his job. The next we hear of Bramman he having taken a property, 1a Wick Road, Homerton, Nottinghamshire, Arthur employed as a surgeon's dispenser of medicine; the fellow though now married living apart from his wife.

Arthur Bramman spent his later years residing in a modest house on the Octagon Road, Surrey, and one would think he often thought back fondly on his years in Henley-on-Thames. War, with all its carnage, came and went, Bramman employed within the field of medicine to experience first-hand the dreadful cost of conflict, many soldiers returning home sorely afflicted by physical injuries, and mental trauma.

The Second World War claimed yet another generation of young men, and now in his dotage Arthur Bramman must have despaired of the loss of so many, he to witness VE Day, dying in the care of a hospital, in the winter of 1946.

As coachman and housekeeper to Doctor George Smith, Charles and Fanny Underwood bore direct witness to their master's involvement in the events of the winter of 1893. On the morning that had followed on from the discovery of Kate Dungeys body, Charles Underwood to convey his employer (Superintendent Francis Keal alongside), to Lambridge Farm. And unsure when his employer would next have need of him, it is probable that Underwood remained in situ, possibly sat within the sitting room of Lambridge House, conversing with those present alongside him. If Doctor Smith, not at that time having a wife to share his troubles with, had cause to unburden himself to his housekeeper, the vision of the murdered body of a patient one that he could never have envisaged seeing; we are not privy to what may have passed between the two.

Once George Smith announced that he was to take Longlands, the Underwood's did not tarry long in his employ, they set to leave the area, taking tenancy of 3 Wellington Road, Winton, Christ Church, Hampshire, Charles Underwood, a competent driver, to avail himself of a Hackney License, horse and cab (kept within a rented stable), he thus able to earn his wage as a cabman. The Underwood's to do as many others did, take in a lodger, George Chapman (a carpenter, widowed in his twenties) adding to the coffers.

The Underwood's moved onto 21 Parker Road, Bournemouth, they to again relocate, taking one of a row of houses known as "Chase Park Cottages", in Yardley, Hastings. And here it was that Charles's mental health deteriorated, he admitted to Berrywood Asylum (opened in 1876, a large and austere building designed by one Robert Griffiths), Duston, Northampton.

Charles Johnson Underwood died aged forty one, on Sunday 19th April 1903 (struck down by general paralysis), and with his body duly released by Berrywoods Assistant Medical Officer (Mr J. Beale Browne), Underwood was buried four days after his demise, within Yardley's churchyard. Up until the time that mental illness had robbed him of his facilities, Underwood had worked hard, but in the end there was little to show for his toils, Charles probate, cleared on 13th August 1903, to see Fanny Underwood inherit assets valued at just four hundred and twenty pounds.

So it was that Fanny Underwood found herself husbandless, a young son dependent upon her care; her solution to this dilemma dramatic in the extreme, within months of Charles's demise, Fanny, with her son and her fourteen year old nephew, George Roberts, in tow, taking herself off to America. The three to take tenancy of a small apartment on Twentieth Street, District 34, San Francisco, Charles (maturing into a tall well-built lad) finding work within the ship building industry, as an iron machine shop worker (alongside cousin George), his mother a self-employed nurse.

In later life Fanny Underwood was to find herself short of funds, she therefore grateful of the assistance, in the matter of a place to reside, of the Ladies Protection and Relief Society, an organisation formed in 1853 by a Mrs A. B. Eaton, to assist women and children, those in need given board. So it was, that on Saturday 26th June 1937, in her cosy room, within the Relief Societies home on Laguna Street, San Francisco, Fanny (a grandmother) died, aged seventy four. Fanny Underwood not to be interred adjacent to her long deceased husband, she, at the behest of her son, buried at Cypress Lawn Memorial Park, San Francisco, in the November of 1975, Fannys only child buried alongside her.

Joshua Watts had been admitted into the inner sanctum, during the preliminary investigation into the horrific events that had played out at Lambridge Farm. And although he was not called as a witness for the prosecution, we can little doubt that the post mortem notes composed by Watts, as he assisted Doctor Smith on the Saturday of 9th December 1893, were tantamount to the success of Robert Woods defence argument.

Tailoring provided a substantial income for Joshua Watts, and by the close of the nineteenth century he had income enough to extensively refurbish his familys apartment (10-12 Bell Street), above the tailors. Though several of the Watts children had flown the nest, Margaret, Thomas (a self-employed carpenter), Harold, Wilfred and Gladys remained at home, the Watts domestic needs met by a solitary housemaid, Mary Herbert. The profession of draper, especially for one as skilled in the craft as Joshua Watts, afforded a good return, and thus allowed Joshua's son, Robert to board at a school on the London Road, Basingstoke (Headmaster, retired draper George Freeman Dunn), his brother, Oliver a boarder at a school in Taunton, Somerset, under the pastoral care of Headmaster, Charles David Whittaker.

Initially, from 1903, a Junior Justice of the Peace, Joshua Watts rapidly advanced to the position of Senior JP, a role he maintained up until his death. He to continue in his role as a councillor, with strong affiliations to the Liberals, being the Honourable Secretary of the Henley Liberal Association, and President of the Liberal Club. Indeed Joshua Watts's views were considered so radical, that during the 1899 Boer War, when he spoke out against the conflict, his premises in Bell Street came under attack from those at odds with his stance, Joshua's tailors shop having to be protected by a line of police constables. Watts, a man not to be daunted, by anything it seems, and in 1902, in opposition to the Education Act (drafted by Arthur James Balfour, the act abolishing School Boards in elementary schools, and thus forward placing control in the hands of local education authorities, under the control of the County and County Borough Councils) he refused to pay his rates, Joshua Watts defiant gesture to culminate in his prosecution.

But politics is a forgiving cause, and in 1894 Watts was returned as Henley Mayor, indeed he sat upon the Town Council until 1901, during his time as a councillor persuading William Frederick Danvers Smith to help fund the rebuild of Henleys town hall. A man of the people, Joshua to strive tirelessly to secure both gravel extraction for building, and the land in which to construct houses for the less well-off inhabitants of the town. Many who wielded influence not to find Watts political and social stance to their liking, but Henley Council was not to be easily done with Joshua Watts, in 1904 he re-elected to fill a casual vacancy, he to finally quit the council in 1907.

In 1909 Joshua Watts was elected a life member of the Charity Trust, he its Chairman until 1926, leaving due to deterioration of his health. Watts, in 1920, to succeed to the position of Chairmanship of the Board of Guardians, a role he held until the work of the guardians was taken over by County Councils, local bodies, known as Guardian Committees, thus formed to assist the councils work, Joshua Watts elected as Chairman.

Watts, like many of his contemporaries, had been drawn to the teachings of the Congregationalists, being a trustee of both Henleys church and adjoining school, never one to limit his commitments, Joshua Watts to also fulfil the role of trustee of both Nettlebed and Peppard Congregational Churches.

The census return of 1911 shows the Watts still beavering away at their business (Henley to have at the time twelve tailoring outlets), several of Joshua and Jane's children still residing at home. Margaret, she having no occupation, assisting her mother in the running of the household, Robert, not following the clothier route, working as a mechanical engineer, he a skilled fellow destined to emigrate to California. Harold trained up as a tailor's cutter, toiling alongside his father, his brother Wilfred an assistant outfitter. There one more, who welcomed into the Watts household had formerly been the company bookkeeper, she being Joshua Watts sister, Jessie.

Christmas Day 1923 proved a sombre occasion for Joshua Watts, with the passing away (at their Bell Street home), aged seventy four, of his devoted wife Jane, her interment, on the twenty eighth, taking place at St James's Bix. Jane, she the principal homemaker, had not had the benefit of a wage, but she had saved what little money she called her own, thus set to leave a resworn of just over one thousand pounds. By the time of his wife's demise, Joshua Watts having long since passed on the running of the business to his sons Harold and Wilfred, the first by now a cutter of some expertise, the latter still incumbent on the shop floor. By the time of his mother's passing, Wilfred Watts relocated to Hungerford, where aged thirty six, the year following Jane Watts demise, he died.

Retired farmer, widower Henry Maynard (his wife Agnes dead since the November of 1910) resided at "Maylands", 7 St Andrews Road, Henley-on-Thames. Maynard not to rattle around his sizable home in isolation, he kept company by his unmarried daughter Agnes Edith (born 1864 in Wargrave, Berkshire), the two having benefit of domestic servant, Ada Ellen Shirley. On 18th April 1918 Agnes found herself deprived of her father, his demise, aged seventy nine, leaving her without male protection. But Agnes Maynard was a shrewd woman, and bolstered by her father's estate of some two thousand two hundred pounds, and his former home in which to reside, she managed to maintain her independence, but all that was to change. In the late summer of 1924, sixty year old Agnes Edith Maynard to take a husband, he the recently widowed Joshua Watts, their nuptials held at St Martins, London.

Whether his new wife was an influence over his decision, the year of his marriage Joshua put pay to any ambitions further generations of the Watts may have had in relation to the family business. When, after some consultation with his sons, Joshua Watts sold his tailoring business, run since the time of his grandfather, thus passing into the ownership of Messer's Silvers of Reading.

Joshua Watts, photographed in later life

Joshua Watts had suffered throughout his life from the affliction of asthma, and with old age upon him he took the decision to winter in Cornwall. Thus while down at the coast, in the winter of 1936, Joshua was taken ill with bronchitis, he conveyed to "The Nursing Home", Penzance, even with benefit of the excellent medical care of one Doctor Ponitt, Watts (aged eighty three) failing to rally, he to die in the arms of his son, Thomas, on Thursday 7th January 1937.

The final gesture that Joshua Watts made on this earth, one he had conveyed to those closest to him. Watts funeral service to take place on the Saturday following his death, as he had so wished his ashes (Watts cremated at Plymouth) scattered at sea. On Thursday 14th January, the Henley Borough Bench to sit for a moment of silent reflection, better to think on the passing of their colleague and friend Joshua Watts. A memorial service (led by Mr E. S. Spooner, and the Reverend T. Wilson), to mark the life of one who had given of himself so unselfishly, thus held within the Congregational Church, at three o'clock the following day.

Joshua Watts will was proved at Oxford on 5th March 1937, the deceased leaving a considerable estate of £7,589 0s 2d. Although his earthly remains were scattered at sea, at the behest of the deceased, Joshua's name to be engraved in perpetuity, below that of his first wife Jane.

Grave of Jane Watts (Joshua's name alongside), St James's Church, Bix

Joshua Watts widow was never to relinquish her father's late Victorian property, after Agnes's demise (aged eighty), on 2nd January

1945 (she leaving an estate in excess of twelve thousand pounds), the house converted into a nursing home; aptly named "St Andrew's Nursing Home". Progress makes for an uneasy bedfellow, and with building land in Henley-on-Thames at a premium, "Maylands" is long since lost to the wrecker's ball.

Sixty Four

The Memory of the Just is Blessed

Augustus Jones, retained to sit as coroner at the inquest held at Lambridge House, in the spring of 1907 resigned all his offices, thus forward concerning himself with voluntary works within Watlington. Augustus Jones retirement not to be protracted, the prognosis of Doctor Thomas Hawkesworth (his practice within Shirburn Street) that his patient was suffering from the effects of bronchial catarrh and gouty asthma, said conditions in turn to lead to cardiac failure. Jones to curtail his duties, what time he had left spent in the company of friends, they sat within the garden of Acacia House, reminiscing. Augustus Jones died at home, aged seventy five, on 9th May 1910, present at the death a clerk from Jones's practice, Mr Arthur Lett. It remarked upon, within the regional newspapers that announced his demise, that Augustus Jones had but a few short days earlier (6th May) borne witness to the passing of King Edward VII. Augustus left neither spouse nor offspring to mourn him, his wife, Mary, having died aged sixty two, on Christmas Day of 1906.

Probate of Augustus Jones estate was granted at Oxford on 20th June 1910, the deceases executors, Frederic John George Jones (itemised within the will as George Jones, Augustus Jones nephew, and Bank Manager of the Ashford Branch of the London & County Bank), and Arthur Lett (Clerk to Justices), thus able to distribute the deceases resworn of £22,476 16s 9d.

Arthur Lett (who had not left his employees side during his final hours) was left a legacy of two hundred pounds (free of Legacy Duty), Augustus Jones's indispensable farm bailiff, Henry Figg (he residing in Watcombe Road, Watlington), better off to the sum of one hundred pounds. A nurse, Mrs Gold, who had no doubt cared for either Mary or Augustus Jones (more than likely the wife of William Gold of Davenport Place, Watlington), in due course to find upon her mat a letter which informed the lady that she had benefitted from a legacy of ten pounds. Augustus Jones had so desired that following his death all his held real estate (together or in parcels), should be disposed of in public auction, after expenses and financial obligations were met the net estate to be divided between his nephew and nieces, if living at his demise. Augustus's late brothers children, Charles Percy and Adelaide (their father John Jones), and his late brother (Frederick Hart Jones) children, George, Alfred, Sidney, Nellie and Montague, and the child of his late brother (Alfred Jones), Florence, the principal beneficiaries of their uncles will. Augustus Jones will (witnessed Friday 21st December 1906, by Clerk in Holy Orders, Sidney Charles Saunders of Watlington, and physician Thomas Hawkesworth) to contain within it a codicil, dated 4th November 1909, his coachman Ernest Brown bequeathed the sum of twenty five pounds, Jones servants, Florence Hedney and Annie Tidmarsh, rewarded for their dutiful care of their master with a legacy, equivalent to a year's wage. Rather touchingly, Augustus not wishing to seem indelicate, to leave a Mary Elizabeth Kent Ward five hundred pounds, she his so called live in "friend and companion".

At the Hare & Hounds (just a few doors up from Acacia House), on Wednesday 17th August 1910, at three o'clock sharp, auctioneers Simmons & Sons disposed of Augustus Jones holdings. The lots consisted of twenty three cottages, all of which let to good tenant's accruing rents amounting to two hundred per annum. Six superior houses in Church Street (sold in six lots), their rental values per annum amounting to one hundred and thirty pounds. Twenty acres of land (suitable for building), close to Watlington, much fought over by bidders, the land at time of auction occupied by agricultural tenants, on an annual rent of fifty seven pounds. The last lot to go under the gavel, Augustus Jones former residence, Acacia House, included in the lot the premises grounds, paddock, and orchard, the auctioneer informing interested parties that the property had a rental value of some fifty pounds per annum. Many moneyed men of the area (and some not quite so moneyed) had crowded into the Fox and Hounds, a Mr Charles Carter securing three cottages and three roods of allotment land for the relatively modest sum of one hundred and twenty eight pounds. This same gentleman to have successfully bid for a further cottage located in Chapel Street, Watlington, though a further seven cottages were to go unsold. Mr H. W. R. Wheeler bid of six hundred pounds to see him secure houses located on Church Street, an additional four semi-detached houses, located in Davenport Place, knocked down for three hundred and eighty pounds, to Mr Raymond Hathaway. A lot, which constituted a pair of houses, secured for the sum of two hundred and five pounds, by one of the houses tenants, none other than Mr Henry Figg. The adage it's a small world never truer, High Wycombe based solicitor, Mr Robert Samuel Wood, successfully bidding on Acacia House, he acting on behalf of a client.

Richard Ovey had been no stranger to the Henley affair, sitting as Chairman of the inquest jury, and upon the Magistrates Bench. As a gentlemen of independent means Ovey to have much time on his hands like many a landed fellow he drawn to civic duties. He sat upon the Rural District Council, founded, and stood as first President of Henley & District Agricultural Association, and formed Henley Rifle Club, the fad of rifle clubs dating back to the early 1840s. In 1899 civilian rifle clubs sprang up (the need of which deemed necessary by the heavy losses in the Boar War, those sent to fight possessed of little skill when it came to discharging a weapon), the Volunteer Drill Hall (built by a Mr Drewett), located at Northfield End, to play host to Henleys rifle club. Still finding time to fill, in 1894 Richard Ovey orchestrated the foundation of Henley Swimming Club, river swimming all the rage, he its first President lending his name to the Ovey Challenge Cup, awarded to those victorious in a monthly held race. The magnanimous gestures of Richard Ovey never to be described as a way to stroke his ego, he was a genuine man, and never one to lack in dedication to his causes, as such he eagerly attending all Swimming Club committee meetings, and come rain or shine a spectator at almost every race, competition, and lifesaving drill. 1895 saw Richard Ovey appointed as High Sheriff of Oxfordshire, he a regular at numerous County Council Meetings, a Governor of Henley School, member of the Charity Trustees, and member of Leander Club, as well as Henley Royal Regatta Steward. In 1896 Ovey returned as President of the Oxfordshire Agricultural Society, the gentleman fitting into his hectic life the time required to attend meetings in his capacity as a prominent member of the Henley Board of Guardians (Chairman 1901), possessed of a keen knowledge of the Poor Law. It of course of no surprise that Richard Ovey was a gentleman of Conservative leanings, he chiefly responsible for the organisation of South Oxon Conservative Association, indeed it is a wonder that Ovey was able to keep abreast of his diary commitments.

Richard Ovey was much attached to his Badgemore estate, as such seldom away from it for any length of time, his former home, Northfield House, tenanted out to a Doctor James Lidderdale. The tail end of the 1890s had seen Richard Ovey purchase, from Mr K. R. Mackenzie, the Hernes Estate, which he had thus extensively adapted. Much fond of sheep Ovey acquiring a flock of pedigree Hampshire Downs (a breed developed by Mr John Twynam), that he grazed at Hernes, Richard intending to take them to leading agricultural shows. Much fond of country pursuits, Richard Ovey, a horseman (one of the initiators of the Whit Sunday Tide Horse Parade) from his college days to drive a tandem (a fast vehicle, consisting of two large wheels), and inspired by the agriculture he saw about him, Ovey founded the Henley Ploughing Match, and Root Show, from which Henley and District Agricultural Association sprung.

But life for this vibrant man was not to be a long one, Richard never to show his prized pedigree sheep. Richard Ovey, having been in failing health for some months, in spring of 1902 to make the decision to relocate his family to their London address (15 Henrietta Street, Cavendish Square) for a time, in order that he might seek out the expertise of leading medical men. Suffering from carcinoma of the intestine (it felt by Doctor S. Molier William, to have been present six months) an operation performed to relieve the symptoms, the Wednesday and Saturday then after telegrams reaching Henley to say Mr Ovey was out of hospital, and back at his London address, he progressing as favourably as could be hoped. But on Sunday 27th April 1902 (eleven days after surgery) news reverberated around the town, Richard Ovey, held within the district in high esteem, at the relatively young age of forty six was dead.

On the Tuesday night following his death Richard Oveys body brought down from London via the Great Western Railway, once back in Henley, by use of a horse drawn hearse, the coffin taken up to Rotherfield Greys. On Thursday 1st May a cortege left Badgemore House, amongst its number the mortal remains of Richard Ovey, a funeral service thus held at St Marys Church. At the conclusion of this sombre service, the coffin of the deceased, borne on a hearse (followed by thirty one mourning coaches), slowly wound its way through Henley (many lining the route), and onward to St Nicholas Church, Rotherfield Greys. At the lynch gate of the churchyard the Reverend A. R. Parker (former Rector of Bix), and Cannon Wood, Rector of Greys, to meet the mourning party, all of whom proceeding in solemnity to the graveside, which had been lined with primroses and evergreens. And here Richard Oveys coffin of polished oak, with brass fittings, was interred, the deceases widow, daughter, and one of three sons (eldest and youngest of which officers in the army seving in India, unable to attend), Henley Councillors, and Richards many friends bid one whom they much cherished, farewell. The deceased had in life employed a large number of domestic servants, and these individuals stood at the graveside, amongst their number the estates gardener Mr Hatton (who residing at Gardeners Cottage, had overseen the adornment of his employers grave), and estate bailiff Mr Ginger, they, after the rest of the mourners had dispersed, stood in quiet reflection within the churchyard, Richard Oveys butler, Mr William Chapman, who stood alongside them, fighting to keep his emotions in check.

Thirty first of May 1902 saw Richard Oveys estate cleared through probate, executors James Moss Howson (of Park House, Regent Parade, Ludgate) and Robert Hunt (of the Elms, Stamford, Lincolnshire) charged to dispose of the deceases assets of £320,322 17s, 6d, Oveys personal estate valued in the region of £160,819 12s 14d. Richard Oveys will stipulated that his wife (during her lifetime), act as guardian of her children during their minorities, dividends to be paid to said children at the age of twenty one, or when any married, the monies for this purpose gleaned from property dividends of Richard Oveys brother Henry, who dying 19th June 1881 had bequeathed said dividends to his brother.

Richards widow to have benefit of the sum of four thousand pounds, she entitled, if she so wished, to occupy her late husband's mansion, Badgemore House, having sole use of the lodge, gardens, orchard, stabling, coach houses, and other out buildings, as well as all fixtures and furniture therein, Clara to receive dividends, to enable her to keep up a suitable household. The will, compiled Friday 8th June 1894, to stipulate that Clara Ovey could, if she wished, take and occupy Northfield House, including its outbuilding's, yard, gardens, adjoining meadows, detached stabling, and coach houses in Hog Lane. At the time of her husband's demise, Northfield House tenanted out (its annual rent £50.00), trustees of Richard Oveys will instructed to thus forward seek his widows permission in writing before granting any further lease. Left to Clara Ovey, for her absolute use and benefit, were all her late husband's watches and jewellery, carriages, horses, wines and consumable stores, a Stradivarius violin (left to Richard Ovey by his father) bequeathed to his daughter Constance Mary.

Ovey not to neglect those in need, two hundred pounds bequeathed to the Royal Berkshire Hospital, Reading; a further five hundred pounds left to the Rector of St Marys (Henley), one hundred of which to be distributed by said rector at his discretion amongst the poor of the parish.

Badgemore Estates lockkeeper received twenty five pounds, Richard Oveys agent, Johnloy Keene, left three hundred pounds in recognition of his invaluable service. All domestic staff, who at the time of their masters death in service not less than one year, to find themselves better off to the tune of five pounds each, those in service not less than three years left ten pounds apiece, Richard Oveys butler, William Chapman, bequeathed an additional forty pounds. All servants employed in gardens or stables (bur not farm labourers), in excess of one year, duly to receive five pounds each.

A small plaque of brass adorns one of the interior walls of Rotherfield Greys Church; it marking the passing of a man who having touched many lives was remembered affectionately. "In memory of Richard Ovey J.P. DL of Badgemore, a constant worshipper in this church, who died April 27th 1902 aged 46 years. The memory of the just is blessed." The mortal remains of Richard Ovey lie within the burial ground that encompasses St Nicholas Church, his grave marked by a simple but affecting monument, a cross adorned with intricately carved flowers.

Clara Ovey was to spend the remainder of her life a solitary figure (choosing not to remarry), residing at Cadogan Gardens Chelsea (Badgemore House to suffer the indignity of demolition in 1946), relocating in later life to the "Beeches" Streatley-on-Thames. And here, on Friday 4th January 1924, she died, her unmarried daughter, Constance Mary, executor to her mother's estate of £11,453 11s. 6d.

Many of those who had sat on the Kate Dungey inquest jury were men of commerce, and Henry Lillywhite, no exception, continued to farm his arable lands at Assenden, he able to sustain the wages of seven men and three boys.

Widowhood could prove to be an isolated existence, but it was not to be so for Lillywhite and as old age bit at his heels Henrys daughter, Clementina and her husband Sidney Miles (a farm overseer, he and his wife residing at New House Farm, Thanington, Kent), took him into their care. Responsibility for an aging parent was tantamount within the Edwardian psych, and it was Henry Lillywhites daughter Priscilla, and her spouse Albert Tucker (an insurance agent), who next took up the mantle, Henry appreciative of a comfortable retirement within the household (Marlow Cottage, Rayleigh Road, Basingstoke, Hampshire) of his son-in-law.

Henry Lillywhites last days were spent in the care of his daughter, Clementina, she on hearing of her father's deterioration in health having rushed down to stay at her sisters. Lillywhite (under the care of Doctor Melville, who practiced out of 2 Church Square, Basingstoke) much weakened by profound arrhythmia, and with little available to alleviate his malady, on Tuesday 21st October 1913, in his eighty third year; Henry Lillywhite expired.

It was a sad occasion that found Clementina and Priscilla within the village of Bix, the women on the afternoon of Saturday 25th October making their way to the Parish Church of St James. Many who had been on cordial terms with Henry Lillywhite while he'd resided in Assenden assembled within the church, some of whom previous employees of the deceased. Once the funeral service was done, the congregation to gather within the churchyard and with the afternoon sun bursting through cloud cover, Henrys Lillywhites daughters stood in quiet contemplation, as their father was interred alongside their late mother.

Grave of Henry and Lucy Lillywhite, St James's Churchyard, Bix

After the one day hiatus, required to attend the inquest hearing which had been held at Lambridge House, Enos Clark returned to his job, carrying out the duties required of him as farm bailiff to Mrs Noble. Park Place an estate that had many acres of agricultural land, stabling, piggeries and such like, Clark having charge of the hiring of labourers, whose wages he administered.   One of those Enos Clark had charge of his very own wife, Ann employed within an attractive partially glazed dairy building; Mrs Noble extremely attached to her dairy herd.

But Enos Clark was to later quit his job (his employer Lily Noble in later life selecting to reside at St George, Hanover Square), and as such the four bedroomed farm house that came with it, by the mid-1890s Enos and Ann tenants of one of a number of small flats, located at 52 Bell Street, Henley-on-Thames.

Enos Clark aspired to all things horticultural, and although now in his sixties was needful of a wage, the fellow thus advertising his services as a gardener. The devoted partnership between husband and wife shattered in the February of 1904, with the passing of Ann; she aged seventy two at death, buried on 29th February, following an intimate service, the deceases niece, Kate Alice Orchard, much saddened.

By the turn of 1907 the premises that Enos Clark had called home was the location of the Reading Industrial Co-Operative (run mainly as a grocers shop, and co-owned by members of a co-operative), Enos having relocated to Rose Cottage on the Reading Road, within an area of Henley known as New Town.

Enos Clark died aged eighty two, on Monday 20th January 1913, within Rose Cottage (his niece Kate in situ), from complications of a cerebral thrombosis, his undoing softening of the brain. Though somewhat puzzlingly Enos Clark's burial does not appear within St Mary's Burial Register, which begs the question of whether he was laid to rest alongside his lamented wife Ann. In July probate of the deceases estate granted to an Edward Berry and Thomas Tunbridge (gardener), a modest resworn of £1,198 7s duly divided amongst the benefices.

Kate Alice Orchard (never to marry), who had known much kindness in the care of her aunt and uncle, relocated to 27 Albert Road, she to die aged seventy three, on Saturday 21st April 1928, Kates last days spent as a patient within Henley Infirmary. And so it was that at Henley Cementry, on 25th April, Kate Orchard was laid to rest; her interment certified by George J. Tomalin, this gentleman acting under the remit of the Burial Law Amendment Act of 1880. One of this acts legislations dictating that a named individual could have charge of the burial of a deceased person, notably without a burial service for the dead, so long as not less than forty eight hours before burial a notice of burial had been displayed at the place of abode of the parish rector affiliated to the cemetery, as was the case with Kate Alice Orchard.

By the spring of 1894, and now in his middle fifties, Thomas Octavius Higgs felt that his physical wellbeing was not as it should be, his doctor diagnosing heart trouble, his patients health failing. Higgs, duly advised to reduce his stress levels, sorely needful of a remedy for his ills, to take himself off to Cirencester for a week. But the change of scene proved of little benefit, and so Thomas Higgs next resolved to take himself off to Bournemouth, the Victorian ethos that bracing sea air cures all ills forward in Thomas's thinking.

Returning to Henley, and never one to forgo a bargain, on Wednesday 7th October 1896 Thomas Higgs resolved to attend a house contents sale, accompanied by his wives niece, Miss Amy Bridges (originally from Bath Somerset, at the time in question aged twenty four), who resided with her aunt and uncle. And so it was that the two set off, their journey but a short jaunt across the road from Caxton House, and onward to "Godiva", an ornately detailed detached property, located towards the top end of Norman Avenue. Higgs, upon entering the house, to take an immediate fancy to a particularly fine stair carpet, and having secured the sale volunteered to assist in its removal. Why, with no doubt many healthier men attending the sale, Thomas Higgs chose to unduly exert himself in the taking up of said carpet, is any ones guess. All went well, and in no time the carpet was free of its grippers, but then Higgs suddenly keeled to one side, and before the eyes of his niece, and those milling about, he collapsed sideways, as if in a swoon. All now was chaos, as the stricken man was removed to an adjoining room, where water was splashed on his face, a Miss Maynard sending for Doctor Browne, while Miss Bridges flew off, her quest to summon her aunt. Mr Thomas Octavius Higgs never to utter another word, it soon to become clear to those clustered about him that his end had come. Eliza Higgs did not tally, she while rushing up Norman Avenue, her niece alongside, halted by two men, Mr Miller and Mr B. Hobbs, both of whom having quit "Godiva" on route to Caxton House. With some difficulty, the two men gently restraining her, Eliza prevented from tearing headlong into the house, where Thomas lay prone, she thus spared the sight of her husbands crumpled body, the countenance of which shocking to see. Doctor Browne, having arrived in haste, failed in all his efforts to bring forth life from death (the deceases doctor, Egerton Baines, upon the death certificate to attribute Higgs sudden demise to chronic heart disease), he shaking his head in dejected admission, Thomas Octavius Higgs was indeed dead, this dreadful occurrence to cause much distress amongst those who had attended the house sale.

At nine fifteen, on Tuesday 13th October, James Harper, landlord of the Bull in Bell Street, drew his cart up alongside the lynch gate of Trinity Church (located at the junction of Church Street and Greys Hill), the precious contents of said cart a coffin which contained the earthly remains of Thomas Octavius Higgs. Several mourners (who awaited the funeral party sat within the church), like the deceased, having experienced certain elements of the events that had occurred as a result of the dreadful murder in the winter of 1893. Sat in close proximity to each other, Alfred Austin, Thomas Riggs and Henry Simons, all of whom had attended Walter Rathalls trial, they conversing in hushed tones with the auctioneer of Lambridge House, Mr William Anker Simmons.

At the conclusion of the funeral service (led by Trinity Churches Curate, the Reverend Thomas Leonard Palmer, a lodger within one of a number of letting apartments in Church Street, under the dutiful eye of the properties proprietor, Mrs Henrietta Brown), six employees of Thomas Higgs lifted his coffin atop their shoulders and carried it back to the vehicle that had borne it. The cortege wound its way up Greys Hill, and on into Greys Road, thus in due course pulling onto the Reading Road, its final destination Henley Railway Station. The Order of Druids (Thomas Higgs their treasurer) to meet the coffin, and before it was placed aboard the ten fifteen to Farringdon one of their party laid a wreath of mistletoe upon it.

At Faringdon a second funeral service, led by Reverend Thompson, was held, after which, in respect of the deceases wishes, Thomas Higgs (as reported within the Henley Standard), "amid manifestations of regret and esteem" was interred in a brick grave, where some twenty two years previously his first wife Emily had been buried. The employees of Henley undertakers Tomalins, to nod respectfully at those who vacated the churchyard, and as required thus placed the floral tributes upon the grave, the message card upon the widows flowers most tender. "With deepest regret, in ever loving and affectionate remembrance of my devoted husband, from his broken hearted wife."

Eliza Higgs, mindful of her responsibilities to both her late husband's staff, and his business interests, shortly after Thomas Higgs demise to issue an announcement of her immediate intentions, via the pages of the paper her late husband had run off his printing presses each Friday.

CAXTON HOUSE, HENLEY-ON-THAMES

MRS T. O. HIGGS

Begs to return her sincere thanks to the Nobility, Clergy, Gentry, and inhabitants of Henley and district, for the support accorded her late husband for the past twenty years, and to inform them that she intends carrying on the business for the present.

Mrs Higgs, in respectfully soliciting a continuance of the confidence so long reposed in her late husband, begs to state that Mr Jacob will retain his post as foreman, in addition to the usual large staff of skilled workmen, and that all orders entrusted to her will be executed with care and despatch.

Eliza Higgs (after probate granted a substantial share of her husband's resworn of £2,030 15s 10d) did her late husband proud, but she did eventually dispose of Higgs, in 1897 selling it to a partnership made up of members of the Hobbs family, and a Charles Luker, this chap having a firm background in matters which pertained to the production of newspapers, his father running the Farringdon Advertiser. Indeed Charles Luker had known Thomas Octavius Higgs exceedingly well, in 1894 taking up an apprenticeship at Higgs, Luker just short of turning eighteen. Before the next year was spent the Henley Conservative Newspaper Company Ltd was dissolved, and the ownership of the Henley Standard passed over to a consortium of prominent Conservatives, it likely William Dalziel Mackenzie (resident at Fawley Court), and Archibald Brakspear (resident at Bellehatch Park), amongst them. Charles Luker served the legacy of his former employer well, and by 1901, when the editor left, Luker, still only twenty five, took on the publishing of the paper, on behalf of the partners. Before much more time had passed Charles Luker negotiating business terms with the partnership, and successful in this endeavour acquired the whole of Higgs & Co. Thus forward a sole trader, although it would appear he did not at the time commit to the added financial burden of purchasing Caxton House, the old stomping ground of Thomas Octavius Higgs.

And as for Eliza Higgs, she relocated to 5 Purdown Road, Horfield in Bristol, residing with widows Mariah Smith and Phoebe Kemberry, both born in Timsbury, the first possibly a sister the second certainly one. Eliza to die, Monday 10th March 1919 (aged eighty three), at 8 Downend Road in Horfield, her assets valued at £2,193 6s 5d.

Robert Carpenter Bratchell, who counted himself a personal friend and confidant of George Dawson, no doubt felt much anguish at the irreparable damage done to his drinking companions character. And if the two men ever met up again, after Dawson quit his position as bailiff of Lambridge Farm and thus forward relocated, we will never be privy to any conversations they may have had regards the fallout from the murder of Miss Kate Dungey.

We next find Robert Bratchell mentioned, within the columns of the local paper, in the September of 1897, when he was granted an occasional licence to sell liquor in a field at Lambridge Woods, on the occasion of the annual volunteer prize shooting, to be held on 2nd October. By the conclusion of the nineteenth century, The Red Cross (a late 18th century flint and brick building, now a private house known as Mill End) closed its doors for the last time, Robert Carpenter Bratchell, popping across the road, installed as publican of the Travellers Rest, its former landlord James Yeatman by that point landlord of The Lamb in Lower Highmoor. But Robert was to relocate again, with the building of a public house, constructed in accordance with plans approved by the magistrates. The Travellers Rest, positioned directly in front of the new build, duly demolished, after what was to be its namesake was completed. Thus the hostelry where George Dawson had agonised over whether to awaken its landlord from his sleep (having failed to rouse Robert Bratchell, tenant landlord of The Red Cross), on the night of Friday 8th December 1893, was no more. Standing at the junction of the Toll Road to Nettlebed, and the Old Road to Assenden, The Travellers Rest (the stopping off point for many a weary traveller, farm labourer, and Bix or Assenden incumbent), to give Robert Carpenter Bratchell a sound living. But it too eventually lost out to progress, when in 1939 the elegant late Victorian structure (which apparently still had not benefitted from an electricity supply) was torn down, to make way for a duel carriageway.

But the eventual demise of the Travellers Rest came long after the time of Robert Carpenter Bratchell, he dying on Wednesday 11th February 1903 (aged fifty nine), within his tenancy, from the effects of a cerebral haemorrhage, George Smith the attending doctor. The death of Bratchell, registered by Henley Registrar, one George Albert Stone, marked by the Henley and South Oxfordshire Standard, the paper to carry within its columns a short obituary. Roberts widow, Mary Ann, to carry on as landlady of her late husband's establishment until 1907, at that time relinquishing the tenancy to a Mr William Grove.

Robert Carpenter Bratchell was laid to rest at Bix on Tuesday 17th February, his headstones wording throwing up somewhat of a quandary. Below the dedication to Robert is another, to a Mary Ann Froud, her epitaph, much worn, discernible at only informing us that she died 22nd August (aged sixty three, the actual year of her demise 1914), below the words "Gone but not forgotten", just visible. The only lady, with a local connection, who held this name the wife of William Froud, he landlord between 1909-1914 of the Old White Horse, which was run out of premises 100 Northfield End, Henley-on-Thames. Mary Ann Bratchell had taken a second husband, Mr William Froud (he himself a widower, his first wife Annie having died in 1904), he and his second wife equal partners in the running of the Old White Horse.

Grave of Robert Carpenter Bratchell
Within the burial ground of St James's Church, Bix

The "Henley Murder" had seen husbands and wives drawn into the ensuing investigation, Walter and Annie Rathall, George and Amy Dawson, and Jessie and Louisa Webb. But the adage life goes on was never truer, and Jessie, reliant on the meagre wage he earned as a carter, carried on much as he had done before. Of course those of Lower Assenden had been sorely affected by the dreadful events within Lambridge Woods, many a villager, on leaving their premises, turning to gaze up at a collection of now smokeless chimneys, just discernible amongst the trees. Lambridge House; deserted by its tenant, before long to be given the dubious nick name of "The Murder House", many, who having cause to be in its vicinity to give the property as wide a berth as possible. Not least amongst them Jessie Webb, he often to convey goods, collected from Henleys retail outlets, to customers who lived not much distance from Lambridge Farm.

The turn of the twentieth century saw Jessie primarily employed in the transporting of corn, the Webb's not destined to leave their two up two down cottage at Bix Folly any time soon. Indeed it seemed at the time that Jessie Webb was never destined to move on from his backbreaking toil as a caman, though it more than probable that by the turn of the century Webb had managed to secure ownership of his own cart (if Jessie Webb possessed a horse to pull said cart unknown), rather than being reliant on renting one by the day.

Advanced age did not sit well with that of a carman, many in the trade to suffer from arthritis, and Jessie Webb did secure other employment, he caretaker at Pishill and Stonor Hospital, which opened between 1904-1928 (a joint venture between Henley and Wallingford) was utilised as a Smallpox Isolation hospital.

On Saturday 25th July 1942 Jessie Webb (aged seventy eight) was taken ill (struck down by a cerebral haemorrhage), Doctor George Smith, who though in his eighties, rapidly on the scene, he unable to revive his patient. And so it was that Jessie Webb died, seemingly a fellow tenant of 78 West Street (the former porters lodge of Henleys workhouse, in the 1940s managed by Frederick Goodwin, and used as a meeting venue for Henley Institution Guardians), Mr H. D. Judge witness to the death.

As for Louisa Webb (the death of her only child having occurred nearly sixty years before her demise), she was reunited, aged ninety one, with those she had loved in 1952.

Unlike Jessie Webb no financial concerns caused William Perrin any sleepless nights, he and Eliza at the tail end of the nineteenth century able to live on their own means, residing at 14 Queen Street. Perrin had relinquished his retail outlet in the latter 1890s, a Francis Frederick Fry (who ironically provided take away fried food) taking over the premises. In the early 1900s 14 Queen Street indeed a lively household, alongside William and Eliza their son, William (a drapers assistant), the coffers assisted by boarders, post office clerk Henry George Wyatt Cowdry, and father and son, widower William Weston (a musical instrument dealer) and Alfred Weston, an auctioneers clerk. By the taking of the census of 2nd April 1911 there to be no sign of any lodgers (family or otherwise) William and Eliza Perrin able to enjoy their home all to themselves.

1918 was to be the year that marked cessation of hostilities in Europe, it also the year that Eliza Perrin died aged seventy six. The year that followed not to bode well either, William Perrin fell ill, Doctor George Smith to diagnosis cancer of the colon, his patient in the August to undergo a colostomy.

Cancer proved an enemy that William Perrin could not defeat, and on Monday 18th December 1922 (under the care of his son Arthur) it claimed him. Probate of William Perrin's estate granted on Saturday 17th February 1923 to his sons, Arthur Edward Perrin (photographer), William Stanley Perrin (draper and clothier), and a Mr Frederick Hussey (grocer), the deceases resworn just short of two thousand pounds.

During the two appearances before the Magistrates Bench of Walter Rathall, hostelries in close vicinity to Henleys town hall had been crammed to near bursting, courtroom spectators, reporters, and the plain curious needful of sustenance. The Kings Arms, under the landlordship of John Charles Wheeler, stood but a stones throw from the centre of the drama, and Wheeler, having sat upon the inquest jury, had benefit of direct insight into the matter of the murder of Miss Dungey. And it is therefore no stretch of the imagination to suppose that some who ambled into the Kings Arms were there solely to glean any salacious titbits from its landlord.

The Wheeler's carried on as tenants of the Kings Arms, by the turn of the twentieth century their barmaid Louisa Wise, she a cousin who hailed from Remenham. Though they were not to be blessed with children, the Wheeler's were to experience parenting, they taking on the care of their niece, Ivy Barker, she born 1894 in Swindon, Wiltshire.

1904 saw John Wheeler relinquish the Kings Arms (Ernest Ivor Hewlett taking on the tenancy), he decanting just around the corner to 6 Kings Road, one of a terrace of late Victorian properties, built by locally based brothers, Thomas and William Hamilton.

John Charles Wheeler was not to experience much of the Edwardian age, he to succumb to Phthisis Bronchitis (chronic bronchitis, known at the time as gangrene of the lungs), dying at his home (aged fifty nine), on Thursday 15th February 1906, his funeral held but four days later.

Caroline Wheeler took on the tenancy of 6 Kings Road, able to manage on her inheritance (just short of six hundred and fifty pounds) and financial contributions from her niece Ivy (by now a draper's assistant), and the rent paid over by boarder, Frank Hampden Sheard.

Caroline Ann Wheeler died aged sixty seven on Sunday 4th November 1917, duly buried three days later at Henley Cementry, Caroline's niece, of whom she had been most fond, benefiting from a share of £433 4s 5d.

By the December of 1894 George Albert Stone had relocated to 57 Market Place, where in 1895 he suffered a grievous blow, with the demise (aged fifty seven) of Harriet; she lay to rest on 3rd August, within Henley Cemetery. But Georges mourning proved a brief affair, and after what can only be described as a less than acceptable period, at St Marys on Wednesday 21st October 1896, he married forty two year old spinster Mary Annie Slade (born in Coofe, Somerset), the daughter of butcher, Samuel Slade, deceased. The nuptials were notably low key, witnessed by Sarah Slade (the bride's sister), John Wick, Frances Harriette Gardner, and none other than Doctor George Smith's dispenser, Arthur John Bramman. The newlyweds made their home at 57 Market Place, Mary Ann's sister, Sarah (as a retired court dressmaker not wanting for a farthing) resident, domestic needs of the three met by servant Fanny Plumridge.

Three of George Stones sons were to marry local young ladies, Albert Ernest Brooks (an accountant), on 5th January 1898 married at St Marys, to Minnie Louise Tomlin. Edward (a bank clerk) married at St Marys, on 18th July 1900, to Fanny, the daughter of David Day gentleman. Arthur Sidney married at St Marys on 11th September 1901, to Miss Ethel Emily Wright, daughter of none other than Emily Wright, former neighbour and friend of Mr Henry Joseph Mash.

1910 saw George Stone step down from his numerous professional roles, passing the mantle to Herbert Fostert, who worked out of his home address in Queen Street. Stone having benefit of a goodly pension thus quitting Henley-on-Thames, retiring to Tubney, Wallis Down, Bournemouth, his sister-in-law, Sarah Slade, still very much part of the equation.

George Albert Stone died aged seventy nine (cause of death senile decay and heart failure), on Sunday 19th December 1926, within his last home (a substantial detached Victorian pile), number 6 Oakwood

Road, Moordown, Bournemouth. George Stones widow, Mary Ann, to remain the rest of her days in Bournemouth, she passing away aged eighty one, in 1935.

And what of Miss Sarah Slade, she relocated to 142 Church Lansport, Portsmouth, and there she died on Saturday 14th December 1940, her brother Edwin executor of his sisters resworn of just short of nine hundred pounds.

John Eustace had experienced something most would not, juror at an inquest into a wrongful death. Of course it could well be that as he lived not much distance from Lambridge Farm, Eustace may well have been on cordial terms with Miss Dungey.

John Eustace did not relinquish chair turning, he to take on his son William as an apprentice. But the latter years of the 1890s did see the Eustace's relocate to Badgemore, Assenden, and here it was in 1904 that John was widowed, with the demise aged sixty three of Ellen. Though the lady had spent much of her life in Lower Assenden, Ellen Eustace not to be buried at St James's, she on Monday 25th January, after a brief service at one of the Cemetery Chapels (which fell under the remit of the Henley Burial Board), laid to rest within Henley Cemetery.

Whether it was financial restraint, or down to feelings of isolation, the close of the first decade of the twentieth century saw John Eustace (a master chair maker) a lodger at the Kings Arms in Market Place, his landlady, publican Elizabeth Ann Hewlett, offering rental terms that were agreeable.

It can be said that John Eustace was never going to retire a man of means, but he always possessed the monies necessary to meet his rent. 23 Church Avenue, Henley-on-Thames, where Eustace last resided, he to die there aged seventy five, on 15th April 1928, from stomach cancer (in his last days under the dutiful care of Doctor George Smith), duly buried at Henley Cementry on 19th April.

The census of 1901 has George Frederick Francis living at Manor Farm in Bix (still a blacksmith), his sons, Frederick and Albert, not having flown the nest. By the end of the decade Francis had retired, and thus chose to occupy one of "Clisby Cottages" on the Fairmile (directly next door to Fairmile Cottage), he and his wife still sharing their home with unmarried sons, Frederick John (a pipe joiner, at times out of work), and Albert, a self-employed wood dealer.

Clisby Cottages on the Fairmile, eclipsed by a gigantic tree
One of which the home of George Frederick Francis

Kate Francis died, aged eighty one, in 1922 (her last address given as Lower Assenden), she on 27th March interred at Henley Cemetery. George Francis was not to last much more than a year after the loss of his wife, dying (his son Albert, who resided at May Cottage, Lower Assenden, in attendance) rather ironically at the last address of Jessie

~ 481 ~

Webb, that being 78 West Street. And here we have the solution to why the two men had this address upon their death certificates; it for the sake of delicacy, both Webb and Francis dying under the care of the Henley Institution. George Frederick Francis end came on Wednesday 9th May 1923 (aged seventy seven), the old gentleman much weakened by the effects of a fibroid (a benign tumour), and deterioration of the heart, the second condition of which Henley Unions appointed Doctor (George Smith), could not alleviate.

And what of George and Kate Francis sons, Frederick John has left no discernible trail, but Albert Henry lived out his days at his parent's former home (Clisby Cottages), and here he died aged sixty six, in the autumn of 1937 (buried 19th August), seemingly not having ever had need of a wife.

And as for the twelfth inquest juror, William George Jackson, who on the morning of Monday 11th December 1893, took his place amongst the tightly packed throng of those who were crammed into the kitchen of Lambridge House, he remains as elusive as ever.

Sixty Five

Shops Closed and Shuttered

Colonel William Thomas Makins continued to pursue that which gentlemen of independent means invariably took part in, commerce, politics, charitable works, and sitting within the magistrate court. One particular case a prime example of the more rudimentary side of that required of a magistrate. On Thursday 26th October 1899 William Makins sitting alongside his son Basil (a fellow magistrate), the two confronted with Raymond Nutt of Harpsden Village. This hapless young fellow summoned for riding a bicycle on 8th October without a light, Raymond fined five shillings he could ill afford to lose.

The Directorship of both the Gas and Light Company, and the Great Eastern Railway, dictated that William Makins was often absent from Rotherfield Court, but when in occupation he gave generously of his time. Henley Grammar School, under the Headmastership of the Reverend Philip Edward Tuckwell, boasted a superior reputation, Makins one of its foremost Governors. He in the July of 1901 elected Chairman of the Board of Governors, upon the demise of the previous holder of the position, Canon North Pinder.

Henley's elegant town hall had in the January of 1894 played host to a multitude, spectators crammed into its gallery, reporters squeezed into any available space at the back of its courtroom, solicitors and magistrates sat behind table and upon the bench, but within four years of Walter Rathalls trial the grand old building was to be no more. In the mid-1890s it being much discussed within Henleys Council Chambers, that the building in which town councillors met had become somewhat dilapidated, many of the opinion that it lacked adequate floor space and facilities. Although the town hall had its defenders, who fought tirelessly to preserve the impressive Georgian structure, their efforts were to no avail, and in 1897 Henley Corporation resolved to demolish and rebuild. The consensus being that a spanking new town hall would be a marvellous way for the town to permanently mark Queen Victoria's Diamond Jubilee. And so it was that in 1898 a building, that had graced Market Place since 1796, was consigned to history, but that is not the end of its story. Councillor Charles Clements (he a spectator at the first appearance of Walter Rathall before the bench) had been much miffed by the loss of a building he considered worthy of preservation. And thus with the benefit of a goodly income Clements purchased much of the town halls façade, porticos, balcony and windows, all of which forthwith incorporated into the construction of Clements new home at Crazies Hill.

Architect Henry Thomas Hare had been fundamental in the design of Oxfords recently completed town hall, and he was duly granted the contract to design a civic building for Henley, a subscription system set up to meet the £9,766 cost involved, a subsequent shortfall leaving the Corporation no option but to borrow a further four thousand pounds. Completed in 1901, on the most part constructed of red brick and Bath Stone, the considerable size of Henleys new town hall had necessitated the demolition of both the Grey Hound and Victoria hostelries (a replacement which bore the latter's name built at the bottom end of West Street), where in the January of 1894 hundreds (who had assembled in Market Place to better observe Rathalls trial) had frequented, to avail themselves of a pie, and a jug of beer. Numerous donators had come forward to help fund the rebuilding of the town hall, not least of which William Makins, who'd handed over a considerable sum. Ironically the gala celebration to mark the opening of Henleys iconic new building (which was not universally admired), due to the death of Queen Victoria, postponed until 13th

March 1901, those who attended (William Makins amongst them) adored with black arm bands.

William Makins was a fellow of strong Christian faith (Church Warden at St Marys), and thus he donated generously to Henley Parish Church, meeting the cost of a new organ, twenty stained glass windows (made at the workshops of Lavers & Westlake), choir stalls and a lectern. Services to his fellowman and his country, to see Makins, on 9th January 1903, created First Baronet of Rotherfield.

Into his seventh decade William Makins was as occupied as ever, but illness would curtail him. In the July of 1905 Makins enduring major surgery, from which he failed to rally, the death of his son, Basil, that same year, to further impede Williams recovery. Makins, ordered to rest and recuperate (at the time residing at his London address, 1 Lowther Gardens Middlesex), proved a stubborn patient, but he grudgingly did as he was ordered by his doctor, and confined himself to Rotherfield Court, but all to no avail, chronic pneumonia, which had hampered William Makins for eight months, to again flare up. On the morning of Friday 2nd Friday 1906, William Makins (aged sixty five) woke feeling much out of sorts, and his son Paul, who having travelled from his Henley seat of Chilterns End to be at his papas bedside sent out for a doctor. Medical practioner, William Longworth Wainwright (who resided at Upton Lodge, on the Reading Road) duly arrived, and in the knowledge that his patient had been suffering from pleurisy (inflammation of the membrane that covers the lungs), did his best to alleviate William Makins discomfort, the man before long to slip peacefully away. As irony would have it the day of Makins demise corresponding with the half yearly meeting of the Gas Light & Coke Company, whose Governorship, due to his health problems, Makins had resigned, those attending set to receive news of their former colleagues death before their meeting closed.

On the evening of Monday 5th February William Thomas Makins coffin taken from Rotherfield Court, and conveyed to St Marys, after a brief service, conducted by the Reverend John Frederick Maul (St Marys illuminated with umpteen candles), the Baronet of Rotherfield to pass the night within the chancel, he oblivious to those sat about him in vigil. The next morning saw the funeral, a report, which appeared within the columns of Friday 9th February's edition of the Henley and South Oxfordshire Standard, to best reflect upon events.

"On the Tuesday, just after twelve mourners and towns people had a funeral service. The body was taken in procession to Rotherfield Greys Church, the grave being lined with Lilies of Valley, White Tulips and White Narcissi. The committal prayer was read by St Mary's Rector, with singing provided by the church choir. Williams Makins body was borne in an unpolished Oak coffin, and bore the words "William Thomas Makins, born 16th March 1840, died 2nd February 1906." The mourners included the widow, his son Paul, Commander Oscar Makins, daughters Mrs Clauson, Miss Makins, Mrs Batchelor, Audrey Makins, and the deceases brother Henry Makins.

At the graveside were the Earl and Countess of Clanwilliam, Lord Claude Hamilton, Chairman of the Great Eastern Railway, Sir Hugh Owen, W.R.D. Mackenzie (Fawley Court), Mr L. Noble (Harpsden Court), Percy Noble (Park Place), the Mayor of Henley W. Anker Simmons, Charles Clements, and indoor and outdoor servants.

The trade's people of the town closed and shuttered their shops during the service, and many towns' people gathered outside St Mary's Church. The funeral was conducted by Tomalins.

Simultaneously to the funeral a memorial service was held at Holy Trinity Church, Prince Consort Road Kensington Gore. A memorial service also held at St Matthews Church, St Peters Street, West Minster, for employees of the Gas Light and Coke Company.

On the Tuesday of the funeral flags were flown at half-mast on the Henley Town Hall, Conservative and Liberal Clubs."

The misfortune of the death of one's children had visited upon the Makins, their eldest son, William Henry, at the time of his father's death, dead near seventeen years, the second born son, Francis Kirby, not to have matured beyond his infancy. And so it was that the Baronetcy and Rotherfield Court came down to Paul Augustine Makins, he to receive a share of his father's estate of £99,776 3s 3d. This fellow, when an undergraduate, having taken advantage of his father's involvement in the infamous "Henley Murder" to secure himself a seat within the reserved portion of the spectators gallery, Paul Makins keen as mustard to witness Walter Rathalls second appearance before the Magistrates Bench.

Dame Elizabeth Makins, thankful of the dutiful care of her unmarried daughter Agatha, and the forbearance of her son Paul, remained on at Rotherfield Court, her every whim met by a considerable number of domestic servants, ladies maid Matilda Greenwood, housemaids Emily Hill and Nellie Louisa Merry, parlour maids Ruth Meredith and Dorothy Russell never short of tasks. Household cook Matilda Reynolds (assisted by kitchen maid Pamela Joyce Ockwell) providing imaginative meals, while house boy Frank Buckett, bottom of the run, did as was asked of him.

Dame Elizabeth Makins not to be long parted from her much lamented husband, she dying aged seventy six, on 3rd November 1911. On the Monday which followed Elizabeth's demise a memorial service to be held at St Marys. Amongst the congregation of mourners (which was considerable), Rector John William Nutt (Harpsden Church), Leonard and Percy Noble (Harpsden Court), Miss Freeman (Fawley Court), and John Hodges of Bolney Court. Tomalins, who acted as undertakers, then onward conveying the coffin to St Nicholas Church, Rotherfield Greys, the deceased buried in a portion of the cemetery reserved for the Makins.

Sixty Six

A Genteel Disposition

Chairman of Henley and Caversham Petty Sessions, Joseph Henry Wilson, found himself often required to sit upon the Magistrates Bench, until that is illness took its toll. Wilson had, from its inception in 1871, been the Chairman of the Reading School Board (taking an active part in prize giving at Kendrick School, only ever having missed two events), and as a resilient fellow remained so until two weeks before his death, he resigning due to rapidly failing health.

The demise of Joseph Wilson to come just over two years on from his startling decision to halt Walter Rahall's trial; the gentleman, aged seventy four, dying on the morning of Monday 25th May 1896. Wilson suffered from a malady that had much plagued him, and it was this that was his undoing, Joseph Wilsons heart to arrest without warning, a Mr Francis Carew Charles Barnett (of the Beeches, Wokingham), present at the death. Many clamoured to pay tribute to the old gentleman, Joseph Wilson a man well liked, one anonymous contributor to the local paper to say of him. "A man who took calm view of matters, showing great discretion in management of public matters, he had a magnetic influence over all he met."

On the afternoon of Wednesday 27th May, a plain oak coffin, adorned with wreaths, left "Marchmont", and lifted atop the shoulders of pallbearers (staff of Messer's Morris & Co Undertakers, Market Place, Reading), thus placed within a hearse. After a small interlude, to allow the widow (Henrica's mental wellbeing still delicate), and mourners to be seated in their carriages, the hearse pulled away, off down the drive, followed by no less than five carriages. The cortege to pull up alongside St Lukes in Caversham promptly at two thirty, the mourning party met by Reverend F. J. Greenham (the Bishop of Reading, Reverend James Leslie Randall, also in attendance), who thus forward conducted the funeral in a manner later to be commented on as a touching and heartfelt mark of admiration to one whom he had oft seen within St Lukes of a Sunday.

At the conclusion of the service Joseph Wilson's coffin taken up by the pallbearers, and once reinstated within the hearse, the cortege to proceed to Caversham, where a burial, within the new churchyard, took place. Joseph Wilson deceased had expressly declared his wish to be buried by the side of his late daughter (Wilson also desiring his wife, upon her demise, be buried the other side of him), his grave elaborately lined with Moss, Maidenhair Fern, and flowers of many varieties, provided by close friends of the deceased, Mr F. G. Saunders of the Grove, and General Robert Parker Radcliffe.

Probate of Joseph Wilsons estate duly granted in London (15th September 1896), to executors Alexander Clark Forbes (esquire) of Swanston House, Whitchurch, and Harold Jennings White (solicitor), of Whitehall Place in the City of Westminster, the men charged with distributing the deceases assets, valued in the region of £10,066 10s 9d.

Upon Joseph Wilsons marriage a trust had been set up for the financial benefit of the newlyweds, it so determined that said trust, upon Wilsons demise, be willed over to any children, with the death of Josephs only issue the monies thus held under the control of the trustees. Joseph Henry Wilson to leave his gold watch, with chain and appendages (an item he was immensely fond of), usually worn about his person, in trust to his nephew Sidney Haigh. Five hundred pounds, raised by the sale or mortgage of Wilson's residency estate, and a small sapphire ring, bequeathed to his goddaughter, Alexandra Forbes. Pictures and household furniture, and effects of every description within Marchmont, left solely to Josephs widow Henrica, her late husband wishing her to have use and enjoyment of them during her lifetime.

The servants of the household not to find themselves neglected, though their legacy was reliant on them still being in the employ of their master at the time of his death, Elizabeth Birt, and Annie Harper, set to receive thirty pounds apiece.

Henrica Wilson did not tally long at Marchmont, the property where both daughter and husband had died, she finding a residence to her liking in Windsor, Berkshire. And thus, under an 1895 codicil of her late husbands will, the household effects of Marchmont, and monies held in it (except Henrica's jewellery, which the lady kept in a case within a plate chest) passed into the guardianship of Joseph Wilsons goddaughter, Alexandra Josephine Forbes, daughter of none other than Alexander Clark Forbes. Whether this late amendment to Wilsons will orchestrated due to his concerns that his wife may again require the care of a private asylum, only he to know.

In the third quarter of 1898 Henrica Wilson died, and thus under the terms of their uncles will (witnessed 1st September 1890, by Sam Preston and George Newton, Clerks to the Reading School Board), nieces Ella and Maude Wilson found the residue and personal estate of their late uncle, including Marchmont, placed in trust for their benefit.

Robert Trotter Hermon Hodge, a keen sportsman and pursuer of country pursuits (member of Berks and Oxon Hunt), could often be seen out in the field, a man of diverse passions he just as content upon the lawns of Henley, during Royal Regatta week. There in fact very little that Hermon Hodge did not favour, he a Free Mason, member of some thirty years of the Queens Own Hussars (Honorary Colonel of the Regiment in 1895), and politician, in the 1895 General Election returned as MP for Southern Henley Division of Oxfordshire.

Saturday 20th November 1897 saw the birth of daughter Nora Carol; the child privileged indeed, on 6th August 1902 her father created

Baronet of Wyfold. As if to acknowledge his elevated status Hodge, on 3rd January 1903, under an assumed Royal Licence incorporating into his surname that of his wife's maiden name, although he had formally used the name for several years.

Wyfold Court, family seat of Robert Trotter Hermon Hodge

But the Baronetcy of Wyfold did not provide Robert with all he wished, in the General Election of 1906 he to lose his seat in the Liberal landslide, the Conservatives under Arthur Balfour relinquishing half their seats. But Hermon Hodge was not a fellow to be cast down, he looked forward, and now having the time to pursue other political interests, in 1908 he found himself returned as Chairman of the National Conservative Association (founded in

1867), it being the first formal Conservative association. In 1909 Robert Trotter Hermon Hodge returned as MP for Croydon, after a by-election, in the December of 1910 (Robert's father dying 7th March, aged eighty four, leaving six thousand pounds) he to resign his seat.

The Great War, hard to endure by those left at home, let alone those who found themselves at the front, to leave an indelible mark, Hermon Hodges son, John (Second Lieutenant in the Oxfordshire and Buckinghamshire Light Infantry), killed in action, on 28th May 1915. Never to return to the shores of Britain, the twenty four year old lay to rest at what is now the Rifle House Cementry, Belgium. John Hermon Hodges personal effects (many items of sentimentality found within his kitbag), itemised in probate, their value £116 7s 7d. And if that was not enough to bear Johns brother, Captain George Hermon Hodge (of the Royal Horse Artillery and Royal Field Artillery), set to appear within the newspapers, he reported as wounded in action. All attempts to save this young man to no avail, on 7th July 1916 George to succumb to his wounds, he buried at Gezaincourt Communal Cemetery, France.

In the May of 1917 Valentine Fleming (MP for Henley-on-Thames) was killed at the Western Front, and though the event was a shattering blow to those who knew and greatly respected Fleming, political necessities dictated that his seat in Parliament be filled. Thus in a June by-election Robert Trotter Hermon Hodge, who had suffered much loss and struggled through a mire of grief, was elected unopposed. Politics proved the tonic Robert needed, and distraction from the humdrum raised his spirits, Hermon Hodge, a striking fellow with his distinctive moustache, a familiar sight within the chambers of Whitehall. At the 1919 General Election Hermon Hodge to retire from politics, on 17th May of that same year created Baron Wyfold of Accrington, in the county Palatine of Lancashire, in recognition of his political prowess. So what was a gentleman of independent means to do with himself, Robert Trotter Hermon Hodge never one to idle away his time taking the opportunity to write a book, "The Upper Thames, some Antiquarian Notes", published in 1923. Lady Frances Caroline of Wyfold died on Tuesday 5th February 1929, and soon thereafter her widower (near eighty) downsized, moving into Wyfold Grange, a comfortably sized house on his estate, alongside Hermon Hodge his elderly butler, Frederick George Eke. Wyfold Court in all sense and purposes left uninhabited, but mindful of the legacy he had received through his wife's line, Robert Hermon Hodge was not neglectful of Wyfold; the property cared for by Mr Jim Knight, its grounds managed by a Mr Pitt.

Advanced age was now upon Robert Trotter Hermon Hodge, and he found himself one of the oldest members of the Hunters Improvement and National Light Horse Breeding Society (conceived in 1885 to encourage the breeding of horses in Great Britain, in an effort to combat the huge expense of importing horses, chiefly to be used by the army), by the time of his demise eighteen years Chairman of the South Berks Hunt Committee, and twelve years Master of Harriers Oxon and Berks. Having been connected with racing for over fifty years, Hermon Hodge retired from the turf, his best performing horse, though not particularly successful, Black Gauntlet. Roberts body had begun to let him down (the cause, according to Doctor Leonard Leslie, Myocardial Degeneration, which in turn led to Arterial Sclerosis, damage of the arteries), and his infirmity limited his getting about, but neither the less Hermon Hodge kept space within his diary to attend Henley Royal Regatta, watching the proceedings from a Bath Chair.

On Sunday 2nd May 1937, Major Robert Edward Udny Hermon Hodge of Wyfold Lodge (Managing Director of Luncarty Bleach Works), having spent some time in Nuffield House, Guys Hospital London (a nursing home), died aged fifty five, leaving his ailing father bereft. Death to claim Robert Trotter Hermon Hodge just a month later, he slipping peacefully away on Thursday 3rd June 1937, at his side old retainer Frederick Eke. Succeeding to the Baronetcy, Robert's eldest son, Lieutenant Colonel, the Honourable Roland Hermon Hodge, he married thirty one years to Dorothy, eldest daughter of Robert Fleming of Joyce Grove, Nettlebed.

Numerous newspapers to pay tribute to Robert Trotter Hermon Hodge, the old gentleman fondly remembered for his eccentricity. "His prodigious moustache made him easy to recognise, it swept in a noble curve almost to the lapels of his coat, the deceased having in his long life never left Britain."

So what of Wyfold Court, in the 1930s it was purchased for the sum of eighteen thousand pounds by Buckinghamshire, Oxfordshire, Reading and Oxford Local Authorities, duly converted into a place of residence for those as being (described very much in the terminology of the time) mental defectives. Hence forward Wyfold, renamed Borocourt (reflecting the first letter of each authority that had purchased it), admitting its initial patients in 1932, Robert Trotter Hermon Hodge, it would seem, still residing within the grounds of his former home. Wyfold Court still stands, a resplendent and extravagant acknowledgement to a bygone age, the now grade two listed building converted into luxury flats, with a luxury price tag.

By the turn of the twentieth century General Robert Napier Raikes had relinquished his tenancy of Harpsden Court, spending the initially portion of his retirement at "Stanford Lodge", Park Road, Watford St Andrew, Hertfordshire. Advancing age was not to be kind to Harriette, she an invalid reliant on others, her husband, wishing to alleviate his wife's symptoms, determining that sea air would be advantageous, the Raikes relocating to number 8 Hartfield Square, Eastbourne.

Though he had benefit of coastal living, Robert Raikes was to be troubled by a recurring cough, thus consulting his doctor, diagnosed with severe bronchitis. All efforts to alleviate Raikes condition failed, and pneumonia set in, the old General to fight a last valiant battle, five days on from his initial prognosis Robert Raikes to succumb.

On Tuesday 23rd March 1909, the Press Association Telegraphs News released to the press that General Robert Napier Raikes, "the father of the British Army" had died (aged ninety five) that same day. It duly noted within the countless newspapers that covered the story of Raikes demise, that the old gentleman had "enjoyed remarkable health and vigour for one of his advanced years, his voice sufficiently strong to enable him to address recently an outdoor gathering of school children."

Robert Raikes widow survived her husband by just one week, she dying on Tuesday 30th March. On the eve of her funeral Harriette mirrored the experience of her late husband a few days previous (his funeral having taken place on Friday 26th March) her body conveyed from London by train, thus onward transferred to Long Hope, in Gloucestershire. Mrs Raikes funeral service officiated by Reverend George Barr; then after she laid to rest alongside her dearest Robert, within the churchyard of Long Hope, where once her husband's father had served as vicar. The demise of two so close together an emotive story, and the editors of numerous newspapers included it within their columns, the sad irony that a couple who had spent nearly fifty five years together had died within days of each other, they, "now to repose together in the same grave, in god's acre of Long Hope Church."

The Probate Register of 1909 included within the listings of those whose affairs had been cleared through probate two individuals, one after each other, Harriette Raikes estate in excess of five hundred and fifty pounds, and Robert Napier Raikes resworn a mere £1,610 11s 10d.

1900 saw Henry Brigham Douglas Vanderstegen still sitting upon the Oxfordshire Bench, he not wanting of a wife, living in happy contentment at Cane End alongside his mother (she a lady in possession of a large fortune living very well indeed), and siblings Frederick and Dorothea. The four not lacking in those to assist with the humdrum of running a large house, cook Ellen Pike whipping up imaginative and tasty meals, general servant Eleanor Pike keeping on top (just about) of cleaning and such like, while footman William Pitt provided the right impression when his employees entertained.

The first decade of the twentieth century proved tumultuous, Queen Victoria died, her heir, Edward, an altogether different character. But by the census of 1911 the king was dead (too fond of cigars for his own good), his considerably more sombre son, George, monarch. Life at Cane End carried on as much as it had before, Ellen (now ninety) in the dutiful care of bachelor sons Henry, Frederick and Ernest, and their spinster sister Dorothea. The women of the house having benefit of a ladies maid Lizzie Dell, while Agnes Hopgood, the cook, and general servant, Florence May Rivers, managed the domestic duties.

Ellen Vanderstegen, the matriarch of Cane End, died aged ninety two on Monday 14th April 1913, her personal monies a mere £37 4s 1d, the families main asset (Cane End) passing into the possession of Ellens eldest son, Henry. The late mistress of Cane End, children did not much change their domestic arrangements, it only death that parted the three, William Frederick dying in 1923, Dorothea the year after.

On Saturday 8th January 1939, at the Caversham Magistrates Court, a gentleman and former magistrate was fined ten pounds, with one pound thirty shillings costs, for causing unnecessary suffering to eleven horses, by failing to provide them with sufficient food and water, the gentleman in question one Henry Brigham Douglas Vanderstegen. The bringing about of his disgrace orchestrated by a random workman, who finding himself travelling down a lane he had often trod, spotted a group of horses pawing at frozen ground and licking desperately at ice within a trough, outranged by the plight of the hapless creatures, the workman informing the police. Thus Vanderstegen, who pleaded not guilty, found himself accused of leaving his horses in a field in severe weather between the 19th and 21st December 1938, their water trough frozen over and grass short. In his defence Henry Vanderstegen to assert that when police had visited Cane End, he had ordered said horses brought in, and insisted in a conversation (later given to a representative of the press) that once in the yard his stable hand found the animals did not trouble to drink from a pond, or grab hungrily at hay. Vanderstegen confounded by his conviction, to relay to the reporter, with whom he conversed, the following. "I sat on this bench between thirty and forty years, and in all that time I never knew a more trivial charge of cruelty. If anyone thought that my horses wanted water or food, they should have gone to my bailiff, instead of informing the police."

Henry Vanderstegen eventually got over his tussle with the law, and lived out his dotage at Cane End. In the spring of 1940 Vanderstegen was to suffer from bouts of abdominal pain, a Doctor Reeds verdict, chronic nephritis (a short term disorder that could result in kidney damage in the elderly); his patient to fall into a coma. Henry Brigham Douglas Vanderstegen did not rally, and with Mr A. E. Bowell of 24 Cane End at his bedside, he died (aged eighty seven), on Tuesday 2nd July 1940. Probate of Vanderstegen's estate granted on 10th December, to Mr Geoffrey Simpson Field, Solicitor, the deceased resworn in excess of thirty thousand pounds.

The 720 acre Cane End Estate to be sold in auction on Thursday 5th December 1940, by Messrs Simmons & Sons of Henley, at the Masonic Hall, Grey Friars Road, Reading, the sale commencing promptly at 2.30pm. The main manorial house, having undergone considerable improvements, detailed within the sales catalogue as possessing a panelled dining room, morning room, drawing room, library, seven principal bedrooms, two dressing rooms, five servants bedrooms, domestic offices, and one hundred and eighty seven acres of garden and grounds. The lot also consisting of stables, barn cattle house, cattle open shed, pig stys and granary. There several other lots besides, arable and pasture land of forty two acres, beech woodlands, plum orchard, tenanted cottages, and Cane End Farm with farm house, not to mention fine villa style houses in Kidmore End, and Sonning Common. It may be that the house that had been the lifelong home of Henry Brigham Douglas Vanderstegen did not find itself disposed of in 1940, or perhaps those who purchased it put it back to the market, for on Wednesday 28th July 1943 it again went to auction.

Whether his profession of brewer and wine merchant proved a factor in early 1893 Henry John Simonds doctor diagnosed his patient as having advanced cirrhosis of the liver. The April of 1895 not to bode well for Simonds; he falling ill, his ailment Dropsy, a term used to describe an internal build-up of watery fluid. The unpleasant symptoms of Henrys illness could not be alleviated, and thus he had no option than to resign his numerous civic duties, such as his seat upon the West Ward of the Urban District Council, and his position as Chairman of the Caversham Conservative Association. Henry Simonds possessed the funds necessary to consult the best medical practitioners, and as such Doctor Cockran, Doctor Deane, Mr Walters of Reading, and Doctor Sharkey of London were all to see Simonds as a patient. But it was to no avail, and Henry Simonds deteriorated, Hypostatic Pneumonia (pulmonary congestion, due to stagnation of blood within the lungs) setting in on 17th January 1896. Henry John Simonds died aged sixty seven (Mr Arnold George Dolton, of Thames Cottage, Church Street, Caversham, present at the death) at his home, "The Rectory", on the evening of Saturday 25th January 1896, leaving his wife, one son, and five daughters, bereft.

And as for the burial of Henry Simonds, the deceased had requested, when it finally hit home that all was hopeless, a simple funeral. On the afternoon of Wednesday 29th January, Simonds coffin was carried, atop the shoulders of six pallbearers (amongst them the deceases infallible butler, Mr George Dolton, the estate gardener, and Mr Willis, the deceases coachman) from his residents, through Mulberry Gardens, and onward to a private lynch gate, that led into St Peters Church, Caversham. The funeral party to be met at three o'clock prompt by both clergy and choir. Many of the deceases direct family attended, such as Blackall Simonds (brewer, of the "Priory" Bath Road, Reading), Henry Adolphus Simonds, Lidel Arthur Simonds, and George Simonds (a renowned sculpture), the Reverend Russell Day (of Horsted Rectory in Norwich), as Henry Simonds oldest living friend, overcome by the loss of one he had held in high esteem.

There also present within the congregation two who had benefit of a reserved pew, they sat alongside the Coroner for South Oxfordshire, Doctor Henry Dixon of Shirburn Street, Watlington. These distinguished gentlemen, like the man they came to mourn, having once sat in on a notorious trial, Mr Robert Trotter Hermon Hodge upon the Henley Magistrates Bench, General Robert Parker Radcliffe within the spectator's gallery. The non-reserved pews occupied by employees of Simonds Brewery, and residents of Caversham, these individuals gazing about the chancel, it filled with flowers selected from Henry Simonds own garden. The reporter who covered the funeral to make particular note that Simonds body had been enclosed (somewhat grandly considering Henry had requested a simple send-off) within three coffins, the outer one of English Oak, with oxidised brass mounting, its plate bearing the inscription, Henry John Simonds, born 23rd March 1828, died 25th January 1896. At the graveside the widow to bid farewell, Mary Simonds in the knowledge that her late husband was to repose for all eternity in a brick grave alongside the remains of his first wife, Julia.

The columns of the Morning Post (London), of Tuesday 7th July 1896, carried details which pertained to the last will and testament of one Henry John Simonds, which drawn up on 24th April 1894, contained a codicil, dated 2nd October 1895. Brewing was a good game to be in, and it was no more so than in the case of Henry Simonds, the deceases estate (under executors Henry Caversham Simonds, and deceases son-in-laws, John Muller, and Francis George Caulfield) valued at £147,556 15s 1d. Henry Caversham had been bequeathed his late father's estate, "The Rectory", and one half of shares in J & G Simonds Ltd, he nominated, at the behest of his father, as the companies director. Mary Simonds, the widow, had benefitted to the sum of five hundred pounds, thus forward charged with her husband's Oxfordshire properties (other than the Rectory), she to also receive an annuity of one hundred pounds. Julia Staveley had benefitted from a legacy of one hundred pounds, John Simonds indispensable butler, George Dolton, bequeathed one hundred and fifty pounds. Simonds, it seems, to have had great fondness for his late wife's sister, Madame Pilati to enjoy, during her lifetime, the dividends of two hundred preference shares of ten pounds each, in J & G Simonds Ltd. All Henry Simonds remaining preference shares and half of his ordinary shares in J & G Simonds Ltd, held in trust for his daughters, Mary Muller, Helen Caulfield, Isa Quarry, Mabel Day and Juliette Mabson. Appointed in trust, for said five daughters, ten thousand pounds from funds settled on Henry Simonds first marriage, and fifteen thousand pounds from funds settled on his second marriage, all residue of the deceases property to be held in trust, equal shares of which to benefit all of Henry Simonds children.

Henry John Simonds a man greatly lamented, a fitting tribute to him made via the pages of the Berkshire Chronicle, of Saturday 1st February 1896. "A man who had been involved in Reading public life for over forty years, he having a genteel disposition and public spirit, kind and good mannered."

Mary Simonds took herself off to live with her sister Rosalie Rix, at the "Limes", Somers Road, Reigate, and here aged seventy five, on 21st September 1903, she died, leaving an estate valued at just short of two thousand pounds.

Alexander Clark Forbes, having stepped down from the law, and his seat upon the County Council, filled his time within his capacity as a Bench Magistrate, a position Forbes was never to relinquish. Old age often brings with it various afflictions, and Alexander Forbes (his household staffed by nine domestic servants, under butler Albert Charlton) was not to be spared, suffering greatly from the unpleasant effects associated with renal calculus (kidney stones.) Twenty one days after the first diagnosis of his condition, on Thursday 22nd August 1901 (having seen the demise of Queen Victoria in the January, who his father had so admirably served) Alexander Forbes died (aged seventy seven), at his beloved Swanston.

The weather of Monday 26th August was best described as boisterous, tree boughs bent by intermittent gusts of wind, and garden flowers cowered by sudden and violent rain storms. As the hour approached two o'clock, residents of Whitchurch-on-Thames emerged from their houses, and made their way to the riverside church of St Marys. It later reported, within the columns of the Reading Mercury, that amongst the congregation were, "A large number of the poorer classes, present to testify respect for the memory of one for many years their friend and benefactor." The funeral service commenced prompt at two thirty, St Marys incumbent, the Reverend Canon Trotter, and Reverend Henry Stewart (the widows brother) leading the service. At the conclusion of the closing hymn mourners to make their way to the churchyard, where in stood the Forbes family vault, the approach to which (owing to the ill health of the deceases gardener) having been decorated with white Dahlias and Asters, on a bed of evergreen and grasses, by Mr Excell, gardener to Robert Grey. Widow and her children, supported by an abundance of close friends, stood in silence, as the English Oak coffin which contained the earthly remains of Alexander Forbes was interred, one person's absence all too obvious. Archibald Jones Forbes, son of the deceased, had just over three months earlier been killed in action (died 13th May), a

Lieutenant in his Majesty's South Wales Regiment, the conflict that had claimed him the Boar War, the location of Archibald's demise, Klerksdorp, South Africa.

Alexander Clark Forbes personal estate, in excess of sixteen thousand pounds, once cleared through probate, duly distributed by the executor, Alexander's son, the Reverend John de Burgh Forbes, Rector of Hemyock, Devon.

Having shared near fifty years in the company of her husband, and to witness his interment within the scenic churchyard of St Marys, Whitchurch; life for Alexander Forbes widow was initially a desolate affair. But time is a healer, and the lady, advanced in years, took herself off to Chudleigh in Devon, poignantly the property she settled on renamed Swanston House. And here it was on Wednesday 5th June 1912, Lillias Miller Forbes died (aged seventy nine), surrounded by the children she had borne, a mother well-loved and sorely lamented, her legacy the relatively small amount of £1,349 13s 10d.

In 1896 John Frederick Cooper took over as Henley Town Clerk, a position he would hold until 27th August 1913, thus being succeeded by his solicitors practice partner, Mr Alfred Caldecott. For the remainder of his life, Cooper to serve as Deputy Town Clerk, on February 12th 1908, succeeding Mr Dixon as Coroner for South Oxfordshire. The Coopers had the financial accruement to enjoy the pick of Henley's finer properties, and thus John Cooper relocated his brood to "Sherwood House" (long demolished), a sizable detached house, in the ownership of the Makins of Rotherfield Court.

Like many others of the town considered a gentleman, John Cooper, outside his work commitments, managing to squeeze in an inordinate amount of activities, such as President of the Henley Operatic and Dramatic Society, and Secretary of Henley Royal Regatta (serving for thirty seven years), Cooper resigning in 1919, then after acting as a Steward. In due course John Cooper reached the landmark of being one of the oldest members of Henley Rowing Club (though not a rower), and as such when he passed away the Vesper Boat Club of America carried an obituary within the American press, the deceased fondly described as one, "Beloved and venerated by all who knew him." To which Mr John Frederick Cooper personally wrote to the Vesper Boat Club, to inform them that he was very much alive.

Henley had a plenitude of voluntary roles, filled by those who had the spare time required, John Cooper stepping up to the mark, acting as Clerk of the Governing Body of the recently relocated Royal Grammar School, it previously located at 6 Northfield End, by 1928 run out of Rotherfield Court, former residence of William Thomas Makins.

John Cooper, as head of the firm Messer's Cooper Son & Caldecott Solicitors (located at 2 West Street), attended, on Thursday 26th January 1928, the Borough Police Court, conducting business as required of one who was Court Clerk. Though seeming his usual robust self on that particular day, the day that followed Cooper fell ill, by the Saturday, and feeling no better, taking to the drawing room couch, within his home, West Hill House, which stood directly next door to the Row Barge. Even with the dutiful attention of Doctor Walter James Susman (who diagnosed Gastro Enteritis), the old gentleman did not rally, and on Monday 30th January, at eleven at night, with his sister Janet at his side, John Cooper (aged seventy two) succumbed to cardiac failure. Immediately upon hearing news of Coopers demise, the Union Jack atop of Henley Town Hall, at the behest of the Town Sergeant, was lowered to half-mast, a hastily prepared tribute read out during the County Bench sitting.

John Frederick Cooper's mortal remains left West Hill House on Friday 3rd February, thus conveyed to St Marys Church, a requiem held at seven thirty in the morning, followed at eight by a communion service. Then after a cortege of cars (many of Henleys shop owners spilling out of their commercial premises to pay their respects) wound their way up Hart Street, turned into Bell Street, and continued onward to the Fairmile. At the Chapel within Henley Cemetery a full funeral service commencing on the dot of twelve fifteen, the deceases widow, children, and John Coopers sisters (Misses Annie and Marion Cooper), sat within the front pew. Many dignitaries, wishing to mark the passing of one who throughout his life had served his community, attended the service, Mayor of Henley, Frederick Butler (resplendent in chain of office), stood alongside Aldermen of the County, Borough Magistrates, and those who sat upon the Henley Corporation. Gentlemen of surrounding estates to also pay the widow the honour of marking her husband's passing, amongst their number, Lord Wyfold, Lord Rathcreedan, Colonel Richard Ovey, Colonel Leonard Noble, and Major William Roderick Mackenzie. Stewards of Henley Royal Regatta stood cheek by jowl (the little chapel very crammed) alongside Mr John Herbert Julius Valpy (Head Master of Henley Grammar School); all to later reflect upon a life well lived, as they witnessed John Cooper's internment.

John Frederick Coopers probate duly administered at Oxford on Friday 7th December 1928; leave to divide the deceases effects of three thousand pounds granted to executors, Mabel Bertha Cooper (widow), and John Cooper (son).

John Cooper had worked within the law his whole adult life, and as such his widow was on cordial terms with many solicitors, one in particular, Charles Oak Crisp (a confirmed bachelor, and son of Frank Crisp of Friar Park, Henley) to catch her eye. In the late spring of 1929, after a modest wedding held in Paddington, Mabel Bertha took the name Crisp, her new husband fourteen years her younger. The Crisp's not to occupy "West Hill House", they selecting to reside at "Oxford Lodge", on the Fairmile, also having benefit of Charles London property, 217 Throgmorton Avenue.

In 1946 the shadow of widowhood was cast upon Mabel for a second time, Charles Oak Crisp dying on 10th May (aged sixty eight), a patient at Dunedin Hospital, Bath Road, Reading. Even with benefit of a share of her late husband's legacy of some forty five thousand pounds, Mabel Crisp struggled, her on going welfare coming under the remit of her devoted children.

Mabel Bertha Crisp died on Sunday 8th August 1954 (just short of her ninetieth birthday, still resident at Oxford Lodge), after probate was granted on 15th October, her son, Lancelot Head Cooper, to distribute his mother's assets of £20,452 7s 10d.

Sixty Seven

The Law of Human Nature

Sydney Brain and Robert Samuel Wood were to again lock horns during a high profile case; the matter they retained to examine to touch upon the very concept of Victorian morality. Amelia Elizabeth Dyer placed adverts within various newspapers, in which she described herself as a kindly soul, who much concerned with the welfare of children was only too happy to assist mothers in need of a place of refuge for their babies. The women Dyer alluded to have one thing that set them apart from that expected of motherhood, they unmarried, the trade in which they (through the necessity to conceal an illigimate child), were drawn toward earning the dubious title of baby farming. But many of those babies who found themselves placed into the care of Amelia Dyer were not to have full lives, their corpses, squeezed into boxes, recovered from the waters of the Thames, the infants (in all seven bodies extracted from the waters) lives snuffed out by strangulation, white tape knotted tight about their throats. The first corpse, a baby girl, dragged from the Thames (found by a bargeman, on 30th March 1896) to give the police a lead, within the box that held the body a piece of paper that bore an address, Mrs Thomas, 26 Piggotts Road, Caversham. The constabulary rapidly to converge on said property, and informed by neighbours that Mrs Thomas (her real name Mrs Amelia Elizabeth Dyer) had moved onto 45 Kensington Road, Reading, they headed on to said address; the date Friday 3rd April 1896. The occupant of 45 Kensington Road seemed innocuous enough, but the police under pressure to resolve the case, took the woman into their custody.

On Saturday 11th April 1896 Amelia Dyer (with more evidence come to light, her moral character the subject of fierce debate within countless newspapers), found herself before the Magistrate, who sat at Reading Police Court. And here is the rub, alongside the woman another on charges of complicity to murder, one Arthur Ernest Palmer, married to Mary Ann, daughter of the infamous Mrs Dyer.

Sydney Brain, as in the trial of Walter Rathall, retained as prosecution solicitor for the Treasury, he to instruct solicitor Mr A. Lawrence, in their sights Arthur Palmer. Robert Wood commissioned to defend Palmer, in what was to be one of his most contentious cases. After a full day in court (the facts presented causing much distress to those present within the spectators gallery), the prisoners to be remanded, Chairman of the Magistrates determining that Dyer and Palmer should again be brought before the bench.

What Robert Wood felt about his client he locked away in his inner thoughts, far from public scrutiny, and as all held before the law had the right of a defence, Wood argued his client's case with passion and utmost professionalism. The next appearance of the prisoners before a string of magistrates, under the Chairmanship of Lord W. B. Monck, the day's dramatic events to conclude with Arthur Ernest Palmer being discharged, freed of all burden upon his character, Amelia Dyer not so fortunate.

And so it was that the villainess Mrs Dyer (after an Old Bailey trial held in May), having been condemned by a jury of her peers, looked on as the judge donned his blackcap, and passed down the sentence of death. Thus Amelia Elizabeth Dyer (within Newgate Gaol), on 10th June 1896, met the hangman and his noose.

With the building of an office block on the opposite side of Friar Street (at the corner of Cross Street), Brain & Brain vacated their commercial premises and moved in as one of its initial tenants, sharing the floor space with Haslam & Sons Auctioneers, Miss Annie Butler, artist, and Joseph Morris, architect. The relocation, and umpteen legal cases, to leave Sydney Brain chasing his own tail, he much grateful of the support of Gertrude, she in 1894 delivered of a son, Francis Sydney, a daughter, Katherine Gertrude, born in 1897.

In the latter years of the nineteenth century Sydney Brain set to experience the courts from a different perspective, that of the bench, he a retained magistrate. With political views of a Liberal nature (at one time working to secure the election of Rufus Isaacs), Sydney was indeed much concerned for his fellow man, though he still possessed a steely resolve when it came to the punishment of those found to have broken the law.

Friar Street in 1913, an area much familiar to Sydney Brain

As the old century drew inevitably to its close, the commencement of the twentieth century saw the Brain's relocate to number 8 Denmark Road (an elegant detached Victorian pile), Reading, better to accommodate their growing family, Ernest Walter born 1903, last born, Helen Mary, arriving in 1906. Those of a certain income were duty bound to convey a particular life style, one necessity of which the retaining of servants, and Sydney Brain did not forego this remit, his children having benefit of a domestic nurse, Elizabeth Ilsley, her sister, Caroline Ilsley, the household cook.

The law was a hard taskmaster, and those who worked within it had need of moments of distraction, following the death of his father (John Brain having died at his address, "St Katherine" Russell Street, Reading, on 12th April 1901, leaving an estate in excess of seven thousand pounds), Sydney Brain to write a touching memoriam volume, published by a family member. It was widely acknowledged that there were still those, who though having the benefit of literacy, did not, due to financial restraints, have the means to access the written word. As a member of the Public Libraries Committee (which met at Reading Town Hall), Brain worked tirelessly to promote its services, many a working man at days end able to facilitate himself of a book. Sydney Brain, it remarked upon, certainly to have a great store of knowledge, which he was only too happy to pass on to others, those who found themselves wined and dined at Sydney's table, finding their host a fascinating and articulate fellow. The reading of books a passion of Brains, he enjoyed the factual, but he particularly loved literature, an avid student of Thomas Hardy, whose books he read several times over. And at his dinner parties, with the ladies retired to the drawing room, and the men left to smoke fine cigars and converse, Sydney Brain was never happier than when he could discuss Hardy's literature. Indeed while on holiday in Weymouth (in the September of 1926), the Brain's attended a performance of The Mayor of Caster Bridge, Thomas Hardy himself present.

The futility of war left many deprived of their sons, the Brain's not spared, with the death of Francis Sydney. Captain within the Princess Charlotte of Wales Royal Berkshire Regiment, Francis killed in action on 3rd October 1918 (poignantly shortly before the armistice), his parents and siblings having to content themselves with the knowledge that his body was at least recovered amongst the mire, duly interred at what is now the Cerisy-Gailly Military Cemetery, Picardie, France.

Advancing years took its toll on Sydney Brain, and with his health not as robust as he had formally enjoyed he retired as Clerk to Reading Borough Bench at the conclusion of the 1929 term, Mr S. F. J. Radcliffe saying of him. "One could not help being impressed by Mr Brain's unfailing courtesy, his great tact, and his shrewd knowledge, not only of the law of human nature. He was fair and impartial."

With their children having flown the nest, Sydney and Gertrude relocated to 'Kelvin', 48 Alexandra Road, Reading, and here it was, on 4th February 1939, that Gertrude (aged seventy five) died, her husband of over forty years lost without her.   Deprived of the unfailing support of his wife, life became a burden for Sydney Brain, and a combination of grief and illnesses (amongst them a very severe attack of shingles) kept him from his practice.   It is often said that the loss of a loved one can inflict a burden upon one that is near impossible to overcome, and Sydney Brain did not tally for long, he sorely affected by recurrent gallstones.   What was to be his final illness made itself known on Thursday 12th October, and with his children much concerned Sydney was admitted to a nursing home, in much pain, he found to have an intestinal obstruction (a hazard of gallstones) quickly put under the knife.   The day that followed the surgery, the resident medical practioner (Doctor Jennings), much heartened, his patient seeming much improved, but Brain was not destined to be discharged.   In the grip of illness did Sydney Brain think back on a life spent within the law, did he ponder on those who he had prosecuted within the magistrates courts, men and women once convicted faced with fine, jail, or trial in a higher court.   One man, Walter John Rathall, having some forty five years previously, wriggled out from under, Sydney Brains legal arguments not sufficient to see a man hung.

On Saturday 21st October 1939 (aged seventy eight, he would have turned seventy nine in mid-November) Sydney Brain died, many to pay homage, not the least of which a tribute that appeared within the columns of the local paper. "An outstanding character and ability, often in pain of late, he was handsomely preserved, vigour and eagerness of mind unimpaired."

Sydney Brain's will was implicate, he wished to be cremated, his funeral to be as simple and inexpensive as possible, no mourning, no flowers, and no public service or ceremony. Thus on Thursday 26th October 1939, the Reverend J. Wilfred Massey led a small intimate funeral service, Sydney Brains earthly remains then after cremated at Reading Crematorium.

John Atkins, Ernest Walter, and Katherine Gertrude, named as their fathers trustees, his estate in excess of twenty one thousand pounds thus divided as he so wished. Aware in late summer that his health was failing, and practical to the last, Sydney Brain had resolved to update his will, and thus on 13th September 1939 the elegantly named Mr Owen Wellbelove (solicitor at Brain & Brain), and the not quite so elegantly named N. W. Darby (clerk at Brain & Brain) witnessed their employees will. Katherine was bequeathed one thousand pounds, and a selection of her choosing of her late parent's household furniture and effects, not to exceed two hundred and fifty pounds in value. A Henry Medway and Catherine Ann Barton of Reading, each receiving one hundred pounds, and in recognition of loyal service to Sydney's family, William Dartreed, Benjamin George Vicars, and Evelyn Welch of Reading, better off to the tune of five hundred pounds each. Brains surviving sons, John and Ernest, received their fixed capital in Brain & Brain, and as trustees were given leave to dispose of their father's property, Sydney Brains trusts to be divided in equal shares amongst his children. The last legacy (an implicate wish of Sydney Brain, and somewhat of an anomaly) to benefit a Helena Muriel Gertrude Ryan, of 36 Saint David's Road Southsea (if still a spinster), she set to receive an annuity of thirty pounds (paid twice yearly) so long as she remained unmarried.

John and Ernest Brain took up their fathers mantle (both solicitors), and the practice thus carried on, after almost eighty years, in the spring of 1960, Brain & Brain relocating from it offices at 156 Friar Street, those running the practice finding to their liking a striking premises "Addington House", 73 London Street. This property (within Reading) is to be remarked upon, so much as its original resident, a Doctor Anthony Addington, was in 1751 involved in another notorious Henley murder, that being the poisoning of one Francis Blandy, at the hands of his only child, Mary, she to feel the hangman's noose.

Trinity Congregional Church used to stand on the corner of Sidmouth Street and Queens Road in Reading, the building lost to demolition, the lands upon which it had stood utilised for a university hall of residence. Much of the churches infrastructure was discarded during demolition, some of which appreciated for its historical worth rescued by workers on the site, not least a plaque. Not an item of monetary value, said plague had worth as an object with a strong local connection, and as such was installed at St Marys Minster Church. And so what marked this object worthy of respect, the answer clear the plague a war memorial dedicated to the fallen of the Great War, who had in life worshipped at Trinity Congregional, one of whom Francis Brain, son of Sydney and Gertrude. Here in death lies a link between father and son, Sydney Brain paid tribute by one of his contemporaries. "His personality radiated goodness, no ostentation or self-seeking deflected him from the right course." The following (taken from a poem), included in the same tribute, having in 1918 been used by Sydney Brain to pay homage to his lost son Francis. "E'en as he trod that day to god, so walk from his birth in simpleness and gentleness, an honour and clean mirth."

After the acquittal of his client, Walter John Rathall, Robert Samuel Wood, having been much consumed by the gravity of the Lambridge case, returned to the humdrum, many a solicitor accepting that though uninspiring, rudimentary litigations paid the bills, Robert to have much need of fees, with the birth in 1894 of a son, Brian Robert Philip, a daughter, Evelyn Maud, born in 1898.

The "Henley Murder" was unresolved, but the attention of those who had read all that had found its way into the newspaper columns, was transitory. Murder (an event regretfully not uncommon) sold papers, and Robert Wood, defence solicitor for the government, name often appeared within the tabloids, he retained to represent those on trial for their lives. On Monday 28th October 1905 Lillian Ann Bakers strangled body was discovered in a garden near the Pheasant Inn in Lent Green, Buckinghamshire, a young fellow, Henry Charles Taylor, quickly arrested and remanded on the charge of grievous murder. Aylesbury Assizes to be where Taylor stood trial, Robert Wood retained to defend him, on this occasion his worthy arguments not to prevail, Henry Taylor sentenced to death. Robert Wood, not one to be daunted, worked tirelessly for a reprieve and he succeeded, only for his client (who languished in a cell) to die at his own hand.

Newspaper editors demanded of their reporter's articules that would catch the reader's attention, the "Platelayer Murder" a point in fact. On Friday 28th August 1914 a seemingly innocuous man, one Tom Gilbert (a railway worker at Great Kimble Station) slayed, without apparent provocation, two of his work colleagues (Charles Busby and Walter Tucker), Robert Wood thus directed to offer a defence. His client (a man in the grip of mania) to cause quite a scene at his trial, when dropping to his knees within the stand Tom Gilbert demanded of the judge, legal teams, and those sat in the jury box, to kneel with him in pray. There never any doubt that the verdict returned would be guilty, the judge compounded to pass down a sentence of death. The prisoner had not had benefit of the opinion of an expert witness on mental affliction, but Robert Wood, an advocate who never gave up, in discussion with the judge and prosecution solicitor, managed with mutual agreement to have the death penalty revoked, as his client was clearly quite insane.

The early years of the so called "Edwardian Era" saw the Woods residing at "Sawpit House", Easton Road, the retaining of domestics to convey a level of income and class. And though Robert Wood was not a man easily impressed by such trifles, he neither the less paid the wage of servants, Beatrice Pusey and Elizabeth Culley.

The census of Sunday 2nd April 1911 to give credence to Robert Woods professional prowess, his wife having benefit of a cook, Rose Silvey. Life was indeed good, the girls educated locally, their brother a boarder at "Felstead School", Essex; an educational establishment (with one hundred and sixty two pupils) that accommodated the sons of the professional elite.

Robert Wood was a man most congenial, and those in his employee were glad of it, none more so than Woods right hand man, Mr Edward Woodward. Having honed his expertise on the Birmingham Circuit, Woodward (he and his wife residing at 49 Roberts Road, High Wycombe) had commenced working for Robert Wood in 1905, he in 1908 invited in as a partner.

In no small part due to the challenges of his youth, Robert Wood was seemingly a man of inexhaustible passions, he throwing himself fully into numerous aspects of High Wycombe's corporate, charitable and social whirl. As well as acting as President of Berks, Bucks and Oxon Incorporated Law Society, he also member of the Solicitors Benevolent Fund, Robert to set aside time to do much more besides. A man most vocal on the subject of the welfare of children, he Honorary Correspondent and solicitor to the Society for the Prevention of Cruelty to Children, appearing, without fee, in many cases. Nor foregoing those who did not possess the words to convey their plight; Wood prosecuting in matters taken up in the courts, by the Royal Society for the Prevention of Cruelty to Animals. Indeed Robert Woods civic duties were so numerous one supposes the fellow was always out of his house, he Clerk to the Joint Committee of the Burial Board (a post Robert Wood held until the Wycombe Borough Corporation took over the role), Director of the High Wycombe and District Chamber of Commerce, Chairman Wycombe High School and Grammar School Governors, Solicitor to the Borough Electric Light Board, and legal adviser to the Elementary Teachers Union of High Wycombe and District. So well thought of was Robert Wood, he to find himself invited in the Parliamentary Election to stand for a northern constituency, he after careful consideration (an independent as far as politics went) to decline the invitation. Many cases which involved those of reduced circumstance came across the desk of Robert Wood, he an ardent churchman (entertained many a congregation with his vocalist skills), greatly troubled by the lot of his fellow man, to offer his support to the Friendly Society Movement, a countrywide mutual aid organisation whose members, within an area, each contributed regular amounts of money, it used to benefit any member who had need of it, say for replacement of a lost cow, funeral expenses and the such like.

So what was a solicitor with a bustling practice to do with his downtime, why enjoy a football match, Robert Wood (one time President of the Wycombe Wanderers Football Club, when it was little more than a junior side) a frequent spectator at Coakes Park. Membership of High Wycombe Bowling Club to allow diversion, a club formed in 1902 (at that time located on the Harlow Road) having none other than Lord Desborough as its President, Robert Wood its Vice President. Wood was much fond of cricket (watching not partaking), on most Saturday afternoons during the summer months he to be found on Wycombe Rye, watching a game. As previously alluded to, Robert a champion of public rights, no more so in the protection of open spaces and walks around High Wycombe, a days labours never to be done without he visiting the Rye to feed the ducks on the Dyke, and if the weather allowed to take a walk on the Rye Mead, or Wenover Way.

Photographic portrait of Robert Samuel Wood
Never without a flower within his buttonhole

Many of commerce sat upon a council and Robert Wood did not prove the exception, he to represent the Eastern Ward on High Wycombe Borough Council, duly acknowledged as one of consummate ability elevated to the Alderman's Bench, in mid-1907 nominated and thus forward elected High Wycombe Mayor. Robert never happier than when keenly debating (sleeves rolled up) in council chambers, alongside his colleagues, Councillor William Neville, Alderman Deacon and Alderman Vernor. The human condition is one which can benefit its fellow man or cast him down, the fallout from the 1914-18 war to catastrophically disrupt the homes of many. The call to arms not to go unheeded by the son of the Wood family, he set to join up, determined to better serve his country. Brian Robert Philip Wood (Second Lieutenant of the Seventh City of London Regiment Rifle Brigade) was shipped to France in the summer of 1915, after scant training appointed as an instructor in bomb throwing, Brian, just five days after his initial day within the role to be killed. On Friday 2nd July, while training an NCO, Wood was much perplexed when the young fellow threw a bomb that failed to explode, concerned for the safety of others, and in the knowledge that the device lay in a trench area, Brian struggled through clinging mud to determine what had happened. Whether it was inexperience in the role that caused Woods error of judgement cannot be conjectured upon, but thinking that the fuse had failed to ignite he picked up the bomb. Brian Wood thus, as reported by those who witnessed the tragic event as it unfolded, trying to light the device, but the fuse had held a flicker of life, and the bomb exploded in the hand of the man holding it, a dreadful wound inflicted to head and chest, causing instantaneous death, Brian Woods demise determined as accidental. Robert (who in due course to receive via the military his sons personal effects of just over thirty six pounds) and Theodora Wood, who were part way through a well-earned break in Folkstone, having had the dreadful news conveyed to them via telephone on the Monday, returning in haste to High Wycombe.

On the morning of Wednesday 14th July 1915, at High Wycombe Parish Church, a considerable congregation attended a memorial service. The man they had assembled to remember one Brian Robert Philip Wood, son of Alderman of the town, Robert Samuel Wood of Easton Street. As chief mourner, Robert, though only in his middle fifties, to seem aged, overwrought by the event and valuing the support of his wife Theodora, daughters Nora and Evelyn (affectionally known by her pet name Poppie), uncles and aunts of the deceased, and High Wycombe's Mayor, Councillor John Gomm. Those who held Brian dear had not body to bury (his remains laid to rest in what is now the Mazingarbe Communal Cemetery, in France), but this did not prevent those in the congregation from (during the solemn service), reflecting on a life, like so many others were to be during the war, cut tragically short.

Return to work seemed the best remedy for Robert Wood, and he immersed himself in his practice, the cusp of the next decade seeing him embroiled in another case that the tabloids seized upon. The case in question, the infamous "Whistling Milkman Murder", the accused, one George Arthur Bailey (a milkman), often to be heard whistling a tune while he went about his round. Now Bailey lived at Barn Cottage (located adjacent to the village church), Little Marlow, Buckinghamshire, and at this address Georges wife, Kate Lilian, was found dead, it determined that she died thereabouts on 29th September 1920. A post mortem revealed the lady had succumbed to the effects of Prussic Acid poisoning (more commonly known as Hydrogen Cyanide, a colourless and extremely poisonous substance), and her widower was quickly taken into custody. Robert Wood (again retained by the Crown to defend) put up a valiant argument, he to ascertain that Mrs Bailey had administered the poison herself, she determined to commit suicide, but this version of the events did not rub. The jury, which most notably sitting for the first time (in Buckinghamshire) with women (three in all) amongst its number, to find after a three day hearing the prisoner guilty. Thus on Monday 17th January 1921, having firstly addressed his thanks to the jury,

Justice McCardie turned his attention to George Arthur Bailey. The Blackcap placed upon the judges head, and the sentence of death by hanging passed down, and so it was that on Wednesday 2nd March 1921 (the prisoner never again to be heard to whistle a cheerful tune), within the walls of Oxford Goal, George Bailey forfeit his life.

One of the last cases that Robert Wood defended one less fatal, but still worthy of mention within the newspapers, this case to involve a dog. The Bucks Herald reported that licensed victualler Thomas John Pashley, of the Kings Head in Haddenham, had been brought before the Magistrates Bench, charged, that on 7th January 1932 having not kept a dog under proper control, the creature observed dashing about amongst a flock of startled sheep. Though Robert Wood put up a good agreement his client thus ordered to keep his dog under control, and fined for the fact that said animal was not furnished with a collar, it tantamount in law that such a collar should display an owner's name and address. With sheep worrying also on the cards, and a policeman's time taken up with apprehending said dog, Thomas Pashley left court some five shillings worse off.

Robert Woods name again to appear in print, many editors picking up on a story alarming in nature, which played out over several days had culminated in the death of a man. For some time Wood had found that his health was not as it had been, his doctor determining cardiac debility. But with benefit of an extended holiday to Hastings, Robert returned home feeling more buoyant, and ready to engross himself in his practice, he on Thursday 8th September 1932 to defend a young fellow from High Wycombe, who had been ordered to appear at Marlow Court.

On Friday 16th September 1932, Theodora Wood took it upon herself to visit the local shops and purchase something for supper, deciding upon a pork pie. Early in the evening of that same day, Robert, his wife and daughter Nora sat at table in the dining room of their home "Bedford House", to partake of said pie, Nora, who commented that the gravy had a funny taste, eating very little. Throughout that Friday night all three suffered, but Robert reluctant to fall behind took himself into work on the Saturday, he set to appear at a case to be held at Aylesbury Police Court. But feeling, as he said to his staff "not up to the mark", Wood passed the case over to his partner Mr Woodward, and took himself back home. Feeling no better on the Saturday evening Robert Wood retired early, just one hour after he found to have died in his sleep. The household was thus in uproar, its master no more, and its mistress, Theodora (not having left her bed) critically ill, while Nora also languished in her sick bed. Doctor Huggins was fetched out, and having examined his former patient he determined that the unfortunate Robert Wood had been dead for some half an hour.

With one man deceased, and others in High Wycombe taken seriously ill after consuming food, the Coroner for South Bucks, Mr Arthur Edmund Webster Charsley, instructed to examine the facts. He to first gather evidence from Miss Nora Wood (the lady giving her testimony sitting up in her bed), from that point, having seized upon the remains of the pie, Charsley determining that it be sent to the Home Office for analysis. Robert Samuel Wood (collected by a local undertaker) was conveyed to a morgue, ready for a post mortem, the coroner to so order that an inquest into his demise be held on Wednesday 21st September, this hearing opened and quickly adjourned, so certain organs of the deceased could be examined in more detail. It now the consensus that those in High Wycombe who had fallen ill in a similar fashion to the hapless Wood family, had been poisoned by Ptomaine, a nitrogenous organic compound, produced by the bacterial petrification of protein.

The day following the inquest adjournment (Robert Wood's body having been released to the undertaker, internal organs returned to him), Roberts funeral held at All Saints Church, High Wycombe. And though the weather was inclement many turned out, a sizable congregation of people squeezed into the church. High Wycombe's Mayor, unable to attend, to send as his representative the Deputy Mayor, Mr W. S. Toms, the deceases daughter, Evelyn Maud Wood, representing her mother and sister, who still most unwell could not be present. Many of the legal profession, including Mr H. J. Blaker of Henley-on-Thames (representing the Berks, Bucks and Oxon Incorporated Legal Society), attended the funeral service, several of whom sorely affected by the ironic and tragic loss of one they counted as a good friend. As a touching tribute those at the graveside to drop flowers on the coffin, to reflect the deceases love of foliage, Robert Wood throughout his career never to be seen without his buttonhole.

The days that followed the inquests adjournment were frenetic indeed, the Ministry of Health conducting inquiries into other poisonings with Ptomaine in High Wycombe, the establishment where Mrs Wood had purchased the pie (checked for hygiene), not found wanting.

On Wednesday 2nd November 1932 the inquest resumed, Arthur Charsley ready to hear what had been determined since last he'd sat. The Home Office, through analysis of the pie, had found the contents of it perfectly sound, and its manufacturing process lacking nothing in cleanliness, but there was a sting in the tail. The man who had made the pie innocently ignorant to the fact that he was a carrier of a particular disease, which emanated from the germ concerned in the case. Many who ate his pies had fallen ill, but Robert Samuel Wood, a man of over seventy and somewhat delicate in health, had been unable to resist the germ which entered his system. Doctor Penrose Huggins, who'd, performed the post mortem, stating to the coroner that although his examination had produced no definitive conclusion, the deceased had succumbed to the effects of Gastroenteritis. Arthur Charsley listened intently, and scribbled down snippets of information he would later revisit, and satisfied of the findings he returned a verdict of death through misadventure, with no blame attached to anyone. Charsley further stating in court that it was "an act of god", little comfort to Robert's wife and daughters.

In due course Robert Samuel Woods probate was granted; his estate valued in excess of forty one thousand pounds. As dictated by the terms of his will Woods widow bequeathed two hundred pounds and all the household furniture, plate, linen, china, glass, books, pictures and other household effects. Robert Wood's daughter Nora also receiving two hundred pounds, and her father's diamond ring, her sister Evelyn Maud to benefit from two hundred pounds, and her father's bracelet. A favourite nephew, Karl Roberts, granted a legacy of fifty pounds, his children, Gordon and David, finding themselves better off to the tune of twenty pounds each.

Robert Wood had so desired that his residuary estate be sold, the annuity raised to befit his daughters to the sum of one hundred and fifty pounds apiece. A man who loved his girls dearly Robert to stipulate that an income, to be paid to his widow, be conditional on her providing a home for her two unwed daughters, if they remained unmarried and desirous of living with their mother. If Theodora later was to remarry a legacy to be paid to her from a trust fund, equalling three hundred pounds, with the capital and income of said fund held for her daughters.

And as for Robert Woods practice, Edward Woodward was bequeathed a legacy of fifty pounds, he at liberty to purchase the solicitors premises (8 Easton Street, High Wycombe), and practice, if he so desired. Each clerk and domestic servant, who had been in service continually for three years immediately prior to their masters death, to find themselves in possession of a legacy of ten pounds each. Thus with assets divided according to Robert Woods wishes (his will witnessed on 10th November 1930), the earthly connection of the man, who as a young solicitor had reversed the tide of vitriol against Walter John Rathall, and in doing so saved him from the gallows, was severed.

Theodora Sarah Sophia Wood resided the rest of her days as Bedford House, 19 London Road. She to die aged eighty nine, on 4th March 1950, at the War Memorial Hospital, High Wycombe, leaving her daughter's, Nora and Evelyn Maud (neither of whom ever married), a share of six thousand three hundred pounds.

Sixty Eight

The Matter of One Hundred Pounds

Frank Ayres had been born in the late November of 1893, but the child had not thrived, and soon after a hastily arranged baptism (held on 4th March 1894), Frank died, he not yet four months old. And so it was that on Saturday 10th March, Joseph and Emily Ayres stood in quiet reflection, as their sons tiny coffin was interred at Henley Cemetery. 1896 saw the birth of another son, named Joseph after his father, but this child fared little better than Frank, he dying aged six months, on 30th April 1897 interred alongside his brother.

By the last decade of the ninetieth century, Greys Brewery, situated at the river end of Friday Street, came under the ownership of Messrs Holmes & Steward (brewers, wine and spirit merchants, and mineral water manufacturers), but on Thursday 29th July 1897 the brewery (which owned fifty four public houses, many of which leasehold) was placed in auction. Prospective purchasers crowded into the Catherine Wheel, the auctioneers (Simmons & Sons) gavel to go down in favour of Brakspears Brewery. Thus the Red Lion Beerhouse came under new ownership, but this fact did not unduly impact upon Joseph Ayres, he remaining on as landlord, in 1899 the Red Lion itemised as one of seven licensed common lodging houses in the borough.

On 31st March 1901 the first census of the twentieth century was taken, on the evening of that date a census collector to find himself within the Red Lion, it rooms let out to those possessed of diverse occupations. William Norris earned his rent as a rag and bone collector, one who went from street to street, having use of a cart, collecting unwanted items. It usual for those disposing of said items to receive payment in goods, such as kitchen utensils constructed out of soapstone. Alongside Mr Norris, Henry Prince and William Jones, both employed as bricklayers, across the hall from them John Wyld, a tinker (a repairman who moved from town to town), who having a paltry income occupied one of the smaller rooms. There were others besides, William Smith, a basket maker, able to afford one of the more substantial rooms. John Gengill, a carman (one, who with the use of a hand pulled cart, transported goods), and Frank Shawkes, a carter (a man who conveyed goods with the use of a horse drawn cart), both renting rooms of a modest size.

The Red Lion had borne witness too much sorrow, and on Friday 3rd April 1904 it was again touched by tragedy, with the sudden death (following a short illness) of Joseph and Emilys seventeen year old son, Edward. The lad, fondly known as Edwin, had been a member of the Henley Company of the Oxfordshire Light Infantry; as such a military funeral deemed an appropriate send off. At two fifteen, on 8th April, thirty of Edwin's comrades assembled outside the Red Lion, under the watchful eye of their instructor Sergeant Cennell, and thus forward they followed the cortege, the route lined by many sympatric onlookers. After an emotional service, led by the Reverend Cyril Balmer (Curate of St Marys), Joseph and Emily Ayres bid farewell to their child, Edwin's coffin (enshrouded with the Union Jack) interred to the discharge of three volleys of rifle fire.

Emily Ayres, who had held up so well before a magistrates court during Walter Rathalls trial, died on Friday 18th August 1905, aged forty five, within the family quarters of the Red Lion, and in the arms of her distraught husband. One can only surmise what had afflicted Emily, but perhaps too much grief and loss took its toll, and she fell into drinking, Emily Ayres in due course having been diagnosed with Cirrhosis of the Liver, her health rapidly deteriorating. Doctor Arthur Edward Peake (Medical Officer to Henley Union Workhouse, he practicing out of premises at Northfield End) having attended Emily in the days leading up to her death, his patient exhausted by the effects of pneumonia, the condition that ultimately killed her. Joseph Ayres was inconsolable, his wife the one certainty in all he had endured, a broken man indeed, to attend Emilys funeral on 22nd August.

The licence of the Red Lion expired on 9th June 1906, and after fraught negations with the Licensing Magistrate, Brakspears agreed to close it. Brakspears to receive compensation of three hundred and eighty two pounds for the loss of one of their most profitable commercial outlets, the Red Lions landlord Joseph Ayres on his uppers. Being a premises of some size and promise, and attached to its neighbours, the Red Lion fared better than other hostelries there abouts (many of which demolished), auctioned off as a freehold property on Thursday 15th August 1907. Mr John Chambers, who had, for the Rathall trial, been commissioned to draft a plan of Lambridge Farm, to dispose of the former hostelry at an auction held within the Catherine Wheel. The premises, by now in residential use and let to tenants (Elizabeth Piercey and her children, her husband Richard having died in the January of 1907), producing a gross rental return of just less than fifty pounds a year, many therefore enticed to bid.

So what became of Joseph Ayres once he lost his livelihood, he had not found himself abandoned, Joseph and his son Frederick (twelve years old at the time) moving into 16 Clarence Road, Henley, home of another of Joseph's sons, John, and his wife Mary. Life had not been a bed of roses for Joseph Ayres, but he found stability in the care of his son, by the 1911 census, John Leonard a tea warehouseman, his brother Frederick earning a crust as an errand boy, while their father, a builder's general labourer, found himself a grandfather to seven month old Leonard Joseph.

Near twenty years after a young fellow named Walter John Rathall had absconded (his wife and baby subsequently dragged from pillar to post) from the Red Lion (one wonders if the Ayres ever received the rent owed by Rathall), Joseph, afflicted by shortness of breath, fatigue and dizziness (diagnosed with Mitral Valve Disease), died. Joseph Ayres aged but fifty three to succumb on Monday 25th August 1913, while a patient at the Royal Berkshire Hospital, Reading.

Joseph and Emily Ayres legacy was seen in their son Charles, who carried on the family tradition, he in the beer and confectionery trade. Though technically it was Charles's wife Minnie who from 1900 was the landlady of the Cannon, located at 31 Market Place her husband (a painter and decorator) not averse to lending her a helping hand.

It is irrefutable that Francis (known as Frank) Walwyn Lillywhites evidence, regards the probable time of the attack upon Kate Dungeys person, proved to be key to the dispelling of the evidence against Walter Rathall. Frank did evidentially leave the bosom of his family, the lady who caused his departure, one Minnie Emma (born 1877 in Canterbury, the daughter of farmer George Miles, who resided at "New House Farm", Iffin, Kent), the couple wed on Wednesday 16th June 1897.

The Lillywhite's, by the close of the nineteenth century, relocated to "Cowcroft", in the protractedly named Upper and Lower Elding by Thain, Herdswick Ogbourne, St George, Marlbourgh. Frank Lillywhite, who provided for his family with wages earned as an employed game farmer, to welcome the birth of a son in the summer of 1899, this child to take his father's name, baptised Francis Douglas. It six years before a second child was born; in 1905 the overjoyed Lillywhite's introducing Ronald Aubrey to his elder brother.

Frank Lillywhite, not a man to sit on his laurels, had ambition, and by the latter years of the first decade of the twentieth century the Lillywhite's had relocated to Oxenwood, Hungerford, Berkshire. The head of the household having taken possession of the impressively sounding "Hippenscombe Manor" Frank (a farmer of game) able to more than handsomely support his growing family, a third son Harold

Clifford to be born in 1910, Minnie Emma therefore grateful of the assistance of domestic servant Mary Drewett. Lillywhite was not to make "Hippenscombe Manor" his family's final place of abode, he to take "Flint House", in Goodworth Clatford, Hampshire. With advancing age Frank Lillywhites health broke down, the prognosis of prostate cancer a devastating blow, Frank (aged eighty one) to succumb to his illness on Tuesday 14th September 1954, his eldest son and namesake, Francis Douglas, at his side. Francis Walwyn Lillywhite had excelled in life, and when in due course his sons, farmers Francis and Ronald, were granted probate, the value of their father's estate exceeded seventy two thousand pounds.

Minnie Emma Lillywhite, who mourned her husband deeply, did not tally many years after Francis demise, she dying at "Flint House", on Wednesday 20th May 1959, her assets in excess of eleven thousand pounds.

Though Thomas Good, who had given evidence in relation to wages paid over to Walter Rathall, held down a job of some stature (that being Head Keeper, in the employ of William Mackenzie of Fawley Court), he has left no discernible trail.

And as for Tom and Maria Brown, and her son Frederick Sutton, never to benefit from any of the reward money put up by Henry Mash, and Maria and Frederick vilified upon the witness stand, well they took themselves back up to London.

Now it is never easy to keep tabs on a family when one has a common surname, and the Browns are a point in fact, the last heard of them within the 1901 census, they residing at 5 Lancing Road Ealing, Brentford, Middlesex. Tom, as before, employed as a bricklayer, his wife Maria still up to her elbows in others dirty laundry, her son Frederick, who it seems was determined not to leave home, a domestic painter. The Browns were never to be flush with money, and as with many who found it nigh on impossible to meet their financial obligations, they had taken in a lodger, sixty year old William Crook, who employed as a watchman, patrolled the streets of Ealing, guarding against disorder and criminality.

So here we leave the Brown's, did they ever, in the decades that followed, think back on the startling events in Henley-on-Thames, during the bitterly cold winter of 1893, that gave cause to their names being sullied within the pages of both regional and national newspapers, the length and breadth of England. Who knows, but it is probable that a Maria Brown, who aged eighty died in Ealing during the first quarter of 1928, is the last discernible link to the family.

By the turn of the century Robert Woods resided at 20 Western Road, Ealing, Brentford, Middlesex, with his wife Sarah Anne, and their son Albert Cecil, the lad, who having in the past curiously taken his mother's maiden name, now using his father's surname. Like the Brown's, who resided within the same borough, money was not abundant, Robert as a domestic gardener at the mercy of the seasons, the Woods lodger, Roberts brother Henry, contributing what he could, he working alongside his sibling.

The Woods eventually quit Ealing, and settled at 18 Osterley Park View Road, Hanwell, Middlesex; Robert, as before, toiling away in the gardens thereabouts. 1906 had seen the birth of little Hilda Maud, her unmarried brother Albert (he resolved to again use the surname Dawson) part way through his carpentry apprenticeship. Many, who had possession of a spare room, to take in lodgers, the Woods lodger a relatively young, childless widower, milk dairy cowman, Mr Charles Watts.

1914, a year that would see the outbreak of war, was also to bear witness to the death of Sarah Ann Woods, she dying aged just forty eight, her youngest Hilda deprived of her mother. Robert cut a sorry figure after the demise of his wife, but he had a little girl to care for, and with the support of his friends he was not found wanting.

Robert Woods, never remarried, and thus spent nigh on thirty years a widower, he dying aged seventy five in 1943 (his death registered in Edmonton in the December), near half a century since he had (provided with travel expenses), travelled to Henley-on-Thames, duly annihilated upon the witness stand, never, as with the Browns, to see any of the reward money.

The Daventry Police Inspector, Harry Webster, who had seen straight through the web of lies spun by a somewhat desperate Walter Rathall, carried on with policing, four sergeants and twenty three constables in his division. In 1895 Arthur Harry was born, the childs life short and traumatic, the little boy, hastily baptised on 14th June, dying within Daventry Police Stations living quarters. Though sorely affected by his sons death, there to be some consolation, with the birth in the winter of 1897 of Florence Sophia, she baptised on 9th February.

By the age of fourteen Harry Webster's son, Montague, had done with schooling, but he was a bright lad and as such, on 7th February 1898 he commenced an apprenticeship as a goods clerk, in the employ of the London & North Western, the lad working out of Daventry Railway Station. The role of railway clerk not to be sniffed at, those who secured the position (paid on average forty pounds per annum) needing to pass numerous exams.

In 1902 the Webster's left Daventry, Harry transferred to Towcester, Northamptonshire, where in the late summer of 1907, after twenty seven years and nine months within the constabulary, he resolved to quit the force. Inspector Webster taking the decision to retire while still relatively young, one of his last duties that of the apprehension of a fellow who somewhat rashly had attempted to steal a motor car, which was parked up in a motor works that stood almost opposite Towcester Police Station. So on 30th September, Inspector Harry Webster was done with policing, an article which appeared within the Northampton Mercury paying him tribute. "A model officer, shrewd, active, kind, able and discreet, never was a fairer or more modest generously minded man in uniform."

The Webster's decanted from Towcester, able, in no small part due to Harry's pension, to pay the rent on 23 Archery Road, Leamington Spa Warwickshire. Montague, still a railway clerk, transferred, his sister Florence placed into a local school.

The last we hear of Harry Webster as a working man, is within the pages of Spennell's Directory of Leamington, he a contented fellow, his family about him, working for a modest wage as a dairyman (delivering dairy products), Harry still running his little enterprise in 1926, far removed indeed from his previous profession. And if Harry Webster ever pondered, as he prepared his produce, on the hours he once spent in the company of a suspected murderer, we are not privy to his thoughts on the matter.

The Family Notices of the Leamington Spa Courier, of Friday 19th November 1937, announced that Sophia "the beloved wife of Harry Webster" had died on the eighteenth, in her eighty third year, her funeral held at All Saints Cementry Chapel on the following Monday.

Harry Webster did not much relish life as a widower, and as such his daughter Florence Gould, dearly fond of her father, took him to reside with her at her residence, 8 Lonsdale Road, in Leamington, Warwickshire.

Harry Webster's health was to break down, diagnosed with Dropsy, an old fashioned term use to describe a painful swelling of the soft tissue, due to accumulation of excessive water. A perilous side effect of Harrys affliction, that of his heart being put under immense stain, myocarditis (inflammation of the heart muscles) the diagnosis of medical practioner, Doctor Alexander Kennedy. Thus on Thursday 10th November 1938 Harry Webster, aged seventy eight, his daughter Florence at his side, lost consciousness, and soon after died.

At three o'clock, on Monday 14th November, Montague and Florence Webster stood arm in arm within the All Saints Cementry Chapel, and struggled vainly to hold in check their emotions, during a short but heartrending funeral service, the earthly remains of Harry Webster laid to rest alongside his late wife.

There were some witnesses at Walter Rathalls trial, though their time on the stand was relatively fleeting; whose recall of facts pertinent to the case proved vital for the defence, Thomas Blake's testimony regards a pair of boots a point in fact.

Thomas Blake at the time of the murder had turned twenty, the son of agricultural labourer Robert Blake. Thomas had grown up in a household literally overrun with children, Harry, the eldest born 1864 in Nettlebed, he soon in the company of Robert, and Thomas. Robert Blake followed the work, and as such had taken a tenancy at "Timbers" in Nuffield, Oxfordshire, his wife Mary Ann (nee Hopkins, born 1842, Swyncombe, Oxfordshire) not long after falling pregnant, yet another boy, Joseph John, delivered in 1871, a fifth son, William, born in 1875. A longed for daughter, Elizabeth, arrived in 1877; she soon joined by a sister Mary Ann, her mother's name sake. Farm owners desired the best labourers they could source, many offering as an incentive higher wages than a rival, thus Robert Blake, who wished to take advantage of this fact relocated, he securing agricultural labouring work in Newham Murren, where in 1881 Frederick was born. But that was not to be the end of it; the Blake's, tenants of a property in Satwell, Oxfordshire, to welcome to the family, John, Charles and Kate, her mother's eleventh and last child, she born 1887. Thomas Blake (he had benefit of some schooling) while still a child joined his father working the land, but with space at home at a premium the lad resolved to secure an alternative place of abode, a hardworking young fellow, agricultural work and farm labouring to keep food in Thomas's belly and a roof over his head.

Walter Huzzey, a cowman, had benefit of arable lands at Pudders Farm, Warren Row (a small hamlet of properties positioned on the road from Knowl Hill to Henley), and by the latter years of the 1880s one Thomas Blake, requiring work and lodgings, took a job on the farm, and a room in the farmhouse, the lady of the house, Elizabeth Huzzey, providing nutritious meals.

With agricultural work at the mercy of the seasons, it seems probable that Thomas Blake took work at Fawley Court Farm in order to feel confident of a regular wage, his position that of cowman, with the responsibility of the grazing of the estates herd. And so it was that this young fellow met Walter Rathall (taken on as a beater), the two, near the same age, no doubt conversing regards their lot in life. And seeing the poor state of Rathalls attire, his clothes shabby, his footwear worn, Thomas Blake magnanimously offered his compatriot the soon to be "infamous" pair of boots.

On 13th October, of what had been the year of Walter Rathalls trial, Thomas Blake married, his bride Emily (born 1867 in Remenham, the daughter of William Saunders, a waterman on the Thames), their nuptials held at St Nicholas Church, Remenham, witnessed by two of the grooms siblings, William and Elizabeth. A son, Frederick, to be born the year that followed (baptised at St Nicholas, 26th May), shortly thereafter the Blake's to up sticks to Henley-on-Thames, tenants of one of a row of distinctive cottages (Havelock Terrace), on Gravel Hill. A second son, Robert Edward, baptised at St Marys on 19th December 1897, his life to be a brief one, the child, ten months old, taken by illness in the September of 1898. The death of their little boy to impact greatly on the Blake's, the hastily arranged baptism of 1st February 1899, of their next born, Thomas William, bitter sweet, the baby to die before the day was spent.

The close of the old century signified a change in circumstance for Thomas Blake; he secured work as a timber feller, and in need of premises in close proximity to his place of work relocated his family to one of a row of cottages on the Fairmile. 1900 saw the birth of Sidney John, the little boy, thankfully robustly healthy, baptised at St Marys on 20th September. On 24th August 1902 the Blake's to again assemble around the stone font of St Marys, a longed for daughter, Elizabeth Emily, received into baptism. Emily Blake, it seemed, was predisposed to carry boys, and in 1905 William was born, the year that followed marred by loss. Frank to be delivered of his mother in the late summer of 1906, all not well, the ailing child baptised on 26th August, ten days after he buried alongside his brothers. Child mortality was regretfully not uncommon, but the Blake's had been sorely tested, and the birth of Flossie in 1909 must have been both joyful and heartrending, the family, on Boxing Day, assembled at St Marys, the last born of the Blake's baptised.

Misfortune had not done with the Blake's, conflict set to take another child from them. With war raging upon the battle fields of Europe, Frederick Blake (he upon leaving school having worked as an oilmans errand boy) joined up, he to be a private in the Oxfordshire and Buckinghamshire Light Infantry. Frederick, not yet twenty, shipped overseas in the July of 1915, then after holed up in a trench in France, and here it was that he was wounded. A telegram boy (sent out at the behest of Henleys Postmaster, Charles Henry Honeysett) arriving at a brick and flint cottage, the Blake's informed that their son lay wounded in a French hospital, Thomas and Emily relieved that their child still lived. Hope however turned to despair, when in the November Frederick took a turn for the worst, he dying, aged twenty, on the twelfth, buried at what is now Etaples Military Cementry.

Thomas Blake had those who relied upon him, and life must carry on, and he finally took up a trade that paid a better wage, that of a bricklayer. But Thomas Blake's life had been fraught with challenges, in the January of 1927 he going down with influenza, duly attended by Doctor Harry Lurgan Brownlow. All was hopeless, and pneumonia soon set in, and on Thursday 27th January 1927 (aged fifty seven), in the bedroom of his home, 34 Fairmile, Thomas Blake died in the arms of his daughter-in-law, duly buried at Henley Cemetery, on the first day of February.

And as for Thomas Blake's widow, Emily, having lived through the Victorian age, she witnessed the cusp of what was to be the "Swinging Sixties", dying at 34 Fairmile, in the late autumn of 1961. Though never seemingly called to appear as a witness at Walter Rathalls trial, Emily Wrights conversion with George Dawson, the afternoon he travelled down to New Street to collect Miss Dungey (she nowhere to be found), was a peculiarity that tabloid editors pondered over, this seemingly innocuous occurrence finding its way into the columns of numerous regional newspapers.

Emily Wright was local by birth, the daughter of Edward Johnson (a fund holder), she born in 1852 (baptised 11th August) at the family home, "Nutfield", on the Fairmile. Emily had nine siblings, her mother, Mary Elizabeth (nee Leaver), having initially given birth in 1837 to Eleanor Elizabeth, her birth followed by that of Edward Sadler, Frank, George, and Walter Henry, he born in 1844. A second daughter, Mary, received into baptism at Henley Parish Church, on 17th June 1846, her birth followed by that of Louisa, and Fred.

In 1854 Edward Johnson took on the landlordship of the Angel Hotel (youngest Agnes Harriet born 1855 in the staff quarters), a formerly domestic premises, nestled adjacent to the Henley side of the towns impressive stone bridge. The business proved a profitable one, and Mary, Louisa, and Emma had advantage of a private education (alongside ten other pupils), at a girls school in Bell Street, run by Miss Sarah Lord and Miss Emma Salisbury. Not many escaped the tribulations of sudden illness, the Johnson's to be a point in fact, thirteen year old Emily much sorrowed at the death of her elder brother Frank, he just twenty five dying in the May of 1866.

Emily Wright matured into an accomplished young lady, and once out in society she met a certain Arthur Wright (born 1851), the son of Henley based accountant George Wright. The two married on 1st May 1876, at Hackney St John, Middlesex, the bride's mother (widowed in 1874, now landlady of the Angel Hotel) proud as punch. Arthur

Wright, a commercial clerk in the employ of Brakspears Brewery, took his new bride to reside at a fine Georgian town house within New Street (opposite his place of work), before 1877 was spent the two parents to Ethel Emily. Sidney Arthur was born in 1879, his mother an enterprising young woman, proprietor of a private school (run out of her home), she the principal tutor, assisted by two domestic servants, both of whom shared the name Charlotte, that being Miss Goodall and Miss Heath. There times when Emily handed over responsibility to others, that being when she was confined, Elsie born in 1885, the child to be later joined by siblings, Mabel and Reginald Leslie, he born 1888, his mother appreciative of the assistance of household servant, Annis Watts.

Arthur Wright, employed by W. H. Brakspear & Son's since he'd turned fifteen, was in due course promoted to the position of Wine Merchant Manager, a sociable man, who alongside his wife liked nothing better than to entertain. The Wright's in the fall of 1889 to meet and much like their new neighbour, Mr Henry Joseph Mash.

The appalling events at Lambridge House in the December of 1893 greatly impacted upon those who resided in Henley-on-Thames, and the Wright's were distressed indeed to hear of the murder of Kate Dungey, a woman who in the course of her duties had often conversed with her employers neighbours. After the trial Henry Mash had taken the decision to rid himself of his tenancy of Lambridge Farm, but he kept ownership of his town house in New Street, Henry, his then unmarried son, taking up residence.

Once she had finished with schooling, Emily Wright's daughter, Ethel joined her mother as a school mistress, her sister Elsie employed as a post office clerk. The census return of 1901 to indicate that the school was of modest proportions, at the time three pupils in its care, Maude, Ethel and Willie Reeland (children of William Reeland, a licensed victualler), all seeming as it should be; the truth of the matter that all was not well.

Arthur Wright had fallen ill in 1898, his health then after delicate, by the spring of 1901 he reliant on a bath chair to get about, only able to attend to his job when his health allowed. Eventually Arthur's health broke down completely, and he was confined to bed, where on Monday 18th November 1901, the hour ten o'clock at night, aged just fifty, he died. Emily left gravely affected by her husband's demise, she too emotionally unwell to attend Arthur's funeral, which took place on 22nd November, at the Chapel of Henley Cementry, the service attended by many who held the deceased in great esteem, Henry Mash amongst them. Emily Wright rallied, bolstered by the support of her children, she had a school to run, and with Arthurs estate valued in excess of one thousand pounds, his widow was not unduly burdened with financial worries.

By the dawn of the twentieth century Henley Workhouse dictated that there would be improved provision made for children in its care. And thus under the dictates of the Henley Board of Guardians, such children were placed into mainstream schooling, and provided with more pleasing living arrangements. In 1908 the Henley Union establishing a children's home at Radnor House (Number 37, still in the ownership of Henry Joseph Mash), eighteen children thus decanted from the workhouse, located off West Street. The Kellys Directory of 1911 to itemise Radnor House as one of the "Henley Union Cottage Homes", a Mrs Cleary in charge, Belmont House, a short distance up New Street, also utilised by the workhouse as a children's home. Alongside Radnor House, Emily Wright to toil away within her school, her son Reginald by now an estate agent and auctioneers clerk, Elsie a telegraphist, household chores seen to by domestic servant, seventeen year old Ethel Soar.

In her twilight years Emily Wright relocated to 18 Thames Side, two of her unmarried sisters, Agnes and Ethel having previously made it their home. Old age was not kind to Emily; she afflicted by angina, her doctor, George Smith, advising his patient to not exert herself.

But Emily Wright would not be contained and carried on as best she could, after a particularly bad attack of ill health she confined to bed. On the morning of Monday 7th December 1931, Emily's son-in-law, Albert Ernest Brookstone, who resided at 62 St Andrews Road, at her bedside, Emily Wright, aged seventy nine, to slip peacefully away. The Henley and South Oxfordshire Standard to pay Emily a fitting tribute; she described as one of the towns older inhabitants, well respected thereabouts. Emily Wright, the paper informed its readership, though taken seriously ill some twelve months previous, having been seen walking out on the Thursday morning before her death. And within the classroom of her town house in New Street, having educated many local pupils, they now adults thought back fondly on their old school mistress, Emily Wright's funeral, held just two days after her demise, well attended by those she had taught. Emilys son, Sydney Arthur Wright (an estate agent), and Arthur Sydney Stone (retired Poor Law Officer, and son of George Albert Stone, who had sat upon the jury at the inquest into Kate Dungeys demise) acting as executors, Emily Wrights assets valued at £659 3s 10d.

Both Belmont House and Radnor House (four properties dividing them) were run as children's homes (under Superintenant Mrs N. F. Cave, affiliated to the Henley Union Workhouse) into the latter years of the 1920s, Radnor Houses children (usually numbering fifteen) pupils at Henley's elementary school.

One Herbert Parker, resided at 13 New Street, but seeing that Radnor House was vacant secured the property, he resident by 1935. This man not to enjoy long life, aged but fifty, dying 17th December 1940, duly buried three days later at Henley Cementry. With an estate valued in excess of six thousand pounds, Parkers executor, and beneficiary, Miss Maude Parker, well able to afford to stay on at Radnor House.

When Miss Parker quit is unclear, but we come across Radnor House again in the 1950s, it under the ownership of a Scot, industrial chemical manufacturer Eric Malcolm Fraser, he born 1896. On 21st July 1960 Fraser applying successfully for planning permission to demolish outbuildings to the rear of Radnor House, in order to build a two storey extension, if the work ever carried out unknown, as shortly after Eric Fraser fell ill. Taken into the care of The London Hospital, Stepney, Eric Fraser was not to return to the home he cherished, he dying 9th December 1960. His widow, Joy Frances, who inherited a sizable share of some twenty eight thousand pounds, not to tally long in Henley-on-Thames; she relocating to Cockermouth in Cumberland, Radnor House throughout the early sixties empty and downcast.

The last usage of the property, outside which Emily Wright and George Dawson had puzzled over the unexpected departure of Miss Dungey, was as Radnor House (Henley) Ltd, the company recorded within the London Gazette of 15th January 1976, as having been struck off, and the business dissolved. Radnor House, a sizable detached structure, fine in architectural detail, like so many others of its era lost to progress, demolished to make way for redevelopment.

Sixty Nine

A Motor Trip to Maidenhead

Subsequent to the auction held at Lambridge Farm attention had been thrust upon William Anker Simmons, he to appear within the columns of innumerable newspapers, but here was a fellow who would not countenance gossip, and following the appalling events of the winter of 1893/94, he kept his own counsel regards his thoughts on the affair. 1895 saw William Simmons stalwart efforts as a town councillor recognised, he elevated to the lofty heights of Henley Mayor (1895 to 1896), the year that followed Williams term of office the Simmons' to welcome the birth of Lorna Yvette. A gentleman of commerce, and much respected, Simmons in 1905 finding himself returned to the civic duty of mayor (a role he again fulfilled in 1906), this second term blighted by the demise of his stepmother Sarah, who on 15th May passed away peacefully, in her sixty fourth year. 1908, the year the Olympics came to Henley-on-Thames (rowing events held on the river), William Simmons again mayor (1907-1908), he presented with a canteen of silver in recognition of the logistical tribulations he overcame. The relentless workload had weighed heavy on Simmons shoulders, and not many days after he had fulfilled his mayoral duties, attended rowing events, and civic dinners, William Simmons health broke down.

Charles Simmons had built up a business of implacable reputation, and content that his son's would carry it forward, the old gentleman, now eighty, quit this mortal coil. On 11th March 1910, within Henley Cementry, William Simmons (now recovered from the malady that had laid him low) sorely lamenting his father's passing, he in due course to benefit from a share of Charles's estate of near six thousand five hundred pounds.

Simmons and Sons had been run very effectively out of 18 Hart Street (the former home of maltster Thomas Riggs), but with Crandem Gate now vacate the decision was made to relocate.

Commercial premises of Simmons & Sons
Formally Crandem Gate, home of Charles Simmons

William Simmons (he needful of live in nurse Mrs Emma Masser, a widow well into her seventies) had no need of Crandem Gate, he in possession of "Bird Place", an elegant premises tucked behind wrought iron gates, just beyond the Remenham side of Henley Bridge. Simmons to value his family time greatly, his unmarried daughters, Irene and Marjory, always to greet their father with a warm smile, while their mother orchestrated the running of the household, ably assisted by a highly proficient cook, Louisa Whiting, and housemaid, Alice Gertrude Porter.

Over years William Anker Simmons had honed his expertise in agricultural and land management, a human catastrophe to see these skills put to use. The Great War inflicted much, not least of which a severe food shortage, those within government to create a new role, William Simmons thus appointed Agricultural Advisor to the Ministry of Food. The job was multi-facetted, primarily existing to monitor good practice when it came to growing food stuffs, and once harvested its carefully rationed consumption. Henley-on-Thames, an area heavily relieant on its agriculture, saw its way through the conflict, though many of its sons did not, one more fortunate son, William Anker Simmons, in 1917 awarded a CBE in recognition of his unfailing dedication to that which the Ministry of Food had demanded of him.

In what was to be the last year of the war, William Simmons stood as MP for Henley, but here was a fellow ready to sacrifice ambition if he thought it in the best interest of his town. Simmons thus withdrawing his candidacy in favour of a man he felt more suited, Conservative candidate, Captain Reginald Terrell, who returned victorious in the 1918 election. The cessation of hostilities did not see Simmons (by now a knight of the realm) released of all burdens upon his time, he duly appointed the Official Arbitrator under the Acquisition of Land Act of 1919 (brought in to resolve bitter disputes, regards compensation payments to owners of land requisitioned for use during the war), a role he resigned, due to ill health, in 1927.

Councillors have oft been subject to allegations of self-interest; Councillor William Simmons not such a fellow, mindful of his obligations he to carry out much of worth, such as the improvement of Henleys bathing place, having in his forty eighth year won Henleys Long Swim. This event, which commenced at Marsh Lock, requiring competitors (ladies excluded) to strike out for Hambledon, and once there swim back to Bushy. The year Simmons entered the race (1906) to see him in the chilled (and not too clean) waters of the Thames a full four hours, his colleagues on the Thames Conservancy Board (there were not many organisations Simmons had no bearing on) cheering him on. In 1921 the Town Council conferred William Simmons with Freedom of the Borough, and much taken with the maintenance of law he often sat as a County Magistrate for Berkshire. Honours were indeed showered down on William Simmons, 1924 he appointed Lord Chief Justice and Master of the Rolls, as well as President of the Surveyors Institute.

Simmons health scares left his children much concerned for their father, and William somewhat reluctantly agreed to a period of rest and recuperation (his maladies anncular fibrillation, a disorder of the heart muscles, and nephritis, an old term used to describe kidney inflammation), away from the vigour's of work. But here was a strong minded individual, this trait sadly to prove William Simmons downfall. The early morning of Thursday 20th October 1927 saw the commencement of a glorious day, and Simmons much gladdened by an upturn in the weather resolved to motor to Maidenhead, wishing to honour an appointment with his tailor. And thus William Simmons arrived at the home of his daughter, Lorna's residence "The Hermitage", Vicarage Road, in Henley. All went well, and the late afternoon saw William, much heartened by a pleasant days driving, decant from his vehicle and stride into the foyer of The Hermitage. But suddenly, and without warning, Simmons staggered, his arm flung out in search of support, without a word uttered he collapsing, and before those about him could summon a doctor, William Anker Simmons (fifteen days since his seventieth birthday) was gone. Doctor Walter Susman (in partnership with Doctor George Smith) arrived in due course, and looked upon his former patient, he of the option that a catastrophic cardiac dilation had caused such a rapid demise.

On Saturday 22nd October 1927 a hearse pulled up adjacent to the front porch of The Hermitage, and in due course a column of people assembled behind it. The casket that lay within the hearse to contain the mortal remains of William Anker Simmons, he to commence his final journey through the streets he had often trudged in life. With the rain intermittently falling, the cortege travelled past heavily lined streets, many having vacated home and workplace to pay their respects. Once reaching the Reading Road, those of the Freemasons joined the cortege, the deceased (three times their Worshipful Master) having helped found the Wargrave and Caversham Lodges.

On into Duke Street, and right into Hart Street, the hearse eventually reached St Marys, its incumbent Canon Allen Edward Dams greeting the mourning party. The appointed hour of the funeral service to see almost all the town businesses suspend trade, while shop owners and customers converged in Hart Street, flags on municipal buildings (flown at half-mast), fluttering gently in the breeze, the sun, on occasion, valiantly breaking through the rain.

William Simmons had desired, when his time came, to be conveyed to his burial within the churchyard of St Nicholas, Remenham, upon the river he so loved (River Thames), and his wish did not go unheeded, at the conclusion of the church service the coffin conveyed to the water's edge. A barge thus drawn up alongside the riverbank of Red Lion Lawn, and the coffin (once down a flight of steep steps), greeted by a guard of honour of local lock keepers, lifted on board. The sorrowful journey (the bells of St Mary's tolling mournfully) to the grave thus commenced, with the Simmons family following behind in a launch.

Landing at the Remenham side of the Thames, Simmons casket met by Reverend Stephen Charles Rees, the coffin conveyed onward to the churchyard of Remenham. The grave, dug that morning, other worldly, beautifully adorned with Moss and Daisies grown by the staff of Culham Court, and interred within said William Anker Simmons bid farewell to this earth, members of the Masonic Brethren dropping sprigs of Acacia (emblematic sprig of the Masons) atop the coffin, one mourner remembering Simmons as such. "The best loved man in Henley, his business abilities, his general manner, his broad mindedness and his kindly sympathy with all who approached him in any kind of trouble, had earned him a great affection from people of all classes."

The third of February 1928 to see the completion of William Anker Simmons probate (executors Egerton Peel Merton, mining engineer, and Charles Carryll Baker, Chartered Accountant), the deceased leaving an estate to the value of £20,832 18s.

Dame Edith Nora Simmons never quit "Bird Place", and aged seventy six, on Wednesday 18th May 1932, she died.

Seventy

Misfortunes of Circumstance

And what of those closest to Walter Rathall, Emilys (Walters half-sister, who had fervently refused to engage with those of the press, on the subject of her siblings predicament) husband, Robert Parker (by the close of the century in his late sixties), still pursued the demanding jobs of both wheelwright and carpenter, he father to a young daughter mindful of his responsibilities. Robert Parker died aged seventy seven, on 18th January 1907, at his home in Lower Assenden, his widow to benefit from the somewhat meagre sum of forty pounds. Staying on at her cottage in Bix Folly, Emily (her neighbours, the Millington's, helpful kindly folk) managing to cover the rent from wages she earned as a cook. Her daughter, Violet (fourteen at the time of her father's demise), like many girls of similar background in service, a general domestic at "Bix Hill House", under its housekeeper Hannah Watts, both women in the employ of a Mr Rawlinson.

It was reported on 14th April 1894 (via a Representative of the Press), that Walter John Rathall still resided in Henley-on-Thames, he, wife and child, taken in hand by the Society of Friends. The Rathalls, Walter with no employment and probably no prospect of gaining any in the foreseeable, through the generosity of the Society of Friends, furnished with a cottage, possibly situated at Northfield End. With the assistance of Charles Singer, and his fellow Quakers, Walter Rathall able to move on from the life shattering events that had ensnared him (one wonders how long the money thrust into his hands, as he had left court a free man, had lasted), he, Annie and Catherine, not long after resolved to quit Henley-on-Thames.

There is no doubt whatever that living so close to the location of all his woes was not one Walter would have relished, and it is no surprise that the Rathall's took themselves off to Annie's parent's home, in Hereford, Hertfordshire. Annie Rathall had borne much, she shortly after her husband's acquittal falling pregnant, Edith Maud born at 10 Berrington Street (home of Annie's father, William Long), on 13th November 1894, there no upturn in fortunes, following the birth of the Rathalls second child. It cannot be ascertained if it was as a result of financial hardship, or possibly the disintegration of Walter (he a domestic gardener, taking work where he could find it) and Annie's marriage, but little Edith Maud was not to be reared by her kinsfolk, she given up for adoption, the arrangement an informal one.

William Lewis resided on the Bath Road, Stratton, Midsomer Norton, Somerset, he a blacksmith. Towards the close of the 1870s William to take tenancy (within Midsomer Norton) of a cottage affiliated to Downside College, and here he took as an apprentice his son Joseph Benedict, the lad born on 23rd January 1868 in Belmont, Hereford.

Joseph Lewis worked hard, and by his early twenties a proficient blacksmith he resolved to marry. Thus in the spring of 1890 Lewis took as his wife Lillie Emma Tyler (born 1866, Writhlington, Somerset), the newlyweds tenants of a property on the Frome Road, Midsomer Norton.

It is not possible to conjecture how long Edith Maud remained in the care of her parents; but she was more than likely placed for adoption before the nineteenth century was spent. This little girl resurfaces within the 1901 census (taken Sunday 31st March), classified as an adopted child, Edith in the care of childless couple, Joseph and Lillie Lewis. As both William Lewis and his son Joseph had been born in Hereford, and subsequently spent some years there, they may have been on familiar terms with the Long's, indeed at the time of Edith's adoption many informal adoption arrangements were made between those known to each other.

But the little girl, who had enjoyed stability in the care of her adoptive parents (the family resided in Brewery Yard, Midsomer Norton, Joseph a blacksmith in the employ of Welton Breweries Ltd), was to have it snatched away; Lillie Emma dying aged forty one, in the summer of 1907. Joseph Lewis not to relish widowhood; he taking a second wife, Julia, the newlyweds settling at 3 Fosseway House, Fosse Road, Clandown, Radstock, Somerset.

If Edith Maud Rathall ever lived with Joseph and Julia, she was not to appear upon their census return of 1911 and her whereabouts not then or since being established, the only tangible link to her the man who had taken Edith in, Joseph Lewis, he dying on 24th April 1948.

Annie Rathall never again resided down south, she on 6th September 1898 marrying (employed as a domestic servant, and still residing at her parent's home in Berrington Street) thirty three year old bachelor William Howells (son of farmer Charles Howells), the groom employed as a woodman. So here is the rub, the marriage certificate issued to give insight into misfortune, Walter Rathall was dead. Much thrown into confusion following the apparent demise of Walter, the most fundamental of which the author of this books failure, though much effort has been put into play, to lay her hands on Walter Rathalls death certificate.

Annie was to have more children, William Charles born in 1899, the subsequent years to witness the births of George Charles, John, Charles (the Howells seemed to favour the name Charles), Arthur Edward, and Tom, who was baptised on 13th September 1908, his mother the sole female within the household. William a wood labourer, providing the funds necessary to pay the rent on a little property in Fishpond, Byford, the Howells home in close proximity to Byford Rectory. Wood labouring by nature an intensive job, it putting much strain on those who pursued it, and with this in mind, as well as the offer of a tied cottage, William took work as an estate labourer, the Howells tenancy close to "School House" in Byford, Hereford.

So what became of William and Annie Howells, it seems they ended their days in Byford, Herefordshire, William a dutiful spouse (far removed in character from his wife's first husband, Walter Rathall), dying aged seventy two, in the late winter of 1938, duly buried on 19th February. If Annie Howells ever thought on the events at Lambridge Farm, it is a matter known only to her, and now turned seventy she did not find herself deprived of her beloved William for long, her death registered in the March of 1938.

There of course is one more, though only a babe in arms at the time, who was mentioned within the newspapers columns in the weeks that followed on from the shocking events at Lambridge House, that being Walter and Annie's eldest, Catherine. What scars her father's trial and untimely death, her sister Edith's adoption, and her mother's remarriage and subsequent new family, left in the psyche of Catherine Rathall, she glad of the opportunity of a fresh start relocated to Wales. Work was plentiful and Catherine soon secured employment, as a domestic servant (more than likely a barmaid) in the household of Mr Evan Morgan, Landlord of the Smiths Arms in Ystalyfera, Glamorgan.

Catherine Rathall found happiness, though it was to be fleeting, marrying Samuel Joseph Mereditch (a collier, who resided at 9 The Square, Nelson) on 28th June 1917; the bride at the time of her nuptials working at the Wellington Hotel in Nelson, Pontypridd. Catherine Rathalls marriage certificate is tantalising by its omission, Samuels father is named (also Samuel, deceased, in life having been a farmer), but the portion of the certificate that should be occupied by the name of the bride's father is glaringly blank. Could it be that the bride, through deep seated resentment, or feelings of shame, was unwilling to include the name of Walter John Rathall?

All, as it is said, comes full circle, and as such having suffered much at the hands of poverty, childhood instability, and loss, on 13th December 1919 (ravaged by the effects of Pulmonary Tuberculosis), twenty six year old Catherine Mereditch (attended by Doctor Alex Duncan), cradled in the arms of her bereft husband, died.

Seventy One

And What of Kate

The edition of the Henley and South Oxfordshire Standard, which hit the newsstands on Friday 19th January 1894, set out to clarify for their readership one crucial matter, that being the exact time the murder at Lambridge House had been committed. The reporter, who composed the article, of the opinion that the human scream heard by Mr Lillywhite had indeed originated from the unfortunate Miss Dungey.

"The witness, who worked at the "Pheasantry", Assenden Hill, had specified that the scream, which he heard at approximately 6.15 on that fateful Friday evening, had lasted several seconds. Lillywhite was located at the time he purported to have heard the scream on a hill, the height of which was akin to that of the cusp of the steep incline on which Lambridge House stood. The wind at the time, blowing in the direction line from Lambridge Woods towards where Lillywhite was engaged in his toil, carried the scream across the rural abyss between victim and witness, and fixed the murder as having occurred in such a time as to allow the murderer, whoever he (or she) may have been, ample time to reach Henley-on-Thames by the hour of seven. It appears that the cowardly ruffian, who so brutally murdered Miss Kate Dungey, will escape the consequence of his terrible crime."

It was, at the time of the issue of the aforementioned paper, exactly six weeks since the tragic events at Lambridge House, and during that interlude the police had only managed to make one arrest. The evidence against the prisoner, Walter Rathall, had been deemed by the magistrates as not sufficient to warrant sending him to trial, and he had been discharged, which was felt to be, by one fellow who wrote for the local paper, the only appropriate outcome.

"It was the best and fairest course the magistrates could take. The circumstantial evidence against Rathall had proved to be weak, and without the merit to enable a jury to convict him, and therefore it had been decided that it was at this point useless to subject the prisoner to a full trial, which if acquitted would have freed him forever."

Though Walter Rathall was not a man released of all burden upon his character, if any evidence against him could be subsequently adduced, through on-going police enquiries, Rathall could have found himself rearrested.

Tabloid hacks, who had forced their way into the local populace's psyche, with the power of their words, had done with the town, and quickly left it via the Great Western Railway, set to pursue whatever salacious new topic caught the interest of their editors.

But the written word was not quite done with Miss Kate Laura Dungey, her murder having the dubious honour of appearing in the form of a short paragraph, on page eighty one, of "Longmans Green, Volume 135 Annual Register of World Events."

A nonagenarian gentleman of the town, who had cause to converse with the author of this book, recalled an event from his boyhood. In the mid-1930s, with the proportion of working class lads out of education by fourteen, many took work as errand boys, employed by the owners or managers of the numerous shops that inhabited the town centre of Henley-on-Thames. The children on the whole enjoyed their jaunts around the local area, duly provided with a bicycle with ample basket, dropping off goods to customers. All except one delivery round, which took them into the heart of Lambridge Woods. The boys would talk amongst themselves, and to their friends, that they did not much relish this route, and tried their upmost to avoid it. The children's sensitivities greatly affected by a story (that hung in the memories of some who had lived through the time in question, or who had heard of the event second hand), that they had been told by their kinsfolk, while sat around the fireside on dark wintery nights. "A lady was done to death in them woods at Lambridge, and her ghostly presence still wanders amongst the trees, her soul not at rest because she got no justice!"

Afterward

In late October of 2015 I took myself off to Kent, to visit the towns and villages that would have been familiar to those of the Dungey family. Walking through the centre of Cranbrook, many buildings as they were in Kate's time, I could not help but imagine the young woman strolling along the High Street, popping into the shops she favoured. Goudhurst also a place Kate Dungey would often purchase provisions (many shopkeepers having known Kate since her childhood), as with Cranbrook, a substantial number of its buildings as they were in Miss Dungeys time, several of them centuries old.

Within the churchyard of Christ Church, Kilndown, several members of the Dungey family are buried, and in the late afternoon of a hazy October day, after much searching, I found the final resting place of Kate Laura Dungey, the sight of her grave one which affected me profoundly. The most emotive aspect of my visit to Kilndown, the sight of the hearse cart (that was used to convey Kate Dungeys coffin), which is located within Christ Church. This item, though having in the course of time lost its original black paintwork and little wooden cross, an object that caused several moments of reflection on my part.

While writing this book (except for an occasional comment), I excluded from my prose any definitive opinion as to who may have been responsible for Kate Laura Dungeys murder. I have theories on the matter, but with much deliberation as to whether I should voice them, I resolved that I wish you the reader to come to your own conclusion.

And as for Lambridge House, the little farmhouse where Kate Dungey so valiantly fought off her attacker before she fled the property (Kate on the bitterly cold night, that was eighth December, subsequently cut down by her assailant), it is no more. In the autumn of 2015 I travelled out to Lower Assendon (as it is now known), and during my exploration of the area I had cause to converse with a long time stalwart of the village. This gentleman to inform me that during his childhood Lambridge House was known as the "Murder House", and many were sore afraid to visit it, or indeed linger for any time in the woods that surrounded it. Subsequently, I was told, Lambridge House, that stood for countless years empty and dejected, was demolished.

Kate Laura Dungeys final resting place
Within the churchyard of Christ Church, Kilndown

Acknowledgements

Publication of this book would not have been possible without the financial generosity of the Greening Lamborn Trust, its objective to promote public interest in the history, architecture, old photographs and heraldry of Oxford and its neighbourhood, by supporting publications and other media that creates access to them.

I am very much indebted to George (grandson of George and Amy Katherine Dawson) and Jenette Dawson, for their stalwart assistance. Living as they do in Australia we corresponded via e-mail, and it was wonderful indeed to meet them face to face, the Dawson's having visited Henley-on-Thames in the fall of 2015.

I also wish to gratefully acknowledge Fiona Fieth (her mother, Jean MacGregor, the granddaughter of Kates brother, Ernest Dungey), she escorting me around Watlington, we trying, with scant success, to establish the location of Augustus Jones former residence, Acacia House. It is uncanny indeed that through happenchance Fiona lives in a village which lies but a short distance from the location of her great aunts murder.

Mr Anthony Mash, the great grandson of Henry Joseph Mash, and grandson of Henry Joseph and Helena (Kate Dungeys sister) Mash; offered invaluable assistance. Anthony resides within the same area where both his grandfather and great grandfather once lived, and he provided me with numerous anecdotes in relation to his grandparents.

Thanks is due to Gill Joyce, she a member of Goudhurst & Kilndown Local History Society. While I was visiting Kent, Gill to spend an afternoon in my company, showing me the parts of Goudhurst that Kate Dungey would have been familiar with.

John Luker, thanks is due to you in relation to the pertinent facts when it came to the history of the Henley & South Oxfordshire Standard, still in print to this day.

When looking into the facts which pertained to Walter John Rathalls dealings with the Society of Friends, Mike Macleod came up trumps, he possessing a keen knowledge of the Quakers.

I am grateful to Richard Wilson, as always a font of knowledge on countless aspects of Henley's commercial and social history.

Many a day and into the evening I utilized Henley Library, its excellent local history section (which contains amongst its collection, historical business directories, auction catalogues, and rare out of print publications) indispensable.

Thanks due also to the numerous local business outlets and residents, who finding me at their doors welcomed me in, and allowed me to explore those premises having been connected with the so called "Henley Murder".

And last, but no means least, thanks is due to my sister, Melanie (and her faithful little Metro), she driving me around about, and never once complaining when I set her to work, trailing around churchyards, in search of pertinent headstones.

Bibliography

Alasia, Valerie (2016) *Henley Union Workhouse,* (Brewin Books).

Allen, Gemma (2004) *The Story of the Henley College,* (Tempus Publishing).

Beeton, Isabella (1861) *Etiquette and Advice Manuels-Mrs Beetons Book of Household Management,* (Victorian London Publication).

Burn, John Southerden (1861) *History of Henley-on-Thames,* (London: Longman & Co).

Climenson, Emily J. (1896) *A Guide to Henley-on-Thames,* (Henley-on-Thames: Gresham Books).

Cottingham, Ann (2000) *The Hostelries of Henley,* (Oxford: Parchment).

Cottingham, Anne & Fisher, Hilary (1990) *Henley-on-Thames, a Pictorial History,* (Phillimore Publishing).

Course, Edwin (1973) *The Railway of Southern England, the Main Lines* (B. T. Batsford Ltd).

Eccles, John R. (1995) *Historical Notes on the Parish of Bix & Assendon,* (Self Published).

Esam, Frank (1906) *The Manors and Farmhouses of Kent,* (The South Eastern Gazette, Maidstone, Kent).

Harrison, J. F. C. (1990) *Late Victorian Britain 1875-1901,* (Fontana Press).

Ireland, William Henry (1829) *A New Complete History of the County of Kent,* (G. Virtue)

Macleod, Michael (2010) *Quakers in Henley 1658-2008,* (Skye Publications).

McKenna, Frank (1980) *The Railway Workers 1840-1970,* (Faber & Faber).

Mosley, Charles, editor (1999) *Burkes Peerage & Baronetage Volume 2,* (Crams Switzerland: Burkes Peerage Genealogical Books).

Noble, Percy (1905) *Park Place Berkshire,* (F. Calder Turner).

Pitt, Alethea (1994) *Henley Quakers, a Short History of the Religious Society of Friends in Henley-on-Thames,* (Henley Preparative Meeting).

Pudney, John (1971) *A Draught of Contentment,* (New English Library).

Railton, Margaret (1994) *Early Medical Services Berkshire and South Oxfordshire, from 1740,* (Polmood Publications).

Reed, A. J. (1982) *Stories & Pictures Associated with Kidmore End & District Oxfordshire,* (Wallingford: Abbey Printing Co).

Richmond, Carol (2004) *Oxfordshire Constabulary Recruitment Register 1863-1878,* (Oxfordshire Black Sheep Publications).

Richmond, Carol (2004) *Oxfordshire Constabulary Recruitment Register 1878-1904,* (Oxfordshire Black Sheep Publications).

Shaida, Margaret (1984) *Views of Henley-on-Thames,* (Spindlewood).

Thacker, Alan editor (2011) *A History of the County of Oxford, Volume XVI, Henley-on-Thames and Environs,* (London: The University of London Institute of Historical Research: Boydell & Brewer).

Tiffin W. Alfred (1937) *The Goudhurst Coronation Book,* (Tunbridge Wells: The Printing & Publishing Company Ltd).

Weinreb, Ben & Hibbert, Christopher, editors (1983) *The London Encyclopaedia,* (London: Macmillan London Ltd).

Whitehead, David (2007) *Henley-on-Thames a History,* (Phillimore).

Willoughby, Mike (2014) *Bringing Them Home, Men of Henley 1914-1921,* (Henley-on-Thames: Printed by Higgs Group)

Newspapers

Aberdeen Journal: Wednesday 21st September 1932
Berkshire Chronicle: Saturday 16th December 1893
Berkshire Chronicle: Saturday 1st February 1896
Berkshire Chronicle: Saturday 30th May 1896
Birmingham Daily Post: Monday 11th December 1893
Blackburn Standard, Lancashire: Saturday 16th December 1893
Bucks Free Press, High Wycombe, Maidenhead & Marlow Journal: Friday 23rd September 1932
Bucks Herald: Saturday 13th January 1894
Bucks Herald: Saturday 17th July 1915
Bucks Herald: Saturday 28th May 1927
Bury Free Press: Saturday 16th December 1893
Cheshire Observer: Saturday 16th December 1893
Daily Telegraph: Monday 11th December 1893
Derby Daily Telegraph: Monday 11th December 1893
Dundee Courier: Monday 11th December 1893
Dundee Courier: Tuesday 12th December 1893
Edinburgh Evening News: Monday 11th December 1893
Evening Telegraph & Star: Friday 5th January 1894
Glasgow Herald: Monday 11th December 1893
Glasgow Herald: Saturday 6th January 1894
Gloucester Journal: Saturday 30th June 1923
Gloucestershire Echo: Saturday 8th September 1900
Hartlepool Mail: Wednesday 2nd November 1932
Henley & South Oxfordshire Standard: Friday 10th November 1911
Henley & South Oxfordshire Standard: Friday 11th December 1931
Henley & South Oxfordshire Standard: Friday 12th January 1894
Henley & South Oxfordshire Standard: Friday 13th May 1910

Henley & South Oxfordshire Standard: Friday 15th December 1893
Henley & South Oxfordshire Standard: Friday 15th September 1939
Henley & South Oxfordshire Standard: Friday 16th September 1921
Henley & South Oxfordshire Standard: Friday 18th April 1930
Henley & South Oxfordshire Standard: Friday 18th February 1898
Henley & South Oxfordshire Standard: Friday 19th January 1894
Henley & South Oxfordshire Standard: Friday 19th May 1899
Henley & South Oxfordshire Standard: Friday 21st April 1961
Henley & South Oxfordshire Standard: Friday 21st October 1927
Henley & South Oxfordshire Standard: Friday 22nd December 1893
Henley & South Oxfordshire Standard: Friday 22nd November 1901
Henley & South Oxfordshire Standard: Friday 26th January 1894
Henley & South Oxfordshire Standard: Friday 28th October 1927
Henley & South Oxfordshire Standard: Friday 2nd May 1902
Henley & South Oxfordshire Standard: Friday 30th April 1915
Henley & South Oxfordshire Standard: Friday 30th October 1896
Henley & South Oxfordshire Standard: Friday 3rd February 1928
Henley & South Oxfordshire Standard: Friday 7th May 1915
Henley & South Oxfordshire Standard: Friday 8th January 1937
Henley & South Oxfordshire Standard: Friday 9th February 1906
Henley & South Oxfordshire Standard: Friday 9th October 1896
Henley Advertiser: Saturday 16th December 1893
Illustrated Police News, London: Saturday 16th December 1893
Illustrated Police News, London: Saturday 20th January 1894
Illustrated Police News, London: Saturday 23rd December 1893
Jacksons Oxford Journal: Saturday 21st November 1857
Jacksons Oxford Journel: Saturday 11th June 1859
Jacksons Oxford Journel: Saturday 21st February 1885
Kent & Sussex Courier: Friday 13th April 1917
Kent & Sussex Courier: Friday 20th May 1904
Kent & Sussex Courier: Friday 22nd December 1893
Lancashire Evening Post: Monday 11th December 1893

Leamington Spa Courier: Friday 11th November 1938
Leamington Spa Courier: Friday 19th November 1937
Lincolnshire Chronicle: Friday 15th December 1893
Lloyds Weekly Newspaper, London: Sunday 10th December 1893
Lloyds Weekly Newspaper, London: Sunday 17th December 1893
London Gazette: Tuesday 16th November 1841
London Standard: Friday 12th January 1893
London Standard: Monday 11th December 1893
Manchester Courier & Lancashire General Advertiser: Tuesday 12th December 1893
Manchester Courier, Supplement: Saturday 16th December 1893
Morning Post, London: Tuesday 12th December 1893
Newcastle Courant: Saturday 16th December 1893
Northampton Mercury: Friday 2nd August 1907
Northern Echo, Durham: Friday 19th January 1894
Northern Echo, Durham: Monday 11th December 1893
Oxford Journal: Saturday 13th January 1894
Oxford Journal: Saturday 22nd October 1870
Oxford Journal: Saturday 28th October 1899
Oxford Journal: Saturday 6th January 1894
Oxford Journal: Saturday 7th July 1888
Pall Mall Gazette: Friday 12th January 1894
Pall Mall Gazette: Friday 19th January 1894
Pall Mall Gazette: Monday 16th December 1893
Portsmouth Evening News: Monday 11th December 1893
Portsmouth Evening News: Thursday 28th June 1923
Reading Chronicle: Friday 27th October 1939
Reading Chronicle: Wednesday 3rd April 1907
Reading Mercury: Saturday 31st August 1901
Reading Mercury: Saturday 3rd May 1902
Reynolds Newspaper, London: Sunday 21st January 1894
Sheffield Evening Telegraph: Monday 11th December 1893

Shields Daily Gazette: Monday 11th December 1893
Sussex Agricultural Express: Friday 15th December 1893
Sussex Agricultural Express: Saturday 16th December 1893
Sussex Agricultural Express: Saturday 20th January 1894
Sussex Agricultural Express: Saturday 23rd December 1893
The Standard, London: Monday 11th December 1893
The Standard, London: Tuesday 12th December 1893
The Times: Friday 12th January 1894
The Times: Friday 19th January 1894
The Times: Tuesday 12th December 1893
Weekly Standard & Express, Blackburn: Saturday 16th December 1893
Western Mail, Wales: Tuesday 12th December 1893
Yorkshire Evening Post: Monday 11th December 1893
Yorkshire Post & Leed Intelligencer: Saturday 3rd February 1906

Business Directories & Journals

Kellys Directory Berks, Bucks & Oxon, 1891 (Published Kelly & Co)
Kellys Directory Berks, Bucks & Oxon, 1893 (Published Kelly & Co)
Kellys Directory Berks, Bucks & Oxon, 1895 (Published Kelly & Co)
Kellys Directory Berks, Bucks & Oxon, 1903 (Published Kelly & Co)
Kellys Directory Berks, Bucks & Oxon, 1911 (Published Kelly & Co)
Spennell's Directory of Leamington, 1926
Temperance Gazette, Volume Two: March 1897
The Comprehensive Gazetteer of England & Wales: 1894/95
The History of Thames Valley Police: Thames Valley Police 2004
The Story of "The Star" 1888-1938, Fifty Years of Progress & Achievement: The Star Publications Department 1938
The Vaccination Officers & Public Vaccinator's Handbook: Walter Bullar Ross 1893
Who Was Who 1929-1940: Adam & Charles Black: 1941

Website Searches

Historic Newspapers: Newspaper Image courtesy of The British Library Board. All rights reserved, with thanks to The British Newspaper Archive. www.BritishNewspaperArchive.co.uk
The Times Digital Archive
www.census1891com/ocupations-all.php
www.gov.uk/order-copy-birth-death-marriage certificates
www.gov.uk/search-will
www.nationalarchives.gov.uk

Illustrations

Kate Laura Dungey: The Penny Illustrated Paper, Saturday 23rd December 1893

Front cover of the Illustrated Police News: Saturday 23rd December 1893

Line drawing of Miss Kate Laura Dungey, line drawing Lambridge Woods, line drawing Lambridge House: Lloyds Weekly Newspaper, Sunday 17th December 1893

Images created courtesy of The British Library Board. Images reproduced with kind permission of the British Newspaper Archive

Henley Cemetery Keepers Lodge: With compliments of Peers & Hilton Estate Agent, Henley-on-Thames

The Red Cross: With thanks to Ann Cottingham, from her book, The Hostelries of Henley

Henley Police Station, Sergeant Thomas Allmond, Superintendent Francis Keal sitting amongst his constables outside Chipping Norton Police Station 1907: All images reproduced with compliments of the TVP Museum

George Dawson, Amy Katherine Dawson, George & Emma Dawson: With thanks to George and Jenette Dawson, Australia

Pattenden Manor, taken from a postcard printed for Miss Midmer, onetime postmistress of Goudhurst, portrait Walter Dungey, taken from Goudhurst Coronation Book by Alfred W. Tiffin, published 1937: Compliments of Goudhurst and Kilndown Local History Society

Park Place, Henley Railway Station, River Terrace, Thameside, Clisby Cottages: With thanks to Mr Richard Wilson

Higgs & Co, Caxton House, Plan Lambridge House: Permission of the Henley Standard

Caversham Priory, line drawing Simonds Brewery, line drawing John Brains commercial premises, photograph Sydney Brain, Belmont House, Wyfold Court: Permission of Reading Borough Council Library

Robert Trotter Herman Hodge: Copyright National Portrait Gallery

Photograph George Richard Fuller, photograph William Simpkins, photograph Joshua Watts: With thanks to Henley Town Council

Henleys Georgian Town Hall: Permission of River & Rowing Museum, Henley-on-Thames

Photograph Henry Joseph Mash, photograph marriage Henry Mash and Helena Dungey: With thanks to Anthony Mash

Portrait William Anker Simmons, premises of Simmons & Sons: Compliments of Simmons & Sons Chartered Surveyors